Merriam-Webster's Guide to International Business Communications

SECOND EDITION

Toby D. Atkinson

Merriam-Webster, Incorporated
Springfield, Massachusetts

Copyright © 1999 Toby D. Atkinson

Library of Congress Cataloging-in-Publication Data

Atkinson, Toby D.
   Merriam-Webster's guide to international business communications /
Toby D. Atkinson.—2nd ed.
      p.   cm.
   Includes indexes.
   ISBN 0-87779-608-4
   1. Business communication—Handbooks, manuals, etc. 2. Communication in
international trade—Handbooks, manuals, etc. I. Title.
HF5718.A765 1998
060'.25—dc21   98-42446
                                                  CIP

Printed and bound in the United States of America

123456QP/M02010099

Contents

Acknowledgments

Many people have helped with the preparation of this book in both its editions, but I would particularly like to acknowledge the contributions of the following advisers around the world: Adriana, Anna-Maria, Annett, Anthony, Anton, Badariah, Beatriz, Bede, Carlos, Catherine & Nigel, Choltanee, Cida, Cor, David, Dieter, Duc, Eleni, Ewa, Fabien & friends, Fabienne, Francisco, Friedrich, George, Gerda, Grazyna, Harsh, Hiroko, Ida, Ismartilah, Ivana, Jasmin, Joelle, John & family, Joss, Kjell & Louise, Lena, Leo, Liliana, Madeline, Marina, MKS, Mary, Matti, Mette, Natalya, Pelin, Péter K, Peter U, Pina, Raija, Ralph, Rolando, STT, Sandra, Seng Ngoh, Siwon, Steve, Susan, Thérèse, Tony, Ursula, Vladimir, Walter, and Zlática. Also Barbara, Françoise, Gwen, Jan, Rhonda, Sunita, Terry, and Yves for various kinds of advice and encouragement; Derri for providing facilities at a critical time; AE Translations in Houston; the Boucris Language School in Paris La Défense; the business libraries of Dallas, Denver, Houston, London, Los Angeles, and Paris; Susan Tapani, Dale Hoiberg, and the painstaking reviewers at Encyclopaedia Britannica International; the professionals of Merriam-Webster, including Jim Rader, Dan Hopkins, Vicki Neufeldt, Steve Perrault, Amy West, Jim Withgott, and Paul Cappellano, who reviewed portions of the manuscript, Rebecca Bryer and Francine Roberts, who proofread the text, and Mark Stevens, who oversaw the project; and finally Alan and Flo for the genetic material.

1. Introduction

Who Needs This Book?

This book is written primarily for a wide range of office workers who deal with organizations in other countries. It is for secretaries, executive assistants, office managers, marketing communications staff, sales assistants, order fulfillment clerks, shipping clerks, mailroom staff, and technical support personnel. It is for employees of international organizations, diplomatic services, the post offices of the world, international delivery services, economic development agencies, airlines, business hotel chains, business travel agencies, and phone companies. In addition, some computer database designers and systems analysts will find information here that will save them a great deal of research time.

The book contains all the information that the Vice President/International vaguely knows but never communicates to back-office staff at home. It is the course that experienced V.P.'s wish they had time to teach. So it will also be useful for beginners in international sales and for anybody else who wants to be V.P./International someday.

The ideal reader would be one person with complete decision-making authority performing all the functions of the international department in a small company. However, to be realistic, the book assumes that you work in a large organization where you do not have complete control over your environment. It will try to help you get your job done, with limited authority, in spite of a number of common internal obstacles.

Why Is It Important?

The globalization of business is proceeding with amazing speed. It is affecting employees and consumers everywhere. More and more companies are buying foreign components and are counting on worldwide sales of their own products. Consumers and businesses increasingly demand the best product regardless of where it is made.

If a product or service is successful in one country, it can probably be successful in others. These days, it is dangerous for a company not to actively promote sales of its products in other countries. To stay at home is to wait for foreign competitors to arrive on your own doorstep.

But even when companies do not actively promote themselves internationally, foreigners find out about them, particularly about American companies. Foreign visitors come to trade shows in the United States and subscribe to the American trade press. Therefore, more and more American companies receive unsolicited inquiries from overseas, from both prospective customers and prospective distributors, and have to be prepared to deal with them. Since you may not know that "Wien" is the way Austrians spell "Vienna," how are you supposed to know which country the fax has come from?

Your colleagues or supervisors will often count on you to take responsibility for a variety of international tasks without offering you much training or information (except when you make an innocent mistake and things go wrong). But their messages have to get through. Contracts and samples have to reach their destinations. And you are expected not to upset foreign executives. Reliable performance makes a lot of difference to your personal reputation and opportunities for recognition and promotion.

There is another reason why the information in this book is timely. Post offices around the world are automating, and thus introducing all kinds of new requirements about how to address mail. Though they are not making any particular effort to publicize this information outside their own countries, it does make a difference to the speed and accuracy with which your mail will be sorted. Everybody in international business has an interest in conforming to these new procedures.

What Has Changed Since the First Edition?

In this second edition we have added chapters on 11 more countries, 9 of which are located in the expanding trading economies of Eastern Europe and Southeast Asia. The 47 countries now covered, representing about 95 percent of international trade, include virtually all the major economies plus a few additions so as to include all the principal English-speaking economies and all the countries of the European Union. However, many other countries have been influenced by Arabia, France, Portugal, Spain, and the United Kingdom; thus, an awareness of the terminology and practices in these countries will help you understand those in many others. (A table summarizing facts about all the countries in the world has been added for this edition.)

As would be expected, information about the postal systems of the world has hardly changed since the first edition. A short summary has been included to reflect the growth of international bulk mail services, which have expanded greatly in the past few years and gained in legitimacy and respectability, to the extent that several foreign post offices have established remailing subsidiaries and are competing for international business in the United States and other countries.

The world's political geography has changed slightly. South Africa has created new provinces and adopted additional national languages. Slovenia has emerged from the former Yugoslavia as a stable economic entity active in European trade. Hong Kong will undergo changes of unpredictable dimensions during the currency of the second edition.

A number of detailed changes to phone system information have been recorded. First, the European Union is standardizing on an International Access Code of 00. Second, more countries are offering toll-free numbers and there is a trend toward adopting variations of the familiar North American 800 prefix to identify them. Also, a number of countries have changed, or are planning to change, their phone-number structure to accommodate the increased demand for fax lines, computer connections, and distinctive ringing signals.

Office equipment is constantly improving. When the first edition was published, for example, plain-paper fax machines were the exception, and now they are the rule in the industrialized countries.

The biggest changes have, of course, occurred in the computer industry. We have retained the section on the problems of older computer systems, since many computer users will continue to suffer the limitations of MS-DOS, UNIX, and mainframe systems for many years. Dramatic progress on standardizing character sets has been made behind the scenes, and the benefits will start to appear during the life of this book. The Unicode consortium has created a reference document defining all the character sets used in the business world, as well as many others of historical or anthropological interest, and the Unicode has been adopted as the native character set of the Windows NT operating system. The TrueType font specification has been expanded to become TrueType Open (for Microsoft) and TrueType GX (for Apple), which among other improvements cover the accented Roman characters of the Eastern European and Turkish languages.

The Internet, which has existed for many years, has exploded into prominence in the business world, mainly because of the new capabilities of the World Wide Web to transmit attractive-looking pages that can mix graphical images with text and contain links to other pages of information. Its primary business uses at present are for electronic mail and the dissemination of livelier corporate marketing information. Without attempting to provide another general introduction to the Internet, we have added information where there were analogies with material already in the book—for example, explaining how Internet addresses are constructed just as we explained how phone numbers are constructed.

Do You Know It All Already?

Test yourself. The following examples show some addresses as they might very well appear on business cards or in trade directories. I have eliminated most of the punctuation—quite a realistic possibility—but I have identified the countries, which might not be obvious in real-world examples. Not all the examples are perfectly correct postal addresses. Can you explain each one and arrange it as it should appear on an envelope?

Country	Address
Argentina	25 de Mayo 359 3° P. "B" Casilla de Correos 238 C.P. 7600 Mar del Plata Pcia. de Buenos Aires
Belgium	Rue F. Severinstraat 62 b 5 1060 Elsene Ixelles
Brazil	SBN Q. 01 Bl. G 70070 Brasília DF
Chile	San Antonio 65 Bellavista Santiago 10
Czech Rep.	Žirovnická č. 23 603 00 Brno
Denmark	Kvægtorvet 19 3.tv 1780 København V
Finland	Ulvilantie 8b A 11 Pl 354 SF-00561 Helsinki
France	Immeuble Valmy 64-68 avenue du Président-Wilson Z.A. Briffaut B.P.154 26027 Valence Cedex
Germany	Landstr. 7/3 45440 Dortmund
Greece	Ag. Annis & 190 Orfeos 105 59 Athens

Country	Address
Hungary	1146 Bp. Bartók B. út 73
Indonesia	Jl. Masyudi III/32 Bandung 40184
Israel	Beit Gibor 53 Rehov Ibn-Gvirol 63143 Tel Aviv
Italy	Palazzo Mantova Via Innocenzo III 21 20138 Milano
Japan	Swan Building 9F 1-2-1 Nihonbashi Hongokuchō Chūō-ku Tokyo 103
Korea	35-2 Sangdaewon-dong Kangnam-ku Seoul 165-010
Malaysia	Wisma Damansara Jalan Sultan Hishamuddin 43200 Kajang Selangkor
Mexico	Lázaro Cárdenas y V. Guerrero Col. San José Insurgentes C.P. 03900 México D.F.
Netherlands	Kerkstraat 21 II Postbus 649 7300 AR Apeldoorn
Norway	Stenersgt. 20 Pb 196 Sentrum 0101 Oslo 1
Philippines	145 Lopez Real Street Mandaluyong M.M.
Poland	00-830 Warszawa ul. pańska 35/37
Portugal	Rua 15 de Agosto 51-55-4° B Apartado 2574 1114 Lisboa Codex
Russia	115203 Moskva Nevsky Prospekt 109
Singapore	Blk. 12 Chai Chee Road #02-13 Singapore 0316
Slovenia	Trstenjakova 12 61000 Lj.
South Africa	256 Market Road Sandton 2199 Private Bag X2581 Gallo Manor 2052
Spain	C/Galileo 38 bis 3° izq 28015 Madrid
Switzerland	Rue des 3 Ponts 26 Case Postale 1213 Genève 13
Taiwan	7F 263 Sec. 4 Chung King N Rd Taipei 10552
Thailand	1058/1 Sukhumvit 101/3 (Soi Wachira thammasathit) Bangjak Prakanong Bangkok 10260
Turkey	Ferah Sok. Ferah Apt. No:19 Kat: 2 D:4 80200 Teşvikiye-İstanbul
United Kingdom	Harcourt Chambers Eton Road Dorney Maidenhead Berks SL6 9DT
United States	3100 Two America Center 1776 Lincoln Ave Mpls. MN 55440
Venezuela	Calle 89 14A-23 Maracaibo 4001 Edo Zulia

How would you address these men (that is, "Dear Mr. ——")?

Country	Name
Argentina	Enrique Rodríguez Estévez
Belgium	Michel Vander Haeghem
Brazil	Mauricio do Prado Filho
France	PIERRE Christophe
Korea	Yu Dai-won
Malaysia	Muhammad Salim Ambak
Mexico	Enrique Rodríguez Estévez
Nigeria	Alhaji Mohammed Abubakao
Portugal	José Correia de Oliveria
Russia	Sergie Gennadyavich Kuznetsov
Singapore	Tan Ming Ho
Spain	Luis Ángel de la Villa y Sangriz
Switzerland	Pierre Christophe
Taiwan	Yu-ching Tan
United Kingdom	Russell Miller-Jones

How would you address these women (that is, "Dear Ms. ——")?

Country	Name
Austria	Anneliese Swoboda Hofer
Denmark	Annett Nielsen Andersen
Finland	Hanna Korpela-Virtanen
Hungary	Fehér Katalin
Ireland	Maureen Keane O'Leary
Malaysia	Siti Hawa Ismail
Philippines	Isabel Reyes-Cruz
Portugal	Maria Martins Rodrigues
Russia	Marina Grigoryevna Tsvetkova
Singapore	Jennifer Chan-Lee Bee Leng
Slovenia	Cvetka Babnik Maroit
Spain	María Aldaca de Hernández
Sweden	Anna Berg Andersson
United States	Karen Swanson Larsen

How would you dial these phone numbers, some of which are out-of-date or contain errors that are commonly made by overseas partners?

Country	Number
Austria	0732/8205-DW 285
Denmark	45 26 02 30
Finland	(90) 692 681
France	(19) 33 (1) 45.35.35.36
Hong Kong	0-218363
Hungary	(1) 125-873
Israel	(03) 513313-5
Japan	(03)438-0382
Malaysia	02-223 8565
Norway	(055) 1 11 57
Philippines	(632) 436-4348
Poland	(48 2) 6651514
South Africa	(092711) 804-1273
Spain	(91) 351 67 50
Turkey	(94) 223 27 00
United Kingdom	081-605 3624

Conclusion

If you are an office worker who responds to foreign inquiries, or deals with foreign vendors, or has colleagues in other countries, this book contains information you may need on a daily basis. The same is true if you work for an organization that serves (or regulates) international companies.

In an area where it is very easy to look ignorant or foolish, the information in this book is intended to help you do your job efficiently.

2. Office
Efficiency

The purpose of this chapter is to provide some concrete and fundamental guidance to help you realize two basic goals.

First, you want to avoid causing problems for foreigners. Your outgoing material should be clear to people who are not familiar with procedures in your country.

Second, you personally don't want to cause expense and delay, even though those two things tend to be unavoidable features of international business.

In one way, this entire book is concerned with these goals; however, this chapter covers five specific areas that often represent obstacles. Since you may not have control over these areas, the book will tell you how to minimize problems even if other people in your organization won't cooperate with you for international requirements.

Business Stationery

"Business stationery" in this context means letterheads, business cards, fax cover sheets, sales literature, product-specification sheets, customer-satisfaction surveys, product-registration documents, dealer and distributor kits, trade-show handouts, direct-mail pieces, newsletters, and anything else that circulates freely outside your organization. It does not include foreign advertising, for which specialist local advice is essential. (The standard paper sheet size in Europe, known as A4, measures 210×297mm, or $8.27'' \times 11.69''$.)

The typical graphic designer wants all corporate materials to be consistent, elegant, and distinctive. There is nothing wrong with any of these three goals, but the international department has three more important considerations: materials must be (1) *clear to foreigners*, (2) *legible after repeated copying and faxing*, and (3) *easy to file*.

EVALUATING DESIGNS

Your rationale for participating in stationery designs is this: international communications are slower and more expensive, and therefore people are less likely to just call up and ask for a few more copies to be sent to them. You will want to encourage people in remote places to copy your correspondence and your sales materials without coming back to *you* for copies.

The way to evaluate any proposed "design" for stationery is to photocopy it on your worst machine, copy the copy, fax it to the least advanced country you deal with, have them fax it back, and photocopy the return fax a couple more times on your worst machine. The following table details some common problems:

Stationery Design Feature	International Considerations
Type size	Anything that will ever be faxed should be in at least 12-point type; anything *intended* for faxing should be in 14-point.
Typeface	Sans-serif typefaces should be used for sales literature in Northern Europe, serif faces elsewhere.
Stroke weight	"Thin"-looking fonts fax and copy badly. Type does not have to be bold, but avoid light type.
Paper color	Darker papers cause smudges on photocopies. Remember that you may be dealing with companies whose equipment is older or not as well maintained as yours.
Ink color	Avoid "screening" (reduced color density) on anything that will be faxed or repeatedly copied.
Four-color artwork	Check a black-and-white photocopy to make sure the sense of the document does not depend on the color.
Embossing	Unless embossed type is also a different color from the background, it will photocopy as a blank space.
Shaded backgrounds	Gray backgrounds make text hard to read after faxing and photocopying and considerably increase fax transmission time.
Ruled lines	Horizontal lines come out jagged after faxing and can make a mess out of an otherwise good design.
Addresses	Print your address *exactly* the way foreigners are supposed to write it, using the shortest possible form. If in doubt, check it with your post office. If you must use a horizontal format, make it clear where the line breaks are supposed to be.
Phone numbers	Print them in the "+ Format" (see Chapter 4). If you feel this is unsuitable for domestic use, print phone numbers twice, once as "Tel.:" according to your usual national convention, then as "Int'l. Tel.:" in the + Format. Use numbers, not letters.
Direct-dial numbers	Do not use them if they are subject to change. Make it clear what they are. Include your main switchboard number as an alternative.
Fax numbers	Use the simple international word "Fax." Provide an alternative fax number along with your main one if you can. Do not add useless information like "Group III" or the model you use.
Toll-free numbers	Make it clear what these are and where they can be used from; be sure to also print a regular number that is accessible from everywhere.
Layout	Keep letterhead information at the top of the page so that you can fax short messages on half-sheets. Don't print important information at the foot of A4 paper when faxing to the United States and Canada (see "Words of Warning" in the "United States" chapter).
Registration numbers	Any registration information mandated by your own government should be kept as inconspicuous as possible so that foreigners do not waste time puzzling over it or translating it.

FAX COVER SHEETS

Fax cover sheets could have been invented by a conspiracy of the world's phone companies to increase their traffic and waste your money. By using them, you may be adding 45 seconds or more to every transmission for very little benefit.

The only time you need a cover sheet is when you fax a magazine article, a contract, or some other preprinted document.

Keep any cover material short and simple! It does not have to be a full page—and do not ramble on in your own language about who to call if transmission is less than perfect. In many cases, all you will need is a plain gummed tag, or a tag preprinted to look like a small cover sheet. Alternatively, you could make a rubber stamp using the same design.

Avoid complicated logos on fax sheets. They increase the transmission time, and they also increase the risk that the fax machines will think they did not communicate correctly. If company standards oblige you to use a logo, make it as small as the standards allow.

I recommend a "memo" format for faxes, printed off the word processor using a text font of 14-point type, with a larger heading:

FAX (3 pages)

TO:	**FRANÇOIS CORDONNIER** International Publishing S.A., Brussels, Belgium Tel: +32-2-233.89.95 Fax: +32-2-234.38.05
FROM:	FRANK SHOEMAKER International Publishing Inc., Los Angeles, CA, U.S.A. Tel: +1-213-869-4630 Fax: +1-213-869-8792
SUBJ:	PURCHASE ORDER FOR ACCOUNTING SOFTWARE
DATE:	January 9, 1997

This style is not to everybody's taste, but whatever design you use, two pieces of information should stand out: (1) how many pages there are, and (2) who it is for. It may be convenient for your own filing to put the destination company (rather than the individual) first in large type, but that does not help the recipients—they *know* what company they work for. Do not make them search for the individual addressee.

Discourage colleagues from sending handwritten faxes to foreigners. People from different countries have difficulty reading each other's handwriting, particularly on a fax. And horizontal guidelines are usually a mistake: everybody wants different spacing, and they look a mess at the other end. If you use them at all, make them as faint and thin as possible.

REPLY-PAID MATERIALS

An International Business Reply Service is available between a limited number of countries. It operates on the same principle as the corresponding domestic service. The card or envelope needs no postage stamp in the foreign country. You deposit money with your local post office, which deducts the postage and a service fee when the reply-paid letter or card is delivered back to you. You must have a domestic license from the post office before you can use the international service, but you cannot use the domestic artwork because the printing requirements are not the same.

From the United States, you can use the International Business Reply Service for more than half the countries covered by this book (Argentina, Australia, Belgium, Brazil, Denmark, Finland, France, Germany, Greece, Indonesia, Ireland, Israel, Japan, Korea, Luxembourg, Mexico, the Netherlands, New Zealand, Norway, Poland, Portugal, Spain, Sweden, Switzerland, and the United Kingdom). Other countries may join in the future. Also, bilateral agreements may exist between other combinations of countries.

There is also a universal worldwide system of reply coupons which you can buy at any post office in any country and send to any other country, where the recipient must take them to the post office and exchange them for local stamps. However, the system is not only expensive but also inconvenient at both ends, because a coupon does not correspond to a letter or any particular weight of package.

For occasions when you feel you should pay for a reply, try enclosing a few American commemorative stamps and a polite personal note asking if a stamp collector in the office would exchange them for local postage. So many people in the world collect stamps that this usually works quite well and will probably even earn you thank-you notes from time to time.

IF YOU ARE NOT IN CONTROL

If you have to use stationery materials that have been designed for domestic use without consideration for the international marketplace, here are some ideas.

You can often improve the legibility of fax cover sheets enormously with the aid of a pair of scissors and a photocopier that will enlarge and reduce. Cut and paste the "official" version until it works better. Correct for unsuitable paper by copying it first on a "light" setting and then copying the copy on a "dark" setting. Some experimenting will be necessary, but you will only have to do it once.

If you believe your company stationery shows misleading address and phone information, you can make up reply labels or imitation business cards on your computer and enclose them with all outgoing correspondence. You should also have a standard paragraph of text in your word processor with correct and legible contact information, which you can include in any outgoing letter on confusing letterhead.

And do not forget that the time-honored rubber stamp is still available very cheaply.

Mailroom Procedures
ENSURING CORRECT POSTAGE

It is essential to have some foolproof way of ensuring that correct postage is put on intercontinental airmail. Nothing is worse for your personal reputation than mail that is returned for additional postage. Nothing is more frustrating for an executive than to discover that an urgent package of sales literature went by sea because the postage was insufficient.

It is only natural for mailroom people to push everything through a postage meter without reading the addresses. You will make the same mistakes yourself if you stamp your own mail at the end of the day. You *must* have some system of identifying letters that require special postage *at the time you seal the envelope*. There are two ways to create a workable system—you should use both.

First, the mailroom should have a separate rack or tray for everything that needs special postage. If you send mail to places in three different postage categories, the mailroom will need a stack of three trays. You, as the international expert, should see that the mailroom has current postage information for all the countries that you deal with. Make sure that the information is clearly posted, so that even casual users like your executives can figure the right postage if they decide to rush something out on a weekend when no support staff are around.

Second, you should have envelopes with colored borders for airmail, and colored airmail stickers as well. This is all for the benefit of your own office more than for the post offices, so that international mail will stand out when it is being franked. If you cannot get colored envelopes or stickers, at least put a bright yellow gummed note marked (or rubber-stamped) "AIRMAIL" on the upper-right-hand corner of the envelope so that it will be noticed at franking time.

COST SAVINGS

There are three traditional classes of international mail: letters, parcels, and "other objects." Any of these three categories can travel by surface or by air. There is also now air express mail. You can save considerable amounts of money by sending out "other objects," officially called *Autres Objets* or *AO* (French being the official language of the long-established Universal Postal Union). Officially, two categories of mail can travel as AO: printed matter and small packets. In practice, this means that almost everything except individual letters is admissible. You will need current local postal information to be sure of the regulations, but as a general rule you can expect to save money sending anything AO that weighs between 4 oz. and 4 lbs. Of the countries covered in this book, only Australia (1 lb.) and Italy (2 lbs.) have lower weight limits. Do not be discouraged if there seems to be a lower weight limit for printed matter; overweight printed matter can travel as a small packet at the AO rate as long as it has an appropriate customs label.

Allowed at AO Rates	Not Allowed at AO Rates
Invoice accompanying merchandise	Invoice alone
Mass mailing	Personalized letter
Diskettes	Blank stationery
Cassettes	Film and microfiche
Videotapes	
Samples	
Computer printouts	
Files and old correspondence	
Sales literature, manuals	

Short greetings, highlighting, underlining, correction of errors, and short instructions like "OK to distribute" do not count as personalization and will not stop a shipment from being considered as printed matter.

There are no practical disadvantages to using AO rates. Delivery times are the same. There are a couple of possible objections, but they should not deter you. One theoretical disadvantage is that AO mail is subject to postal inspection and must be easy to unseal and reseal. Europeans generally meet this requirement by using pressure-sensitive envelopes, and Americans do so by using clasp envelopes. Your international mail is subject to customs inspection anyway, whether it is AO or not. The second theoretical disadvantage is that the treatment of undeliverable AO mail may be different, and worse. However, most of your mail *is* deliverable, and, for that matter, the treatment of undeliverable international first-class mail is not wonderful.

All you need to do is to write (or rubber-stamp) on the envelope **AO PRINTED MATTER** or **AO SMALL PACKET**. You will still need your airmail labels, because there is an AO surface rate, too. If you are a perfectionist, you could write (rubber-stamp) on the flap **Unsealed packet, open for inspection**. If you are an *extreme* perfectionist, you could add French translations, which are, respectively: **AO Imprimés**, **AO Petit Paquet**, and **Envoi non clos, peut être ouvert d'office**. "Airmail" is the well-known **Par Avion** in French. Envelopes are sold in some countries with preprinted messages for AO rates.

If you have significant quantities of mail for another country, you will need to evaluate a specialist service which will put it into the mailstream of the other country with local postage. Refer to the chapter on "Useful Products and Services."

SPECIAL POSTAL SERVICES

The post offices can trace your mail if you send it *Registered* (letters) or *Insured* (parcels). There is a simpler and cheaper system, equivalent to U.S. Certified Mail, called *Recorded Delivery*, but it is not universally available by any means. From the United States, it is available only to Belgium, China, Czech Republic, Italy, Korea, Malaysia, the Netherlands, New Zealand, Spain, Turkey, and Venezuela, of the countries covered by this book. Registered and insured mail (but not recorded delivery mail) is kept in a secure area and a trace is kept of its travels. You can request a return receipt on any of these special mailings.

It is unusual for registered and insured mail to get lost, even in countries where the regular mail is unreliable, but it does travel more slowly. It is well worthwhile to insure a parcel for a nominal value, just to get the trace and secure handling. However, actually tracing anything or making a claim takes months. On the other hand, the international return-receipt system works poorly, even in advanced countries. Local letter carriers do not recognize the international documentation. Do not be surprised if your return receipt never comes back.

ENVELOPE DESIGN

A casual mailer cannot deal with all the different envelope dimensional requirements of different countries, and it is not really safe to rely on the international standard margins because many individual countries are more restrictive. However, it is important to comply with margin requirements, because you will want Optical Character Recognition equipment to read your envelopes so as to avoid delays. If you leave a top margin of 40mm (1.6″), side margins of 15mm (0.6″), and, most important, a bottom margin of 20mm (0.8″), most countries' equipment should be able to read the address. If you have special airmail envelopes printed for your company, consider putting faint gray margin lines or corner indicators at these positions. Avoid printing advertising or other messages on envelopes, and certainly keep them well clear of the address.

Refer to Chapter 8 for additional advice about making addresses acceptable to OCR equipment.

There should be a return address on every letter leaving your office, since it is a fact of life that letters get returned. Your address should be printed or rubber-stamped at the top left corner. If you are a perfectionist, you could also stamp it on the flap for the United Kingdom, Ireland, and Spanish- and Portuguese-speaking countries.

Bulk Mail

If your office is mailing more than about 10 lbs. (5 kg) of international mail per day, you should probably seek specialist advice. There are two options for reducing costs. First, most post offices have special programs for international mail deposited in quantity. In the United States, the term used is *ISAL* (International Surface Air Lift). The alternative is a service known as *direct entry* or *direct injection,* offered by third-party remailers, in which your mail is freighted to the country of destination outside the postal system and deposited in the foreign country as though it were their domestic mail. Mail for direct injection obviously has to be prepared strictly in accordance with local bulk-mail requirements. For example, it must have a local return address and it must be sorted and grouped for the particular country, whereas international mail rules do not require you to know these details. The handling of undeliverable directly-injected mail will be different from undeliverable ISAL mail, probably worse. Nevertheless, cost savings can be appreciable. Remailers often act as consolidators for ISAL mail and can advise you and assist with preparation.

People sometimes question the legality of remailing services. In the early 1990s, the system for settling charges between postal administrations gave rise to strange opportunities for arbitrage. For example, a major Swiss corporation was dispatching large quantities of mail to its domestic Swiss customers from the Mediterranean island of Malta. There were cases in which post offices blocked remailers on technicalities. However, the growth of remail services has been impossible to ignore. Some Third World countries have profited handsomely, and some European postal administrations have joined in enthusiastically and established their own remailer subsidiaries. The Seoul Congress of the Universal Postal Union attempted to put the system of international settlements on a more rational and commercial basis. This is making remailing more universally acceptable, while removing some of the potential for savings that existed during the last few years. Changes in international mailing costs are to be expected over the next five years as more and more post offices in the world adopt commercial accounting practices. You will need help from intermediaries who are familiar with current practice as well as current regulations. Local letter shops (mass-mailing services) can put you in touch with international remailers.

Export Documentation

For the most part, export documentation is a specialist subject, and you will have banks and freight forwarders to help you with it. This section is written strictly for the amateur who occasionally sends air freight packages that need additional documentation or who handles occasional special billings.

The most common *customs declaration* is a small green label you have to attach to most mail except letters and printed matter. The United States has at least three different labels for different types of larger package, and also a *Shipper's Export Declaration* for business-to-business packages valued at over $500. In the "Export License No." blank, write **G-DEST** ("General Destination") unless you know that exports of your products are controlled.

A *certificate of registration* (U.S. terminology) is obtained from customs officials (ask the post office where to find them) and is advisable for anything valuable that is going to be returned to you—for example, trade-show stands and materials.

An *international air waybill* is formally a receipt for the package you hand over to an airline or an air courier service. You can get a supply of them from the air freight company. Many companies have a short form for packages that only contain documents.

A *pro-forma invoice* (also known as a *commercial invoice* or a *customs invoice*) is generally required whenever you are shipping anything other than business correspondence. Every country has its own regulations specifying when a pro-forma invoice is required, and the air freight company will have detailed information to guide you. It is best to assume one is required—you cannot go wrong by including it, but you can go wrong by not including it.

Think of the pro-forma invoice as a preview of the real invoice your accounting department will send to the consignee. It is required even if you have no intention of billing the consignee, because it is a statement of the value and contents of the package, and customs relies on it. It can be typed up on your letterhead, or an air freight company may offer you a recommended standard form. It does not have to look like your accounting department's invoice. It needs to show who you (the shipper) are (make sure your country is in the address), who the consignee is, a description of the consignment, its value, and the name of the carrier and the air waybill number. You usually provide a signed original and two photocopies in a transparent envelope attached to the package, and keep a copy for yourself.

A pro-forma invoice is usually a pure formality, and shippers run one off a word processor without much thought. However, if a letter of credit is involved, you will need to be careful with it.

Letters of credit are the key component of an international payment system operated by the banks of the world. Your company would ideally like to insist on payment in advance from foreign customers, and often the customers will agree to this for small orders. However, since they do not necessarily trust you any more than you trust them, you arrange for banks in the two countries to referee the transaction. Your customer pays its local bank, and you then have to prove to *your* local bank that you really have shipped what the customer ordered. The foreign bank sends you a document that should be called in full an Irrevocable Confirmed Documentary Letter of Credit; the letter of credit will probably not be satisfactory to your company unless it is explicitly marked as *irrevocable* and *confirmed* and *documentary*. A letter of credit is rather difficult to handle. You must check it carefully when it arrives and protest immediately to your customer if there is anything you cannot comply with. In order to get paid, you will have to comply *exactly* with it—there is *no* tolerance! If the letter of credit says you have to ship in a wooden box, you will have to prove to your bank (by means of the air waybill) that the box was wooden and not plastic. If it says you have to present a certificate of inspection, you had better have a document in the file headed "Certificate of Inspection." See Alan Branch's *Import and Export Documentation* (New York: Chapman & Hall, 1989) for a long and excellent checklist of all the things that can go wrong.

The *single administrative document*, or SAD, is a combined export declaration, transit document, and import declaration used in Europe. If you are shipping within the European Community, you will need to be familiar with your national version of the SAD.

IMPORTANCE OF CONSISTENCY

There are several additional things to be careful about.

If you declare a "value for carriage" above the normal default value on the air waybill, there may be an extra charge.

Watch out for all value and weight limits on official forms. If you can justifiably value something at $499 instead of $500, or divide a large package into two smaller ones, you may sometimes be able to avoid trouble and delays.

The values and the description of the goods must be identical on your air waybill and your pro-forma invoice; otherwise you risk causing customs delays.

The values and the description of the goods on the shipping documents must also be identical to those on the letter of credit; otherwise you will cause serious delays in obtaining payment.

When you ship diskettes and computer media, you are supposed to declare separate values for the media and the data. If you ship such materials regularly, be sure you know what your company's policy is.

Always note the waybill number for tracing purposes. If the consignment is critical to the recipients, fax them the waybill number, the name of the carrier, and the date as soon as the shipment is picked up by the carrier (and not before, in case something changes).

Unless somebody instructs you differently, sign shipping documents yourself with a suitably impressive title, such as "International Shipping Specialist." (Executives do not usually want to be bothered with shipping details unless the consignment has a high value and a letter of credit has to be complied with.)

Most countries now require you to file export documents under a national tax identification number (Federal Employer Identification Number in the United States, Value-Added Tax Registration Number in Europe), and these are increasingly being used to look for inconsistencies between different shipments and to compare your customs declarations to your other tax returns.

WHAT TO DECLARE

When you want to know how to describe your goods, always ask a freight forwarder rather than a government agency. Government officials will either simply read the rules to you or throw the problem back in your lap by asking you to choose from among thousands of code numbers. The staff of an international freight forwarder knows how to get a consignment through customs with the least fuss. Your primary goal is to reduce delay rather than to reduce costs. Customs duties are mostly low, but customs procedures can be time-consuming and have great nuisance value for businesses. To be a good trading partner, you and have great nuisance value for businesses. To be a good trading partner, you need to make export paperwork look as innocuous as possible without actually breaking anybody's laws.

Similarly, if incoming parcels are held up by customs, get help from a customs broker who deals with that port or airport all the time. Your own well-intentioned efforts to extract badly documented shipments from customs can easily make matters worse.

Do not exaggerate values for insurance purposes. Your package probably will not get lost, and if it does you will probably not succeed in collecting outrageous compensation. However, you run a very real risk that customs officials will base their duties and taxes on your exaggerated value, even if your proforma invoice has a lower figure. Always declare the lowest value that you can justify, because foreign charges will usually be based on your declared value unless the officials have some reason to investigate more closely.

Fax Selection

USEFUL FEATURES

Most people regard all fax machines as somewhat interchangeable, although whole books have been written about their selection. If you have any chance to influence the purchase of equipment, here are some features that make a fax machine good or bad for international needs:

Fax Feature	International Considerations
Unattended operation	Essential. It must be able to receive faxes at night and on weekends.
Integrated telephone handset	Essential. Overseas fax operators will sometimes answer, and you will feel like a fool if you can hear them but have no way of replying.
Manual redial	Very useful to have a one-touch last-number redial key on either the fax machine or its accompanying telephone equipment.
Automatic redial	Limited usefulness. If you cannot get through in two or three manual attempts, auto redial probably cannot get through either. Also, unless the machine reads your fax into memory, auto redial obstructs other users.
Delayed transmission	Limited usefulness, unless the machine can read your fax into memory. If you have to leave documents in the feeder, it obstructs other users, and you can only trust it for a single document. The idea is to take advantage of cheaper phone rates. If you have heavy traffic, you may be able to cost-justify an expensive fax machine with a lot of memory.
Error correction mode (ECM)	Saves a little time. Essential if you are dealing with countries with less-developed telecommunications networks (e.g., in South America).
Speed	Reliable transmission at 9600 baud can often be achieved. Transmission on a machine limited to 4800 baud potentially doubles your time and cost.
Automatic speed fallback	Mixed usefulness. Most current machines have this feature. It is acceptable to drop from 9600 baud to 4800, but if speed drops below 4800 you should consider redialing, especially if the fax is long.
Speed indicator	Highly desirable if the machine has Automatic Speed Fallback, for reasons stated in the previous entry.
Answerback display	Seeing some confirmation that you have dialed the right fax before you transmit is highly desirable, so as to avoid sending confidential documents to the wrong office.

Fax Feature	International Considerations
Speed dial	Highly desirable if you call a few numbers frequently: international numbers are longer than domestic ones.
Fine resolution; image enhancement	Consider what kind of documents you will be transmitting. If you send drawings or 16-pitch computer printouts (e.g., spreadsheets), you will need these features.
Plain paper	Thermal paper is adequate for most users, but plain paper is worth the extra expense if you frequently receive faxes that need to be filed. (Thermal paper is likely to fade after six months and needs to be photocopied onto plain paper for permanent filing.)
Activity report	Check that it gives you whatever information you need for usage reports or cost allocation. It is desirable to have an immediate display or printout of the duration of each international transmission so that every user gets a feeling for the costs.
Error reporting	You will have more line errors than domestic users, so find out how the machine notifies you when transmission or other errors occur: Is it clear or are there complicated codes? Does it warn you during a long transmission that errors are occurring?
Potential disadvantages of "personal" fax machines	Paper roll size too small. No document feeder. No paper cutter.

Another consideration, which can help you to judge the machine and its instructions, though it is not specifically for international use, is ease of setup. How easy is it to change the time or the answerback on the machine?

In addition to the selection of the fax machine itself, you should consider whether you need an *uninterruptible power supply*. Does it matter if there is a power outage during the night and people cannot get through to you for a while?

Since fax machines are improving rapidly, some features not listed above will probably become economical in the next year or two. More memory will certainly be beneficial. For example, the ability to read a document into memory and transmit it unattended saves a lot of time, and a machine with a large memory and a second phone line is able to transmit and receive at the same time.

Processing Orders from outside the United States

Many foreign companies purchase American components directly in the United States, either because no distributor exists in their home country or else to obtain better prices or the latest versions. American employees who are unfamiliar with export procedures, or afraid of them, often raise three unnecessary objections, each of which is addressed below.

1. *Do not demand a certificate of exemption from sales tax from foreign customers*. As a general principle, sales tax is not charged on any shipment leaving the country. A foreign customer does not have to provide a certificate of exemption. You can confirm this with your sales tax hotline.

2. *Do not demand unnecessary export licenses.* If you are trading in weapons, food, dangerous substances, fakes, military equipment, pornography, or live animals, then clearly you are subject to real trade barriers which you are probably familiar with. Most ordinary purchases are covered by the "general license G-DEST," and you can simply write "G-DEST" in any blank where an export license number is required. If you are in doubt about the status of any of your products, check with the local office of the U.S. Department of Commerce.

3. *Do not raise difficulties about selling outside your territory.* Some manufacturers do impose restrictions on distributors, or on themselves, to avoid creating a "gray market" overseas. The restrictions may or may not be enforceable. Remember that your overseas customers may have genuine difficulty obtaining the product locally. It is also true that they may be trying to defeat the manufacturer's restrictions, but you should only refuse business if you are sure of your facts and of your company's policy. Just because you cannot sell into the next state does not mean that you cannot sell overseas.

Foreign companies that do a lot of purchasing in the United States often deal through an intermediary or establish their own purchasing office. If you are shipping substantial quantities of products to an obscure customer located near an international border or just outside a major international airport, you can guess that they are ending up overseas. Unless your product is subject to national-security controls, you should probably accept such business at face value.

Conclusions

International executives and salespeople often depend heavily on support staff to follow up quickly and efficiently on the deals they have struck and the promises they have made. After they have spent money and effort to get a foreign company to cooperate in some exercise, any delays and mistakes become very frustrating. Office staff must be knowledgeable and competent and must have access to detailed information about the regulations of the post office and of air courier companies. You do not need to learn the contents of thick manuals, but you do need to know what information exists and where to look for it. You also need to take responsibility and use common sense, as though you were spending your own money and sending messages and packages to people who are important to you personally.

3. Useful Products and Services

This chapter will attempt to identify a variety of books, services, and other resources ranging from the merely convenient to the indispensable.

Bibliography

Your bookshelf should contain the following:

Any *world atlas*.

A *map of Europe* with a multinational list of places, such as the *Europa Strassenatlas mit Orts- und Namenverzeichnis* ("Europe Road Atlas with Index of Places and Names"), published by Hallwag, Bern, Switzerland. Local maps can be obtained from specialized bookstores, such as:

Traveller's Bookstore
75 Rockefeller Plaza
22 West 52nd Street
NEW YORK NY 10019
Tel.: 800/755-8728
Fax: 212/397-3984

Stanfords
12-14 Long Acre
LONDON WC2E 9LP
U.K.
Tel.: +44-1-71-836-1321
Fax: +44-1-71-836-0189

A *road atlas of the United States*, such as the *Rand McNally Road Atlas*.

The *postal regulations of your own country*. In the United States, the *Domestic Mail Manual* and the *International Mail Manual* are published every six months and are available on subscription (allow plenty of lead time) from:

Superintendent of Documents
P. O. Box 371954
PITTSBURGH PA 15250-7954
Tel.: 202/512-1800
Fax: 202/512-2250

The *national postcode directory* of any country that you deal with extensively, if you can understand it. In the United States, the USPS book is republished as the *National Five-Digit ZIP Code and Post Office Directory* by:

National Information Data Center
P. O. Box 96523
WASHINGTON DC 20090-6523
Tel.: 301/816-8950
Fax: 301/816-8945

In other countries, you will need to activate your local contacts to get post-office publications. Requesting them by mail is a long and frustrating process in most cases.

The *AT&T Direct Service Worldwide Calling Guide,* a concise pocket guide to international dialing. It is available free of charge from AT&T by calling 800/428-8468.

Phone books for at least the capital cities of any countries you deal with regularly. Most foreign phone books are obtainable from:

M. Arman Publishing Inc.
P. O. Box 785
ORMOND BEACH FL 32175
Tel.: 904/673-5576
Fax: 904/673-6560

A *national trade directory* for any country that you are interested in. For most countries in this book, the most readily available directory is the one published by Kompass AG, Zürich, Switzerland, and its international associates. For the United States, industry-specific directories (such as *Data Sources,* published by Ziff-Davis, for the computer industry) are more useful and accurate than general directories. One informative general reference work for the United States is the *Directory of Corporate Affiliations,* available from:

National Register Publishing Co./Reed Reference
121 Chanlon Rd.
NEW PROVIDENCE NJ 07974
Tel.: 908/464-6800
Fax: 908/665-6688

The *Japan Company Handbook,* an English-language book on Japanese corporations, is published by:

Toyo Keizai America Inc.
380 Lexington Ave., Suite 4505
NEW YORK NY 10168
Tel.: 212/949-6737
Fax: 212/949-6648

Stock-exchange directories, in particular the *NASDAQ Fact Book and Company Directory* in the United States, available from the National Association of Securities Dealers (202/728-8000); and the (London) *Stock Exchange Official Yearbook* in the United Kingdom, available from the London Stock Exchange by phone (+44-71-797-3306) or fax (+44-71-410-6861).

An *international airline guide,* of which there are two in English: the *Official Airline Guide* (Oak Brook, Ill.: Official Airline Guides) in the United States, and the *ABC World Airways Guide* (Dunstable, Beds.: Reed Travel Group) in the United Kingdom.

A *schedule for European railroads,* such as the *Thomas Cook European Railway Timetable,* which is available from certain offices of the Thomas Cook travel agency chain, or more easily in the United States from:

Forsyth Travel Library
P. O. Box 2975
SHAWNEE MISSION KS 66201-1375
Tel.: 800/FORSYTH
Fax: 913/384-3553

A *guide to holidays and time differences*, such as the *World Holiday and Time Guide*, published by:

Corporate Communication Dept.
J. P. Morgan & Co.
60 Wall Street, 45th floor
NEW YORK NY 10260
Tel.: 212/648-9607

A *guide to shipping documentation*, such as Alan E. Branch's *Import and Export Documentation* (New York: Chapman & Hall, 1989).

A *guide to international business etiquette*, such as Roger Axtell's *Do's and Taboos around the World*, 3d ed. (New York: John Wiley, 1993). *Do's and Taboos of International Trade: A Small Business Primer*, by the same author (Wiley, 1994), is another helpful guide.

Cost-of-Living Information

You can spend a small fortune on specialized research services and personnel consultants to advise your organization about costs of business travel and expatriate living in foreign countries. There are also the following excellent sources of less detailed information.

A free booklet called *Prices and Earnings around the Globe* is intermittently available from the Union Bank of Switzerland, which has offices in major cities everywhere, including:

444 S. Flower St., Suite 4500
LOS ANGELES CA 90071
Tel.: 213/489-0600
Fax: 213/489-0637

Information compiled by the U.S. government for its own overseas personnel policy is available to the public. There are two particularly useful documents entitled *Maximum Travel Per Diem Allowances for Foreign Areas* and *U.S. Dept. of State Indexes of Living Costs Abroad*. Copies are available from:

Superintendent of Documents
P. O. Box 371954
PITTSBURGH PA 15250-7954
Tel.: 202/512-1800
Fax: 202/512-2250

Prices in these publications are a very good guide to comparative costs and are themselves good budget figures for professional staff who are traveling to countries they are unfamiliar with. Someone with local knowledge, or who speaks the local language, or who is on a tight budget can travel a little more cheaply, at maybe 75 percent of the cost. On the other hand, a senior executive using the major international hotel chains can easily spend double the government allowances.

A source of detailed practical information for business travelers is the *Multinational Executive Travel Companion,* published by:

Suburban Publishing of Connecticut
P.O. Box 1293
STAMFORD CT 06904-1293
Tel.: 203/324-3007
Fax: 203/967-8404

and republished by other organizations, including the Union Bank of Finland. Be aware that information on "Local Customs" in publications of this type is apt to be very subjective.

Associations

Someone in your organization may be interested in belonging to one of the following associations, which all publish interesting newsletters, even if you are not able to play an active part:

International Telecommunications
 Users Group
31 Westminster Palace Gardens
Artillery Row
LONDON SW1P 1RR
U.K.
Tel.: +44-1-71-799-2446
Fax: +44-71-799-2445

International Communications
 Association
2735 Villa Creek Drive, Ste. 200
DALLAS TX 75234-7419
Tel.: 214/233-3889
Fax: 214/488-9985

International Facsimile Association/
 International Facsimile
 Consultative Council
4019 Lakeview Drive
LAKE HAVASU CITY AZ 86406
Tel.: 520/453-3850
Fax: 520/453-9234

Foreign-Language Correspondence

If you intend to try and write in another language, you should equip yourself with the best local dictionary you can afford, the best bilingual dictionary you can afford, and, if there is one available, a commercial dictionary. A good test of a bilingual dictionary is to see whether it translates accounting terminology. Look up *receivables, payables, ledger, journal entry.* If it passes that test, try some warehouse terminology: *skid, gantry, lift truck.*

You will also need a secretarial handbook and a book of sample letters from the foreign country.

Most multilingual (as opposed to bilingual) dictionaries and phrase books contain an inadequate level of detail. However, two books worth knowing about are the *Handbook for Multilingual Business Writing,* 2d ed., distributed in the United States by NTC Business Books, and a series in several volumes called the *Bilingual Guides to Business and Professional Correspondence,* distributed in the United States by Franklin Book Co. Neither is perfect, but the idea behind them—to provide a structured vocabulary of phrases that you can assemble into a routine letter with a very limited knowledge of the foreign language—is very good. Microsoft publishes a technical glossary which is useful for anyone localizing computer programs or manuals.

Translators

When should you have outgoing material translated, and who should do the work?

In most business situations, all sales and promotional literature should be translated, unless the market is highly technical. Instruction books should also be translated unless you are sure that the users are professionals who will be fluent in English. All safety warnings should be translated.

It is always difficult to decide whether to have internal documentation or detailed maintenance instructions and product specifications translated. Often, engineers in your foreign affiliates, distributors, and major clients would rather have up-to-date documentation in English than out-of-date or poorly translated versions in their own language. Maintaining a long description of an evolving product in several languages over a period of years represents a significant cost and effort which is not to be underestimated. You should consult the readers before committing resources to it; they might tell you that they only want an index or a glossary in their own languages.

Advertising, unless it is extremely factual, should never be translated, for a different reason. Advertising styles differ greatly from country to country. A design or an idea that catches the eye of an American may not work at all in other countries, including Britain. Advertising generally needs to be rethought by local specialists.

Promotional literature presents a similar problem. A translator is unlikely to be a competent direct-mail copywriter. At worst, you may find translators whose real interests are literary and cultural and who are mildly antibusiness. Your carefully worded letter expressing enthusiastically the advantages of your product or service and detailing the immense benefits of placing an immediate order may return from the translation agency with a distinct loss of color and persuasiveness. A marketing person with a limited knowledge of the foreign language can negotiate with the translator to restore the sales pitch to the letter. If nobody understands the foreign language well enough to do this, you should plan on a two-stage process in which the translator produces a literal translation and then a foreign copywriter (even a distributor's sales representative) improves it. Again, it may help the translator if you can collect some samples of direct-mail letters in the foreign language.

Technical material should really be translated by people who understand the subject matter. Nobody will know how to translate "twisted-pair" unless he or she is familiar with the terminology of the telecommunications industry. To keep up to date, a professional will subscribe to foreign-language trade publications and search them carefully for terms that are not yet accepted into dictionaries. Specialized translators for a particular subject and language may be difficult or impossible to find. You should plan for a joint effort between your engineers, your own technical writers, and the translators; you cannot expect good results if you just unload material onto a translator without an explanation of your specialized vocabulary.

Translation agencies and individual professional translators can be found in all major cities through the Yellow Pages. Amateurs, such as immigrants and students, can also be useful, especially for rarer languages, and for incoming translations at less than publication-quality. You can find amateurs through associations, such as a Swedish-American Chamber of Commerce or a Chinese-American Voter Registration Project. Organizations like these often are not listed in the phone book, but consulates, universities, immigrant churches, ethnic restaurants, and often local newspapers and politicians will know them. You can also look overseas for translators, particularly if you need an industry specialist or a press watch.

AT&T can set up a conference call with an interpreter while you wait. The AT&T Language Line can be reached at 800/752-6096 or, from outside the United States, at +1-408-648-5861. You will need a credit card.

CompuServe (800/848-8199) offers both automatic and manual translation services for electronic mail. Other e-mail services are likely to appear during the currency of this book.

Further information and guidance is published by

American Translators Association
1800 Diagonal Road, Suite 220
ALEXANDRIA VA 22314
Tel.: 703/683-6100

Computer Products

NON-ROMAN FONTS

The following companies offer fonts and word-processing programs in a wide variety of alphabets.

Timeworks
625 Academy Dr.
NORTHBROOK IL 60062
Tel.: 708/559-1300

Data-Cal Corporation
531 East Elliot Rd., Suite 145
CHANDLER AZ 85225-1118
Tel.: 602/813-3100
Fax: 602/545-8090

Linguist's Software
P. O. Box 580
EDMONDS WA 98020-0580
Tel.: 206/775-1130
Fax: 206/771-5911

CIMOS
73, avenue Gambetta
75020 PARIS
FRANCE
Tel.: +33-1-43.66.88.48
Fax: +33-1-43.66.51.13

Wright & Associates
P. O. Box 994
KENT OH 44240-0994
Tel.: 330/673-0043
Fax: 330/673-0738

Diplomat Software
P. O. Box 9878
NEWPORT BEACH CA 92658
Tel.: 714/775-1229
Fax: 714/448-0895

Gamma Productions Inc.
12625 High Bluff Drive, Suite 218
SAN DIEGO CA 92130
Tel.: 619/794-6399
Fax: 619/794-7294

TRANSLATION SOFTWARE

Translation software originated as a productivity aid for professional translators. At the time of writing, PC translation products are not suitable for ordinary office use. They can be valuable for an organization that translates large volumes of rather uniform material. But to work well, they need to be specialized very carefully over a long period of time with the technical vocabulary of their users, and the output needs to be reviewed manually. It is not currently realistic to expect to produce automatic translations of average business correspondence, especially marketing materials. However, it would be worth evaluating translation products if you are interested in scanning foreign-language text just to see what you want to have professionally translated. Products of this type are likely to improve over the next few years. The following are specialist companies:

Globalink, Inc.
9302 Lee Highway, 12th floor
FAIRFAX VA 22031
Tel.: 800/255-5660
Fax: 703/273-3866

Polygon Industries, Inc.
P. O. Box 24096
NEW ORLEANS LA 70184
Tel.: 504/451-5721
Fax: 504/486-2371

Linguistic Products, Inc.
P. O. Box 8263
THE WOODLANDS TX 77387
Tel.: 713/298-2565
Fax: 713/298-1911

Microtak Software
4375 Jutland Drive, Suite 110
SAN DIEGO CA 92117
Tel.: 619/272-5700
Fax: 619/272-9734

To test a product of this type, do two things. Take an article from the foreign trade press, scan it, transfer it to the translation package by whatever means the producer recommends, translate it, and see if you can understand it. Then take a standard business letter—for example, a cover letter that accompanies brochures you send out—and use the product to translate it into a foreign language and back again. Do not accept translations of text prepared by the vendors as a valid test—they are usually carefully written to be easy to translate.

A magazine called *Multilingual Computing* is a source of information about new products and services in this field. For information call 208/263-8178, fax 208/263-6310, or e-mail info@multilingual.com. Expect it to support vendors' optimism about who can realistically use their products.

Address Hygiene

"Address hygiene" and "(mailing) list hygiene" are the computer industry's jargon for the level of accuracy and standardization of postal addresses. The U.S. Postal Service operates an Address List Correction Service based on its Carrier Route Information System (CRIS), and also licenses its National Change of Address (NCOA) system information to a variety of private vendors. More and more U.S. software products incorporate NCOA address correctors. One reseller with a personal-computer *Address Corrector* based on this system is Alpha Software Corporation (800/622-7105), vendors of the Alpha Five database.

A prominent mainframe vendor is Group One Corporation (800/368-5806 or + 1-301-731-2300). Products of this kind greatly assist the elimination of duplicate addresses as well as economizing on postage for bulk mailings.

In 1996, the correction of addresses in other countries is still far more difficult. National software is available from the post offices of the United Kingdom, Germany, and Japan (though not for Roman-alphabet Japanese addresses), and others will probably follow suit during the currency of this book. Two independent software vendors providing national address hygiene software are AFD Ltd. (at + 44-1924-823221, fax + 44-1924-822905) for the United Kingdom, and Corradress S.A. (at + 33-1-40.77.54.67, fax + 33-1-40.77.54.68) for France.

A multinational address correction software product is Global-Z, created by Dasgar Systems Inc. (at 802/447-3978, fax 802/442-3473).

Government Information Services

Most countries' governments make at least a show of providing assistance to their taxpaying exporters. But the taxpaying exporters often have an unrealistic idea of what they can expect in the way of assistance.

The inexperienced exporter will usually be looking at a number of likely countries, wanting market research, information about local regulatory requirements, general information about market opportunities, specific contacts with major customers, and specific information about distribution channels and individual distributors.

A typical *embassy* is located in a capital city and consists, at the lower levels, of consular, commercial, and information departments. *Consular officers* issue (or refuse to issue) passports, visas, birth certificates, death certificates, and the like. *Commercial officers* are there to assist exporters from their own country. *Information officers* report home about the foreign political situation, distribute positive information about their own country, and arrange cultural exchanges of various kinds. Any of these officers may have the title of consul or vice-consul. A *consulate-general* is a branch of an embassy, usually located outside the capital city, and also performs the above functions. A *consulate* is a sub-office with a limited set of functions and may well not have a commercial department. (Spell these words correctly: if you confuse consuls and councils and counsels, you will look ignorant to diplomats.) Embassies may also have military and technical specialists on loan from various government departments, who may be valuable contacts on regulatory and procurement matters. Some countries (not the United States) call their commercial organization a *trade commission* and keep it physically separate from embassies and consulates-general, but all the same comments apply to it. Individual provinces and regions of some countries, including many states of the United States, have established their own overseas commercial representative offices because of dissatisfaction with their national organizations. For simplicity, all these functions will be referred to below collectively as a *Foreign Service*.

Exporters can theoretically get information about foreign market conditions and opportunities from the commercial departments of their own Foreign Service. The entry point into the system in the United States is through the International Trade Administration of the Department of Commerce, which has offices all around the country. In case of difficulty, call 202/482-3809 in Washington, D.C., for the location of the regional office responsible for your area. The corresponding organizations for U.K. exporters are the British Overseas Trade Board (071-215 5000) and the Department of Trade and Industry. If your interest is in a specific country or two, you can bypass the ITA (or BOTB) by writing to your embassy in those foreign capitals. The U.S. embassies usually have special domestic addresses you can use (for example, "AmEmbassy Moscow, PSC 77-FCS, APO AE 09721"), which you can obtain from the U.S. State Department (202/647-4000).

The Japanese External Trade Relations Organization (JETRO) is the one foreign trade commission that may assist you to export. Generally, Foreign Services of other countries have no mandate to promote U.S. exports, and ours does not encourage imports.

What can an exporter expect? You will be able to obtain basic factual information from the Foreign Service about the economy of the country, business hours, the most popular trade shows, and addresses of national regulatory agencies. It may have specific information about retail trade distribution channels. The Foreign Service may sponsor occasional exhibitions or participate in trade shows. It may have lists of the names of some local translators, lawyers, accountants, and consultants of various kinds. Their standard information may or may not be up-to-date, depending on the trading importance of the country. Whether they can do more for you will depend on the individuals; if you are lucky, local staff with business backgrounds may have useful suggestions and contacts. But the official systems for finding trading partners for you produce very haphazard results.

If you are an importer, on the other hand, you must turn to the Foreign Service of the country that you want to buy from. Write politely to their commercial department, explaining what you want, and expect to make an appointment. Someone is quite likely to visit you if you appear serious. They will write a report on you, and the information is supposed to circulate to exporters in their home country. Do not hold your breath waiting for the official system to work. However, again, individuals may be knowledgeable and may provide useful background information.

If you want standard information about a foreign country, any of the above sources (commercial and information departments of your Foreign Service or theirs) will probably be willing to look it up for you in Yellow Pages, almanacs, or trade directories. Their information may not be very recent. You must have precise questions; it is not reasonable to ask these people to study your business and make recommendations.

Contact with consular departments is usually frustrating for businesspeople. Regulations are constructed to control immigration, without making many allowances for the legitimate needs of international business visitors. Visas, residence permits, and work permits are processed at a pace that may have been appropriate in the nineteenth century. Many business executives therefore travel around as tourists on the borderline of illegality, because it is just impractical to comply with official requirements, particularly when executives are relocating for overseas assignments. If you do research for relocations, be particularly careful to find out about permits for spouses and live-in companions. Regulations are invariably written with the assumption that an accompanying companion is a nonworking female, legally married to the principal male applicant.

There is another category of government organizations whose object is to encourage you to establish manufacturing and similar facilities in their country. This is often a regional or local function with varying degrees of central government coordination. Commercial departments will be able to tell you who to contact concerning their own regions. Well-known examples of economic development organizations active in the United States are Locate in Scotland (formerly the Scottish Development Agency) and the French DATAR.

In other countries, financial information published by large public companies is less carefully controlled than it is in the United States by the SEC. However, private companies in most countries have to file annual financial statements with their governments, and these are generally public records. Getting access to them may be difficult and time-consuming, particularly if there is a language barrier, but local intermediaries can obtain them for a fee. Local Foreign Service people should know how you can obtain financial information about individual companies.

Nongovernment Information Services

If you have a precise target market, the local *chamber of commerce* can usually provide lists of local companies. Do not underestimate them as sources of information. In many European countries membership is mandatory, and therefore their information about local businesses is the most comprehensive.

Controlled by or cooperating with chambers of commerce are some 250 *World Trade Centers* in principal cities around the world, which largely duplicate the functions described in the previous section. They have libraries and databases, provide office space and hotel discounts for visitors, organize trade missions, and help to find trading partners. Your local WTC probably has reciprocal membership facilities with its counterparts overseas.

The *national trade association* for your industry may have an international business department, or it may belong to some international federation that can supply market information. Always request lists of publications from organizations like these.

Call the *trade journals* of your industry. Many of them have sister publications overseas or links with similar publications in other countries, or at least staff members who cover international news.

Specialized consultants can be extremely valuable, but are hard to find. Someone who is really familiar with your market or activity can give you advice in a few days that would otherwise take you months or years to discover. An example in the computer industry is EMS (111 Pine Street, San Francisco CA 94111; tel.: 415/433-4344). Find such consultants through the trade press or through major manufacturers in your industry.

The *Big Six accounting firms* are an excellent source of information about overseas business matters of all kinds. In the United States, the Big Six are known as Arthur Andersen, Coopers & Lybrand, Deloitte & Touche, Ernst & Young, Peat Marwick, and Price Waterhouse. Each one has related firms, usually with similar names, all over the world, and each one publishes information about tax and other business matters in dozens of countries. You can take all

kinds of business problems to their international management consulting partners. (Finding the right people to deal with can be a little difficult outside of
major cities—insist on seeing an internal directory if necessary.) These organizations combine a multinational perspective with the detailed local business
knowledge and the local contacts to solve the typical problems of the inexperienced exporter. Of course, their services are not free by any means.

Banks possess some of the same capabilities but are less organized internationally to give general business advice, and it is not what they sell. Their in-
house knowledge of your sector of industry may be very good, but it may be
hard to locate and benefit from. *Law firms* with international connections may
have access to excellent knowledge of major companies overseas, but are likely
to be specialized in strictly professional matters.

Credit information about overseas companies is offered by the principal
U.S. companies in the business, but it is expensive and at least as erratic as it is
in the United States. Basically, you are not going to trust anybody, anyway, because of the difficulty of enforcement. Refer to the information on letters of
credit under the heading "Export Documentation" in Chapter 2.

In summary: If you are a newcomer to international business and cannot
find an international specialist who knows your exact business, the Big Six are
the most effective place to commission practical help. Commercial services organized by governments are apt to be of limited usefulness, although many individual officers will do their best to be helpful.

4. Getting Phone Calls, Faxes, and E-Mail Through

Here is a real example of a series of phone numbers from the "Italy" section of a directory published by a large, professional, well-funded, multinational organization in the United States:

```
049/669121
089-871.578
80 5216643
(0923) 869148
055. 217461
(091) 6371830
(396) 6879568
(0344) 40456
(041) 5260130-5261457
```

Someone uncritical has copied these numbers from information received directly or indirectly from Italy. Apart from failing to standardize their punctuation, the editor has not noticed that two of the contributing Italians have tried to be "helpful": one has taken the zero off the beginning of the number, and the other has changed 06 to 396 to include the country code. This is typical of what happens whenever name and address information has passed through the hands of people who do not understand it.

The Structure of Domestic Numbers

> **Long-Distance Access Code + City Code + Local Number**

MOST COUNTRIES OUTSIDE NORTH AMERICA

In most places outside the North American (Bell) system, each city, with its surrounding area, has a prefix. For consistency, it is always called a *city code* in this book. Inside one city area, the caller just dials the local number, which is usually from four to eight digits long. In some places, the local number does not have a fixed length within one city area. There may very well be both five-digit and six-digit numbers even for lines going into the same office.

To dial from one city area to another within the same country, the caller dials a *long-distance access code*—usually a single 0 (zero), but not always—then the city code for the distant city, and then the local number of the distant phone. In the terminology of this book, the long-distance access code and the city code are two different parts of the number. However, national terminology often has one name for the whole prefix; for example, 071 is often called locally the "dialing code" for central London. City codes are commonly one, two, or three digits long (after the 0 or other long-distance access code), but they can be longer. The following table provides some examples of domestic long-distance dialing.

City	Long-Distance Access Code	City Code	Local Number
Tokyo, Japan	0	3	54217698
Brussels, Belgium	0	2	6490141
Barcelona, Spain	9	3	6362880
Helsinki, Finland	9	0	647920
Hamburg, Germany	0	40	229873
Salzburg, Austria	0	662	975015
Gouda, Netherlands	0	1820	972810

In a few countries, the number for a long-distance call is always the same length. For example, a complete Spanish domestic number is always nine digits long; if the city code is longer, the local number is shorter in order to compensate.

When more numbers are needed in a growing city, most countries will lengthen the local number by adding a one-digit prefix.

There is no standard practice at all for directory information or other services. One country's directory-information service cannot usually be dialed direct from another country.

NATIONAL NUMBERS

Led by France, there is a trend away from city codes and toward national numbering systems, in which the same fixed-length number is used for both local and long-distance calls. Denmark, New Zealand, and Norway have changed to an eight-digit national dialing system, and Israel and undoubtedly other countries intend to change.

NORTH AMERICA

The United States and Canada, along with a number of Caribbean and Pacific islands, use a slightly different system. Local numbers are always seven digits long. The long-distance access code is 1, not 0. It is followed by an *area code*, which is always three digits long. Currently, the second digit of an area code is always 0 or 1. An area code covers a state or province or part of one; area codes never cross state or province boundaries. When more numbers are needed in an area, the phone companies introduce a new area code. For example, in 1991 San Francisco's 415 area-code zone split into two and the city's surrounding areas took the new area code 510. From 1996, area-code splits will not always be strictly geographical. An "overlay" area code can now be allocated to a major city, which will mean that close neighbors, or even a single office, may have phone numbers with different area codes.

SPECIAL PREFIXES

Many countries are introducing prefixes for special purposes, such as business information services and mobile phones. The prefixes sometimes (not in every country) look like city codes but are not geographic in nature. There is no consistency at all between countries.

Until recently, toll-free information services were accessible only within a given country, but they are now starting to open up to international calls, providing that the business offering the service agrees to pay the international call charges. Selected U.S. 800 (toll-free) and 900 (chargeable information) numbers may now be accessed from overseas.

IN-HOUSE DIRECT-DIAL LINES

When a subscriber has multiple lines, an incoming call should be able to "roll over" from one line to another until it finds a free line. This is usually a function of the equipment the subscribers have installed on their own premises. You cannot count on automatic rollovers when calling smaller offices in countries with less-developed telecommunications systems. For example, in some places it may be technically possible to roll calls over only to consecutive numbers.

Some countries allocate a block of numbers to a large office so that all the direct-dial numbers look similar. If all direct-dial numbers begin 264-7———, you can guess that the main switchboard operator is 264-7000. Only in Austria, Finland, Germany, and Italy is there sometimes a systematic way of identifying the operator.

The Structure of International Numbers

IAC + Country Code + City/Area Code + Local Number

The *international access code (IAC)* is a number sequence that warns your national phone system that you are about to dial another country. The system therefore interprets the next few digits as a country code rather than as a city code or a local exchange. The most widely used IAC is 00.

The *country code* is a one-, two-, or three-digit number that uniquely identifies the called country, regardless of where the caller is. From each nation, callers dial their own IAC followed by the unique country code. Thus, since France's country code is always 33, the Germans dial 0033 for France and the Irish dial 1633. After the country code, the caller dials the city code *without* the long-distance access code. "Drop the zero" is a good rule of thumb, but it is not universally true.

The country code of the North American phone system is 1, which is convenient because it makes North American numbers look the same domestically and internationally. An American company will often quote its phone number as, for example, 1-713-222-3131, because that is exactly how you would dial it from out-of-state. From overseas, you would dial your IAC and then that same number. The 1 is thus interpreted as the long-distance access code if you dial in from out-of-state, and as the country code if you dial in from overseas.

All the countries in this book can be dialed from all the other countries, but by no means every country in the world can be dialed *direct* from every other country. When we call Myanmar (Burma) from Houston, we hear an AT&T operations center in Pittsburgh talking to operators in Singapore, whose equipment plays music from *Dr. Zhivago* to soothe us while the operators try to reach Myanmar.

THE + FORMAT

A very sensible convention that is being adopted by businesses all over the world is called in this book the +*(Plus) Format.* By writing a plus sign (+) at the beginning of a number, you announce that you are starting with your country code and are giving the complete international number—except, of course, for the IAC, which will be different for each caller's country. The following four examples illustrate differences between domestic and international dialing.

City	Domestic	International
Tokyo, Japan	(03)5421-7698	+81-3-5421-7698
Houston, Texas	(713) 522-0450	+1-713-522-0450
Helsinki, Finland	(90) 869-0898	+358-0-869-0898
Monterrey, Mexico	(9183) 16 89 01	+52-83-16-89-01

I strongly advocate the use of the + Format, which tells foreigners clearly what they are supposed to dial and removes a whole class of possible misunderstandings.

Signals (Tones)

With a little practice, you can estimate how far your call has progressed. After you finish dialing, there will be complete silence for a few seconds while your local phone system waits to see if you dial any more digits. It probably does not know at this stage how many digits you should dial. (Some equipment lets you press # to show that the number is complete.) Then you will hear a click and a change of sound when it opens an international line for you. There will be a second or two before the foreign phone system reacts, which you may hear as an increase in background noise. In some places, you will hear foreign equipment redialing or connecting the number. If the foreign number does not start to ring within about 15 seconds, something has gone wrong. It is important to pay attention to the normal sequence of sounds, because it will help you to decide what to do when something does go wrong.

There are four basic signals you will hear from most national phone systems. People often have difficulty distinguishing unfamiliar signals from other countries, and do not know whether to wait or hang up. Unfortunately, a certain amount of misinformation is circulated by seemingly authoritative sources. It is best not to completely trust anything one country says about other countries' signals.

A *busy signal* (called an "engaged tone" in British English) tells you the distant phone is in use or unplugged or otherwise unavailable for reasons which are not the phone system's fault. *Almost all busy signals in the world are subsecond beeps, evenly spaced.* The pitch and the speed both vary, but not enough to be confusing. A half-second beep followed by a half-second silence is a common pattern. If the beep is as long as the pause, you are probably not listening to a ringing signal. Exceptions do exist, but are rare; the principal variation among the countries in this book is in Denmark.

There are three *ringing signals* in the world, with minor variations and exceptions. What they have in common is that *the pause between rings is noticeably longer than the ring*. In Europe, the ring is a pure tone lasting about one second, followed by a silence of three or four seconds. In North America and many Asian countries, the ring is a *brrrrr* sound formed by mixing two frequencies; it is meant to imitate a muffled bell. The third system is the British one: each ring is a mixed-frequency *brrrrr* split by a brief pause, and a long pause occurs between complete rings ("brrr-brrr, pause, brrr-brrr").

A *congestion signal* means the phone companies have not been able to reach the line you are dialing, because of equipment overloads or some other reason. Not every country has a distinctive congestion signal. Some prefer to use recorded messages, and some use their busy signal. If a busy signal begins after a delay, it probably means congestion. An extended period of background hiss is also a de facto sign of congestion. A true congestion signal, when one exists, is usually noticeably faster than the country's busy signal.

A *number-unobtainable signal* means that the number you have dialed does not exist or is disconnected. Again, some countries use recorded messages. There is no internationally standardized signal. If you hear a continuous tone or if the tones are much longer than the pauses, you are probably listening to a number-unobtainable signal.

In the individual country chapters I include warnings about unusual signals that could be confusing for foreigners. However, you may come across obsolete or nonstandard equipment that is not described here, particularly when calling rural areas.

One piece of good news is that Group III fax machines sound the same everywhere in the world.

Troubleshooting

Phones are so easy to use that people tend to panic when an international call does not go through immediately. When something goes wrong, ask yourself the classic troubleshooting questions: What was different between this call and all the international calls I have made before? Is my information reliable? Which of the possible explanations can we eliminate?

There are two ways to approach the problem. First, consider the symptoms:

Symptom	Solution
No outside line.	Read "Office Problems" section below.
A recording in your own country, refusing the call.	The IAC, country code, or city code is not correct. Read "Impossible Numbers" section.
A recording in a foreign language that you cannot understand.	Read "Foreign Recordings" section.
A busy signal before you have finished dialing.	Read "Office Problems" and "Impossible Numbers" sections.
A busy signal very quickly after you finish dialing.	Retry a few times over five minutes, then read "Impossible Numbers" section.

Symptom	Solution
A busy signal after a delay.	Retry a few times over five minutes, then read "Failure to Get Through" section.
A foreign signal that you do not understand.	Read "Signals" section above. Retry twice, then place operator-assisted call.
Silence or "white noise."	Retry a few times over five minutes, then read "Impossible Numbers" section.
A congestion signal, your own or the foreign country's.	Keep retrying. Try a different long-distance carrier if you are in a country that offers you a choice.
A continuous or near-continuous tone (or other number-unobtainable signal).	Retry once. Read "Verifying Numbers" section.
A recording after the foreign number has rung.	Read "Foreign Recordings" section.
A human being answering when you expected a fax machine.	Ask clearly for the fax. Read Chapter 5 and "Verifying Numbers" section.
An unexpected person answering in a language you don't understand.	Read Chapter 5 and "Impossible Numbers" and "Verifying Numbers" sections.
A ring that is not answered.	Retry once. Read "Foreign Holidays," "Foreign Business Hours," "Time Differentials," "Verifying Numbers," and "Failure to Get Through" sections.
A person in your own country answering.	Read "Impossible Numbers" section.
A poor-quality line (noise or echo).	Hang up and redial as soon as possible, particularly if you have a long fax, unless you have had a lot of difficulty getting through at all.

Second, examine what mistakes you could be making:

Mistake	Result
Your extension is not authorized for international calls.	You will get an immediate busy signal.
Your call-accounting code is not good.	You will get an immediate busy signal.
You did not dial what you meant to dial.	Anything could happen. Retry all failed calls once, very carefully.
You are dialing too fast (in places with older equipment).	You will get a long silence.
The number you are dialing is too short.	You will get a recording or a busy signal, possibly from your own country's phone system.
The number you are dialing is too long.	The excess digits will be ignored, so the call will probably go through to a wrong number.
The number you are dialing is legitimate, but not the one you want.	There will be no answer, or a stranger will answer.
The foreign company has relocated or changed its number.	You may get a foreign recording, a continuous tone, no answer, or a stranger.

Mistake	Result
Circuits are busy in the foreign country.	You will get a foreign recording or a foreign busy or congestion signal.
They have forwarded their calls to someone else.	An unexpected person will answer.
You are calling outside of office hours.	No answer.
You are calling on a national holiday.	No answer.
You are misunderstanding a foreign ringing signal.	Have patience.

OFFICE PROBLEMS

Consider the possibility that your own office phone system might be the culprit. Is this the first time you have ever dialed an international call from this extension? Has anybody been reconfiguring the phone system in your office? Do you need any special authorization or call-accounting code to make international calls from this extension? If the answer to any of these questions might be yes, try the call on an executive's phone or on a fax machine with a direct outside line.

IMPOSSIBLE NUMBERS

Consider first where you got the phone number from. If the number is from your own address file and you have dialed it many times before, then it is highly reliable. If it has come out of a five-year-old trade directory, it is highly suspect.

The two commonest occurrences of misplaced trust are:

- *You are trusting a phone number that has not come to you directly from its own country.* When such information passes through the hands of nonnatives, mistakes tend to be made. A trade directory that covers multiple countries is unreliable, as is a list of foreign subsidiaries or dealers of a multinational company.

- *You are trusting foreigners to tell you how to call in to them from other countries.* They never do that themselves, so they do not really know whether they are correct or not. However, anyone who gives you a number in the + Format is more likely to be correct. Its use is an encouraging sign that they understand what they are doing.

If the symptoms indicate that you have a number which cannot exist, as opposed to one that is simply disconnected, here are the most likely causes of the problem:

- *You forgot to dial your international access code.* From the United States, 16127359159 is in Minnesota but 01-16127359159 is in Sydney, Australia.

- *You are dialing the wrong country.* Ridiculous? It happens all the time! Which do you want—Northern Ireland or the Republic of Ireland? North Korea or South Korea? the Republic of China or the People's Republic of China? and an American specialty: Austria or Australia?

- *You could be dialing the wrong country code*. It can't happen? You can't look a number up wrong in the phone book? Your boss would never interrupt you between looking up the code and dialing it? The easiest way to get a wrong code is to ask somebody who doesn't want to admit ignorance—"What's Switzerland again?" "39, I think"—and there you are, dialing Italy.

- *You might not have dialed the country code*. Apart from just plain forgetting, this is how it can happen: You are dialing the number 45 59 53 98 in Denmark; the country code for Denmark is 45, so you assume the 45 is the country code, but in fact Denmark has eight-digit domestic numbers.

- *You could have dialed the country code twice*. This may happen because you think the number you are looking at is a domestic number but it actually includes the country code already, as in the example at the beginning of this chapter. The second country code you dial will be taken as the city code, which is probably not valid.

- *You could have dialed the other country's international access code*. Lots of people assume that IACs are the same everywhere. Thus, a "helpful" South African will tell you to dial (092711) 804-1273; you drop the 0, dial your IAC to begin with, as you always do, and it doesn't work!

- *You could have dialed the other country's long-distance access code*. Automatically dialing 0 between the country code and the city code is not only a beginner's mistake. The foreign country's long-distance access code may not be 0! (Watch out for Finland, Spain, and Mexico.) Also, if you are dialing a North American number from overseas, do not dial 1 twice—no area code begins with 1.

- *You could have the wrong city code*. People do know their own city codes. The danger here occurs when you have had to look the code up yourself or get it from an operator. Which Freiburg? Or was it Friedberg? Or Freiberg? Are they in Neukirchen or Neuenkirchen? Which Newcastle? Which San Lorenzo?

- *You could have an out-of-date city code*. The city code for central London is now 71, not 1, and will change again in 1995. In the United States, area codes 312, 415, and 213 have split recently.

- *You could have dropped a 0 that you needed*. A few city codes really do begin with 0, which you need to dial. Helsinki and the Australian state of Tasmania are examples.

- *All local numbers in that city could have changed*. For example, Tokyo numbers have recently increased from seven to eight digits.

VERIFYING NUMBERS

Could you really have a wrong number? Where did you get it from? Was it a clear, recent letterhead or was it an unclear fax or an old trade directory?

Getting foreign directory information is often painful. Many countries are slow to respond. There may be a language barrier. (Spell very slowly; see Chapter 5.) Operators are inclined to tell foreigners there is no listing, in order to get rid of them and move on to an easier customer. You may have better luck calling for directory information in the middle of the foreign country's night, when they are less busy.

Where else can you get foreign numbers? Another difficult source of information is the foreign country's embassy in your capital city, or its associated organizations, such as consulates or trade commissions. They probably have phone books from home, at least old ones, but they may consider it beneath their dignity to look something up for you. Maintain firmly that you want to buy something urgently from the company you are inquiring about, because they are supposed to help their own exporters.

Major business libraries, chambers of commerce, and similar organizations may have foreign phone books that you can consult in person, or may offer to look up foreign numbers if you call them by phone.

You probably deal with a small number of countries regularly. Get their phone books if you can. You may be able to order them from your local phone company, if you have the patience. Another source is listed in the chapter on "Useful Products and Services." You could also ask traveling executives to bring or ship you phone books from overseas. (It will not be the primary task on their minds, so fax their hotel to remind them and suggest that they ask the hotel to take care of it.) All you will generally need is the capital city's phone book. However, Germany is so decentralized that you will need a national trade directory; refer to Chapter 3. The United States is also highly decentralized, but fortunately phone books are less necessary because the phone companies' directory information services work well, provided you know where the business is located. Locating the home of a U.S. business can be quite difficult. However, consolidated U.S. listings on CD-ROM are available off-the-shelf in many U.S. bookstores and software stores.

FOREIGN RECORDINGS

Always listen to a recording to the end; if you are lucky, an English translation will follow. The Norwegians, for example, are aware that few foreigners understand Norwegian messages, so they kindly repeat them in English. However, French and German telecommunications officials never record an English word.

You must pay attention to when the recording starts. Did the number ring or not?

If it rang, you are dealing with an answering machine or voice-mail system, which will beep and wait for your message. Leave your name, country, and number very clearly; leave a fax number too, if appropriate. If you want to send a fax but a recording answers, press START anyway. It may be one of those systems that can recognize a fax tone and connect you to a fax machine. You have incurred a charge already, so do not give up until the line disconnects without the paper moving through your machine.

If the recording is a phone-company recording, it is almost certainly telling you one of three things: (1) circuits are busy, (2) the number is no good, or (3) the number has been changed.

A changed-number recording is usually easy to identify because you will hear a computer-generated voice saying digits slowly in its own language: "incomprehensible (pause) yksi (pause) kaksi (pause) kolme (pause) nelyä." At this point, the official solution is to call your international operators and force them to call an operator in the other country to listen to the recording and interpret for you. Ultimately, the same is true for other recordings. (But see also "Conclusion" below.)

FOREIGN HOLIDAYS

A surprisingly common reason for getting no answer from a foreign number is that you are calling on one of their national or local holidays. Local holidays are impossible to keep track of without an annual world guide (see p. 369). However, the principal holidays observed every year by businesses in the countries in this book are as follows (see table of ISO abbreviations, p. 382):

FOREIGN HOLIDAYS	
January	1(everywhere), 2(CH,KR,TW), 6(AT,DE,ES,FI,GR,IT,SE), 7(RU), 15(JP), 20(BR), 25(BR), 26(AU,IN)
February	5(MX), 6(NZ), 8(SI), 11(JP), 3d Mon.(US)
March	1(KR), 8(RU), 15(HU), 17(IE), 19(ES,VE), 21(MX), 25(GR), 29(TW)
April	5(KR,TW), 6(TH,ZA), 9(PH), 12–14(TH), 19(VE), 21(BR), 23(TR), 25(AU,IT,NZ,PT), 29(JP), 30(NL)
May	1(almost everywhere), 1st Mon.(GB), 3(JP,PL), 5(JP,KR,MX,NL,TH), 8(CS,FR), 9(RU), 17(NO), 19(TR), 21(CL), 25(AR), 28(LU), 29(TR), 31(ZA), penultimate Mon.(CA), last Mon.(GB,US)
June	3(MY), 5(DK), 6(KR), 10(PT), 12(PH,RU), 18(BR), 20(AR), 23(LU), 24(Quebec,VE), 25(SI)
July	1(CA), 4(US), 5(CS,VE), 6(CS), 9(AR), 14(FR), 17(KR), 21(BE), 24(VE), 25(ES)
August	1(CH), 1st Mon.(CA,IE), 8(HU), 9(SG), 12(TH), 15(AT,BE,CH,CL,ES,FR,GR, IN,IT,KR,LU,PL,PT,VE), 17(AR,ID), 27(PH), 30(TR), 31(MY), last Mon.(GB,HK)
September	1(MX), 1st Mon.(CA,US), 7(BR), 11(CL), 15(JP), 16(MX), 18–19(CL), 23(JP), 28(TW)
October	1(NG,CN,HK), 2(IN,CN,HK), 3(DE,KR), 5(PT), 10(JP,TW,ZA), 12(AR,BR, CL,ES,MX,VE), 2d Mon.(CA), 23(HU,TH), 25(TW), 26(AT,NZ), 28(CS,GR,TR), 29(TR),31(TW), last Mon.(IE)
November	1(AT,BE,CH,CL,DE,ES,FR,IT,LU,MX,PL,PT,SI,VE), 2(BE,BR,LU,MX), 3(JP), 7(RU), 10(TR), 11(BE,CA,FR,PL,US), 12(TW), 15(BR), 3d Wed.(DE), 20(MX), 23(JP), 24–26(CS), 4th Thurs.(US), 30(PH)
December	1(PT), 5(TH), 6(ES,FI), 8(AR,AT,CH,CL,ES,IT,PT), 10(TH), 12(MX), 16(ZA), 23(JP), 24(FI), 25–26(almost everywhere), 30(PH), 31(AR)

There are also international holidays that are not tied to the Western calendar: Chinese New Year (usually February), Good Friday (usually April), Easter Monday (usually April), Ascension (sixth Thursday after Easter), Pentecost (Whit) Monday (eighth Monday after Easter), Corpus Christi (ninth Thursday after Easter), plus numerous movable Chinese, Muslim, and Israeli holidays.

FOREIGN BUSINESS HOURS

Detailed lists of business hours are meaningless. Opening hours and lunch breaks vary more from one company to another than from one country to another. Business hours are typically 8 a.m. to 5 p.m. in smaller towns every-where, and 9 a.m. to 6 p.m. in the largest cities. Executives in all countries often stay in the office later. Lunch is a time-consuming event around the Mediterranean (leave people alone between their noon and 2 p.m.) and in Spanish-speaking countries (try to get them before 2 p.m.). Expect offices in Muslim countries to be closed on Thursday afternoons and Fridays.

TIME DIFFERENTIALS

The following tables, based on Chicago (i.e., Central) time, will help you to identify good times to call during the winter and the summer. Because different countries change to summer time at different dates, there is always doubt about the time differences in the spring and fall; consult the *World Holiday and Time Guide* (see Chapter 3) for precise dates. Obviously, southern-hemisphere countries "spring forward and fall back" on an opposite schedule from northern-hemisphere countries, which creates a double time shift. (In the tables, *tmw* stands for "tomorrow," and *prev.* stands for "previous.")

Country	TIME DIFFERENCES, NOVEMBER–FEBRUARY			
	Chicago's 8 a.m. is their:	Chicago's 5 p.m. is their:	Their 8 a.m. is Chicago's:	Their 5 p.m. is Chicago's:
Europe:				
Ireland	2 p.m.	11 p.m.	2 a.m.	11 a.m.
Finland	4 p.m.	1 a.m. tmw	midnight prev. night	9 a.m.
Greece	4 p.m.	1 a.m. tmw	midnight prev. night	9 a.m.
Russia (Moscow)	5 p.m.	2 a.m. tmw	11 p.m. prev. night	8 a.m.
Turkey	4 p.m.	1 a.m. tmw	midnight prev. night	9 a.m.
United Kingdom	2 p.m.	11 p.m.	2 a.m.	11 a.m.
Other Europe	3 p.m.	midnight	1 a.m.	10 a.m.
Middle East:				
Israel	4 p.m.	1 a.m. tmw	midnight prev. night	9 a.m.
Saudi Arabia	5 p.m.	2 a.m. tmw	11 p.m. prev. night	8 a.m.
Southern-Hemisphere America:				
Argentina	11 a.m.	8 p.m.	5 a.m.	2 p.m.
Brazil (Rio, São Paulo)	noon	9 p.m.	4 a.m.	1 p.m.
Chile	11 a.m.	8 p.m.	5 a.m.	2 p.m.
Northern-Hemisphere America:				
Mexico (Mexico City)	8 a.m.	5 p.m.	8 a.m.	5 p.m.
Venezuela	10 a.m.	7 p.m.	6 a.m.	3 p.m.
Northern-Hemisphere Pacific:				
China	10 p.m.	7 a.m. tmw	6 p.m. prev. day	3 a.m.
Hong Kong	10 p.m.	7 a.m. tmw	6 p.m. prev. day	3 a.m.
Indonesia (Jakarta)	9 p.m.	6 a.m. tmw	7 p.m. prev. day	4 a.m.
Japan	11 p.m.	8 a.m. tmw	5 p.m. prev. day	2 a.m.
Korea	11 p.m.	8 a.m. tmw	5 p.m. prev. day	2 a.m.

Country	Chicago's 8 a.m. is their:	Chicago's 5 p.m. is their:	Their 8 a.m. is Chicago's:	Their 5 p.m. is Chicago's:
Malaysia	10 p.m.	7 a.m. tmw	6 p.m. prev. day	3 a.m.
Philippines	10 p.m.	7 a.m. tmw	6 p.m. prev. day	3 a.m.
Singapore	10 p.m.	7 a.m. tmw	6 p.m. prev. day	3 a.m.
Taiwan	10 p.m.	7 a.m. tmw	6 p.m. prev. day	3 a.m.
Thailand	9 p.m.	6 a.m. tmw	7 p.m. prev. day	4 a.m.
Other:				
Australia (Sydney)	1 a.m. tmw	10 a.m. tmw	3 p.m. prev. day	midnight prev. night
India	7:30 p.m.	4:30 a.m. tmw	8:30 p.m. prev. day	5:30 a.m.
New Zealand	3 a.m. tmw	noon tmw	1 p.m. prev. day	10 p.m. prev. day
Nigeria	3 p.m.	midnight	1 a.m.	10 a.m.
South Africa	4 p.m.	1 a.m. tmw	midnight prev. night	9 a.m.

Country	TIME DIFFERENCES, MAY–AUGUST			
	Chicago's 8 a.m. is their:	Chicago's 5 p.m. is their:	Their 8 a.m. is Chicago's:	Their 5 p.m. is Chicago's:
Europe:				
Ireland	2 p.m.	11 p.m.	2 a.m.	11 a.m.
Finland	4 p.m.	1 a.m. tmw	midnight prev. night	9 a.m.
Greece	4 p.m.	1 a.m. tmw	midnight prev. night	9 a.m.
Russia (Moscow)	5 p.m.	2 a.m. tmw	11 p.m. prev. night	8 a.m.
Turkey	4 p.m.	1 a.m. tmw	midnight prev. night	9 a.m.
United Kingdom	2 p.m.	11 p.m.	2 a.m.	11 a.m.
Other Europe	3 p.m.	midnight	1 a.m.	10 a.m.
Middle East:				
Israel	4 p.m.	1 a.m. tmw	midnight prev. night	9 a.m.
Saudi Arabia	4 p.m.	1 a.m. tmw	midnight prev. night	9 a.m.
Southern-Hemisphere America:				
Argentina	10 a.m.	7 p.m.	6 a.m.	3 p.m.
Brazil (Rio, São Paulo)	10 a.m.	7 p.m.	6 a.m.	3 p.m.
Chile	9 a.m.	6 p.m.	7 a.m.	4 p.m.
Northern-Hemisphere America:				
Mexico (Mexico City)	7 a.m.	4 p.m.	9 a.m.	6 p.m.
Venezuela	9 a.m.	6 p.m.	7 a.m.	4 p.m.
Northern-Hemisphere Pacific:				
China	9 p.m.	6 a.m. tmw	7 p.m. prev. day	4 a.m.
Hong Kong	9 p.m.	6 a.m. tmw	7 p.m. prev. day	4 a.m.
Indonesia (Jakarta)	8 p.m.	5 a.m. tmw	8 p.m. prev. day	5 a.m.
Japan	10 p.m.	7 a.m. tmw	6 p.m. prev. day	3 a.m.
Korea	10 p.m.	7 a.m. tmw	6 p.m. prev. day	3 a.m.
Malaysia	9 p.m.	6 a.m. tmw	7 p.m. prev. day	4 a.m.

Country	Chicago's 8 a.m. is their:	Chicago's 5 p.m. is their:	Their 8 a.m. is Chicago's:	Their 5 p.m. is Chicago's:
Philippines	9 p.m.	6 a.m. tmw	7 p.m. prev. day	4 a.m.
Singapore	9 p.m.	6 a.m. tmw	7 p.m. prev. day	4 a.m.
Taiwan	9 p.m.	6 a.m. tmw	7 p.m. prev. day	4 a.m.
Thailand	8 p.m.	5 a.m. tmw	8 p.m. prev. day	5 a.m.
Other:				
Australia (Sydney)	11 p.m.	8 a.m. tmw	5 p.m. prev. day	2 a.m.
India	6:30 p.m.	3:30 a.m. tmw	9:30 p.m. prev. day	6:30 a.m.
New Zealand	1 a.m. tmw	10 a.m. tmw	3 p.m. prev. day	midnight prev. night
Nigeria	2 p.m.	11 p.m.	2 a.m.	11 a.m.
South Africa	3 p.m.	midnight	1 a.m.	10 a.m.

An obvious error is to call from the Americas to Asia or Australia on Friday evening, or back from there on Monday morning; crossing the International Date Line, your call will reach an empty office on the weekend.

LANGUAGE BARRIERS

Refer to the chapter "How to Make Your English More Understandable."

FAILURE TO GET THROUGH

Maybe you really cannot get through. Any of several problems on the other end could cause a foreign busy signal: All their lines could really be busy. Their fax could be out of paper. Their phone could be switched off. Their power could be out. Their phone could be off the hook. Their switchboard could be down.

Before you give up on an important call, try any other number you know in the same company. If you do not know one, try another office of the same company and ask whether they are having any problems, and whether they have any internal way of communicating (such as an electronic mail system). Also, do not forget that telexes and telegrams still exist.

Internet and Web Addresses and Electronic Mail

Computers connected to the Internet are assigned unique numbers, just as telephones have always been assigned unique numbers. A typical computer number consists of four parts of three digits each, although leading zeros are sometimes dropped (e.g., **194.89.21.23**). This is called an "IP (Internet Protocol) address." For ease of use, an IP address is translated by Internet software into a "domain name," such as **microsoft.com**, which identifies a *site* called **microsoft** in the **com** *domain*. A site is a group of computers under common administrative control. A top-level domain like **com** comprises a huge number of sites of a certain type: **com** sites are commercial companies, and other common domains are **gov** (government agencies), **edu** (educational institutions), **org** (nonprofit organizations), and **net** (network organizations). An e-mail address like **angela@harpo.adviser.com** means that the Internet user **angela** logs on to a particular computer called **harpo** at a site called **adviser.com**. Normally, one computer at a site is nominated to receive all messages from the Internet. It maintains a list of known users at the site, along with the name of the particular computer each person collects mail from. So it is usually unnecessary to specify the computer, and even counterproductive because your correspondent could have changed computers inside the organization without notifying you. However, if you must address a department because you don't have the name of an individual there, try to be specific. For instance, rather than sending a message to **info@lotus.com** (*info* being a frequently used address element signifying "general information"), try to narrow it down to **info@sales.lotus.com** or **info@techsupport.lotus.com.**

The last element of a complete Internet address is the two-letter ISO code for the country (see the "Country Identification" chapter), as in **suyama@mpt.go.jp**. Not all countries have Internet domains, and those that do often use two-letter codes such as **co** and **go** instead of **com** and **gov**. The United States is assumed to be the country addressed unless otherwise specified (just as, in an earlier era, it was agreed that all countries except Britain would print their names on their postage stamps). Each site establishes its own convention for individuals' e-mail names. A man called Robert H. Owen is likely to be ROwen, RobO, or simply Rob. Other styles are Owen__Rob, Rob__Owen, and RHO. You can tell from the way a message is refused whether you gave, for example, the right site name but the wrong user name. If you want to find a person's log-on name at a site called **rain.org**, send a message to **postmaster@rain.org**. Every Internet site is supposed to have an administrator called **postmaster**; however, you will find they vary a lot in responsiveness.

World Wide Web addresses are built on the Internet addressing system, and are called URLs (Uniform Resource Locators), pronounced "U-R-L" by some and "earl" by others. A simple URL of the top-level contents or index page of a Web site looks like **http://www.sncf.fr/**, in which **http://** identifies it as a World Wide Web address, **www** is the name of the particular computer that serves the Web (www is almost invariably chosen as the name), **sncf** is the name of the site, and **fr** is the country. After the final slash, you could place the name of the page you want to access, if you know it, but it is almost always simpler to use your Web browsing software to connect to the page you want by clicking on a hyperlink. Web browsers also allow you to create an organized list of "bookmarks" or "favorites" so that you can return to a site that you often visit simply by choosing its name from a menu. If you need information about a World Wide Web site that cannot be found on the site itself, you can try sending e-mail to **webmaster@www.sncf.fr**, **webmaster** being the equivalent of **postmaster** (note that many web sites include "feedback" or "customer service" links to simplify the sending of e-mail questions and comments). Web administrators are usually more responsive than the mail administrators because their job descriptions and culture are to make information available to the outside world.

It does not matter whether you capitalize any or all letters in an e-mail address or URL.

The problem of international document exchange is becoming more acute as more and more computer users attach themselves to the Internet and the World Wide Web. There are so many commercial products in use that it is difficult to be precise about capabilities and specific obstacles.

A message travels through the Internet by a somewhat unpredictable path. It will traverse different communications systems and different computers along its way. It is switched through the network by programs known as "mailer daemons," which vary considerably in their ability and willingness to detect transmission errors and correct them. If you are unlucky, your message might pass through old equipment or an old mailer which assumes that a European character like é is a transmission error and replaces it with a question mark or a ■. So even if the sender's and receiver's computers or printers agree on the meaning of a particular character, there is a chance it will get lost in transit.

There is usually a way around such problems, because messaging systems usually need to be able to transmit computer programs and images, which also need protecting from unwanted changes. There may be a "binary mode" of transmission (this is the case in *ftp* programs, the file-transfer protocol commonly used on the Internet), or there may be a way to send your document as an "attachment" to a plain-text message, or "encapsulated" within it. If you are lucky, your e-mail software may use one of these techniques automatically. Another resource to be aware of in older systems is a pair of programs called *uuencode* and *uudecode*. They use their own system of encoding, which may double the size of your document but guarantees the safe arrival of unusual characters.

It is also possible to send a scanned image over the Internet, and this occurs very commonly in pages you obtain from the World Wide Web. The disadvantage is that the computer does not really understand an image. An å character in an image is just an arrangement of dots. The computer can show it on the screen and enlarge or reduce or rotate it, but it has no idea that it is showing a letter of the alphabet, or that å is equivalent to Å. Thus, you cannot search an image looking for a particular word until you put the image through Character Recognition software, which is time-consuming and introduces more errors than transmission problems ever do.

Conclusion

Failing to reach someone by phone or fax can be discouraging and frustrating. There are two ways you can try to prepare to overcome telecommunications problems. One way is to find any cooperative company, institution, or library in your town that has a good collection of foreign phone books and trade directories. The second way is to cultivate people you deal with in other countries, regardless of what their official relationship to your company is. You need a personal network of people you can trade favors with. It is *much* easier for friends in the other country to track down a relocated company or fight their way through their local phone system. A business-card collection is an important personal asset for anyone who wants to make a career in international business.

5. Making Your English More Understandable

How much of what you say and write in English is really understood by people who have learned English as a foreign language?

A language is not something that you simply "speak" or "don't speak." Most people, unless they have a special talent for or interest in languages, learn and retain the minimum for their immediate needs. For planning purposes, you can assume that business executives and engineers from other cultures understand something like 80 percent of what you write and 50 percent of what you say, provided, first, that you are clear and, second, that they are interested in your subject matter. If you are not clear, their minds will be wandering during your presentations, your handouts and mailings will be thrown away, and they will call your hotline all the time instead of reading your manuals.

Most of this chapter consists of advice about how to be clear. Unless you know at least one other language really well, you probably do not realize how difficult it is to find equivalent words and expressions in another language, even for truly bilingual people and for professional interpreters. Many years ago, General de Gaulle made an important speech about British entry into the Common Market, in which he said he would "tenir à cœur" (literally, "hold in my heart") the position of the British government of the day. A journalist challenged the official translation of the speech, and for days people debated in the British media what exactly a Frenchman of President de Gaulle's age and background meant by "tenir à cœur." How strong a commitment was it? What phrase in English would have the same strength?

Judging Their English

Nonnative speakers' command of English varies in several different ways. It is absolutely useless to ask people whether they understand you—they will always say they do. Pretend you are an English teacher: Make them talk. Make them introduce themselves in a meeting. Make small talk with them on the phone for a minute. Listen for mistakes and estimate their vocabulary, without paying too much attention to their accents.

- *Everybody reads English better than they speak or write it.* Therefore, make sure you provide American speakers with good handouts. Prepare scripts for foreigners who are going to make presentations in English. Write and circulate the minutes of important meetings. When you make critical arrangements or reach important decisions on the phone, confirm them immediately by fax.

- *People who are quiet in meetings may know good English.* They may have learned the rules and may be able to write good English, but they have to think about it too much and so their spoken English is hesitant. Do not ignore them; they may be quite influential in decisions, and they may help to convey your message to colleagues who listen less carefully or understand less well.

- *Someone who writes broken English may communicate quite fluently in person.* Some individuals pick up fairly natural, colloquial English from frequent contact with English-speaking people. Because their grammar is poor, however, they make a lot of mistakes; these are not very noticeable in speech, but they make any written English look terrible.

- *Most people understand English better than they speak it.* However, there are exceptions that you have to watch for. Some outgoing people with intermediate-level knowledge of English and poor listening skills appear to speak quite well but will not understand you.

- *Pronunciation is misleading.* Good pronunciation and intonation may make you overestimate somebody's English, and bad pronunciation may make you underestimate it. Some individuals are natural mimics; others feel foolish about putting their tongue to their teeth to make our *th* sound. Spanish-speaking and Japanese-speaking people typically have a lot of difficulty learning to pronounce English and may give the impression that they know less than they really do.

One sure sign that you have a problem is when foreigners tell you that they have learned British English and that American is a different language, or even accuse you of speaking bad English yourself. These are always face-saving excuses made by people whose English is poor. Of course, some Americans are indeed hard to understand because of their regional accents, unclear diction, or use of slang, but exactly the same is true of some British people.

Making Yourself Understood

SPELLING AND GRAMMAR

The most basic requirement for dealing with nonnative speakers is that your grammar and spelling need to be perfect. Do not send them searching in vain through a dictionary for a word like *superseed* or *supercede*, which would not stop an American reader for a moment.

The importance of grammatical correctness in international usage is that people may have different natural word order or sentence construction. In simple sentences, it is helpful that English grammar is so flexible. You *register* in a *register*, making a *register* entry, right? But if a sentence is complex, foreigners may be searching for "the verb." There is no space in this book to repeat guidance on grammatical correctness, but all the advice written on the subject applies with increased force to international English usage.

Most of the examples in this chapter were taken from a sample group of American product brochures that have been circulating freely in Europe. They are all fine, professionally produced materials adequate for their purpose, but they contain a lot of words and sentences that only the most fluent Europeans could understand in detail.

VAGUENESS AND COMPLEXITY

Sales literature frequently seeks to convey a general impression that the product is modern, advanced, and useful. It may deliberately not seek to convey much solid factual information. Out of context, this sentence may look worse than in its original setting:

> [The XYZ product] allows for efficient and cost-effective monitoring of systems and applications because it is based on the occurrence of specific events throughout the system, rather than having administration continuously looking at each part of the system in the hopes of discovering problems.

This is intended to sound positive without being precise. The authors expect their readers to skim it quickly and not question it too closely. However, people with intermediate-level knowledge of English will become discouraged and stop reading after a few sentences like this. They cannot skim; they have to try to understand everything that they read. The following version would stand a better chance of being understood and keeping their attention:

> [The XYZ product] monitors systems and applications more efficiently because it is activated by specific events. Thus, administration will no longer waste resources by continually looking for problems in each part of the system.

An additional benefit is that simpler and grammatically correct sentences are much easier to translate into other languages. Vagueness is difficult to translate correctly. A translator may have to think for minutes about every phrase, at your expense. Common examples of words and phrases often used vaguely are *in the area of, relevant, arrangements, sophisticated,* and *profile.*

COMMON SOURCES OF DIFFICULTY

People whose English is "intermediate" complain about several of our common writing habits. Though most of these habits are thought by business writers to make material easier for Americans to read, they have the opposite effect on international readers.

- *Do not use contractions.* Surprisingly, many courses and texts teaching English to foreigners pay little attention to all the contractions that we use so frequently in speech (*can't, don't, wouldn't,* etc.), so intermediate-level foreigners frequently have to stop and think, "Now what is that in full?" Do not use contractions even in quoted speech. Above all, expand contractions of verbs, as in "We should've priced lower," "The answer's obvious," or "Where'd that one come from?"

- *Try to avoid two-word (phrasal) verbs.* Consider "come around." "The car came around the corner" will be perfectly clear, since "around" here does not form part of the verb. "Would you like to come around for supper?" will be factually clear, although the casual nature of the invitation will probably be lost on a foreigner. However, "Our lawyers have come around on Paragraph 7.1" will only be clear to the most fluent people. Two-word verbs are not found in pocket dictionaries in other countries, and English-language courses often do not stress them. But it is difficult to write English without them. The only practical concession we can make is to avoid the usages that a foreigner would find hardest to interpret:

Pull down: The Purchasing Manager pulls down a good salary.
Pull for: We are all pulling for the success of the new product line.
Pull off: Rochester pulled off a big funding increase at the budget meeting.
Pull out: The Greek agent has pulled out of the cooperative advertising program.
Pull through: The revamping project is so tough that it may not pull through.
Pull over: R&D was going a hundred miles an hour until the auditors pulled them over.
Pull up: Management pulled them up short after they failed the design review.

The general sense of sentences like these is clear to fluent speakers, but intermediate-level speakers will only half-understand.

• *Do not write casual, informal English.* This admonition is closely related to the preceding one. My sales-literature sample contained the expressions *to flag, to route, to thumb through, to steer clear, to make a splash, to bog down, to kick into overdrive, to get your people up to speed, to trigger.* Though the general sense may often be clear from the context, the precise meaning is probably lost on many foreign readers, and some of them will just not understand at all. Above all, do not use cultural references, such as sports expressions—"two strikes against them," "way off-base," "out in left field," or (British) "we were stumped"—and certainly not references to television programs, characters, or personalities. A European executive told me that on one of his first overseas trips, an American told him to look for her in a June Cleaver station wagon, and the British told him to stop his taxi when he saw the zebra crossing after the Green Dragon. Nothing in engineering-school English classes prepared him for expressions like these.

• *Do not drop the words* that *and* which. We are in the habit of writing sentences like:

The one or more customers we deal with in each country serviced by our Amsterdam representatives account for over half of the questions we receive about new release implementations.

To understand this sentence, the reader must connect the subject *customers* to the verb *account*, which is quite far away. Our tendency to drop the words *which* and *that* makes such sentences much harder to follow. This version would have been clearer:

The one or more customers that we deal with in each country which is serviced by our Amsterdam representatives account for over half of the questions that we receive about new release implementations.

(And note that even this latter version could have been improved quite a lot:

Of all the questions about implementing new releases, half are addressed to our representatives in Amsterdam.

Half the reading time and twice as clear.)

- *Explain abbreviations.* Assume that foreigners, even those from other English-speaking countries, do not understand any abbreviations. They do not understand that CA is California, USDA is a government agency, ASE is a stock exchange, and UL is a certification. They certainly do not understand colloquial abbreviations like SRO or CYA. Foreign engineers usually *do* understand common American abbreviations in their industries, like CAD/CAM or RDBMS (and an amazing number of people in the world understand WYSIWYG, of all things), but remember that they naturally use different abbreviations in their own languages and there is no advantage in slowing them down or running risks of misunderstanding.

- *Try to avoid long strings of nouns.* Three nouns together is about the most that foreigners can stand, and Americans themselves balk after four or five, but many business writers love to pile up nouns as adjectives in English: *service success factor, word search retrieval methods, quality control procedures recommendations, office equipment maintenance seminar reimbursement.*

- *Do not coin your own terms.* If you feel obliged to put anything in quotation marks, it is too unusual to use. Every time you hyphenate two words, ask yourself whether their meaning is clear and whether you would find it in a dictionary. Newly invented terms like *co-editions, relevance-ranked, production-scale,* and *PC-centric* will not be understood reliably. Nouns newly used as verbs *(to keyword, to password)* may be clear in a simple context, but they may make long sentences confusing, and of course they will not be found in an English–German pocket dictionary. It is difficult to know at what point a new term is used by enough people to be accepted. Fashionable jargon terms like *downsizing, scalability, legacy systems,* and *seamless integration* should be well-known in the international computer industry, but they will not be found in local dictionaries yet.

- *Capitalize or clearly identify product names.* Make it clear to people that this is not an ordinary word that they would find in a dictionary.

- *Avoid unusual words and expressions.* Nobody who reviewed my collection of sample sales literature understood the word *linchpin,* which refers back to fourteenth-century technology, after all. Many of them had to guess from the context the meaning of *merely* (why not say *only?*), *uneven* (try *variable?*), *upwards of* (*over?*), *encompass* (*include?*), *disparate* (*varied?*), *news wires, similarly minded, toothcomb, bottleneck, off-load, drudgery, cumbersome, fumbling,* and *devise.* But at least they may find these words in their dictionaries, if they are interested enough to spend the time. Informal expressions are worse, because it is difficult to find explanations: *on the spot, sticky note, from the ground up, in a flash, best of breed, geared toward.*

The advice in this section is not at all intended to encourage you to write completely colorless English. One author in the sample used the phrase "an island of information." This is great: *island* is a well-known word, the image is concise and clear, and we were saved from reading about "a discrete localized region of higher information concentration, isolation-barrier-delimited from principal neighboring continuous extents of lower-significance data point clusters."

LENGTH AND STYLE

Is it better to be concise or repetitive? The advantage of being concise is that it helps nonnative speakers who read more slowly. But some technical and business writers believe that there is less likely to be a misunderstanding if you say the same thing in three different ways. There is truth in both points of view. I know I prefer concise documents, particularly when my knowledge of the language is poor. If you do not choose to be concise, at least insert clear headings at frequent intervals so that people can easily find the parts that they want to spend time reading. Also, a summary in simple English can be really helpful.

A related debate concerns writing style, particularly in letters. An elaborate and flowery style is standard in some countries. You will sometimes receive a letter of casual inquiry in this kind of eccentric English:

> We consider ourselves fortunate to have learned of the magnificent reputation of your esteemed company from our many close friends and long-standing trading partners in all parts of your country and we beg from you the favor of furnishing us with information about your export prices and delivery dates for your widely-acclaimed Model T380. In anticipation of your kind attention we await anxiously your reply.

Some advisers will tell you to reply in similar terms. However, it is difficult to do so, and it is not at all certain what the effect will be. Americans have the reputation of being direct and to the point, which is grudgingly appreciated by businesspeople from other cultures even if they are not about to imitate it themselves. You should compromise. It is orthodox American business practice to thank someone for their inquiry and to say that you look forward to doing business with them; in response to a flowery letter, just expand a little on your conventionally polite opening and closing sentences:

> We were particularly pleased to receive your inquiry, and we would very much appreciate your opinion on the market opportunities in [country] for our Model T380. . . .

> In conclusion, may we express the hope that this correspondence will be the beginning of a long and successful business relationship between our two companies. We are at your disposal for any additional information.

Contract Language

Contracts, letters of intent, memoranda of understanding, and similar documents present the most acute language problem, for several reasons. They are naturally complicated. It is particularly important that they be understood clearly. Furthermore, the size and complexity of American contracts frequently horrify foreigners.

Most lawyers write competently, and many of them take a lot of trouble to write clear and precise English. Unfortunately, language that was originally simple and clear becomes more and more complicated as its details are negotiated in a succession of contracts and it is adapted for reuse in one document after another.

Realistically, there is not much you can do to improve a contract without the consent and cooperation of your legal department. It is dangerous to provide any kind of interpretation or explanation or even translation, in case it is held to constitute part of the agreement. However, for a base document that is clearly international in character, such as an overseas distributorship agreement, the international department should be entitled to insist on a language review. If you do not understand it, what chance is there that your foreign trading partners will?

Consider a typical sentence from a contract that has been the subject of negotiation:

> Vendor its employees agents representatives distributors subcontractors consultants officers directors investors and ex-employees shall upon notice given in accordance with Paragraph 35.9 release publish and/or disclose to Purchaser or its duly authorized representatives all documents including but not limited to invoices delivery notes travel expense reports purchasing records accounting journals correspondence files and machine-readable electronic mail logs concerning expenditures approved under Paragraphs 3.1, 4.6 (a), Appendix B Part II or as otherwise demanded in writing in accordance with the notice provisions of Paragraph 35.9 provided that such release publication and/or disclosure shall take place during Vendor's normal business hours and in compliance with Vendor's customary reasonable security procedures, provided further that Vendor's consent shall be required for the examination of any records relating to the sale of goods and services to the United States Government or any political subdivision thereof, which consent shall not be unreasonably withheld.

There are two root causes of this logical and linguistic complexity: (1) a lack of proper definitions, and (2) the failure to group provisions according to the business agreement. A commercial contract should have a structure like this:

1. Definitions.
2. What your side is agreeing to do and to pay, and when.
3. What their side is agreeing to do and to pay, and when.
4. What you both will do if the agreement breaks down in the future (how you will compensate each other, how you will support orphan customers, etc.).
5. Procedural provisions, in very small type (separability, governing law, indemnities, notices, etc.).

The commercial negotiators should be primarily responsible for the content of the three middle sections, and the lawyers can write what they like in the fifth part. The definitions should be a joint effort and should look like this:

> The capitalized word VENDOR shall mean [company name, address, tax identifier].
> The capitalized word AGENTS shall mean employees agents representatives distributors subcontractors consultants officers directors investors and ex-employees.
> The capitalized word DISCLOSE shall mean release publish and/or disclose during VENDOR's normal business hours and in compliance with VENDOR's customary reasonable security procedures.

Then later in the body of the contract you can rewrite the original sentence like this:

> After NOTIFICATION from PURCHASER, VENDOR and/or its AGENTS shall DISCLOSE all PROJECT RECORDS, provided that VENDOR's consent shall be required for the examination of any GOVERNMENT RECORDS. Such consent shall not be unreasonably withheld.

You should keep reusing the capitalized words so that the real agreement is simple and uses ordinary commercial words, which have been defined to the lawyers' satisfaction in the introduction.

Understanding Their English

English-speaking people are quite tolerant of mistakes, in the sense that we can easily understand sentences containing unnatural errors of grammar like "He send us two time same book" or mixed expressions like "Waiting forward to see you." It is rare to receive messages that are totally incomprehensible, but the details can sometimes be puzzling.

A translator or someone who is fluent in the originator's language can probably help you to understand strange phrases. If foreigners faxed you to complain that their team was wiping the plasters for your engineering department, you would probably have no idea what they meant, but a bilingual person would see immediately that they had translated an expression from their own language word for word into English.

People whose native languages are derived from Latin (French, Spanish, Italian, Portuguese, etc.) present a particular problem because they firmly believe that many of their words exist in English with the same meaning. Even the most fluent people make the most surprising elementary mistakes. Sometimes it is clear what they mean. For example, French-speakers commonly invent the word *performant* in English. Considering that both languages use the same word *performance*, it is indeed surprising that English does not have *performant* as a corresponding adjective. But other examples are not clear at all until someone explains them to you. French-speakers use the word *park* when they mean *customer base*, and Spanish-speakers invent the English word *capacitation* when they mean *training*. Speakers of these languages also tend to use certain unusual English words like *polyvalent*, sending you running to your English dictionary. It is not that they are highly educated and have a wide vocabulary—it is that the word is common in their languages and they do not realize it has a changed or specialized meaning in English.

There are two words that cause so many real misunderstandings between English-speakers and Europeans that you should avoid them yourself and politely question their use by foreigners. European executives who say "we will fund this project eventually" are giving you a very weak, conditional commitment. They think *eventually* means "in the event that it is necessary." When they say "this is our actual policy," they are very likely giving you their *current* policy, with the implication that it could change at any time. Similarly, when you use the words *eventual(ly)* and *actual(ly)*, many Europeans will misunderstand you. With these two exceptions, you should ignore the possibility of words' being misunderstood. Write clear, correct English; it then becomes their responsibility to realize that, for example, *versatile* is not at all derogatory in English.

Telephoning

This section offers advice on dealing with people who speak very little English. It could be subtitled: "I don't believe it! They hung up on me!"

Speak up, as if you were talking with a loud noise outside the room. Speak slowly, one word per second, separating your words clearly. It is difficult for most people to speak slowly and simply. It is easier to read slowly, so you might try writing down a phrase you expect to use: "This is International Publishing calling from the United States. Is Mr. Degermann available?" Practice a speed of one word per second by your watch.

If you know someone's extension number, ask for it slowly, one digit at a time, rather than asking for the person by name.

When you want to ask a switchboard operator for a person, say only the name, as best you can, slowly, followed by *please*. Do not race through a long explanation:

> Hi! How are you! This is Mary Beth calling from Geyser Oil in Broken Arrow, Oklahoma, trying to reach my boss, Arthur Steinberg, who's visiting with Emilio Breghenti, who I think is the head honcho of your exploration operation out there?

There is no serious chance that they will pick out *Breghenti*, the one word they need to hear, especially not with your pronunciation of it. They will hang up on you. When that happens, do not be mad at them. Remember that all they have heard is an incomprehensible babble from you, while ten other lines are waiting to be answered.

A British receptionists' specialty is a style of rambling politeness spoken at express speed:

> Oh I'm terribly sorry you're having to wait, oh I'm afraid actually his extension is still engaged, could you please hang on for just a sec, will that be all right, are you quite sure, right then, he won't actually be very long, that's ever so lovely, thanks ever so much. [click]

All of which leaves foreigners, including Americans, thinking to themselves in their own dialects, "Huh, say what now again?"

When you dial a wrong number and disturb some individual, apologize slowly and carefully; "Pardon" and "Excuse me" are more international and more likely to be understood than "Sorry."

English-speakers should take care to pronounce consonants clearly. English seems to foreigners as though it consists mostly of vowels with frequent use of clear *s*, *sh*, *ch*, *k*, and *j* sounds. People from other major language groups think that we articulate most other consonants with "lazy lips."

To spell out names, here are two systems. The orthodox one is the international Air Traffic Control standard known as "A for Alfa." Personally, I have a hard time remembering it, so I usually use geographical names that I expect everybody to know. This has one other advantage over the orthodox system: if people don't understand it, you can provide more information.

Me: "P for Paris."
Them: "What?"

Me (taking care to articulate superbly): "P like Paris."
Them: "What?"
Me (louder and slower): "You know, the capital of France!"
Them: "What?"
Me: "PARIS! EIFFEL TOWER! PIGALLE! THE LOUVRE!"
Them: "Ah! Ho! Paris! P! Yes!"

But what do you say next if they do not catch "P for Papa"?

For international use you should take care to choose names that are similar in all the major languages. For example, "F for France" is fine, because everybody calls France something like *France,* but "G for Germany" would be poor, because Germany is called everything from *Alemagna* to *Saksa* to *Tyskland* in other languages.

	Orthodox	Unorthodox		Orthodox	Unorthodox
A	Alfa	America	N	November	Norway
B	Bravo	Berlin	O	Oscar	Osaka
C	Charlie	Canada	P	Papa	Paris
D	Delta	Denmark	Q	Quebec	Quebec
E	Echo	Ecuador	R	Romeo	Romania
F	Foxtrot	France	S	Sierra	Swiss
G	Golf	Granada	T	Tango	Turkey
H	Hotel	Hamburg	U	Uniform	U.S.A.
I	India	Italy	V	Victor	Venezuela
J	Juliett	Japan	W	Whiskey	Washington
K	Kilo	Kansas	X	Xray	Xerox
L	Lima	London	Y	Yankee	Yokohama
M	Mike	Mexico	Z	Zulu	Zurich

Conclusion

Should you learn other languages? You are up against two difficulties—the number of languages in the world, and the length of time it takes to learn one. In the countries covered by this book, business is conducted in some 20 languages and the populations speak dozens of minority languages and dialects. To learn an "easy" language well enough to participate effectively in a business meeting takes many hundreds of hours of study and practice. A "difficult" language may take several thousand hours. It could easily take ten full years of your life to learn 20 languages. Where would you start? The time you might spend learning German is wasted if you are transferred to the Japanese desk.

Rather than learn languages, a little effort in speaking and writing English more clearly will be more constructive and a better investment, unless you are going to live in another country.

By the way, General de Gaulle's "tenir à cœur" turned out to be a rather weak commitment.

6. Customer Database Design

The purpose of this chapter is to tell you how to construct computer-based mailing lists and database entries for international names and addresses. It is intended to help you not only to create applications on a PC for your own use, but also to state your requirements precisely to computer professionals. If you are not reasonably familiar with computer issues, you may find some of this material hard to follow. However, this chapter should help even the novice to get an idea of what is involved in creating a customer database.

When you write a single letter, the address block in it is free-form text. It could fill the width of the page and occupy as many lines as you like. However, if you intend to use a window envelope or an address label, you have to accept some constraints on the width and length of the address. When you plan a computer database, you have to establish a maximum size that will limit all the addresses you store in that database, and you have to make some choices about how the address block is divided up. Computer professionals will usually want to separate the address block into at least three parts: the name of the person, the name of the company, and the address itself. They will probably want to subdivide the address into at least another three parts: the country; the postcode, and the rest. They will want to associate any number of personal names with each address, and any number of addresses with each company. They will only carry one title with a person, but they may want to carry several phone numbers with each person, each address, and each company.

Before studying a problem such as this, computer professionals generally have little idea what sizes and structures to choose. They rely on guidance from the people who understand the information and all the variations that can occur.

Information to Be Stored

Most international business addresses can be contained in a total of eight lines, of which the domestic delivery address itself is four lines:

1. Name
2. Title or Department
3. Company
4. Building
5. Street
6. Locality
7. Postcode, City, State
8. Country

} Domestic delivery address

Addresses in Japan, Korea, Taiwan, and the United Kingdom may need to be compressed to fit into four lines by writing two address elements on the same line even though they would more naturally occupy separate lines. The addition of a fifth domestic-delivery address line (treat it as a province/country name) should be enough to cover most addresses outside of the United Kingdom, some of whose addresses will still need compression.

You will frequently also need to record a postal address, which means that line 7 will have to be repeated, because a P.O. Box usually has at least a different postcode than the street address, and may have a different city (post-office) name, too.

You will probably need to keep a salutation line ("Dear Mr. Andersen") for each person.

You must keep at least one voice phone number and one fax phone number for each person. If your database is structured for multiple contacts for each company, there should be a company switchboard number and a company fax number. Even if there is only one contact per company, you should have a minimum of four phone numbers: fax, switchboard voice, direct-dial voice, and one spare field which might be used for a backup fax, a secretary's direct-dial number, or a toll-free number. Six phone numbers per person is not excessive if your end users are really going to phone the people in the database.

Finally, you will probably need to sort lists and reports by the name of the person, the name of the company, and in a geographic sequence. To do this, you should provide sort key fields with default values that can be manually overridden.

Data-Entry Errors

It is hard to standardize international addresses in a comprehensive way. There are so many legitimate variations, and in many countries the residents do not observe the local conventions themselves. When addresses are copied by foreigners, errors are invariably introduced.

The two address elements that are most important to identify are the postcode and the box number. Anyone entering international addresses should at least be trained to recognize the postcode formats of all countries concerned and the local words for "P.O. Box."

The most common data-entry errors are:

Error	Wrong Example	Corrected
Confusing building numbers and postcodes.	Bielstrasse 1 8050 Zürich	Bielstrasse 1 8050 Zürich
Confusing building numbers and suite numbers.	Rua do Funchal 134B	Rua do Funchal 13 - 4°B
Putting the postcode in the wrong place.	PARIS 75010 or 60606 CHICAGO IL	75010 PARIS CHICAGO IL 60606
Using a local layout.	CHICAGO Illinois 60606	CHICAGO IL 60606
Putting office information in the locality position.	10776 East London Avenue Suite 230 KITCHENER ON M6B 1K1	10776 E. London Ave., #230 or Suite 230 10776 East London Avenue

Error	Wrong Example	Corrected
Incorrect spaces in postcodes, particularly in Israel, Greece, Sweden, Canada, the Netherlands, and the United Kingdom.	63 143 TEL AVIV 10559 ATHENS 12351 STOCKHOLM TORONTO ON M5A3W5 1101MN AMSTERDAM LONDON SE1 23AB	63143 TEL AVIV 105 59 ATHENS 123 51 STOCKHOLM TORONTO ON M5A 3W5 1101 MN AMSTERDAM LONDON SE12 3AB
Not separating the country name.	PARIS France 75116	75116 PARIS FRANCE
Placing the building number wrongly.	21 Via Terenzio or Chislehurst Way 180	Via Terenzio 21 180 Chislehurst Way
Confusing British towns and counties.	Reading BERKS	READING Berks
Confusing 0 and 1 with O and L in British postcodes.	CROYDON CRO LDT	CROYDON CR0 1DT
Including irrelevant foreign words, copied from letterhead.	Siège Social Besöksadress Código Postal	(omit)
Entering unauthorized country prefixes.	GB-LONDON WC1V 3XX	LONDON WC1V 3XX United Kingdom
Inconsistent use of country prefixes in a list.	A-1010 WIEN 1040 BRUXELLES L-1859 LUXEMBOURG	1010 WIEN 1040 BRUXELLES 1859 LUXEMBOURG or A-1010 WIEN B-1040 BRUXELLES L-1859 LUXEMBOURG
Inconsistent phone-number layouts in a list.	+44 (0628) 71668 32 (2) 723-1912 (47) 56.11.35.61 33 (1) 40.50.40.50	+44-628-71668 +32-2-723-1912 +47-56.11.35.61 +33-1-40.50.40.50
Failure to recognize "Inc."	International Verlag A.G. Schillerstrasse 159	International Verlag AG Schillerstrasse 159
Imprecise country.	BELFAST, Ireland TAIPEI, China	BELFAST, United Kingdom TAIPEI, Taiwan

Record Layout

The following table sets out recommendations for the field definitions in an address record which is intended to contain international names and addresses. It is a starting point which will be adequate for applications of average complexity, but examination of your data may indicate that different field lengths or definitions are more suitable. For simplicity, the record is designed for a single name and a single address.

Seq.	Field (No. of Chars.)	Contents	Possible Default Value	Possible Validation Rules
		INTERNATIONAL ADDRESS RECORD LAYOUT		
1	Title (20)	Honorific Title	"Mr." or a local equivalent.	Query if not on an approved list. See text.
2	Name (30)	Given name(s) Family name(s) Degrees or decorations	Not practical.	Not practical.
3	Department (35)	Department or job title	Not practical, unless you know that some value like "Chief Financial Officer" is the most likely.	Not usually practical.
4	Company (35)	Company name	Not practical.	Query if no "Inc." or equivalent. See text.
5	Building (35)	Building name Office internal address	Not practical.	Query if not usual practice in the country. See next table.
6	Street (35)	Street Building number Office internal address	Not practical.	Query if no "Street" word. Query if no building number in appropriate position (see next table). Query if "P.O. Box" or equivalent is included.
7	Locality (35)	Locality name	Not practical.	Query if not usual practice in the country. See next table. Query if "P.O. Box" or equivalent is included.
8	Postcode (10)	Postcode	Not practical.	See Table 5 in the Keyword Index.
9	City, state (25)	City State/province abbrev.	(1) The name of the principal city associated with the postcode (see "Assisting Data-Entry" below), or (2) the name from the previous address, hoping that input entries are grouped by city.	Not practical.

INTERNATIONAL ADDRESS RECORD LAYOUT

Seq.	Field (No. of Chars.)	Contents	Possible Default Value	Possible Validation Rules
10	Spare line (35)	Province, county	Not practical.	Query if not usual practice in the country. See next table.
11	Country (2)	ISO abbreviation	The name from the previous address, hoping that input entries are grouped by country.	Query if not on an approved list.
12	P.O. Box (20)	Number or code	"P.O. Box" or a local equivalent.	Not practical.
13	POB post-code (10)	Postcode for P.O. Box	Field 8	Not practical.
14	POB city, state (25)	City State/province abbrev.	Field 9	Not practical.
15	Salutation (30)	Name as it is to appear in correspondence	See "Assisting Data Entry" below.	Query if no word matches a word in Field 2.
16	Phone numbers (12 or 20; see text)	Principal phone number	Not practical.	Cross-check country code and Field 10. If possible, cross-check postcode and city code at least for major cities.
17–19	Alternative phone and fax numbers (12 or 20; see text)	Fax number Switchboard number Toll-free number	Field 16.	Query any difference in country code or city code. Do not check Field 19.
20	Personal-name sort key (20)	Correct position of name in an alphabetic list	See "Assisting Data Entry" below.	Not practical.
21	Company sort key (20)	Correct position of name in an alphabetic list	Field 4, excluding any first word which is "Inc." or an equivalent.	Not practical.
22	Geographic sort key (10)	Correct position of name in a geographic list	Field 8; if absent, Field 13; if absent, Field 9. See text.	Not practical.

The following table shows which address elements may be expected to occur in different countries. (The "Length" columns indicate the total number of lines in the address.)

| Country | DOMESTIC DELIVERY ADDRESS CHARACTERISTICS | | | | | | | |
	Building Names?	Building Number	Specify Office?	Locality?	Postcode	Region?	Usual Length	Max. Length
Argentina	Unusual	Right	Yes	Unusual	Left	Province	2–3	4
Australia	Yes	Left	Yes	No	Right	No[1]	2–3	3
Austria	No	Right	No	No	Right	No	2	2
Belgium	Unusual	Right[2]	Unusual	Unusual	Left	No	2–3	4
Brazil	Unusual	Right	Yes	Unusual	Left	No[1]	2–3	4
Canada	Yes	Left	Yes	No	Right	No[1]	2–3	3
Chile	Unusual	Right	No	Yes	None	No	3	4
China	Unusual	Left	Unusual	Yes	Right	No	3	4
Czech Rep.	No	Right	No	No	Left	No	2	2
Denmark	No	Right	Yes	No	Left	No	2	2
Finland	No	Right	Yes	No	Left	No	2	2
France	Yes	Left	Unusual	Unusual	Left	No	2–3	4
Germany	No	Right	No	No	Left	No	2	2
Greece	No	Left	No	Unusual	Left	No	2–3	4
Hong Kong	Yes	Left	Yes[3]	Yes	None	No	3	3
Hungary	No	Right	No	No	Left	No	2	2
India	Yes	Left	Yes[3]	Yes	Right	No	3–4	4
Indonesia	Yes	Right	Unusual	Unusual	Right	No	2	3
Ireland	Yes	Left	Unusual	Yes	None	County	2–3	4
Israel	No	Left	No	No	Left[2]	No	2	3
Italy	Unusual	Right	Unusual	Unusual	Left	No[1]	2	4
Japan	Yes	Left	Yes[3]	Two	Right	No[4]	3–4	5
Korea	Yes	Left	Yes[3]	Two	Right	No[4]	3–4	5
Luxembourg	No	Left	No	No	Left	No	2	2
Malaysia	Yes	Left	Unusual	No	Left	Province	2–4	5
Mexico	Unusual	Right	Unusual	Yes	Left	No[1]	3	4
Netherlands	No	Right	No	No	Left	No	2	2
New Zealand	No	Left	No	Yes	Right	No	3	3
Nigeria	Yes	Left	No	Yes	None	State	3–4	5
Norway	No	Right	No	No	Left	No	2	2
Philippines	Yes	Left	Unusual	Yes	Left	Province	4	6
Poland	No	Right	No	No	Left	No	2	2
Portugal	Unusual	Right	Yes	Unusual	Left	No	2–3	4
Russia	No	Right	No	No	Right	No	2	2
Saudi Arabia	No	Left	No	No	Right	No	2	2
Singapore	Yes	Left	Yes	No	Right	No	2–3	3
Slovenia	No	Right	No	No	Left	No	2	2
South Africa	Yes	Left	Unusual	Yes	Right[2]	No	3–4	4
Spain	Unusual	Right	Yes	Unusual	Left	No[1]	2–3	4
Sweden	No	Right	No	No	Left	No	2	2
Switzerland	No	Right	No	No	Left	No	2	2
Taiwan	No	Left	Unusual	Yes[5]	Right	County	2–3	5
Thailand	Yes	Left	Unusual	Two	Right	Province	3–5	5

Country	Building Names?	Building Number	Specify Office?	Locality?	Postcode	Region?	Usual Length	Max. Length
Turkey	Unusual	Right	Yes	Yes	Left	No	3	4
United Kingdom	Yes	Left	Unusual	Yes	Right	County	2–5	6
United States	Yes	Left	Yes	No	Right	No[1]	2–3	3
Venezuela	Yes	Right	Yes	Yes	Right[6]	No	3–4	4

1. State or province abbreviation can be considered as part of city name.
2. Recommended, but local usage inconsistent.
3. Usually added to building name, not street name.
4. Prefecture name can be treated as city name.
5. Extra line needed for additional street information, not locality name.
6. State or province abbreviation follows postcode.

Record Contents

This section contains some additional comments on how data should be stored in the recommended record layout.

The field lengths proposed above assume that you are aiming to produce address labels or similar printouts, 35 characters wide, which will cover a high proportion of the international addresses you will encounter. To save space, most of the lengths could be reduced.

The length of a phone number depends on how you intend to store it. An adequate length is 12 unpunctuated digits or 20 positions if you intend to include punctuation. It is possible, with difficulty, to supply or validate phone-number punctuation automatically. There is information in every country chapter to allow you to do so.

You could omit country codes from the phone numbers. Country codes are fairly stable, but there are two possible reasons for changes over the next few years. First, there will probably be some reorganization of numbers in Europe; current proposals would lengthen all phone numbers. Second, phone ownership has increased greatly in some countries since the original allocation of country codes. Some governments whose countries received three-digit codes now feel they deserve two-digit codes, particularly if a nearby rival nation has a two-digit code already.

ISO two-letter country codes (see the first table in the "Country Identification" chapter), on the other hand, are exactly as stable or unstable as the political areas they describe. The ISO codes are recommended for the country not only because they save space and keystrokes but also because you may want to produce lists or labels or letters in which the country name appears in another language. As an example, if your French and German subsidiaries may both invoice a Swedish customer in the database, you need to print SE as "Suède" and "Schweden" on the respective documents. You should keep this table in your database and allow space for translations of the names.

Remember that, by international convention, you should force uppercase onto Fields 9, 11, and 14, at least for mailing purposes. Take care when printing addresses from a multinational list that the postcode is in the correct position, preferably with blank spaces as required by OCR equipment or local custom, and that blank lines are dropped.

Assisting Data Entry

This section concerns the choice of default values to present to a terminal operator.

It is implicit in these recommendations that you know which country the address is supposed to be in. If you are not working with batches of data from one country at a time, you must capture the country name first, so that your validation rules will be appropriate. Preferably, you should present a screen panel with fields suitable for the particular country.

It is rather difficult to prepare default values for the Salutation and Personal-Name Sort Key fields, but without any, a lot more data entry will be needed. The simplest rule is to take the last word of Field 1 followed by the last word of Field 2. If you add the following rules, in this precise order, the results should be quite good. (*Accept* in these rules means "Deliver the selected word and exit." *Ignore* in these rules means "Retrieve the next word to the left.")

- Ignore the word "Don" in Field 1.

- If one word in Field 2 is in capitals and the others are not, accept the word in capitals.

- Remove "-san" and similar Japanese suffixes from the last word of Field 2.

- Ignore the last word of Field 2 if the country is Spanish-speaking (except Argentina).

- Ignore the last word of Field 2 if it contains any periods (this eliminates qualifications).

- Ignore the words "Jr," "Sr," "Filho," "Esq," "II" and "III" in Field 2.

- Ignore the last word of Field 2 if it contains a hyphen and the country is Chinese- or Korean-speaking.

Information in every country chapter will help you to refine this algorithm.

Terminal operators should be allowed to override any validation rule. For example, you should not absolutely reject a title of "Signor" in Spain, because there might be an Italian executive in a Spanish subsidiary. You can give a warning, but you should allow the terminal operator to respond "I insist." Similarly, it is not practical to check company names rigidly. You may expect every company in Sweden to be an "AB," but you might occasionally have a charitable trust or some other quite different entity in your records.

It is tempting to expect the computer system to propose the name of a city based on the postcode. Unfortunately, there are several obstacles. Postcode systems vary in precision from one country to another. Generally, there is by no means a one-to-one relationship between postcodes and city names. In half the world, the postcode follows the city name, whereas for data entry we would prefer it to come first. Still, there is a significant potential for improvement in speed and accuracy of data entry, especially when operators are typing unfamiliar city names. You need not necessarily create or acquire on-line postcode directories for all the countries that interest you. If you are revamping an existing application, you should extract a table of the most commonly occurring pairs of postcodes and city names and use it for proposing default city names. If you are creating a new application, you could let it learn the pairs as they are entered. It is even worthwhile to simply retrieve the city name which was used the last time a given postcode was entered.

Duplicate Elimination

The elimination of duplicates is a specialized task if complete automation of large lists is required. However, it is relatively easy to produce reports of suspected duplicates which can be examined manually. First, for countries with extended (precise) postcode systems, a postcode sort is usually good enough, assuming you do indeed have the complete postcode. Precise-enough postcode systems exist in Canada, Korea (six-digit), Luxembourg, the Netherlands, Sweden, the United Kingdom, and the United States (nine-digit). The following countries could also be considered to have precise-enough systems unless you have unusually heavy concentrations of records for them: China, Czech Republic, Finland, Greece, Hungary, India, Indonesia, Israel, Japan (five-digit), Malaysia, Philippines, Poland, Russia, Saudi Arabia, Singapore, Slovenia, Taiwan, Thailand, and Turkey. In all the other countries, postcode sorts alone are not very helpful unless your database is small. You are almost bound to have a considerable number of duplicate postcodes in major cities. In the United States, a sort using the street line as a subsidiary key is surprisingly effective, because the combination of a building number and a five-digit zip code is quite likely to be unique. The same principle does not work in other countries because the building numbers are all low: you will have many occurrences of a number like 1.

For large international lists, try the following procedure for duplicate elimination: Sort by Fields 11 and 22. Ignore any records that produce unique keys. Then compare Field 6 of each group of potential duplicates that remain. If any word occurs in two members of the group, report them as duplicates. Consider any characters between white-space delimiters as a word, in order to include building numbers, for example, in the comparison. However, do not consider "Street" or "Suite" or local equivalents as words in the comparison. You could also compare successive Field 4s in the same way, eliminating "Inc." and its equivalents. The report you produce will still need manual examination. If too many legitimate duplicates are reported, you could either indicate them explicitly as unique or refine the Field 6 and 4 comparisons.

This method will break down for giant consumer lists of the kind that an international insurance company or magazine publisher would produce.

Duplicate elimination is not the only reason for sorting name-and-address records. It is very useful for many purposes to produce lists in several sequences, particularly in geographic sequences. A geographic sort must obviously use the country as a key as well as Field 22. A geographic sort by postcode is not very useful for France, Spain, or the United Kingdom, nor for the countries without postcodes—Chile, Hong Kong, and Ireland—but north-to-south transformation tables can be created for any of these six countries if they are important to you.

Conclusion

Handling name-and-address files is surprisingly difficult, even within a single country. Many large organizations cannot efficiently change a customer's address or eliminate duplicate mailings even in their home markets. When staff are handling unfamiliar data in unfamiliar formats the risk of error is immensely greater. The alternative of decentralizing all record-keeping to local affiliates is increasingly unattractive to globally oriented businesses, and is just impractical for smaller exporting organizations. In the major industrial countries, automation of mail is starting to force a closer scrutiny of domestic name-and-address files. Similar procedures will have to be put in place increasingly for multinational files.

7. Printing European Characters

Western European languages use about 30 special characters (such as å, ç, é, î, ñ, ö, ù). The computer industry calls these *national characters*. They are also commonly called "accented characters," but this term is not strictly correct. The marks under or over the letters are called *diacritical marks*, some of which (é,è,ê) are considered *accents*, but others of which (å, ã, ç, ü) are not. A pair of letters coupled together, such as œ, is called a *digraph*.

Generating national characters and processing them correctly has been a very troublesome problem for the computer industry, because early standards were established without considering the requirements of any language other than English. Various makeshift solutions were adopted, which we still have to live with. Fortunately, new standards are being set, and computers and software are improving.

Here are some problems commonly encountered by anyone trying to maintain a document such as a multinational mailing list.

- *The character you need to type may not be on your keyboard*. Keyboards in English-speaking countries do not usually have keys corresponding to European national characters. There is no standard "European" keyboard either, so in every country some special characters are missing.

- *Foreign-language text may print differently on different printers*. Older printers sometimes cannot print national characters correctly.

- *National characters may get changed when you send a file from one application to another*. For example, if you cut and paste between a word processor, a spreadsheet, and a database package from different software vendors, you may find that the national characters have changed or disappeared. The same problem can occur if you download material from a mainframe computer to a workstation.

- *National characters may get changed when you send a file from one country to another*. Even when you think you are using the same computers and the same software, your colleagues in other countries may have equipment set up differently for their local language needs.

- *National characters may be refused in a data-entry screen*. Some programs may check that you are only using the 26 letters A–Z in a name. The computer considers é to be a different letter from e.

·• *Uppercase and lowercase national characters may confuse your computer.* When you search a document or a database for a name, you usually expect a command like FIND + TERESA to find both "Teresa" and "TERESA." You would also like FIND + THÉRÈSE to find "Thérèse," "THERESE," and "THÉRÈSE," but it rarely does.

• *Lists of names containing national characters may be sorted out of sequence.* It is impossible to satisfy everybody in a multinational listing. · For example, the letter ä comes in one place in the German alphabet and in a different place in the Swedish alphabet, and an American would expect it to count as an unmarked a.

This chapter is intended primarily for (1) people who want to write names and addresses (or other low-volume material) in the language of several foreign countries, and (2) people who need to assemble a document from contributions in other countries, such as a multinational-company phone book, a list of distributors or customers in many countries, or a standard collection of specification sheets in different languages.

Of course, the authoritative sources of information about your computer are the help text, manuals, and technical support services of your software and equipment vendors. This chapter is intended to tell you what is likely to be possible and what information is worth searching for.

Basic Methods

Before computers existed, there were three techniques available for producing national characters on a typewriter. All three have influenced computer designers. First, some countries simply substituted their commoner national characters for keyboard characters that they rarely used. For example, the left bracket [on an American keyboard is replaced by an Ä on a German keyboard and by a ¡ sign on a Spanish keyboard. Second, the typist could make a character like ä by typing double quotation marks '' , then backspacing and typing the letter *a* in the same position on the paper. Third, European typewriters were built so that certain keys, called *dead keys,* did not advance the carriage when the typist pressed the key. Since the accent or other mark was on a dead key, the following keystroke automatically overtyped it on the paper. Some manufacturers built international keyboards on which the dead keys could be activated or deactivated by a switch.

If you do not have a particular character on your keyboard, there are several possible ways you may be able to create it. The two most useful (but refer also to "Alternative Methods" below) are as follows:

1. There may be a special sequence of characters called a *compose sequence* that will produce the character. A compose sequence should imitate the dead keys of a typewriter. You type some unusual code to signal to the computer what you are about to do, and then you press, for example, '' followed by **o** to produce an ö.

2. There may be a way of entering the computer's *internal code* for the character. When you enter an internal code, you are bypassing the keyboard. The computer knows many more characters than there are keys on

the keyboard, and there is usually some obscure way of entering them all directly. There are two principal internal code systems in the computer industry: *EBCDIC*, which is used by large and mid-range IBM computers, and *ASCII*, which is used by everything else. Basic ASCII lacks many national characters, and several attempts have been made to extend it. The two principal variations on ASCII are called *PC–850* (occasionally referred to as *ISO 8839/1*) and *ANSI* (occasionally referred to as *ECMA-94*).

Specifically, this is what you have to do on some well-known systems:

- *PCs running DOS or OS/2:* Hold down the ALT key and type the three-digit code from the ASCII column of the following table. Then release the ALT key. You must use the numeric keypad, not the numbers from the typewriter part of the keyboard. On some computers, NUMLOCK must be set while you are doing this. If there is no code in the table, try the code from the PC-850 column. (It may not appear correctly on the screen, and your printer may need to be initialized in a PC-850 mode.) The specific software producers mentioned below have their own solutions. Comments on DOS apply to all variants: MS–DOS, PC–DOS, and DR–DOS.

- *WordPerfect for DOS:* Press CTRL+V and then the two characters from the Compose column in the following table. Alternatively, press CTRL+V and then the code from the Perfect column in the table below, including the comma, and then press ENTER.

- *Lotus products for DOS:* Press ALT+F1 and then the two characters from the Compose column in the following table. Alternatively, try ALT+F1 and then the code from the ANSI column in the table below, and then ENTER.

- *Ventura Publisher:* Press < and then the three-digit code from the Ventura column in the table below, and then >.

- *PCs running Windows:* Hold down the ALT key and press 0 and then the three-digit code from the ANSI column of the following table. Then release the ALT key. You must use the numeric keypad, not the numbers from the typewriter part of the keyboard. NUMLOCK must be set on. ASCII codes (three digits with no preceding 0) also work under Windows.

- *IBM AS/400:* Press ALT+F7 and then the two-character code from the EBCDIC column of the table. If you do not have a PC-style keyboard, try pressing ALT+HELP or ALT+x, where x is the key at the top left of the typewriter keyboard, to the left of the 1 key. If you do not have an ALT key, try pressing CMD,x.

- *Apple Macintosh:* Press OPT and then the compose sequence from the Apple column in the table. Release OPT after typing the first character. In other words, to get À you press OPT+~,A. The combinations in the table may apply only to U.S. keyboards.

Letter	ANSI	ASCII	PC-850	EBCDIC	Compose	Ventura	Perfect	Apple
à	224	133	133	44	`` `a ``	133	1,33	~a
á	225	160	160	45	'a	160	1,27	ea
â	226	131	131	42	^a	131	1,29	ia
ã	227	N/A[1]	198	46	~a	176	1,77	na
ä	228	132	132	43	"a	132	1,31	ua
å	229	134	134	47	*a[2]	134	1,35	aa
æ	230	145	145	9c	ae	145	1,37	'
ç	231	135	135	48	,c	135	1,39	c
è	232	138	138	54	`` `e ``	138	1,47	~e
é	233	130	130	51	'e	130	1,41	ee
ê	234	136	136	52	^e	136	1,43	ie
ë	235	137	137	53	"e	137	1,45	ue
ì	236	141	141	58	`` `i ``	141	1,55	~i
í	237	161	161	55	'i	161	1,49	ei
î	238	140	140	56	^i	140	1,51	ii
ï	239	139	139	57	"i	139	1,53	ui
ñ	241	164	164	49	~n	164	1,57	nn
ò	242	149	149	CD	`` `o ``	149	1,65	~o
ó	243	162	162	CE	'o	162	1,59	eo
ô	244	147	147	CB	^o	147	1,61	io
õ	245	N/A	228	CF	~o	177	1,83	no
ö	246	148	148	CC	"o	148	1,63	uo
ø	248	(237)[3]	155	70	/o	179	1,81	o
ù	249	151	151	DD	`` `u ``	151	1,73	~u
ú	250	163	163	DE	'u	163	1,67	eu
û	251	150	150	DB	^u	150	1,69	iu
ü	252	129	129	DC	"u	129	1,71	uu
ij	(255)[3]	(152)[3]	(152)[3]	(DF)[3]	ij	216	1,139	(uy)[3]
ß	223	(225)	225	59	ss	217	1,23	s
a	170	166	166	N/A	_a	166	4,15	9
o	176	167	167	N/A	_o	167	4,16	0
À	192	N/A	183	64	`` `A ``	182	1,32	~A
Á	193	N/A	181	65	'A	199	1,26	eA
Â	194	N/A	182	62	^A	200	1,28	iA
Ã	195	N/A	199	66	~A	183	1,76	nA
Ä	196	142	142	63	"A	142	1,30	uA
Å	197	143	143	67	*A[2]	143	1,34	A
Æ	198	146	146	9E	AE	146	1,36	''
Ç	199	128	128	74	,C	128	1,38	C
È	200	N/A	212	71	`` `E ``	201	1,46	~E
É	201	144	144	72	'E	144	1,40	eE
Ê	202	N/A	210	73	^E	202	1,42	iE

Letter	ANSI	ASCII	PC-850	EBCDIC	Compose	Ventura	Perfect	Apple
Ë	203	N/A	211	78	"E	203	1,44	uE
Ì	204	N/A	222	75	`I	204	1,54	~I
Í	205	N/A	214	76	'I	205	1,48	eI
Î	206	N/A	215	77	^I	206	1,50	iI
Ï	207	N/A	216	69	"I	207	1,52	uI
Ñ	209	165	165	ED	~N	165	1,56	nN
Ò	210	N/A	227	EE	`O	208	1,64	~O
Ó	211	N/A	224	EB	'O	209	1,58	eO
Ô	212	N/A	226	EF	^O	210	1,60	iO
Õ	213	N/A	229	EC	~O	184	1,82	nO
Ö	214	153	153	80	"O	153	1,62	uO
Ø	216	N/A	157	FD	/O	178	1,80	O
Ù	217	N/A	235	FE	`U	213	1,72	~U
Ú	218	N/A	233	FB	'U	214	1,66	eU
Û	219	N/A	234	FC	^U	215	1,68	iU
Ü	220	154	154	B1	"U	154	1,70	uU
£	163	156	156	B2	L–	156	4,11	3
¥	165	157	190	N/A	Y"	157	4,12	y
IJ	159	N/A	N/A	N/A	IJ	N/A	1,138	(uY)³
œ	156	N/A	N/A	N/A	oe	N/A	1,166	q
Œ	140	N/A	N/A	N/A	OE	N/A	1,167	Q

¹N/A: Not Available.
²If * does not work, try @ or o.
³The code in parentheses will produce a different letter, but it may look similar to the one you want.

Alternative Methods

- *Character selection window:* Modern systems with Graphical User Interfaces, such as Windows and the Apple Macintosh, can usually open a window that displays all the characters known to the computer or to the program you are running. The disadvantage is that selecting a character typically requires a lot of keystrokes or mouse movements. The technique is very easy to use and looks great in product demonstrations, but it slows you down significantly if you have to activate the window for every individual character. Windows that allow you to prepare a whole word and then copy it into your main document are significantly more useful. At the time of writing, WordPerfect for Windows is a rare example of a product with a character selection window that is convenient for international use.

- *Overstrike techniques:* Word-processing programs often have a function called *overstrike* or *backspace* that enables you to create national characters. For example, WordStar for DOS can produce an Ø if you type the sequence /,CTRL+P,H,O, and WordPerfect for DOS can produce a Korean won sign from the sequence SHIFT +F8,4,5,1,Y, = ,F7,F7. This technique has the advantage that it may work with older printers that cannot print all the national characters.

- *Keyboard remapping:* A computer has to know which national keyboard is in use. For example, under DOS the *keyb* statement in the *autoexec.bat* file changes the keyboard. Individual programs may have similar capability. The advantage of changing to a foreign keyboard is that you immediately get keys (or dead keys) for all the national characters of that country. The disadvantage is that other keys change position, too, and therefore you may not be able to touch-type correctly any longer. The only time you really need to remap a keyboard is if you have foreign visitors in your office who want to touch-type with the layout that they are accustomed to.

- *Individual key remapping:* Many programs and add-on products also offer you a way of changing the keyboard key by key. This is something to consider seriously if you need a small number of national characters frequently. Replacing the ~ key with the Spanish ñ would be an obvious improvement for many people. To do this in WordPerfect for DOS, you would press SHIFT + F1,5,1, select your usual keyboard name (try *enhanced* if you do not know it), press 8, set the cursor under ~, press 5,1,COMMA,5,7 (1,57 is the code for ñ from the Perfect column of the table), and then press ENTER,F7,F7. If there is no explicit remapping capability in a product, you may be able to achieve the same result by creating hot-keys or single-key macros, so that, say, ALT+N produces Ñ. One disadvantage of this technique is that you cannot easily substitute more than a few characters without getting confused. Another disadvantage is that your keyboard becomes different from other people's.

How Important Are National Characters?

The "Country Identification" chapter contains a table showing which characters are used by which languages.

Omitting diacritical marks altogether will have two effects on your foreign readers. It will slow them down, and it may cause them to misunderstand certain words. It is like reading text containing a lot of spelling mistakes. The severity varies from language to language: for example, it is quite common to drop some diacritical marks from capital letters in some languages. However, it is generally somewhat dangerous to omit diacritical marks. Norwegian Mr. Høst will not appreciate at all being called "Mr. Host."

If you have no way of printing or entering national characters, there are ways of substituting for most of them. Adding the marks by hand usually looks bad and may be inaccurate if you are not familiar with the language. Do not add marks by hand when they are described as optional in the following notes.

Catalan: It does not prevent understanding if marks are dropped from addresses or short passages of text. However, try at least to create ç and Ç by pressing C,OVERSTRIKE,COMMA. Marks are optional on capitals. The raised dot exists an ANSI 0183 but may also be typed as a period (e.g., 1.1 instead of 1·1). The Catalan letters L and l· are defined in WordPerfect as 1,151 and 1,150 and in the Unicode as U + 0141 and U + 0142 respectively. Depending on your font, it may still be clearer and easier to use the raised dot, which, like all ANSI characters, is carried over into the Unicode.

Czech: Diacritics can be omitted without causing serious misunderstanding. Instead of placing a haček sign ˇ on the letters d and t, you can write a single closing quote (') after the letter. The letters d' and t' are available in the Multinational Extensions font of Windows, but you can also type any recognizable apostrophe. Vowels like á can also be typed a'. Diacritics are written on both capitals and lowercase letters in Czech.

Danish: It is acceptable to substitute ae for æ, oe for ø, and aa for å. Marks are expected on capitals.

Dutch: It is acceptable to substitute ij as two separate characters for the digraph ij. On many computer typefaces you can hardly tell the difference. Do not substitute ÿ. An initial capital must be written IJ, not Ij or Ÿ. If you use the digraph, check your printout, because it may display as ij but print as ÿ.

Finnish: You may omit the marks from ä and ö if you must, but try not to. Finns may understand if you substitute ae and oe, but it will look strange to them, particularly in the many words that have double vowels. You cannot write aeae for ää. Marks are expected on capitals.

French: It does not prevent understanding if marks are dropped from addresses or short passages of text. Marks are optional on capitals.

German: It is acceptable to substitute ae for ä, oe for ö, ue for ü, and ss for ß. If you cannot produce a ß, try a Greek beta β; computer printers often use the same or a very similar dot pattern for both. Marks are expected on capitals.

Hungarian: The accents on á and é are important. If you cannot produce them, type apostrophes instead: a' and e'. Other diacritical marks are less important. If you can't produce ő and ű, then ö and ü are better substitutes than o and u. Diacritics are written on both capitals and lowercase letters in Hungarian.

Italian: In place of an accented letter, it is acceptable to write an apostrophe after the unaccented letter; for example, you can write **società** as **societa'** . Marks are optional on capitals.

Norwegian: It is acceptable to substitute ae for æ. For Ø try to substitute O,OVERSTRIKE,/. Otherwise, substitute oe for ø and aa for å. Marks are expected on capitals.

Polish: Diacritics can be omitted without preventing understanding of addresses and short passages. If you cannot add an accent to a consonant, it helps to write an apostrophe after the unmarked letter, thus: write ć,ń,ś,ź as c',n',s',z'. Diacritics are written on capitals in Polish.

Portuguese: It does not prevent understanding if most marks are omitted from addresses or short passages of text, except that the tilde marks on ã and õ are really needed, and unfortunately these are often the most difficult to produce. Substituting ä and ö is somewhat acceptable. Try also to produce ç and Ç by pressing C,OVERSTRIKE,COMMA. Marks are expected on the Ä, Ç, and Ö, but other marks are optional on capitals.

Slovenian: Diacritics can be omitted from addresses and short passages. Diacritics are written on both capital and lowercase letters in Slovenian.

Spanish: It is permissible to drop marks from addresses or short passages of text, except that the tilde mark on ñ is really necessary. Substitution of *ny* is not acceptable. Try pressing N,OVERSTRIKE,~. The tilde is expected on capital Ñ, but other marks are optional on capitals.

Swedish: It is acceptable to substitute ae for ä, and oe for ö. The mark on the letter å should be retained if possible. Try pressing A,OVERSTRIKE,°. If you substitute an unmarked a, however, the meaning of the word should be clear from the context. Some Swedish people seem to reluctantly accept aa as a substitute for å. Marks are expected on capitals.

Turkish: If you cannot produce Turkish letters, omit the diacritical marks. Both national and international keyboards are used in Turkey, so Turkish business people are relatively accustomed to seeing documents without diacritical marks.

Currency symbols: Older computer systems have only the dollar, pound, and yen symbols. There are a number of other currency symbols that you can produce only if you have an overstrike capability or Unicode-based computer software.

Currency	Overstrike sequence	Unicode
Korean won	W,OVERSTRIKE, =	U + 20A9
Nigerian naira	N,OVERSTRIKE, =	U + 20A6
Philippine piso	P,OVERSTRIKE,/	U + 20A7 (see text)
Thai baht	B,OVERSTRIKE,/	U + 0E3F

The Unicode standard currently provides for the Philippine piso symbol only as an alternative glyph of a rarely used Spanish peseta symbol, so it is largely a matter of luck whether it will appear correctly in Unicode-based software.

If you cannot produce the above symbols, it is acceptable to use a simple capital letter: W, N, P, or B. Similarly, Y is acceptable for the Japanese yen. The pound sign was used in the past for Italian and Turkish lira, but L. is current usage. However, the pound sign is still the standard symbol for British and Irish pounds, in which countries L, with or without overstrikes, is likely to be misunderstood.

Miscellaneous: It is acceptable to substitute oe for the digraph œ, which occurs in several languages. The marks on ë and ï, which also occur in several languages, only serve to separate successive vowels (as in "Noël") and are always optional. It is acceptable to substitute underlined a̲ and o̲ for the ordinal signs ª and ° found in several languages.

Collating Sequences

Catalan: The combination l·l comes between l and m in the alphabet.

Czech: Consonants with the haček sign ˇ are considered to be separate letters in the Czech alphabet; thus, for example, *Košeca* follows *Kostoliště*. The combination ch is also considered a separate letter falling between h and i; thus, *Cheb* follows *Huty*. However, diacritics on vowels do not affect the collating sequence.

Danish: The letters æ, ø, and å follow z in the alphabet, in that order. Words that contain aa are sorted as though å was written instead.

Finnish: The letters ä and ö follow z in the alphabet, in that order. If Swedish and Finnish names are mixed, Swedish å will be sorted between z and ä.

German: The letters ä, ö, and ü used to be sorted as though they were written ae, oe, and ue, but this practice is disappearing under the influence of computer technology. The letter ß is sorted as though it was written ss.

Hungarian: All marked vowels are considered separate letters of the alphabet, though you may see variations in collating sequence in practice. The consonant groups cs, dz, dzs, gy, ly, sz, ty, and zs are also considered separate letters. From among these, the two cases noticeable to a foreigner are that *Csér* follows *Cún* and that *Zselic* follows *Zuzmó*.

Norwegian: The letters æ, ø, and å follow z in the alphabet, in that order.

Polish: All marked letters are considered separate letters of the alphabet and follow the corresponding unmarked ones. Thus, *Łodz* follows *Lublin*. The three last letters of the alphabet are z, ž and ż.

Slovenian: The marked letters č, š, and ž are considered separate letters of the alphabet and follow the corresponding unmarked ones.

Spanish: The letter ñ comes between n and o in the alphabet. The combination ch used to come between c and d, and the combination ll used to come between l and m, but the Association of Spanish Language Academies recommended in 1994 to end this distinction in the interests of international compatibility.

Swedish: The letters å, ä, and ö follow z in the alphabet, in that order.

Turkish: Any letter with a diacritical mark follows the unmarked letter in the Turkish alphabet. The dot on an i is considered a diacritical mark, so all words beginning with i follow all words beginning with dotless ı. There are two rare exceptions to this rule. The letter é occurs in some words of foreign origin, and the letter â in some older words, particularly proper names. Diacritical marks are used on capital letters, including İ. (Dotless I is the capital of dotless ı.)

Multinational Document Interchange

If you receive a file or document from another country, will you be able to display it and print it correctly? Historically, the computer industry has found this difficult to achieve, but recently designed products are much better. WordPerfect files should exchange correctly. Files created by any products running under Windows should exchange correctly. Apple Macintosh documents should exchange correctly. If a document from one of these systems does not print or display correctly, that is probably due to limitations of your printer or your terminal. Letters that do not display correctly may still print correctly.

Older systems have had difficulty because displays and printers lacked the necessary characters and therefore had to be modified for different countries. They were not modified in a compatible way. For example, the "official" ASCII character code for the Spanish ñ is now 164. However, before the official code was decided upon, the Spanish started to use 92, which is the "official" code for the backslash \. They changed the backslash key on their keyboards, and they changed their printers and displays to display ñ when a 92 was received from the computer. Inside Spain, this worked fine; however, the Portuguese used code 92 for their ç character. Therefore, documents typed in Spain on older computer systems will print wrong in Portugal, because all the ñ characters will be replaced with ç characters. There have been many such examples.

Sometimes older printers appear to go wrong if you try to print European characters on them. For example, old models of one well-known brand of dot-matrix printers were unable to print î because they interpreted that character (140) to mean "Space to the next vertical tab." The result was that the printer threw paper forward until it jammed whenever you tried to print a word containing an î.

There is a solution, called *codepage 850*, for multinational document interchange in DOS systems, provided you have relatively recent software (MS-DOS 4.0 or later), an EGA or better monitor, and a modern printer such as a Hewlett-Packard or compatible laser printer or an IBM Proprinter or Quietwriter or compatible dot-matrix printer. This is what you have to do to use codepage 850 (do not use it with WordPerfect or Lotus or any other products that are solving the interchange problem their own way, outside of DOS):

- Make sure you have a COUNTRY statement in your CONFIG.SYS file. In the United States and Canada it is usually missing. It should read (assuming all your files are in the c:\dos directory):
  COUNTRY = 001,437,C:\DOS\COUNTRY.SYS
- You also need a "display device" statement, which should read:
  DEVICE = C:\DOS\DISPLAY.SYS CON = (EGA,437,1)
- Now set up a procedure called INTL.BAT which contains:
  NLSFUNC
  MODE CON CP PREP = ((850)C:\DOS\EGA.CPI)
  CHCP 850

This procedure will switch your display and IBM-compatible printer to the PC-850 code set. Laser printers must usually be switched over at their control panels. To switch a Hewlett-Packard LaserJet III, for example, set it *off-line*, press *menu* until you see SYM SET, press + until you see SYM SET = PC-850, press *enter*, and press *on-line*. If your application is capable of initializing a printer, send an HP-compatible printer the decimal sequence 27,40,49,50,85 or the hex sequence 1B,28,31,32,55.

- To return to normal running, execute the DOS command CHCP 437 (or whatever other number has to be in your COUNTRY statement), and reset the printer's SYM SET.

You can always create amateur solutions to document interchange problems, as long as you have some way of producing the national characters locally. If the Spanish ñ and the Portuguese ç are both appearing as \, for example, you can go through the Spanish file changing \ to ñ and the Portuguese file changing \ to ç before merging the two files.

Microsoft Windows

By adopting the ANSI standard in place of ASCII, Microsoft Windows has effectively enabled us to produce Western European characters without the earlier confusion. By defining "locales" it has also provided an underlying mechanism for sorting and capitalizing marked characters. If programs running under Windows continue to have problems with Western European characters, it is the fault of their authors and not of the operating system. However, all the traditional problems continue to plague us when we wish to produce or process Eastern European characters. Comments in this section about Eastern European characters apply equally to Turkish characters.

A TrueType font called "Multinational Extensions" (MULTIEXT.FOT/ .TTF) is available for all current versions of the Microsoft Windows operating system. It is an extension of Times New Roman which includes all the individual Eastern European characters that are needed for the languages described in this book. You install it like any other font from the Fonts icon of the Control Panel group; any program that allows you to change fonts from a toolbar or menu can use it.

The simplest way to produce Eastern European characters under Windows is to copy them one at a time from the Character Map panel of the Accessories group. However, this method suffers from the same inherent problems as all earlier character-replacement systems. For example, ANSI 0070 is usually the letter F, but MULTIEXT uses it to represent the marked letter č. The letters F and č appear differently (correctly) on your screen, but in your document they are the same character, ANSI 0070. Consequently, a function like Find or Replace does not work properly. To find *česka* you would have to search for *Feska*. Also, the uppercase and lowercase letters do not have the same relationship that programs expect. Unless the program specifically recognizes MULTIEXT as being different from all other fonts, ľ will be uppercased to ğ, not Ľ, because the program sees ANSI 0122 as z, not ľ, and therefore changes it to ANSI 0090, which is normally Z, but is ğ in MULTIEXT. The most severe operational disadvantage of MULTIEXT is that you cannot type an entire Eastern European word in one font: you have to copy in the marked characters one at a time. (A tip: if you have to type a Slovenian address, first go to the Character Map panel and select čšž, copy them, and paste them several times into your document, so that you have a pool of useful characters to drag around with your mouse.)

The above advice applies to almost all Windows programs from all sources, but WordPerfect for Windows remains the honorable exception, as earlier versions of WordPerfect were an honorable exception in the MSDOS/PCDOS environment. WordPerfect continues to use its own character-encoding system in defiance of all standards, and it works quite well and is still the most practical of well-known word-processing products for multinational use.

The only solution to all the problems described in this chapter is an agreed system under which different characters are represented by different internal codes. There is at last a solution on the horizon, and it is called the Unicode.

Microsoft Windows 95

Windows 95 is not itself based on the Unicode, although it does have provision to run applications written for the Unicode. For some time, most people will still be running ANSI applications designed for earlier versions of Windows. Windows 95 offers ANSI applications three fonts with Central European (Czech, Hungarian, Polish, and Slovenian) characters, called Arial CE, Courier New CE, and Times New Roman CE. Times New Roman CE should be an adequate substitute for the earlier Multinational Extensions. To add these fonts if they were not chosen during the original installation procedure, follow the sequence: Start, Settings, Control Panel, Add/Remove Programs, Windows Setup, Multilanguage Support, Details, Central European Language Support.

For most purposes, these CE fonts are adequate. Though you must change font when you switch from Western European words to Eastern European words, the person who sees the finished document will be unaware of the change and English words appear correctly in both.

There are local editions of Windows 95 (and other Windows variants) on sale in other countries, and any of them can be special-ordered from outside the country for which it is intended. In particular, there is a "Pan-European Edition" that supports a further generalization of the font system, known as Windows Glyph List 4 (WGL4). A WGL4 font contains all Western European, Eastern European, Cyrillic, Greek, and Turkish characters. Read the file called PANEURO.TXT on distribution disks (including the Microsoft Developer Network CD-ROMs) for current limitations, because the details are subject to change.

It is not advisable to install special fonts and software editions on a network without consulting M.I.S. professionals and allowing some time for experimentation. Do not assume you can immediately send WGL4-based documents from one computer to another. The nature of the problem is changing. In the days of MS-DOS and mainframes, the computer industry offered very incomplete solutions to international-character-set problems, but amateurs could often find creative solutions. Now, good solutions are becoming available, but to obtain them users are increasingly at the mercy of their computer network administrators.

The Unicode Standard

The computer industry has developed a new international character encoding standard that defines over 34,000 characters. It covers every major language written today and many sets of mathematical and technical symbols. The largest part of the standard is devoted to a unified set of the thousands of ideographs used by the Chinese, Japanese, and Korean languages. In principle, the Unicode standard creates a marked character, such as ô, by combining a character (o) and a diacritic (ˆ), but for compatibility with earlier codesets it provides single ("precomposed") codes for many marked Roman characters. In practice, every possible marked character a business correspondent might use in Europe has a single Unicode representation. Each character or other text element is allocated a four-digit hexadecimal number; for example, ô is written as U+00F4 (which is decimal 244, the same as the ANSI value). Applications based on the Unicode standard will go far beyond current capabilities; for example, you will be able to embed an Arabic quotation in European text, even though its directionality is right-to-left.

The Unicode project has laid the foundations for a complete solution to the historical problems described in this chapter, but it will take some time before Unicode-based applications are widely available. Components designed to assist software developers to upgrade their applications are becoming available. Upgraded applications will follow as time goes by. One vendor that can provide a Unicode-enabled word-processing program is Gamma Productions Inc., listed in Chapter 3.

The Microsoft Windows NT Operating System uses the Unicode internally. You can see the range of languages and symbols covered in the Unicode by looking at the Character Map (in the Accessories group) and pulling down the "Subset" list. Your monitor is probably unable to display most of the non-Roman subsets, but you should be able to see and use the "Latin Extended-A" characters for Eastern Europe.

Equipment Selection

The list of problems at the beginning of this chapter can be used as a checklist in evaluating computers and software. Current systems based on the ANSI or EBCDIC codes are likely to be satisfactory for Western European languages. ASCII-based systems need to be checked carefully, using Norwegian and Portuguese characters as a test. If you need national characters for areas outside the present scope of this book, you will probably need to turn to a specialized vendor. Some suggestions will be found in Chapter 3.

Although most systems and software can now process national characters, there are considerable differences in how easy or natural the entry of these characters is. Vendors frequently offer keyboard remapping or font changes as inappropriate answers to all questions about international characters. Ask for a demonstration of how to write a Norwegian or Portuguese address in the middle of a page of English (or other local language). Make sure it will print in bold and italic and in different type sizes. You should also check whether you can use a national character in any special windows or dialogs. For example, can you use them in file names, passwords, authors' names, document summaries, electronic mail destination names, and text searches? Minor problems with search-and-replace operations when the target text contains national characters are still quite common and may be unavoidable.

A possibility that is often overlooked is to equip an international department with Spanish keyboards and matching software. The advantage of the Spanish keyboard is that its layout is similar to the U.S. layout but it has three dead keys with six diacritical marks on them, including all the characters needed for French, German, and Italian as well as, obviously, Spanish.

Most printers now have all the Western European national characters in their resident fonts, but that feature matters less and less because most software now controls the printer dot by dot rather than by telling it to print a character at a time. Still, it is worthwhile testing the compatibility and performance of a total system. Include a few national characters in a multipage document, and make sure not only that they print correctly but also that the system is still working at the printer's rated number of pages per minute.

If you are selecting application packages, rather than office software, for international use, then there are two levels of localization to check. The first question is whether the product can produce dates, times, measurements, currency amounts, and sorted reports, all according to local expectations. The second question is whether the application needs are different for international use. Any computer application that has to deal with the government, with the banking system, or with customers' and suppliers' computer systems probably needs extensive modifications for international use. Even within the Western European "Single Market" there are a lot of detailed differences in Electronic Data Interchange standards, Generally Accepted Accounting Procedures, Value-Added Tax rules, local document layouts, banking procedures, and government controls and reporting of all kinds. You may also require functions that you have never needed domestically, such as the automatic calculation of foreign currency gains and losses.

A product designed for international use should obviously be able to present data-entry screens, reports, and help text in the language of the foreign operators. But remember that you may also have a customer whose language is different from that of the computer operator. For example, many organizations need to keep product descriptions in several languages so that their computer systems can produce correct export invoices for different destinations.

Conclusion

Attention to typographical detail is important for your image and reputation both inside and outside your own organization. If you cannot produce accents and other marks correctly, it generally looks to foreigners just as though you were making spelling mistakes. It also reinforces their natural feeling that they would rather be dealing with a local organization or with somebody who understands their customs rather than with you.

Inside your organization, it is always to your personal advantage to be an accurate source of detailed information about how equipment works and about how international requirements should be taken into account.

8. Guide to the Country Chapters

This chapter is a step-by-step introduction to the treatment of names and addresses in the 47 individual country chapters that follow.

Address Formats

Each of the following country chapters starts with an example of a typical business address and then provides more detailed information about each part of it. A name and address, as you would write them on an envelope, constitute an *address block*. Each part of it is called an *address element*. To show all the address elements you might see in a street address, here is a composite example of a street address in a fictitious place:

      Illustris[1]
      Dom.[2] Spurius[3] Flavius[4]
      Editores Interpopulares[5] S.A.[6]
      Aedificium[7] Domitiani[8] Off.[9] 2300[10]
      Via[11] Decumanus[12] 137-139[13]
      Vicus Medius Rerum Venalium[14]
      30032[15] NEMAUSUS[16] (NB)[17]
      ROMA DAITEIKOKU[18]

Key:

    [1] Honorific.
    [2] Title.
    [3] Given name.
    [4] Family name.
    [5] Company name.
    [6] "Inc." in the local language.
    [7] "Building" in the local language.
    [8] Building name.
    [9] "Suite" in the local language.
    [10] Office number inside the building.
    [11] "Street" in the local language.
    [12] Street name.
    [13] Building (house or lot) number(s).
    [14] Locality name (suburb or village).

[15] Postcode.

[16] City or delivery-post-office name.

[17] State/province abbreviation.

[18] Country name in the sender's language.

Any instructions in *italic type* that appear in the "Key" Section should be followed to assist automated mail processing.

NOTE: The last address line, which should always show the country's name *in the language of the country from which the mail is being sent*, is omitted from the rest of the display addresses throughout the book, precisely because it will be spelled differently depending on where the mail is originating. However, a country name should appear in the address on *all* international correspondence. See "Country Names" on page 85.

Address Elements

PERSONAL NAMES

Three distinct systems of naming individuals are in use in the countries covered by this book, each with numerous small variations.

The European tradition has been that parents would choose one or several names for a child at birth or at a Christian baptism ceremony. If the local custom was to give several names, the second and subsequent names were usually the names of relatives or godparents. Unlike the other traditions described below, given names in the European tradition are almost always distinctive words; there is generally no object or concept called an "allan" or a "rhonda"—these are unmistakably personal names. The European child also has automatically inherited a *family name* from its father, and a woman has automatically taken her husband's family name when she married. If an individual has more than one given name, only one (normally the first) is ever used, except that in many countries compound given names are common and are considered as single names: **Jean-Pierre** is never called Jean. Compound family names are common in Argentina, Brazil, and Portugal (**Correia de Oliveira**), and are found occasionally in all Spanish-speaking countries and in the United Kingdom (**Luxton-Jones**). Russia and Spain evolved their own variations on the Christian tradition. In Spain and most Spanish-speaking countries (but not Argentina), a child takes its mother's family name after its father's family name. It is still known familiarly by its father's name; therefore, **Francisco Rodríguez López** is **Mr. Rodríguez**, not "Mr. López." In Russia, a person's second name is a *patronymic*, derived from the father's given name. The given name and the patronymic are used together to identify someone precisely and respectfully.

The traditional European system is still strong in many countries but is changing as women's independence increases. In most countries, a married woman now has the legal right to keep her own family name, change to her husband's, or combine them in various ways. Children may be given their father's family name, their mother's, or both. The extent to which this freedom is really used varies a lot from country to country. As more children receive compound names, there will presumably be even more choice for future generations. When a woman uses two family names and you do not know what her preference is, it is safest to use both: thus, **Maria Keller Haussmann** should be called **Ms. Keller Haussmann**. If a woman hyphenates her names, it is certain she wants you to use both parts. More-specific guidance is given in the appropriate country chapters.

The Chinese tradition has been that a child's name consists of three characters of the Chinese language. The first character has been the family name, inherited from the father. The second character has been a name given to all the children of a generation in that family. (The boys would have one name and the girls another.) The third character has been the true given name of the individual. The generation names were often planned many generations ahead. The names of successive generations might, for example, form a poem. Any character in the language could theoretically be used as a part of a name, although some are preferred, and a particular given name is felt to be characteristically masculine or characteristically feminine. Chinese women have not traditionally changed their family names on marriage, although they have sometimes used their husband's name to Westerners to avoid confusion.

The traditional system is still strong but is breaking down to some extent in some places as parents are starting to choose given names more freely for their children. Unfortunately, many Chinese-speaking people in business change their names into the European sequence when dealing with Westerners, so there is always some doubt as to which is their family name. Guidance on this problem is given in the individual chapters on China, Hong Kong, Singapore, and Taiwan.

The Arab tradition, which is largely followed in all Muslim countries, is that most individuals are described as the son or daughter of their father: **Rashid ibn Fayad** is Rashid, the son of Fayad, and **Zahra bint Fayad** is Zahra, Fayad's daughter. Given names are normally ordinary Arabic words: thus, **Kareem** means "generous and noble." **Al-Kareem**, however, is a name of God and can only be used by a man when prefixed **abd Al-Kareem**, meaning "the servant of the Generous and Noble God." This, like many other similar names, has been compressed into a modern given name, **Abdelkareem**. In classical times, other elements were added to names: for example, **abu Rashid** means "the father of Rashid," and **al-Quchayri** means "from the Quchayr tribe." These and many other honorific, professional, and religious descriptions have been adopted as family names in the modern world. Muslim women do not change their names on marriage.

TITLES

The commonest equivalents of "Mr." in Europe are **Herr, Monsieur, Señor, Signore,** and **Senhor.** The equivalents of "Mrs." are **Frau, Madame, Señora, Signora,** and **Senhora.** Except in the case of "Herr" and "Frau," it is a little more polite to use these local forms in addresses and written communications than to use "Mr." and "Mrs."

There is no easy answer to the question of whether "Ms." is appropriate in international English. Obviously, it was not in English textbooks when your foreign business contacts were in grade school, but most of them will recognize it as an American usage, without realizing how standard it has become. All reactions are possible, ranging from appreciation through incomprehension to resistance. This book tries to give specific guidance about current practice in each culture, but unfortunately any of the three titles "Miss," "Mrs.," or "Ms." may give offense, and so may immediate use of a given name. In the absence of specific information, you can either be conservative and use "Mrs." for a few more years, or be progressive and call all women "Ms."

Italian-speaking and Portuguese-speaking people often write an *honorific* in front of names: **Ill.mo**, or **Ilmo.**, is a common example. The word **Don** is a respectful additional title in Spain. The suffixes **-sama** and **-dono** indicate respect in Japan.

The title **Dr.** is used in many countries. In some countries it is confined to researchers, but in others it is a common title for business executives. Depending on the country, the holder may or may not have really studied for a doctorate. A common academic title all over Europe, except in the United Kingdom and Ireland, is **Ing.** or close variations of it. It is an abbreviation for the French word **ingénieur**, translated into English as "engineer." However, you must not assume that the person is a professional engineer. Any business executive might have this type of degree, which is at least equivalent to a U.S. master's degree. **Lic.** and **Dipl.** are other common European titles related to degrees, less prestigious than "Ing."

FORMALITY

Formality varies enormously from country to country. Given names are almost never used in business in Japan or Korea or by Chinese-speaking people. However, Chinese-speaking people may adopt Western given names, which they fully expect you to use. More guidance is given in the chapters on China, Hong Kong, Singapore, and Taiwan.

At the other extreme, given names are almost always used in Australia, Canada, Denmark, Finland, Ireland, Israel, Norway, Sweden, and the United States. Even in these informal countries, it is advisable to be cautious on a first contact with someone outside your own organization. However, the social risk in the informal countries is that you will appear distant and unfriendly if you are not quick enough to start using given names.

Malays and Indonesians do not distinguish between given and family names in the Western sense, and in Russia the patronymic rather than the family name is used to identify someone more exactly and respectfully. Further explanation will be found in the chapters about these three countries. In all the other "intermediate" countries, practice varies. Given names are commonly used by people who work together closely and are at roughly the same level of responsibility. Beyond that, it is dangerous to generalize. Corporate cultures vary. Younger people, smaller companies, and employees in American-dominated industries (such as the computer business) are usually more informal.

Executives from formal and intermediate countries are usually aware that Americans expect to use given names. They may like the practice or they may not, but they accept it as a feature of the American language. You will hear foreign executives call each other by their given names in an English-speaking environment even though they would not do so in their native languages.

When dealing with people at a distance, by phone or mail, it is best to be cautious and avoid given names, particularly with Asians, unless it is part of your corporate culture to assert informality, or unless your contact is with one of the countries listed as informal above. However, you also need to be sensitive to how familiar a person is with the United States. For example, many

Latin American executives have studied in the United States, worked for U.S. companies, and traveled there extensively on business. It is more courteous to treat such people informally, as honorary Americans, regardless of how you think they may be treated in their home countries.

COMPANY NAMES

The abbreviations **Inc.** and **Corp.** are characteristically American. The commonest equivalents elsewhere are **Ltd.** and **S.A.** Other local equivalents are **AB**, **AG**, **AE**, **A/S**, **BV**, **GmbH**, **KK**, **NV**, **OY**, and **PLC**. Many other rarer legal forms exist for smaller companies.

Most countries have two types of corporation, which could be summarized crudely as "small" and "large." It is important to know which you may be dealing with. Unfortunately, a lot of misinformation circulates on this subject, because national practices are not what you would expect from a study of the regulations. An AG in Austria or Germany really is a large company, but an AG in Switzerland could be any size. An NV in the Netherlands is probably large, but an NV in Belgium could be any size. Most companies in France and Spain are S.A.s, the "large" type. Most companies in Germany and the United Kingdom are GmbH and Ltd., respectively, which are the "small" type.

Another mistaken belief is that all of the "large" corporations, such as AGs and PLCs, are necessarily publicly traded. They can be private. S.A.s are frequently private. It is true that the "small" type of corporation cannot be publicly traded, but such an entity may very well be the subsidiary of a publicly traded company.

The individual country chapters contain more detailed information about what you can deduce from a company name in a particular place.

OFFICES

In many countries every company in a shared office building has to have its own maildrop at the entrance, and therefore no information is needed in the address to explain where the office is located inside the building. In Denmark, Spain, Portugal, and Latin America, internal directions are regularly included in addresses. In English-speaking countries and in Asia, floor numbers are common. The U.S. system of suite numbering is rarely used, except in a modified form in Singapore and India.

BUILDING NAMES

Building names are common in the United Kingdom and somewhat common in France and in other places which those two countries have influenced. In other countries, only the name of a landmark building would be included in an address. The commonest local names for buildings outside the United States are **Bâtiment**, **Edificio**, **House**, **Immeuble**, **Palazzo**, **Tour**, and **Torre**.

In some countries, again led by the United Kingdom and France, industrial areas are named and used in addresses. The commonest expressions are **Industrial Estate**, **Polìgono Industrial**, **Trading Estate**, **Zone d'Activités Commerciales**, and **Zone Industrielle**.

BUILDING NUMBERS

Except occasionally in the United Kingdom, Ireland, and Spanish-speaking countries, addresses must include building numbers, or "house numbers." In half of Europe, the building number follows the street name; elsewhere the number is written first. In Japan and Korea, the building number is accompanied by a district number. Building numbers are allocated on a grid system in many newer cities throughout the Americas, as explained in the "United States" chapter. With these exceptions, buildings are numbered more or less consecutively along a street, with even numbers on one side and odd numbers on the other.

Where there is no grid system, buildings may have multiple numbers. **12-14 High Road** indicates that two buildings have been combined, or a single new building has replaced two older ones. A building may also have multiple entrances. Subsidiary entrances are called **12a**, **12b**, etc., in most countries. The words **bis** and **ter** also indicate subsidiary entrances. The precise implications vary a little from country to country.

STREET NAMES

The commonest equivalents of the word "Street" are **Calle**, **Laan**, **Road**, **Rue**, **Rua**, **Straat**, **Strasse**, and **Via**. In the Afrikaans, Danish, Dutch, Finnish, German, Norwegian, and Swedish languages, the word is usually suffixed to the name of the street; for example, "High Street" is **Hoogstraat** in Dutch. The commonest suffixes are **–gade**, **–gate**, **–gatan**, **–katu**, **straat**, **–straße**, and **–tie**.

Words and suffixes like the above are called *street designators* in this book. (The U.K. Post Office uses the term *thoroughfare designator*.) The particular street designator used in an address sometimes gives you an idea of the surroundings of a company. For instance, the word **Boulevard** normally implies a major business street in all the countries where it is used. Information like this is mentioned wherever appropriate in the country chapters. However, there is always some uncertainty and inconsistency about the meanings of street designators. In English-speaking countries, **Drive** in a business address implies a boulevard, but many "drives" also exist in residential subdivisions. (No systematic attempt has been made in this book to interpret all the street designators you might see in residential or rural addresses.) Also note that the implications of some words—in particular, **Allée**, **Chaussée**, **Road**, and **Weg**—vary from country to country.

The street designator is customarily omitted in Greece, Israel, Spanish-speaking America, and the southwestern United States.

In a number of countries, there may be two street names in an address, implying that one is a small alley leading off a larger and better-known road. Countries where this is the custom (listed here with the lesser street designator in parentheses) are Malaysia (**Lorong**), Taiwan (**Alley, Lane**), Thailand (**Soi**), Turkey (**Sokaği**), and older areas in the United Kingdom (**Court, Mews, Place, Yard**).

LOCALITY NAMES

The word *locality* is used in this book to describe whatever comes between the street and the city in an address block. In some countries, a locality is not needed. In many others, it is used occasionally or often to resolve ambiguities. Ambiguities occur because there are often streets of the same name in different parts of a city; thus, before postcodes were introduced, it was necessary to specify the district of the city to be sure that the letter arrived at the intended address. Postcodes should eliminate the need for locality names in time.

In Japan and Korea, localities are all-important as the addressing system is based on successive subdivisions of an area rather than on street names.

CITY NAMES

City really implies "delivery post office." City names should be written in capitals, by international convention.

STATE/PROVINCE/ETC. NAMES

Most countries are divided into states, provinces, prefectures, or counties. In the past these regional names were necessary in addresses because towns with the same name occurred in different parts of the same country—for example, Denver, Colorado, and Denver, Tennessee.

The development of postcode systems should eliminate the need for regional names. Where they are still required, most countries have standard abbreviations for them which are locally very well known.

POSTCODES

A *postcode* is a code that assists the post office to sort and deliver mail. A basic postcode system identifies the post office responsible for delivery to the addressee. The postcode typically has a structure, which it can be useful to know. For example, a U.S. zip code beginning with 77 refers to the Houston, Texas, postal region. 77006 is the code for a particular post office, known as the "Fairview station." A French postcode beginning with 77 refers to the Seine-et-Marne prefecture to the east of Paris. The French postcode 77010 refers to a government office complex in the town of Melun in Seine-et-Marne. A British postcode beginning with RG refers to the city of Reading and its surrounding towns. Post-office boxes, at least in major cities, usually have their own postcodes. High-volume mailers in most countries have their own postcodes.

An *extended postcode*, in the terminology of this book, is a postcode that not only identifies the delivery post office but is also used within the delivery post office to sort the incoming mail according to delivery routes. The code for local delivery is generally set off by a space or a hyphen. The principal examples of extended postcodes are these:

Canada	M5A 1N1
Japan	386-04
Netherlands	7300 AR
United Kingdom	SL6 7DP
United States	77006-1119

Postcodes are written after the city name at the end of the last line of the domestic address in English-speaking countries, and at the beginning of the last line, in front of the city name, in most others. Countries with non-Roman alphabets have mostly adopted the American postcode position for international mail.

In most countries, postcodes are allocated in a loosely geographical sequence. In many cases, the capital city is out of sequence. In spite of the irregularities that are found everywhere, it is usually meaningful and useful to sort a mailing list by postcode. The exceptions are France, Spain, and the United Kingdom, where sorting is not very useful without specialized computer programs.

P.O. BOXES

Post-office boxes exist everywhere. In some countries they are frequently used by businesses and in others they are not. In countries where they are not common, there is sometimes a suspicion that a P.O. Box address is not quite respectable and the business may not be real. This is a possibility, but a remote one. Boxes are perfectly usual in many countries, and in any event it is probably much easier in most places for a dishonest business to arrange a street address for itself than to rent a P.O. Box.

Where boxes are common, it is either because mail is obtainable from them earlier in the day, or because the deliveries to street addresses in the area are unreliable. Therefore, if you know a box address, you should always use it. It is a waste of time and space to add the street address, and specifically against the rules of many national post offices.

However, only post offices can deliver to P.O. Boxes. *You must not make the mistake of giving box addresses to air courier services or to freight forwarders!*

Many countries use or accept the English expression **P.O. Box** or **POB**. The most common translations are **Apartado**, **Apartado Postale**, **Boîte Postale**, **Caixa Postale**, **Case Postale**, **Casella Postale**, **Casilla de Correos**, **Postboks**, **Postbus**, **Postfach**, and **Postilokero**.

In Hong Kong, Norway, and Singapore, it is customary to add the name of the post office where the box is located. Other detailed variations are mentioned in individual country chapters.

COUNTRY NAMES

Most national post offices ask that you write the full name of the country, in your language, alone, in capitals, as the last line of the address on international mail. There are a few conflicts between national post-office requirements. South Africa, the United States, and the United Kingdom would prefer that you write their postcodes after the country name.

There is a system of *country prefixes* in Europe dating from the 1960s which is quite widely used, at least by business mailers. For Belgium, France, and Switzerland, for example, prefixed postcodes will look like **B–1040**, **F–26320**, and **CH–8021**, respectively. The prefixes are based on the long-established system of automobile identification in Europe. Europeans who drive outside their own country are supposed to attach an oval sticker to the back of their automobile showing which country issued their license plates. Consequently, these abbreviations are well known to the general public, much better known than the "official" ISO abbreviations. (Separatists everywhere produce their own oval stickers as a peaceful protest against the central government.) There is no proper list of internationally accepted country prefixes, and most European post offices still want the country name in full even if you use the prefix. Automatic sorting equipment cannot always process the country prefixes. The system was a good idea, but in practice it is a waste of effort to reproduce these prefixes.

Letterheads

It is standard or customary in Northern European countries to print various items of information on company letterheads. Examination of a letterhead can help to give you an idea of the type of company that has sent you an inquiry. Where appropriate, the individual country chapters translate and explain the usual phrases that you will see.

Dates, Money, Typographical Conventions

Material from other countries sometimes contains confusing abbreviations and punctuation, because people do not realize that habits differ around the world. The best-known examples are dates: 12/1/97 means December 1, 1997, in the United States and 12 January 1997 in most other places. In many countries, the month number is sometimes written in Roman numerals, as in 1 XII 97 or 1 xii 97. About one third of the countries in this book use decimal points and thousands commas (1,999.99) and about two thirds reverse the punctuation (1.999,99). Some local variations are mentioned in the individual country chapters.

Currency units generally have a local, domestic abbreviation, such as F for the French franc, an ISO standard three-letter abbreviation (FRF) based on the two-letter ISO country abbreviation (FR), and various informal local conventions (such as FFR). The ISO abbreviations have very varied levels of acceptance in different countries: SEK has more or less driven out the informal alternatives in Sweden, whereas TWD is unknown or even disliked in Taiwan.

Envelopes

There is an international requirement that you leave 40mm (1.6″) clear space between the top of the envelope and the first line of your address, and a 15mm (0.6″) margin to the right and left of the address and also underneath it. Some individual countries require a little more space. The space underneath is particularly important, because that is where the post-office equipment prints its own codes so that the address does not have to be read repeatedly.

Automated equipment can read most typewriter and computer fonts in most likely sizes. There is a risk that older or poorly maintained equipment may not read proportionally spaced type or the type from draft-quality dot-matrix printers. The absolutely safest choice is 10-pitch Courier. International and local regulations are what you might expect from common sense: You must not mix fonts in the same address. You must not use italic or script fonts. You must not underline anything or space letters out or leave blank lines in the address. The address must not be tilted or faded or slanted. You should not use colored ink or colored paper, except that airmail envelopes are conventionally and correctly identified by colored borders.

The majority of countries require return addresses to be written in the top left corner of the envelope. This is accepted even in countries that prefer the return address to be written on the flap.

As an exception to the general assumption throughout this book that your correspondence will be in English, translations are provided for a half-dozen words that you might want to write on an envelope to attract the attention of a mailroom in places where local employees may not read English. The abbreviation **c/o** ("care of") is widely used, often more so than local translations, but many people are confused about its use and may write incorrectly "Mr. [Local] c/o Mr. [Visitor]" rather than the other way around.

Conclusion

This introduction to the individual country chapters that follow has summarized the principal variations that exist in names and addresses in the world. Many of the countries that are not covered in detail in this book were influenced by Arabia, China, England, France, Portugal, or Spain, and much of the information is therefore common to other countries. With an awareness of the habits of 47 countries, you will acquire the flexibility to guess at the meaning of what you see originating from others.

ARGENTINA

Address Summary

Example of a street address:

Sr.[1] **Juan**[2] **Pérez**[3]
Editorial Internacional S.A.[4]
Sarmiento[5] **1337,**[6] **8º P.**[7] **"C"**[8]
1041[9] **BUENOS AIRES**[10]

Key:

[1] **Sr.** = **Señor**, meaning "Mr."
[2] Given name.
[3] Family name.
[4] **S.A.** = **Sociedad Anónima**, signifying a corporation.
[5] Street name; **Calle**, meaning "street," is omitted.
[6] Building number.
[7] 8º means 8th; **P.** = **Piso**, meaning "floor."
[8] Room or suite C; sometimes a number instead of a letter.
[9] Four-digit postcode *(required)*.
[10] City or delivery-post-office name.

Example of a mixed postal and street address in a suburban or provincial location:

Sr. Ricardo Sabatini Ruiz[11]
Editorial Internacional S.A.I.C.[12]
Calle 29[13] **No.**[14] **2867**
Casilla de Correos[15] **238**
7600 MAR DEL PLATA[16]
Pcia.[17] **de Buenos Aires**[18]

Key:

[11] Two family names; thus, **Mr. Sabatini Ruiz**.
[12] **S.A.I.C.** is a variation of S.A., meaning it is a corporation.
[13] 29th Street (**Calle** is only used with numbered streets).
[14] **Nº** or **No.** separates street number and building number. *Use this line, not the following line, for freight and courier deliveries.*
[15] **Casilla de Correos** means "P.O. Box." *Use this line for postal delivery, not the line above.*

[16] City name, all three words in this case.

[17] **Pcia. de** = **Provincia de**, meaning "Province of"; optional.

[18] Province name, usually added (but not required) when the city name is not the same as the province name.

Address Elements

PERSONAL NAMES

Although most names in Argentina look Spanish, there are also many families of British, German, and Italian origin in Argentina. Presumably as a consequence, Argentinians do not follow the convention of other Spanish-speaking countries, where a person's full name includes the family names of both parents. Many people use a single given name and a single family name.

However, double family names do occur. **Mr. Luis Rodríguez Estévez** would be called **Mr. Rodríguez Estévez**. His father was probably also Mr. Rodríguez Estévez. Possibly his great-grandfather was an immigrant from Spain called Mr. Rodríguez and his great-grandmother was an immigrant called Miss Estévez.

A man's name may include the word **de**, meaning "of," which just indicates a compound name and is no special indication of social status in Argentina. A married woman may also use **de** to join her family name to her husband's.

Double given names exist, such as **José María** (a man) and **María Liliana** (a woman). Different people have different preferences: he may want to be called José and addressed **Dear José** in a letter, or he may want to be José María. She may prefer to be María, María Liliana, or Liliana. If you do not know which they prefer, you should not be calling them by their given names anyway.

Argentinian businesspeople do not usually use their given names except with people they know well.

Academic and professional titles are sometimes used in business circles, and you should be careful to copy them. **Dr.** (**Dra.** for women) is commonly used by lawyers, economists, researchers, and other professionals. **Ing.**, **Arq.**, and **Ctdr.** stand for "Engineer," "Architect," and "Accountant," respectively. **Lic.** indicates a university degree, more or less equivalent to a master's.

COMPANY NAMES

Legal Entities	Abbrev.	Explanation
Sociedad Anónima	S.A.	Most common designation for a corporation, either publicly traded or privately owned
Sociedad de Responsabilidad Limitada	S.R.L.	Smaller corporation
S.A. Industrial, Comercial y Financiera (and other qualifiers)	SAICF, etc.	S.A. is sometimes qualified by the activities of the company (Industrial, Trading, and Finance Co., etc.)

OFFICES

An office in a shared building is usually identified by giving its floor (**Piso**, abbreviated **P.**), followed, if necessary, by a letter that indicates the individual office: for example, **Esmeralda 319, 3º P. "B"**.

Offices sometimes have numbers instead of letters, and the word **Oficina** or its abbreviation **Of.**, meaning "suite," is sometimes inserted: for example, **25 de Mayo 359, 7º Piso, Of. 24**. You might see other Spanish-language variations as described in the chapter on Spain.

BUILDING NAMES

Edificio means "building," but such names are not required in a postal address and are only used when the building is a local landmark.

BUILDING NUMBERS

A street number is written after the street name. It is sometimes preceded by **No.** or **Nº**—for example, **Rivadavia Nº 1290**—but this is optional, and **Rivadavia 1290** is acceptable.

Combined street numbers occur: **Av. F. Lacroze 1973/81** means the building occupies numbers 1973 through 1981. The full name of the street is Avenida Federico Lacroze; given names are often abbreviated when a street is named after a person.

STREET NAMES

The most common designation for a street is **calle**, which is almost always omitted. A major business street may alternatively be called an **Avenida**, abbreviated **Av.** Rural plants can be addressed by a highway name: for example, **Ruta Nacional 9, Km. 655**.

The city of **La Plata** has a grid system whose streets have numbers in place of names, and numbered streets are found in other places occasionally. The word **Calle** must be included when the street is numbered (e.g., **Calle 10 Nº 154**).

LOCALITY NAMES

Locality names were once widely used but are being made obsolete by the postcode system. Individuals may still use neighborhood names beginning with **Villa**, **Barrio**, or **Colonia** in a residential address, but businesses generally do not.

CITY NAMES

Most international business is done with **Buenos Aires**, sometimes abbreviated **Bs. As.** or, colloquially, **B.A.** Other business cities are listed under "Postcodes" below.

Addresses in the city of Buenos Aires, which is the country's capital, often have **CAPITAL FEDERAL** on the city line instead of Buenos Aires. Addresses in the large surrounding urban area are part of the province of Buenos Aires, but not part of the city.

STATE/PROVINCE/ETC. NAMES

Argentina is divided into the following 23 **provincias** (provinces) plus the Federal Capital District.

Buenos Aires	Entre Ríos	Misiones	Santa Cruz
Catamarca	Formosa	Neuquén	Santa Fé
Chaco	Jujuy	Río Negro	Santiago del Estero
Chubut	La Pampa	Salta	Tierra del Fuego
Córdoba	La Rioja	San Juan	Tucumán
Corrientes	Mendoza	San Luis	

The post office does not require the province name in an address, provided you have the correct postcode. Historically, Argentinians are in the habit of writing the province name, except when the city and province have the same name. Because there are a considerable number of duplicate place-names, try to include the province name for smaller towns if you know it and you have space. It is written under the city name, like this:

8000 BAHÍA BLANCA
Pcia. de Buenos Aires

There are no standard abbreviations for the provinces.

POSTCODES

Postcodes are necessary in Argentina. Officially the postcode is called a **número postal**, but it is usually referred to as a **código postal**.

It is a four-digit number, written in front of the city name. Postcodes start at 1000 (through 1499) in the Federal Capital district and are then allocated counterclockwise around the northern half of the country back to Buenos Aires province, and then from north to south over the southern half of the country.

In a trade directory or a list of addresses, it is common to see the abbreviation **C.P.**, short for Código Postal. Do not copy the "C.P." into the address, but make sure you have a correct city name. Use of "C.P." is a sign that the editors think it is obvious which city the address is in. For example, **Pavón 3062 (C.P. 1253) CAP** means you should write:

Pavón 3062
1253 CAPITAL FEDERAL

As another example, **SALTA - Juramento 101 (C.P. 4400)** should be written on an envelope:

Juramento 101
4400 SALTA

If you deal with rural areas, be aware that there is a lot of duplication of names of towns and villages. There are about 60 places called San Antonio or San Antonio de Something, including duplicates in the same province. Postcodes are the only practical way for a foreigner to specify an address unambiguously.

The states and postcodes of the principal business cities are:

8000 Bahía Blanca, Buenos Aires
5000 Córdoba, Córdoba
1900 La Plata, Buenos Aires
7600 Mar del Plata, Buenos Aires

5500 Mendoza, Mendoza
3100 Paraná, Entre Ríos
2000 Rosario, Santa Fé
3000 Santa Fé, Santa Fé
4000 Tucumán, Tucumán

P.O. BOXES

P.O. Boxes do exist but are not common. A box is called **Casilla de Correos**. The street name should not be included if you write to a box address.

COUNTRY NAME

The short name of the country is Argentina. Postage stamps say **República Argentina**.

Letterheads

There is no standard layout or convention. **Su referencia** and **Nuestra referencia**, abbreviated **S/ref.** and **N/ref.**, mean "Your reference" and "Our reference," respectively. **Sede Central** means "head office." The phrase **Cotiza en Bolsa** may be used to indicate that the company is publicly traded.

Dates, Money, Typographical Conventions

DATES AND MONEY	
Date format	Day, Month, Year
Typical date abbreviation	29-2-92
Currency unit	peso
Cents	centavos
Domestic currency code	$
ISO international currency code	ARS
Other international codes	none
Decimal separator	comma
Thousands separator	period
Typical currency amount	$5.879,50 (note no space after the $)

Until January 1, 1992, the currency was the **austral** and its symbol was **₳**.

Envelopes

International rules apply: top margin 40mm (1.6″); other margins 15mm (0.6″). Return addresses are usually written on the flap of the envelope.

See the chapter on Spain for mailroom messages that can be written on envelopes.

Phone Numbers

PHONE SYSTEM INFORMATION (SEE CHAPTER 4)	
Country Code	+54
International Access Code	00
Long-Distance Access Code	0
Typical City Codes	one-digit (only 1 = Buenos Aires) two-digit (e.g., 51 = Córdoba) three-digit for rural areas
Typical number formats	(051) 45-6157 (01) 923-3012
Ringing and busy signals	European

Local numbers can be as short as four digits in rural areas. A number like 87-7547/5205 means there are two lines, 87-7547 and 87-5205. Businesses often do not quote their city codes on stationery, because long-distance dialing is not universally available in Argentina, although foreigners can dial every city from outside the country.

Word of Warning!

Both telephone and postal services in Argentina have some shortcomings. Businesses there have difficulty getting enough phone lines, and connections are unreliable. If you need to send something that is at all important or valuable, be sure to use certified mail or an air courier service.

AUSTRALIA

Address Summary

Example of a street address with P.O. Box included:

Mr. Roger[1] Lewis[2]
International Publishing Pty. Ltd.[3]
166[4] Kent[5] Street,[6] Level[7] 9
GPO Box[8] 3542
SYDNEY[9] NSW[10] 2001[11]

Key:

[1] Given name.
[2] Family name.
[3] **Pty. Ltd. = Proprietary Limited**, signifying a (privately owned) corporation.
[4] Building number.
[5] Street name.
[6] **Street** is the usual word.
[7] **Level** means "floor." *Use this line, not the following line, for freight and courier deliveries.*
[8] **GPO Box** means a P.O. Box in a city center. *Use this line for postal delivery, not the line above.*
[9] City or delivery-post-office name, *in capitals. Two spaces must follow the city name.*
[10] State abbreviation, *without periods. Two spaces must follow the state abbreviation.*
[11] Four-digit postcode (for the box address); *essential.*

Address Elements

PERSONAL NAMES

Most Australians have two given names, and call themselves by one given name, usually the first, followed by their family name. A few people use their two initials, British-style; for example, **R. T. Bennett**. You would assume this was a man. Also, a few people, both men and women, use an American-style middle initial (e.g., **Andrew J. Robertson**). The majority of Australians have British family names, but there are substantial communities whose origins are in Asia and Southern Europe. People of all backgrounds have British given names.

Australians are informal and almost always use their given names with each other. However, it is usual to use **Mr.** or **Mrs.** on a first contact or with people of significantly greater seniority in business. "Ms." is understood but rarely used. Say and write "Mrs." unless you know a woman prefers "Ms." or "Miss."

Most women adopt their husband's family name. A woman might use both names if, for example, she was well known in a company before she married. You would address **Sarah Carter Morgan** formally as **Mrs. Morgan.** If she writes a hyphen, address her as **Mrs. Carter-Morgan.**

Australians sometimes add university degrees or professional qualifications after their names on a business card, but it is not necessary to reproduce them unless you want to be particularly careful or respectful.

COMPANY NAMES

Companies doing international business are invariably corporations, designated **Ltd.** ("Limited") or **Pty. Ltd.** ("Proprietary Limited"). Most privately owned companies have the "Pty. Ltd." form; a "Ltd." company is likely to be publicly traded.

OFFICES

An office in a shared building is usually identified by the word **Level**, meaning "floor," written as either **Level 21** or **21st Level**. **Floor** is also used. The word **Suite** is also used to identify an individual office in a shared building.

BUILDING NAMES

Building names are quite common in major cities. **Building, House, Place,** and **Centre** are all used.

BUILDING NUMBERS

Street numbers are written in front of the street name, without a comma.

Combined buildings are quite common (e.g., **183-193 Collins Street**), and buildings are sometimes split (e.g., **183A Alfred Street**).

STREET NAMES

Street Designator	Abbrev.	Explanation
Street	St.	Most common designation.
Avenue, Road, Drive	Ave., Rd., Dr.	Major business streets. Also used in residential areas.
Circle, Circuit, Close, Crescent, Lane, Parade, Place, Terrace	Cir., Cct., Cl., Cr., La., Pd., Pl., Tc.	Usually residential areas.

LOCALITY NAMES

Names of localities are not used. All addresses can be written on two lines: (1) a street or P.O. Box, followed by (2) a city, state, and postcode.

CITY NAMES

City names should be written in capital letters. Principal business cities are listed in the following section.

STATE/PROVINCE/ETC. NAMES

Australia is divided into eight states and territories, for which the following abbreviations are always used in postal addresses. (Periods should not be used—the automated equipment doesn't like them.)

State/Territory Name	Abbrev.	Principal City
Australian Capital Territory	ACT	Canberra
New South Wales	NSW	Sydney
Northern Territory	NT	Darwin
Queensland	QLD	Brisbane
South Australia	SA	Adelaide
Tasmania	TAS	Hobart
Victoria	VIC	Melbourne
West Australia	WA	Perth

POSTCODES

A four-digit postcode must follow the state abbreviation, separated from it by one or two spaces. Postcodes are allocated roughly from east to west across the southern part of the country, with exceptions. High-volume mailers have their own special series of postcodes, as shown in the right-hand column below.

State Abbreviation	Regular Postcodes	Special Postcodes
ACT	2xxx	02xx
NSW	2xxx	1xxx
NT	08xx	09xx
QLD	4xxx	9xxx
SA	5xxx	58xx, 59xx
TAS	7xxx	78xx, 79xx
VIC	3xxx	8xxx
WA	6xxx	68xx, 69xx

P.O. BOXES

P.O. Boxes are commonly used by businesses, and are usually written **PO Box** in suburbs and small towns and **GPO Box** (General Post Office) in the major cities. GPO Boxes have postcodes ending in 1; thus, street addresses in central Adelaide have the postcode 5000, and GPO Boxes in Adelaide's main post office have 5001.

A **Private Box** or a **Private Bag** is a P.O. Box used by a high-volume mailer. Its postcode will be in the "special" series.

COUNTRY NAME

Australia is the full name of the country.

Letterheads

There is no standard convention or requirement except that all business stationery must show an **ACN** ("Australian Company Number") registration number.

Dates, Money, Typographical Conventions

DATES AND MONEY	
Date format	Day, Month, Year
Typical date abbreviation	29/2/92, 29.02.92
Currency unit	dollar
Cents	cents
Domestic currency code	$
ISO international currency code	AUD
Other international codes	A$, $A
Decimal separator	period
Thousands separator	comma
Typical currency amount	$5879.50 (note no space after the $)

The thousands comma is often dropped from numbers below one million. Spelling conventions are predominantly British.

Envelopes

You are supposed to leave 15mm (0.6″) left, right, bottom margins and a 40mm (1.6″) top margin (this is not necessarily always observed). Return addresses should be written at the top left, but are often omitted.

Phone Numbers

PHONE SYSTEM INFORMATION (SEE CHAPTER 4)	
Country Code	+61
International Access Code	0011
Long-Distance Access Code	0
Typical City Codes	one-digit (e.g., 2 = Sydney) two-digit (e.g., 89 = Darwin)
Typical number formats	(062) 39 0431 (01) 358 5976
Ringing and busy signals	British

(008) is a prefix for toll-free numbers, (018) is for mobile phones, and (0055) is for chargeable information numbers, equivalent to U.S. 900 numbers.

City codes in the state of Tasmania begin with 0. For example, a Hobart number written domestically as (002) 42 9337 must be dialed from overseas as +61-02-42-9337.

Australian phone numbers are changing to an eight-digit system within four single-digit area codes. The first digit will be 2 for New South Wales and the A.C.T., 3 for Victoria and Tasmania, 7 for Queensland, and 8 for South Australia, the Northern Territories, and Western Australia. In many cases, this will simply mean transferring a digit from the area code to the number, but in other cases the old number will be lengthened.

AUSTRIA

Address Summary

Example of a street address:

Herrn[1]
Dipl.-Ing.[2] **Johann**[3] **Gerdenitsch**[4]
International Verlag[5] **Ges.m.b.H.**[6]
Glockengasse[7] **159**[8]
1010[9] **WIEN**[10]

Key:

[1] **Herr** means "Mr.," **Herrn** means "to Mr."; usually on a line by itself.
[2] **Dipl.-Ing.** is an engineering degree.
[3] Given name.
[4] Family name.
[5] Company name.
[6] **Ges.m.b.H.** signifies a corporation.
[7] Street name; many names in older areas end in **-gasse**, meaning "street."
[8] Building number.
[9] Postcode.
[10] City or delivery-post-office name, not usually capitalized in domestic usage. **Wien** is Vienna.

Address Elements

PERSONAL NAMES

Austrians nearly always write one given name or initial followed by their family name.

"Mr.," "Mrs.," and "Miss" are **Herr**, **Frau**, and **Fräulein** in German. "Fräulein" is obsolete in business, and therefore "Miss" should not be used.

Although corporate cultures vary, most Austrians only use given names with their personal friends and with people they have worked with for a long time.

The academic and other titles listed in the chapter on Germany are also common in Austria. **Mag.** (**Magister**) in Austria is a regular university degree. People may like to use multiple degrees, as in **Mag. Dr. Josef Toth** (who would be addressed as **Dear Dr. Toth**).

Government officials in Austria use a variety of special titles, which are important to include. If you see "Oberamtsrat Dr. Nikolaus Huber" or the abbreviated form "OR Dr. Nikolaus Huber" on a business card, you would address a letter:

Herrn Oberamtsrat
Dr. Nikolaus Huber

on two lines, and the salutation would be **Dear OR Dr. Huber.**

Women increasingly use their own family names as well as their husbands' names. **Maria-Theresia Karlovits Hofer** will have been born Maria-Theresia Hofer and is now probably known as **Frau Karlovits**, but she might prefer **Frau Karlovits Hofer**. Her husband will probably object to being called "Herr Hofer."

A substantial minority of Austrians have Czech family names (e.g., **Swoboda, Nowotny, Prohaska**), and smaller minorities have other Slav origins (**Vukovits, Lomosits**) or Hungarian names (**Nagy, Szabó**).

COMPANY NAMES

Legal Entities	Abbrev.	Explanation
Aktiengesellschaft	AG	Large corporation, usually publicly traded or government-owned.
Gesellschaft mit beschränkter Haftung	Ges.m.b.H.	Most common designation of a corporation.

There are few AGs in Austria. Most companies are Ges.m.b.H. Several other rare forms of legal organization, such as **KG**, exist for smaller companies.

OFFICES

No internal office designation is given in a postal address.

BUILDING NAMES

Building names are not used in postal addresses.

BUILDING NUMBERS

Building numbers follow the street name, without a comma.

STREET NAMES

Streets are usually designated by suffixes, which are similar to those in Germany, except that small streets in Austria are frequently called **-gasse** or **-weg**.

Street Designator	Abbrev.	Explanation
-straße	-str.	Most common designation for a street.
-gasse	-g.	Usually a smaller street in an older area.
-ring, -damm, -allee, -bahn	not used	Major business streets.
-platz	-pl.	Square.
-weg	not used	Usually a smaller street.

When a street is named after a person, which is common, the "street" word is not suffixed, but stands alone, with or without a hyphen:

Albert Schweitzer-Gasse 4
Dr. Otto Neurath Gasse 5
Karl-Kapferer-Straße 5

LOCALITY NAMES

Names of localities are not used.

CITY NAMES

In domestic correspondence, city names are not usually written in capital letters.

The principal business cities are **Graz**, **Innsbruck**, **Klagenfurt**, **Linz**, **Salzburg**, and **Wien** (Vienna).

Salzburg is occasionally abbreviated to **Sbg.**, and **Wiener** (the adjective from Vienna) is often abbreviated to **Wr.**, as in **Wr. Neustadt** ("Vienna New Town").

STATE/PROVINCE/ETC. NAMES

Austria is divided into provinces, but their names are not normally used in postal addresses.

POSTCODES

A four-digit postcode (called a **Postleitzahl**, abbreviated **PLZ**) is written in front of the city name. Postcodes are allocated roughly from 1000 in the west (Vienna) across the northern part of the country to Bregenz in the east and then again west to east starting from 7000 through the three southern provinces of Burgenland, Steiermark, and Kärnten.

P.O. BOXES

Box addresses are written in the form **Postfach 2005**. "Postfach" is sometimes abbreviated to **Pf.** or **Postf.**

COUNTRY NAME

Austria's full name is **Republik Österreich**, which is what appears on postage stamps.

The country prefix **A-** is often written in front of the postcode.

Letterheads

Words you may see on letterheads are listed in the chapter on Germany.

Dates, Money, Typographical Conventions

DATES AND MONEY	
Date format	Day, Month, Year
Typical date abbreviation	29.2.1992
Currency unit	Schilling
Cents	Groschen

Domestic currency codes	S, Sch.
ISO international currency code	ATS
Other international codes	öS.
Decimal separator	comma
Thousands separator	period, space
Typical currency amount	S 2 300,50
	(note one space after the S)

Even amounts are usually written **S 8,—** or **S 8,--** rather than **S 8,00**. The abbreviation **Sch.** is written after the amount (e.g., **2 000,— Sch.**).

Dates are also sometimes written in the order year–month–day, as in **1992-02-29**.

Envelopes

You are supposed to leave left, right, and bottom margins of 15mm (0.6″) and a top margin of 40mm (1.6″) around the address block.

The return address should be in the top left corner.

See the chapter on Germany for mailroom messages that can be written on envelopes.

Phone Numbers

PHONE SYSTEM INFORMATION (SEE CHAPTER 4)	
Country Code	+43
International Access Code	00 or 900
Long-Distance Access Code	0
Typical City Codes	1 = Vienna
	three-digit (e.g., 662 = Salzburg)
	four-digit (everywhere outside the major cities)
Standard number formats	84 75 86
	0662/22 9 41
Ringing and busy signals	European

In many Austrian offices you can dial the internal extension as part of the external number. A number written like **070/88 42–21 32** implies that 2132 is the extension and that you could reach the switchboard by dialing **+43-70-8842-0**. Another way of writing internal numbers is **0732/8205-DW 285**. (**DW** is short for **Durchwahl**, "extension.")

Phone numbers in Vienna and Linz are invariably written with 0222 and 0732 prefixes in domestic business literature. Foreign phone companies usually give these two city codes as 1 and 70 respectively, and you sometimes also see them in materials from Austria in English. Either +43-1 or +43-222 should work from most locations, but if not, try the other one.

BELGIUM

Address Summary

Example of a French-language street address:

Monsieur[1] L.[2] Bogaerts[3]
Éditions Internationales S.A.[4]
Rue[5] P. J. Delcloche 19[6]
4020[7]   LIÈGE[8]

Key:

[1] **Monsieur** means "Mr."
[2] Initial letter of first given name.
[3] Family name; sometimes written first (then usually in capitals).
[4] **S.A.** indicates a corporation.
[5] **Rue** is the most common word for "street"; initial capital customary.
[6] Building number.
[7] Four-digit postcode (*essential*); may have a **B-** prefix. *Five spaces should follow the postcode*.
[8] City or delivery-post-office name; *must be capitalized*.

Example of a Dutch-language street address:

Dhr.[9] W.[10] Sterckx[11]
Internationale Uitgeversmaatschappij N.V.[12]
Pelikaanstraat[13] 104[14]
2018   ANTWERPEN

Key:

[9] **Dhr.** = **De heer**, meaning "Mr."
[10] Initial letter of first given name.
[11] Family name.
[12] **N.V.** indicates a corporation.
[13] Street name; the suffix **-straat** means "street."
[14] Building number.

Example of a mixed-language address in Brussels, as commonly printed on business stationery:

Georges van Wilderoode[15]
S.A. International Publishing[16] **N.V.**
Rue de la Fusée 58 Raketstraat[17]
Bruxelles 1040 Brussel[18]

Key:

[15] **Georges** is a given name of French appearance and **van Wilderoode** is a family name of Dutch appearance.

[16] Many Belgian companies have English-language names.

[17] **Raketstraat** is the Dutch street name and **Rue de la Fusée** is the French street name; you don't need both in an address.

[18] **Brussel** is Dutch and **Bruxelles** is French; again, you don't need both.

Language

People living in the southern part of Belgium speak French and those in the northern part speak Flemish, which is a group of dialects of Dutch. A foreigner cannot tell the difference between written Flemish and written Dutch. The capital city, Brussels, is officially bilingual. A small area in the east of the country is German-speaking, but you are unlikely to deal with it in international business.

Each major business city except Brussels has one predominant language. If you are enclosing translated material, it is essential to use the correct language. Local languages are listed below under "City Names."

Address Elements

PERSONAL NAMES

Belgians usually give their first given name (or more often just its initial letter), followed by their family name, but the sequence can be reversed. If it is, the family name is usually written in capitals. You cannot reliably tell from their names whether they prefer to speak French or Dutch. Flemish family names may belong to families that have been French-speaking for generations. To further complicate things, Dutch-speaking Jan may call himself Jean when he is with French-speaking people and John when he deals with foreigners.

Belgians who work together use their given names with each other, and the use of given names is widespread in offices that are wholly or partly English-speaking. (Brussels is a favorite location for the European head offices of multinational corporations.) However, it is safest to address Belgians as **Mr.** and **Ms.** until you know their individual preference.

Words like **van** and **de** (meaning "from") preceding people's names may be spelled with or without initial capitals, depending on the individual. For example, different people will prefer **De Schrijver**, **de Schrijver**, **Deschrijver**, and **De Schryver**.

Academic titles are not usually used in business.

COMPANY NAMES

Most Belgian companies engaging in international business are corporations, designated by the abbreviation **S.A.** in French and **N.V.** in Dutch. Both abbreviations are often included with the company name. Other corporate forms do exist. You might encounter **S.P.R.L.** (French) and **B.V.B.A.** (Dutch), indicating probably a small family-owned company. P.V.B.A. is an obsolete Dutch abbreviation for the same structure. There is no way of identifying a publicly traded company: S.A./N.V.s exist in all sizes in Belgium.

OFFICES

In a shared building, individual tenants are sometimes indicated by **boîte** (abbreviated **bte.**) in French or **bus** in Dutch, meaning "box." Both words may be abbreviated to **b** or **B**, especially in bilingual addresses (e.g., **Av. van Volxem 542-B1**). Apartment or other internal numbers may also be used (**Av. van Overbeke 218/15**). Internal addresses are not common, however; most mail is delivered by business name.

BUILDING NAMES

Some modern high-rise buildings in Brussels and other major cities have names. The English word **Building** is used, as are **Tour** (French) and **Gebouw** (Dutch). Otherwise, building names are rare; the street name and building number alone normally identify the building.

BUILDING NUMBERS

The building number always follows the street name in Dutch-language addresses and usually in French-language addresses, but some French-speaking people prefer to write the number first. Divided buildings are usually indicated as A and B (e.g., **Steenovenstraat 1A**).

STREET NAMES

Street Designator (French/Dutch)	Abbrev. (Fr./Du.)	Explanation
Rue/-straat	not used/-str.	Most common designation for a street
Avenue/-laan	Av./-ln.	Major business streets
Chaussée/-steenweg Drève/-dreef	Chée./-stwg.	Highway
Place/-plein	Pl./-pl.	Square (English word also used)

Other street designators mentioned in the chapters on France and the Netherlands may also be seen. **Chaussée** is the Belgian equivalent of **route** in France, which is also used occasionally. Every suburban community near Brussels has a **Chaussée de Bruxelles**, meaning "Highway to/from Brussels" (**Steenweg op Brussel** or **Brusselsesteenweg** in Dutch). A number of streets in Antwerp end in **-lei** (e.g., **Amerikalei**), which is equivalent to **-laan**.

Streets in Brussels have both French and Dutch names. Most companies print their letterheads and business stationery in both languages. The two versions of the address are often run together, which is confusing for foreigners. Thus **Rue F. Severinstr. 62** is short for **Rue F. Severin 62** (French) and **F. Severinstraat 62** (Dutch).

In this case, F. Severin was presumably a person, and so the street names are very similar in the two languages. Unfortunately, this is not always the case.

The street names can be translations which are highly misleading for foreigners: **Av. du Martin-Pêcheur 52** and **IJsvogellaan 52** are the same address. The bird called a "kingfisher" in English is a "martin-pêcheur" in French and an "ijsvogel" in Dutch.

There is no point in slavishly copying both languages onto your reply letter or envelope. If you can distinguish them, use the one you are more familiar with or the one you are less likely to make spelling mistakes in. It would be a courtesy to use the preferred language of the person you are dealing with, if you know which it is; however, the choice of language is not critical for a foreigner, although domestically it is a sensitive subject.

LOCALITY NAMES

Locality names are not used in cities. The name of a village sometimes precedes the post town in a rural area.

CITY NAMES

City names must be written in capital letters.

Many cities have different names in French and Dutch. This is confusing for visitors but does not affect business correspondence. The only bilingual business city is **Brussels**, which is spelled **Bruxelles** in French and **Brussel** in Dutch.

Many businesses are located in suburban communities that are not part of the city of Brussels but are inside the bilingual Brussels region. The suburb names most likely to be seen are:

French Name	Dutch Name
Auderghem	Oudergem
Forest	Vorst
Ixelles	Elsene
Molenbeek-Saint-Jean	Sint-Jans-Molenbeek
Saint-Gilles	Sint-Gillis
Schaerbeek	Schaarbeek
Woluwe-Saint-Étienne	Sint-Stevens-Woluwe
Woluwe-Saint-Lambert	Sint-Lambrechts-Woluwe
Woluwe-Saint-Pierre	Sint-Pieters-Woluwe
Uccle	Ukkel

The principal French-speaking cities are **Charleroi**, **Liège**, **Mons**, and **Namur**.

The five principal Flemish cities have well-known English-language names because of the ancient trading relationship between England and the area that is now Belgium. Note the correct local spelling of **Antwerpen** (Antwerp), **Brugge** (Bruges), **Gent** (Ghent), **Leuven** (Louvain), and **Oostende** (Ostend); international postal regulations require you to use the Belgian spellings. Belgian cities also have German and Spanish names, which should also not be used.

STATE/PROVINCE/ETC. NAMES

Belgium is divided into provinces, but their names are never used in postal addresses.

POSTCODES

A four-digit postcode precedes the city name and is essential to avoid delays in the mail. Belgians usually insert a number of spaces between the postcode and the city name. The limit is supposed to be five spaces. Postcodes are allocated roughly in a clockwise spiral around the country, starting from Brussels.

P.O. BOXES

P.O. Boxes exist, but are rare. "P.O. Box" is written **Boîte Postale** (abbreviated **B.P.**) in French and **Postbus** (abbreviated **P.B.**) in Dutch. The English term is also used.

COUNTRY NAME

Belgium is called **Belgique** in French and **België** in Dutch. Postage stamps use both names.

In English, "Belgium" is the name of the country, and "Belgian" is the adjective. ("*Belgium* makes the best chocolates in the world," but "*Belgian* chocolates are the best in the world.")

The country prefix **B-** is often added to the postcode.

Letterheads

Belgian letterhead must show a company registration number, written out **Régistre de Commerce de Bruxelles** (or other city) in French and **Handelsregister van Brussel** in Dutch. These expressions are usually abbreviated (e.g., **RCB/ HRB**). Stationery often shows the Value-Added Tax registration, abbreviated **TVA** in French and **BTW** in Dutch. It also usually shows a bank account number and/or a postal account number for electronic funds transfers, which are very widely used in Belgium by both businesses and individuals. A number like **GB 210-0359200-81** would be a bank account. You may see other words as listed in the chapters on France and the Netherlands, but it is also quite common to have English translations.

Dates, Money, Typographical Conventions

DATES AND MONEY	
Date format	Day, Month, Year
Typical date abbreviation	29-02-92, 29/9/92, etc.
Currency unit	franc
Cents	not used
Domestic currency codes	FB, BF (see text)
ISO international currency codes	BEF, BEC, BEL (see text)
Other international codes	BFR, FRB (see text)
Decimal separator	comma
Thousands separator	period
Typical currency amount	BF 2.300 (see text) (note one space after the BF)

The currency's symbol is usually **BF** in English or Dutch, written in front of the amount, and **FB** in French, written after the amount. The principal international currency code is **BEF**. The alternative codes **BEC** and **BEL** also exist because there are slightly different exchange rates used for different types of transactions (convertible francs and financial francs).

Envelopes

You are supposed to leave left and right margins of 15mm (0.6″), a bottom margin of 18mm (0.7″), and a top margin of 40mm (1.6″). The whole address is supposed to be contained in an area 54mm (2.2″) high and less than 130mm (5.1″) wide. The postcode is supposed to be between 30mm (1.2″) and 50mm (2″) from the bottom edge of the envelope. The return address should be at the top left.

See the chapters on France and the Netherlands for mailroom messages that can be written on envelopes.

Phone Numbers

PHONE SYSTEM INFORMATION (SEE CHAPTER 4)	
Country Code	+32
International Access Code	00
Long-Distance Access Code	0
Typical City Codes	one-digit (e.g., 2 = Brussels) two-digit (e.g., 91 = Gent)
Typical number formats	055/31.37.70 03/238.79.86
Ringing and busy signals	European

Phone numbers are sometimes written with spaces instead of periods, and prefixes are sometimes written differently: **011-75 61 01** or **(011) 75.61.01**.

Numbers prefixed **017** are for mobile phones, **0800** (formerly 078) numbers are toll-free, **0900** (formerly 077) numbers are chargeable information numbers like U.S. 900, and **070** indicates a nationwide number with a special tariff.

BRAZIL

Address Summary

Example of a street address with P.O. Box included:

> **Ilmo.**[1] **Sr.**[2]
> **Gilberto**[3] **Rabello Ribeiro**[4]
> **Editores Internacionais**[5] **S.A.**[6]
> **Rua**[7] **da Ajuda,**[8] **228**[9] **- 6º**[10] **Andar**[11]
> **Caixa Postal**[12] **2574**[13]
> **20040-000**[14]　　**RIO DE JANEIRO**[15] **- RJ**[16]

Key:

[1] Honorific (**Ilmo.** = **Ilustríssimo**).
[2] **Sr.** = **Senhor**, meaning "Mr."; not usually abbreviated.
[3] Given name.
[4] Family names; probably addressed as **Mr. Ribeiro**.
[5] Company name.
[6] **S.A.** = **Sociedade Anônima**, signifying a corporation.
[7] **Rua** is the most common word for "street."
[8] Street name.
[9] Building number.
[10] **6º** means "6th."
[11] **Andar** means "floor."
[12] **Caixa Postal** means "P.O. Box."
[13] Box number.
[14] Eight-digit postcode (*essential*), for the P.O. Box. *Four spaces must follow the postcode.*
[15] City or delivery-post-office name; not always capitalized in domestic usage.
[16] Two-letter state abbreviation, usually after a hyphen.

Example of a street address in Brasília:

> **Ilmo. Sr.**
> **Maurício do Prado**
> **Editores Internacionais S.A.**
> **SOFN**[17] **Q**[18] **01**[19] **Bloco**[20] **D**[21]
> **70070-000**　　**BRASÍLIA - DF**

Key:

[17] Sector abbreviation (this one stands for "North Office Sector").
[18] Q = **Quadra**, meaning a complex of buildings.
[19] Quadra number.
[20] **Bloco**, translated as "block," is a subdivision of a quadra.
[21] Block number or letter.

Address Elements

PERSONAL NAMES

Brazilian businesspeople usually give their first given name followed by one or two family names. **Mr. Gilberto Rabello Ribeiro** is the son of Mr. Ribeiro, who married Miss Rabello. It is safe to address him as **Mr. Ribeiro**, but an individual may prefer to be called "Mr. Rabello Ribeiro." Women's names are constructed in the same way.

The word **Filho** at the end of a name means the man has the same names as his father; thus, it is used like "Jr." in the United States. Nobody is called "Mr. Filho"! **Júnior, Neto** (grandson), and **Sobrinho** (nephew) are also used in this way.

Family names are sometimes connected by the words **da, de,** or **do** ("of"), not capitalized. These connectives do not indicate any claim to social status. You do not use them in a salutation: José de Paula da Silva would be addressed as **Mr. Silva** in English unless you found out he preferred something different.

"Mr.," "Mrs.," and "Miss" are **Senhor, Senhora,** and **Senhorita,** respectively, in Portuguese; the abbreviations **Sr., Sr^a,** and **Srt^a** are often used. Women in business are now usually addressed as "Senhora," regardless of marital status. The titles **Dr.** (a male Doctor), **Dra.** (a female Doctor), **Eng.** (Engineer), and **Arq.** (Architect) are seen in business. Not all the people who call themselves "Dr." really do have doctoral degrees as they are understood in other countries.

The honorific **Ilmo.** is commonly used in front of "Senhor," and **Ilma.** in front of "Senhora."

Many women's names end in **-a** and many men's names end in **-o**, but a foreigner cannot tell reliably whether a name belongs to a man or a woman. Double given names are common, especially for women (e.g., **Maria Isabel**).

COMPANY NAMES

Legal Entities	Abbrev.	Explanation
Sociedade Anônima	S.A., S/A	Larger company, almost certainly publicly traded
Sociedade por quotas de responsibilidade limitada	Ltda.	Smaller (private) company

OFFICES

An office in a shared building is usually identified by its floor number:

1º **Andar** (1st floor)
2º **ao** 9º **Andares** (2d through 9th floors)
5º **e** 6º **Andares** (5th and 6th floors)

A room number may also be given (e.g., **Sala 130**).

BUILDING NAMES

Modern high-rise buildings have names, which appear in postal addresses (e.g., **Edifício Faria Lima, 9º Andar**) but a street name and number are still required.

The name of a planned industrial area called a **Parque Industrial** (abbreviated **Pq. I.**), may also be given.

BUILDING NUMBERS

A street number is written after the street name, usually preceded by a comma: for example, **Avenida Brigadeiro Faria Lima, 1962**.

Occasionally there is no number because the address is in a new area or on a freeway, in which case **s/n** ("without number") is written in place of the number.

STREET NAMES

Street Designator	Abbrev.	Explanation
Rua	R.	Most common designation for a street
Avenida	Av.	Major business street
Rodovia, Estrada	Rod., Estr.	Highway
Praça	Pç.	Square

Rural plants are often addressed by their position on a highway: **Rodovia BR-116 Km. 148, 1780** means building 1780 near kilometer post 148 on Federal Highway 116. **RS-122** would be a state highway. The same two-letter abbreviations that are used in addresses (see below) are used for highway names.

Streets in the master-planned capital, Brasília, and the nearby state capital, Goiânia, have names like **Avenida W5 Norte**, which means it is north of the major east–west axis called the **Eixo Monumental** and west of the major north–south axis called the **Eixo Rodoviário**. Addresses in Brasília are described under "Locality Names" below.

LOCALITY NAMES

There are neighborhood names in the cities. It is not strictly necessary to use them if you have a correct postcode, but people still usually include them. Many locality names begin with **Jardim** ("Garden"), **Parque** ("Park"), **Via** ("Road"), or **Cais** ("Port").

In rural areas, villages with the same name are distinguished by including in parentheses the post town through which their mail is routed. **Morro Grande (Meleiro) - SC** is thus distinguished from **Morro Grande (Jaguaruna) - SC**. Again, the postcode has made this convention obsolete, but it is still commonly used.

Addresses in Brasília rarely use street names. The city and its satellites are divided into many **setores** ("sectors"), all of which have abbreviated names. Sector names beginning **C**, **EQ**, **H**, **Q**, or **SQ** are residential. Most business addresses are in the following sectors:

Sector Abbrev.	Permitted Activity
SBN	Banking
SCEN	Sports
SCN	Retail
SCTN	Cultural
SDN	Recreational
SGCV	Garages, auto dealerships
SHN	Hotels
SMHN	Hospitals
SOFN	Offices
SRTN	Media

For every sector ending in **N** (North), there is usually a similarly named one ending in **S** (South). Sectors are divided into **quadras**, which are large building complexes. Quadras are numbered in various ways. They, in turn, are divided into **blocos** ("blocks"), which are also numbered or lettered. Finally, except for large organizations occupying one or more blocks, there is an identification of the individual office or dwelling. Therefore, a residential address might look like **HIS Q. 706 Bl. N Casa 28**: this would be house 28 in block N of quadra 706 in sector HIS, which would be a southside area of individual houses.

CITY NAMES

City names are not always capitalized in domestic mail. Most international business is done with **Rio de Janeiro**, **São Paulo**, **Recife**, **Belo Horizonte**, and the capital, **Brasília**.

STATE/PROVINCE/ETC. NAMES

Brazil is divided into 27 "Federal Units" (states). Each has a two-letter abbreviation for postal and other purposes:

State, etc.	Abbrev.	State, etc.	Abbrev.
Acre	AC	Paraíba	PB
Alagoas	AL	Paraná	PR
Amapá	AP	Pernambuco	PE
Amazonas	AM	Piauí	PI
Bahia	BA	Rio de Janeiro	RJ
Ceará	CE	Rio Grande do Norte	RN
Distrito Federal	DF	Rio Grande do Sul	RS
Espírito Santo	ES	Rondônia	RO
Goiás	GO	Roraima	RR
Maranhão	MA	Santa Catarina	SC
Mato Grosso	MT	São Paulo	SP
Mato Grosso do Sul	MS	Sergipe	SE
Minas Gerais	MG	Tocantins	TO
Pará	PA		

The state abbreviation is usually written after the city name, separated from it by a dash. The principal cities are in the following states:

BELO HORIZONTE - MG
BRASÍLIA - DF
RECIFE - PE
RIO DE JANEIRO - RJ
SÃO PAULO - SP

POSTCODES

There is an eight-digit postcode system, which is now in general use. (The three-digit extension is a 1992 innovation.) The postcode is called the **código de endereçamento postal**, frequently abbreviated **CEP**. Postcodes are allocated roughly counterclockwise around the country, starting in São Paulo.

In typed and computer-printed addresses, the postcode is usually placed in front of the city name, separated from it by three or four spaces, or by a dash and spaces:

70020-020   BRASÍLIA - DF

or

70020-020 - BRASÍLIA - DF

It is also acceptable on the next line:

BRASÍLIA - DF
70020-020

Major buildings and high-volume mailers have their own postcodes.

P.O. BOXES

P.O. Boxes are used by businesses. The Brazilian term is **Caixa Postal**. The postcode is the postcode of the post-office building where the box is located, not the postcode of the street address. The street address should not be included if you use a P.O. Box.

COUNTRY NAME

The short name of the country is **Brasil**, which is what appears on stamps.

Letterheads

There is no standard layout or convention.

Dates, Money, Typographical Conventions

DATES AND MONEY	
Date format	Day, Month, Year
Typical date abbreviation	29-2-92 or 29/2/92
Currency unit	real
Cents	centavos
Domestic currency code	R$
ISO international currency code	BRL
Other international codes	none

Decimal separator	comma
Thousands separator	period
Typical currency amount	R$ 10.879
	(note one space after the $)

Envelopes

You are supposed to leave a top margin of 40mm (1.6″), side margins of 21mm (0.8″), and a bottom margin of 20mm (0.8″). Return addresses are usually written below the flap.

See the chapter on Portugal for mailroom messages that can be written on envelopes.

Phone Numbers

PHONE SYSTEM INFORMATION (SEE CHAPTER 4)	
Country Code	+55
International Access Code	00
Long-Distance Access Code	0
Typical City Codes	two-digit (e.g., 21 = Rio de Janeiro)
	three-digit in rural areas
Typical number formats	011-557-1532
	0124-42-0178
	sometimes (0124) 42-0178
Ringing and busy signals	European

CANADA

Address Summary

Example of an English-language street address:

> **Jane[1] MacAllister[2]**
> **International Publishing, Ltd.[3]**
> **249[4] Adelaide[5] St.[6] E.,[7] Suite 203[8]**
> **TORONTO[9] ON[10]   M5A 1N1[11]**

Key:

[1] Given name.
[2] Family name.
[3] **Ltd. = Limited**, signifying a corporation.
[4] Building number.
[5] Street name.
[6] **St. = Street**.
[7] **E. = East** (of the grid origin).
[8] A **Suite** is an office in a shared building.
[9] City or delivery-post-office name; not usually capitalized in domestic use.
[10] Two-letter province abbreviation (*recommended*); an older system is in more general use domestically. *Two spaces must follow the province abbreviation.*
[11] Six-character postcode (*essential*); *one space must separate the two parts. The last three elements should be on the same line.*

Example of a French-language street address:

> **Réjean[12] Lapointe[13]**
> **Éditions Internationales Ltée.[14]**
> **1901[15] rue[16] Notre-Dame[17] O.,[18] bur.[19] 785[20]**
> **Case Postale[21] 1123[22]**
> **MONTRÉAL PQ   H3A 2T7[23]**

Key:

[12] Given name.
[13] Family name.
[14] **Ltée. = Limitée**, signifying a corporation.
[15] Building number.

114

[16] **rue** is the most common word for "Street"; no initial capital.

[17] Street name.

[18] **O. = Ouest**, meaning "West."

[19] **bur. = bureau**, meaning "Room" or "Suite."

[20] Office or room number. *Use this line, not the following line, for freight and courier deliveries.*

[21] **Case Postale** means "P.O. Box."

[22] Box number.

[23] Postcode for the box number. *Use this line and the line above for postal delivery.*

Language

The official languages of Canada are English and French. About a quarter of the population is of French origin. The principal language of business is English in all major cities except Montréal. If you do not have specifically Canadian documentation, you can use American, British, or (in Montréal) European French materials.

Address Elements

PERSONAL NAMES

Most Canadians write one given name and their family name. A few people use either British (two initials) or U.S. (middle initial) conventions.

Canadians are somewhat informal and fairly quick to use their given names. The titles **Mr.**, **Mrs.**, **Miss**, and their French equivalents, **Monsieur**, **Madame**, and **Mademoiselle** (the French titles are better not abbreviated) are used. A large and increasing number of women prefer to be called **Ms.** At a first business contact with someone outside your own organization, particularly if you are selling something, it is safer to use a title rather than a first name.

Women sometimes give you three names in full. It is most likely that **Sylvie Villeneuve Gauthier** was born Sylvie Villeneuve and is married to a Monsieur Gauthier. She is addressed formally as **Dear Madame Gauthier**, or informally as **Dear Sylvie**.

COMPANY NAMES

Registered names of companies usually include the word **Limited**, its abbreviation **Ltd.**, or the French equivalent **Limitée**, abbreviated **Ltée**. Alternatively, **Inc. (Incorporated)** and **Corp. (Corporation)** are also sometimes used. There is no distinction between the names of public companies and private ones.

The English words **Company** or **Associates** or their abbreviations **Co.** and **Assocs.**, or the French words **Société (Soc.)**, **Compagnie (Cie.)**, or **Associés**, unaccompanied by "Inc." or the equivalent, indicate unincorporated businesses.

OFFICES

An office in a shared building is called a **Suite** in both English and French. In a large organization, it is usual to quote a **Room** number. In French **bureau**, sometimes abbreviated **bur.**, may be used for either "Room" or "Suite."

An office/warehouse in an industrial area is usually described as a **Unit** (e.g., **710 Dorval Drive, Unit 2**).

The suite number should follow the street address, but many Canadians write it first. They may also attach it to the building name, if there is one, rather than to the street name, and they sometimes insert a superfluous number sign: **Suite #503** or **Unit #5**.

BUILDING NAMES

High-rise office buildings are commonly called **Centre** or **Plaza**, and named after a principal tenant or financing organization (e.g., **Aetna Centre, Royal Bank Plaza**). A name like **One First Canadian Place** implies a complex with several separate buildings. However, it is often hard to be certain what such names indicate without further information.

In practice, mail will be delivered to major buildings without the street address, especially if you have the correct postcode, but it is safer to include the street address.

BUILDING NUMBERS

The western cities of Calgary, Edmonton, Regina, and Vancouver are laid out on a grid system, in which the building number tells you which block it is located in. Building numbers in Eastern cities are allocated more or less consecutively, as in Europe.

STREET NAMES

Street Designator	Abbrev.	Explanation
Street	St.	Most common English-language designation for a street
rue	none	Most common French-language designation for a street
Avenue, Boulevard, Highway	Ave., Boul., Hwy.	Major business streets
Road, etc.	Rd., etc.	Residential streets

Compass directions (**North, South, East, West**) or abbreviations (**N., S., E., W., N.E., N.W., S.E:, S.W.**) are very common in addresses and are essential. Even in a city like Toronto, which does not have a true grid system, all major east–west streets start counting in either direction from Yonge Street, so **500 Richmond Street West** is nowhere near **500 Richmond Street East**. In Montréal, the French words and abbreviations **Est, E., Ouest, O.**, are used for "East" and "West."

When streets have numbers rather than names, building numbers are usually separated by a hyphen to avoid confusion (e.g., **777 - 8th Avenue S.W.**).

Street names are usually named after people or places and are therefore not translated. Any given street has either an English or French name. A street in a French-speaking area could have an English name, including the word "Road." Sometimes a street name may be used alone (e.g., **250 Sherbrooke**) to avoid committing to either "rue" or "Street."

LOCALITY NAMES

Locality names are not used.

CITY NAMES

By international convention, and to assist automated mail processing, city names (strictly speaking, it is the name of the delivery post office that appears) are supposed to be written in capitals, without punctuation. Domestically, Canadians often use lowercase.

Most international business is done with the following cities:

Calgary AB	**Montréal PQ**	**Toronto ON**
Edmonton AB	**Ottawa ON**	**Vancouver BC**
Halifax NS	**Regina SK**	**Winnipeg MB**

Smaller business cities in Southern Ontario are **Guelph**, **Hamilton**, **Kitchener**, **London**, **Oshawa**, **Sarnia**, **Waterloo**, and **Windsor**. In addition, many internationally active companies are located in the Toronto suburbs of **Bramalea**, **Brampton**, **Markham**, and **Mississauga**, and **Scarborough** (which is actually part of Toronto).

STATE/PROVINCE/ETC. NAMES

Canada is divided into ten provinces and two territories. Several styles of addressing are in use. It is quite common to spell out the province name: **Toronto, Ontario**. French-speaking people usually write the province name in parentheses: **Toronto (Ontario)**. Certain traditional abbreviations are very common (see the table below): **Toronto, Ont**. However, the current Canadian Post Office standard is a two-letter code: **Toronto ON**.

English Name	Old Abbrev.	New Code	French Name
Alberta	Alta.	AB	
British Columbia	B.C.	BC	la Colombie britannique
Manitoba	Man.	MB	
New Brunswick	N.B.	NB	le Nouveau Brunswick
Newfoundland	Newf.	NF	la Terre-neuve
Northwest Territories	N.W.T.	NT	
Nova Scotia	N.S.	NS	la Nouvelle Écosse
Ontario	Ont.	ON	
Prince Edward Island	P.E.I.	PE	
Quebec	P.Q.	PQ, QC	Québec
Saskatchewan	Sask.	SK	
Yukon Territory	Y.T.	YT	

The Canadian Post Office prefers **QC** for Québec province, but most Canadians use **PQ**. The code **LB** is accepted for the Labrador part of Newfoundland province.

POSTCODES

Postcodes are universally used and are required to avoid delays in the mail. The postcode should follow the two-letter province abbreviation, separated from it by two spaces. This is a relatively recent requirement, and many Canadians are still writing it on a line by itself, after the city and province name.

Postcodes always have the format letter–number–letter [space] number–letter–number (e.g., **K1A 3B1**). Postcodes are allocated across the provinces in an orderly manner from **A0** in Newfoundland in the east to **V9** on Vancouver Island in the west.

P.O. BOXES

P.O. boxes are used to some extent by businesses. They are sometimes followed by the name of a post office (e.g., **P.O. Box 1000 Station M**).

In Québec, a P.O. Box is officially called a **Case Postale**, abbreviated **C.P.**, although people also use the expression **Boîte Postale**, abbreviated **B.P.**

COUNTRY NAME

Canada is the name of the country in both languages. "Dominion of Canada" is obsolete.

Letterheads

There are no requirements that any particular information be printed on business stationery.

Dates, Money, Typographical Conventions

DATES AND MONEY	
Date format	Day, Month, Year
Typical date abbreviation	29-02-92
Currency unit	dollar
Cents	cents
Domestic currency code	$
ISO international currency code	CAD
Other international codes	CDN$, Can.$, C$, $C, $Can., etc.
Decimal separator	period
Thousands separator	comma
Typical currency amount	$10,253.19 (note no space after $)

Measurements in Canada are metric, with some exceptions such as paper sizes.

Envelopes

You must leave a bottom margin of 19mm (3/4″), side margins of 15mm (0.6″), and a top margin of 40mm (1.6″). The postcode is supposed to be written within 45mm (1.8″) of the bottom edge. The return address must be positioned in the top left corner.

Phone Numbers

PHONE SYSTEM INFORMATION (SEE CHAPTER 4)	
Country Code	+1
International Access Code	011
Long-Distance Access Code	1
Typical City Codes	All three-digit (e.g., 416 = Toronto)
Typical number formats	(416) 864-0300
Ringing and busy signals	North American

Area codes are always three digits long, and local numbers are always seven digits long. Directory information for every area code xxx is obtained by dialing xxx/555-1212, which can be called directly from overseas.

Area code **800** indicates a toll-free number.

Words of Warning!

Paper sizes: People outside North America should be aware that Canada uses U.S. paper sizes, not metric sizes. See "Words of Warning" in the U.S. chapter if you are not aware of the implications of this difference.

Currency: If you quote prices in dollars, they will be assumed to be Canadian dollars. If you are going to send a standard U.S. price list to Canadians (which they tolerate), it must specify the currency as U.S. dollars.

U.S. Phone numbers: It is frustrating for Canadians to see a telemarketing-oriented ad in a U.S. trade journal which shows, as the only means of contact, an 800 number that does not work in Canada. To find out where the firm is, they must find an acquaintance in the United States who will call the 800 number. Always print your regular phone number and your address on anything that might circulate in Canada.

CHILE

Address Summary

Example of a street address:

> **Sr.**[1]
> **Juan**[2] **Pérez**[3] **García**[4]
> **Editores Internacionales**[5] **S.A.**[6]
> **Av.**[7] **Providencia**[8] **N⁰**[9] **920,**[10] **Of.**[11] **12**
> **Las Condes**[12]
> **SANTIAGO**[13] **10**[14]

Key:

[1] **Sr.** = **Señor**, meaning "Mr."; usually on its own line.
[2] Given name.
[3] Family name; thus, **Mr. Pérez**.
[4] Mother's family name.
[5] Company name.
[6] **S.A.** = **Sociedad Anónima**, meaning "Inc."
[7] **Av.** = **Avenida**, meaning "avenue."
[8] Street name.
[9] **N⁰** or **No.** = **Número**, meaning "number."
[10] Building number.
[11] **Of.** = **Oficina**, meaning "Suite."
[12] Neighborhood name (not always present).
[13] City name, in capitals.
[14] Postal district number (Santiago only).

Address Elements

PERSONAL NAMES

Chileans usually follow the traditional Spanish convention of writing their given name, followed by their father's family name, then their mother's family name; thus, people are referred to by the middle name on their business card.

For more information on names, refer to the chapter on Spain.

COMPANY NAMES

Legal Entities	Abbrev.	Explanation
Sociedad Anónima	S.A.	Most common designation for a corporation, either publicly traded or privately owned
Sociedad de Responsabilidad Limitada	Ltda.	Smaller corporation, privately owned

OFFICES

An office in a shared building is usually called an **Oficina**, abbreviated **Of.**, written after the building number: **Ahumada 131, Of. 102**. The abbreviation **Depto.** (for **Departamento**, "department" or "room") and the word **Piso** ("floor") are also used in internal addresses.

BUILDING NAMES

Building names exist but are not usually included in postal addresses. **Edificio**, abbreviated **Edif.**, is the word for "building."

BUILDING NUMBERS

A building number is written after the street name. It is common to precede it with Nº or # (e.g., **San Antonio Nº 65, San Antonio #65**).

STREET NAMES

Major streets in Santiago are called "avenues." The Spanish word is **Avenida**, abbreviated **Av.** A smaller street is called a **calle**, but the word **calle** is always omitted.

A cross-street is sometimes included in an address to help visitors: **Santa Rosa 101 y París** means the address is close to the intersection of Calle Santa Rosa and Calle París.

LOCALITY NAMES

Neighborhood names in Santiago—for example, **Las Condes**, **Lastarria**, **Bellavista**, **Ñuñoa**, **Barnechea**—are often included in an address.

CITY NAMES

Apart from the capital, **Santiago**, other business cities are **Valparaíso**, **Concepción**, **Talcahuano**, and **Temuco**. **Curicó** is a small town in the south of the wine-growing and -exporting district.

Santiago is divided into postal districts, written as a number after the city name; for example, **Santiago 4**.

STATE/PROVINCE/ETC. NAMES

Chile is divided into regions and provinces, but their names are never used in postal addresses.

POSTCODES

There is no postcode system, except for the postal district numbers in Santiago.

P.O. BOXES

P.O. Boxes are used by businesses. A box is called a **Casilla Postal**, usually abbreviated to **Casilla** (e.g., **Casilla 314**).

The street address and the box number should not be used together.

COUNTRY NAME

The short name of the country is **Chile**. **Chile Correos** ("Chile Postal Service") is printed on postage stamps.

Letterheads

There is no standard letterhead layout or convention.

Dates, Money, Typographical Conventions

DATES AND MONEY	
Date format	Day, Month, Year
Typical date abbreviation	29-2-92
Currency unit	peso
Cents	not used
Domestic currency code	$
ISO international currency code	CLP
Other international codes	none
Decimal separator	comma
Thousands separator	period
Typical currency amount	$23.350 (note no space after the $)

Prices are often quoted in U.S. dollars or in an arbitrary local currency called the **Unidad de Fomento**, abbreviated **UF**. Its ISO international code is **CLF**. The agreed amount is not converted to pesos until the time of purchase.

Envelopes

There are no national rules. By international convention, the top margin is supposed to be 40mm (1.6″) and the other margins 15mm (0.6″).

See the chapter on Spain for mailroom messages that can be written on envelopes.

Phone Numbers

PHONE SYSTEM INFORMATION (SEE CHAPTER 4)	
Country Code	+56
International Access Code	00
Long-Distance Access Code	0
Typical City Codes	one-digit (only 2 = Santiago) two-digit (e.g., 32 = Valparaíso)
Typical number formats	281-2734 33-2300 8-6953 9504
Ringing and busy signals	European

City codes are not always written for domestic use. Santiago businesses often write their phone numbers for foreigners in the form **(562) 281-2734**, which includes the combined country and city code. Do not prefix it with another +56.

The hyphens in local phone numbers are sometimes omitted.

Word of Warning!

Mail service to Chile is slow and letters sometimes go astray. It is advisable to use certified or insured mail for anything you care about, or to use an air courier service.

CHINA

Address Summary

Example of a street address:

**Xia[1] Zhiyi[2]
International Publishing Ltd.[3]
14[4] Jianguolu[5]
Chaoyangqu[6]
BEIJING[7] 100025[8]**

Key:

[1]Family name.
[2]Given name.
[3]**Ltd. = Limited**, signifying a corporation.
[4]Building number.
[5]Street name; the suffix **-lu** (sometimes a separate word) means "street."
[6]District name; the suffix **-qu** means "district."
[7]City or delivery-post-office name; *should be capitalized*.
[8]Six-digit postcode.

Language

Mandarin Chinese is the spoken language of Beijing (Peking) and the official written language of all China, although dialects and minority languages are spoken in the provinces. In the People's Republic, unlike other Chinese-speaking countries, the language is usually written from left to right and transliterated into the Roman alphabet using the Pinyin system throughout the country. There can always be mistakes, typographical errors, and differences of opinion when romanizing Chinese words and also variations based on local dialects.

Address Elements

PERSONAL NAMES

A romanized Chinese name in the People's Republic consists of the person' family name followed by the given names. Unfortunately, individuals occasionally reverse the order to be helpful to Westerners. In the most commonly used convention, the two given names are joined together into a single two-syllable romanized word. Then the single-syllable word is the family name and the two-syllable word is the given name. Thus, **Chen Qiang** (the usual presentation) would be **Mr. Chen**. But **Yongsen He** would be **Mr. He**, who has reversed his name for you. Another variation is that given names are sometimes written separately, with or without a hyphen. You know that Guoyang or Guo-yang is a given name, but there is some ambiguity about Guo Yang. Assume that the first word of the name is the family name unless it clearly has two syllables and the last word is clearly a single syllable.

Job titles may be added to a name. **Zhuxi** means "Chairman," a **Lishi** is a senior manager ("director"), **Changzhang** is a term for a factory manager, and a **Shuji** is a Communist Party official. The title **Xiansheng** is equivalent to "Mr." but is used for foreigners only.

A significant number of women hold responsible positions in China and should be addressed as **Ms.** in English. Married women do not take their husbands' names in China.

COMPANY NAMES

The words **Corporation**, **Company**, or **Limited** (**Ltd.**) may all be used to indicate an incorporated company.

OFFICES

Floor and room numbers are occasionally included in an address in a large building. **3/F** means "3rd floor."

BUILDING NAMES

Large office buildings sometimes have names which are used in addresses:

> **Jinmao Mansion**
> **Lido Commercial Building**
> **China World Tower**

It is also quite usual for a company's representative office to be located in a hotel.

BUILDING NUMBERS

The building number precedes the street name, with or without a comma following.

STREET NAMES

Street Designator	Standard Translation	Explanation
Lu	Road	Major business street
Jie	Street	Major business street
Dajie	Avenue	Major business street
Malu, Hutong	none	Smaller side streets
Yuan	Square	Square

The distinction between **Lu**, **Jie**, and **Dajie** is not very clear. All indicate major business streets. Any of them may be suffixed to the preceding words, particularly in compounds like **Beilu** ("North Street") and **Nandajie** ("South Avenue"). It is useful to be able to recognize the following components of street and place-names:

Chinese Word	Translation
Bei	North
Dong	East
Duan	Section (one stretch of a road)
Gongyuan	Park
Jiao	Suburb
Nan	South
Nei	Inside
Qiao	Bridge
Wai	Outside
Xi	West
Zhong	Central

A few streets are numbered: for example, **Yi Lu** is "1st Street."

LOCALITY NAMES

The name of a district (**qu**) or suburb (**jiao**) may be written after the street name in an urban address. For example, **Dongchengqu** is an area of Beijing whose name means "East City District."

CITY NAMES

China's principal business cities are the following:

Beijing (Peking)   **Shenyang**
Chengdu   **Tianjin (Tientsin)**
Guangzhou (Canton)   **Wuhan**
Nanjing (Nanking)   **Xian**
Shanghai

Shenzhen is an economic development area in Guangdong province where many internationally oriented businesses are located.

The suffixes **-cheng** and **-shi** mean "city"; thus, **Tonghua** and **Tonghuashi** are the same place.

STATE/PROVINCE/ETC. NAMES

China is divided into the following provinces and **zizhiqu** ("autonomous regions"). Their names are not usually included in postal addresses, but you may come across them in other contexts.

Anhui	**Henan**	**Qinghai**
Fujian	**Hubei**	**Shaanxi**
Gansu	**Hunan**	**Shandong**
Guangdong	**Jiangsu**	**Shanxi**
Guangxi Zhuangzu (AR)	**Jiangxi**	**Sichuan**
Guizhou	**Jilin**	**Xinjiang Uygur (AR)**
Hainan	**Liaoning**	**Xizang (AR)**
Hebei	**Nei Monggol (AR)**	**Yunnan**
Heilongjiang	**Ningxia Huizu (AR)**	**Zhejiang**

AR in the above list stands for "Autonomous Region." Guangdong, Sichuan, and Xizang are better known in English as Canton, Szechuan, and Tibet, respectively. Nei Monggol is Inner Mongolia. The urban areas of Beijing, Shanghai, and Tianjin are municipalities under the direct control of the national government.

POSTCODES

There is a six-digit postcode system in use. The postcode should be written after the city name in an address. However, in advertisements and directories, it is frequently separated from the address and written with the phone number or other information.

P.O. BOXES

Numbered P.O. Boxes do exist in China but are very rarely seen in business addresses.

COUNTRY NAME

The full name of the country is translated as **People's Republic of China**, often abbreviated in addresses to **PRC**.

Letterheads

Letterheads used for international correspondence are usually printed with English transliterations or translations.

Dates, Money, Typographical Conventions

DATES AND MONEY	
Date format	Year, Month, Day
Typical date abbreviation	92/02/29
Currency unit	renminbi (yuan)
Cents	fen
Domestic currency code	RMB
ISO international currency code	CNY
Other international codes	none
Decimal separator	period
Thousands separator	comma
Typical currency amount	3,450.50

Envelopes

International rules apply: top margin, 40mm (1.6″); other margins, 15mm (0.6″).

See the chapter on Taiwan for mailroom messages that can be written on envelopes.

Phone Numbers

PHONE SYSTEM INFORMATION (SEE CHAPTER 4)	
Country Code	+86
International Access Code	00
Long-Distance Access Code	0
Typical City Codes	one-digit (only 1 = Beijing) two-digit 2X (e.g., 21 = Shanghai) three- or four-digit outside major cities
Typical number formats	(021) 52315 (029) 635161 (01) 3573944
Ringing and busy signals	European

Czech Republic

Address Summary

Example of a postal address:

Mr. Jiří[1] Tichý[2]
Mezinárodní Nakladatelství[3] a. s.[4]
Kodaňská[5] 48[6]
110 00[7] PRAHA[8] 10[9]

Key:

[1] Given name.
[2] Family name.
[3] Company name.
[4] **a. s.** = **akciová společnost**, indicating a (larger) corporation.
[5] Street name. The word **ulice**, "street," is usually omitted.
[6] Building number.
[7] Five-digit postcode *(required)*; a space must follow the third digit.
[8] Name of the city or delivery post office.
[9] Postal district number (only for Prague).

Another example:

Ms. Zdeňka Kučerová[10]
Mezinárodní Nakladatelství spol. s r. o.[11]
Mendlovo nám.[12] 5
603 00 BRNO

Key:

[10] **-ová** indicates a woman's name.
[11] **spol. s r. o.** = **společnost s ručením omezeným**, indicating a (smaller) corporation.
[12] **nám.** = **náměstí**, meaning "square."

Address Elements

PERSONAL NAMES

Czechs usually write a single given name followed by their family name. Some prefer to use only the initial of their given name. Use of given names is mainly limited to family and personal friends, but people who work regularly together and know each other well, and whose ages and levels of responsibility are similar, will probably be on first-name terms.

129

Women's names generally end in -a and men's generally do not. A large majority of Czech wives adopt their husbands' family names, but some keep their own names, and a few use both, in which case the husband's name will come second. If a Czech woman does not adopt her husband's name, her children eventually have the right to choose which family name they prefer.

Married or not, a woman's family name is grammatically feminine; thus, for example, the wife or daughter of a Mr. Novák is called **Nováková**. Certain spelling contractions occur; for example, the masculine names **Vrána** and **Spaček** have the feminine equivalents **Vránová** and **Spačková**. Some masculine names end in -ý; the feminine equivalents of **Krátký** and **Nový** are **Krátká** and **Nová**. There are very few exceptions to the rule that a woman's name ends in -á; one is **Janů**, which is the same for both men and women.

Pan (abbreviated **p.**) and **paní** (abbreviated **pí**) mean "Mr." and "Mrs.," respectively. The title **slečna** means "Miss" but is less often used. It is appropriate to address all Czech women as **Ms.**

Many Czech executives write their academic titles in front of their names, and you should use them in written communications. **Dr.** (Doktor), **Mgr.** (Magister), and **ing.** (Inženýr) are the principal academic degrees. Variations indicate the subject of the qualification; for example, **JuDr. Jarmila Růžičková** would be an attorney ("doctor of law").

COMPANY NAMES

Czech companies have one of two corporate forms, following current European Union practice. The "larger" type is identified by the abbreviation **a.s.** (akciová společnost), and the "smaller" type is called **společnost s ručením omezeným**, abbreviated either **spol. s r.o.** or **s.r.o.** (note the difference in punctuation). The abbreviation **s.p.** indicates a public-sector enterprise, **k.s.** and **v.o.s.** are forms of partnership, and a **v.d.** is a cooperative.

OFFICES

Individual offices are not separately identified in postal addresses. You might see an expression like **kančelar č. 22** ("Room 22") after a department name in a government agency or other large organization. The word **hala** implies a building or section of a building in a factory.

BUILDING NAMES

Buildings in Czech cities do not ordinarily have names.

BUILDING NUMBERS

The building number follows the street name without an intervening comma. Numbers are simple, but can be high (for example, **Žirovnická 2389**). The abbreviation **č.** ("no.") is occasionally inserted (**Žirovnická č. 2389**).

STREET NAMES

By far the most common word for "street" is **ulice**. A major thoroughfare may be called a **třída** (abbreviated **tř.**), and a square is called a **náměstí** (abbreviated **nám.**). Street names are often feminine adjectives formed from proper names, with the noun "ulice" understood. Thus, **Masarykova** means "Masaryk('s)

Street" (Masaryk was a famous statesman) and **Olomoucká** means "Olomouc Street" (street from Olomouc, a town name).

Unless a word like "třída" is specified, the word "ulice" is understood. There are a few exceptional types of name in which "ulice" must be included, as when the street is named after an important historical date (**ul. 17. listopadu 2**, for instance, means "2 17th of November Street"). Czechs use traditional Slav names for months; thus "listopadu"means "the fall (of leaves)."

Some Czech prepositions that occur frequently in street and other place-names are:

K (lesu)	near (the forest)
Na (mlatech)	on (the threshing floor)
Nad (kašnou)	above, near (the fountain)
Pod (kapli)	below (the chapel)
U (viaduktu)	close to (the viaduct)
V (koutku)	at (the corner)
Za (mostem)	behind (the bridge)

There are many similar phrases, which are usually quite indicative of the location of the street to a Czech-speaker.

LOCALITY NAMES

No locality name is necessary between the street address and the city name. In rural areas, the name of a small village may take the place of a street name. Thus **Sklené 19** would be house no. 19 in the village of Sklené, which does not have its own post office and postcode.

CITY NAMES

The Czech Republic's principal business cities are the following:

Brno	**Olomouc**
České Budějovice	**Ostrava**
Hradec Králove	**Pardubice**
Jihlava	**Praha (Prague)**
Karlovy Vary	**Plzeň**
Liberec	**Ústí n. Orlicí**
Litovel	**Zlín**
Most	

A number of Czech towns and cities used to have alternative German names. The German names are sometimes very well-known in other countries, particularly those of old established spas such as Karlsbad (Karlovy Vary) and Marienbad (Marianské Lazně), and those associated with famous breweries, such as Budweiser (České Budějovice) and Pilsen (Plzeň). The Czech name must always be used in postal addresses and in any business dealings with Czechs, except that the French and English spelling "Prague" is acceptable.

The word **pošta** in front of a city name indicates that the post office responsible for delivery is in that city but the addressee is not, probably because the final destination is a small village nearby.

The largest Czech cities are divided into numbered districts for administrative purposes. In Prague only, the number is used as a postal district number and follows the name of the city (e.g., **Praha 5**). The name of the neighborhood is sometimes added (e.g., **Praha 8-Karlín**), but the postcode is in fact precise enough that this additional information is redundant.

In domestic usage, city names are sometimes underlined or spaced out. This practice is not approved for international usage.

STATE/PROVINCE/ETC. NAMES

No regional name ever appears in postal addresses, but it is useful to recognize the traditional names of the two provinces that make up the present-day Czech Republic: Bohemia and Moravia. Moravia is the eastern third of the country.

POSTCODES

The postcode is a five-digit number written in front of the city name. The Czech term is *Poštovní Směrovací Čisla*, abbreviated PSČ. There must be a space between the third and fourth digits. Prague city postcodes start with 1, those of the surrounding region with 2. Succeeding postcodes are allocated roughly clockwise around the country, starting in the south. Since the system was established under the Czechoslovak administration, codes 800 00 and above are now located in Slovakia, not in the Czech Republic.

The Czech Post Office regularly assigns individual businesses its own postcodes.

In domestic usage, postcodes are sometimes written to the left of the address block rather than in the same column as the other lines; in international usage, all the lines are supposed to begin in the same position.

P.O. BOXES

The use of P.O. Boxes is not very widespread. The Czech term is **poštovní přihrádka**, abbreviated **PP**.

COUNTRY NAME

The Czech Republic calls itself **Česká Republika**, abbreviated **ČR**. It came into existence on January 1, 1993, when Czechoslovakia divided itself into two independent countries. The other part is now called Slovakia. Its postcodes start with 8 or 9 and its telephone city codes start with 7, 8, or 9. The automobile code for the Czech Republic, **CZ**, is sometimes used unofficially as a prefix to the postcode.

The name "the Czech Republic" is inconveniently lengthy but there is no convenient noun corresponding to the adjective "Czech." Czechs themselves sometimes use the unofficial name "Česko" for their country and foreigners have invented a correspondingly artificial name, "Czechia," which also has no official standing.

The abbreviation ČSFR and the automobile code CS refer to the former Czechoslovak republic and are obsolete.

Letterheads

The following are some words and expressions that you might see on Czech business stationery:

Czech	English
Vaše značka	Your reference
Naše značka	Our reference
Datum	Date
Vyřizuje	Person to contact
Bankovní spojení	Bank account number
Číslo Účtu, č. ú.	Account number
IEO	Company registration number
Dálnopis	Telex
Linka, kl.	Telephone extension
Generalní ředitelstvi	Main office
Odbor	Department
Oddělení	Department
Prodejna	Store
Kancelář	Office
Výrobní podnik	Factory
Sklad	Warehouse
Počet stran	Number of pages

Dates, Money, Typographical Conventions

DATES AND MONEY	
Date format	Day, Month, Year
Typical date abbreviation	29.02.1996
Currency unit	koruna (česká)
Cents	haléř (rare)
Domestic currency codes	Kč
ISO international currency code	CZK
Other international codes	not used
Decimal separator	comma or space
Thousands separator	period
Typical currency amount	2 500,- Kč

The currency is sometimes referred to as the "crown" in English.

Kčs and CSK were the domestic and international abbreviations for the Czechoslovak currency, which no longer exists.

Envelopes

International convention requires a top margin of 40mm (1.6″) and other margins of 15mm (0.6″). The return address should appear in the top left corner, but it is also accepted on the flap.

MESSAGES FOR THE MAILROOM	
English	Czech
Urgent	Naléhavé
Please forward	Prosím, obraťte list
Confidential	Důvěrné
Please do not bend	Nepřehýbat, prosím
Fragile	Křehké
(Visitor) c/o (employee)	(Employee) k rukám (visitor)

Phone Numbers

PHONE SYSTEM INFORMATION (SEE CHAPTER 4)	
Country Code	+42
International Access Code	00
Long-Distance Access Code	0 or 8
Typical City Codes	one-digit (2 = Prague, 5 = Brno) two-digit for other cities three-digit elsewhere
Typical number formats	048/215 38 02/42 21 44 82 068/541 33 69
Ringing and busy signals	European

The Czech phone system is being rapidly modernized. A routing signal (rapid beeps) may still be heard in addition to the usual sounds. Do not hang up if you hear it; wait until the equipment completes the call.

Local phone numbers are being extended to eight digits in Prague and Brno.

City codes beginning with 7, 8, or 9 are in areas that are now in Slovakia, outside the Czech Republic.

DENMARK

Address Summary

Example of a street address:

> **Anders[1] Sørensen[2]**
> **Internationalt Forlag a/s[3]**
> **Vesterbrogade[4] 8,[5] 5.th[6]**
> **1780[7] KØBENHAVN[8] V[9]**

Key:

[1] Given name.
[2] Family name.
[3] **a/s** indicates a corporation.
[4] Street name; the suffix **-gade** means "street."
[5] Building number.
[6] 5th floor; **th** means "on the right."
[7] Four-digit postcode for sorting (*essential*); may have a **DK-** prefix.
[8] City or delivery-post-office name; not usually capitalized in domestic use.
[9] Postal district (**V** means "west").

Address Elements

PERSONAL NAMES

Danes usually write their (only) given name followed by their family name. Double given names like **Jan Peter** do exist but are not common. However, many Danes have a middle name, particularly when their family name is a common one. The middle name is likely to be the name of a village or even a farm from which their ancestors came. Some people have dropped the original family name, some hyphenate the middle name and the family name, and others just use both: **Jan Østergård Nielsen** would be addressed informally as **Dear Jan** or formally as **Dear Mr. Nielsen**, unless you knew he had a different preference.

Married women increasingly use their own family name as a middle name, in front of their husband's family name.

Danes are relatively informal. In business, they use their given names with each other, except possibly when addressing people of higher rank or seniority in the organization. They expect to use their given names in any dealings with

135

English-speaking people. Translations of "Mr." and "Ms." are **Hr.** and **Fr.** ("Frk.," meaning "Miss," is obsolete, and English "Miss" should not be used.)

Professional degrees and titles are not commonly used, except that individuals who have no management titles may show their professional qualifications on business cards and correspondence. **Cand.**, **Lic.**, and **Dr.**, followed by a subject abbreviation, correspond to a master's, a Ph.D., and a "post-doctorate," respectively. Subject abbreviations seen in business include **Sci.** (Scientist), **Ing.** (Engineer), **Merc.** (Economist; may occupy a position an M.B.A. would have in the United States), and **Jur.** (Lawyer). **Civ. Ing.** indicates a prestigious qualification, not a civil engineer as it is understood in English-speaking countries. **Rev.** or **Revisor** in a degree or title indicates an accountant.

A foreigner cannot automatically tell from a Danish given name whether the person is male or female.

COMPANY NAMES

A Danish company engaging in international business is usually a corporation, or **aktieselskab**, designated by the abbreviation **a/s**, usually written in lowercase. An a/s may be public or private.

There is also a rarer legal form for a smaller privately owned business—**anpartsselskab**, abbreviated **ApS**—and an even rarer **K/S**.

OFFICES

Offices in large organizations may be identified by some code after the street address, representing a room number or a mail station: for example, **Måløv Vej 1, 6A.1.201.**

Smaller businesses (and residences) commonly specify a floor in their addresses. The words **etage** (**et**) and **sal** both mean "floor"; thus, the following lines all mean the same thing:

> **Kristianagade 8, 2**
> **Kristianagade 8, 2.**
> **Kristianagade 8, 2. sal**
> **Kristianagade 8, 2. etage**
> **Kristianagade 8, 2. et**

The ground floor is called **stuen** or **stuetage**, abbreviated **st.**

Abbreviations like **5.th** and **5.tv** means the office is on the fifth floor to the right (**til højre**) or to the left (**til venstre**).

BUILDING NAMES

Buildings rarely have names, and they are never needed in postal addresses.

BUILDING NUMBERS

Building numbers are written after the street name, without a comma. When a building has been divided, or a lot has been split, the addresses look like

> **Lystrupvej 21a**
> **Lystrupvej 21b**
> **Lystrupvej 21-1** (rare)

Combined addresses are written in the form **Lystrupvej 23-25.**

STREET NAMES

Street Designator	Explanation
-gade	Most common designation for a street
-vej	Larger street
Allé	Major street
-stræde	Narrow street
-pladsen, -torvet, -gården	Squares

Examples:

Frederiksborggade 26
Platinvej 8
Klostergården 35
Park Allé 373
Kvægtorvet 19
Banegårdspladsen 1

The suffixes **-en** and **-et** are the equivalent of "the" in English. The "street" word is written separately when the street is named after a person:

Martin Vahls Vej
Mikkel Bryggers Gade
Herman Triers Plads.

Standard prefixes and their abbreviations seen in street (and town) names are:

Prefix	Abbreviation	Translation
Gammel	Gl.	old
Ny	Ny	new
Lille	L.	small
Store	St.	big
Nordre	Ndr.	north
Sønder	Sdr.	south
Øst	Ø	east
Vest	V	west
Sankt	Skt.	Saint
Station	St.	station

LOCALITY NAMES

Names of localities are not usually used. A rural address may occasionally include a village name when the village does not have its own post office and postcode.

CITY NAMES

In domestic usage, city names are not required to be written in capital letters.

Copenhagen is spelled **København** in Danish, often abbreviated to **Kbh.** The other principal business cities are **Odense**, **Århus**, and **Ålborg**.

The larger towns are divided into postal districts; for example,

> 5000 Odense C
> 5270 Odense N
> 5210 Odense NV

where "C" is **Centrum** (Center), "N" is **Nord** (North), "NV" is **Nordvest** (Northwest), and so on. Many business addresses are located in the neighborhood of Copenhagen called **København K**. The "K" refers to **Købmagergade**, the street where the district post office is located.

STATE/PROVINCE/ETC. NAMES

An abbreviation occasionally follows a city name to distinguish between towns of the same or similar names in different regions of the country. Geographical areas used in this way, and their abbreviations, are:

Djursland	Djurs
Falster	F
Fyn	Fyn
Jylland	J or Jyll
Lolland	L
Mors	M
Sjælland	Sj

POSTCODES

Except in the Faeroe Islands, the postcode is a four-digit number written in front of the city name. Postcodes are allocated roughly in ascending order from 1000 in the east (Copenhagen) west across the islands and then from south to north on the Jylland (Jutland) peninsula.

There are different postcodes for box numbers in the major cities. A few dozen postcodes are allocated to high-volume mailers, individually or in small groups.

P.O. BOXES

P.O. Boxes are much less common than in other Scandinavian countries. Most businesses give their street addresses.

"P.O. Box" is **Postboks** in Danish, but the English spelling is often used, particularly in international dealings. Mail will be delivered to the box, so it does not matter whether you include the street address, except that certified mail should theoretically be taken to the street address to obtain a signature.

When Danish letterhead or business cards give you both the street address and a box number, they usually include only the *box's* postcode. Postcodes reserved for boxes are:

København	1000–1049 and 1500–1549
Odense	5100
Århus C	8100
Ålborg	9100

Theoretically, you should not use these postcodes for air freight, but in practice the deliverers can figure them out.

COUNTRY NAME

Denmark is spelled **Danmark** in Danish. Greenland (**Grønland**) and the Faeroe Islands (**Færoerne**) are dependencies of Denmark.

The country code **DK** is often written in front of the postcode (e.g., **DK-2100 KØBENHAVN Ø**). Faeroe Islands addresses sometimes use the country code **FR**, which is not necessarily recognized by foreign postal authorities (e.g., **FR-100 TORSHAVN**).

Letterheads

Danish Expression	Meaning
Deres ref.	Your reference
Vor ref.	Our reference
Dato	Date
Tlf.	Telephone
Moms	Value-Added Tax
Postgirokonto	Postal checking account

Dates, Money, Typographical Conventions

DATES AND MONEY	
Date format	Day, Month, Year
Typical date abbreviation	29/2/92, 29.02.1992
Currency unit	krone
Cents	øre
Domestic currency code	kr
ISO international currency code	DKK
Other international codes	none
Decimal separator	comma
Thousands separator	period
Typical currency amount	5.879,50 kr
	(note one space before the kr)

Envelopes

MESSAGES FOR THE MAILROOM	
English	Danish
Urgent	Haster
Please forward	Send Venligst
Confidential	Fortroligt
Please do not bend	Må ikke bøjes!
Fragile	Forsigtig
Care of	(use c/o)

Return addresses are always placed in the top left-hand corner.

You are supposed to leave left, right, and bottom margins of 15mm (0.6″) and a top margin of 40mm (1.6″).

Phone Numbers

PHONE SYSTEM INFORMATION (SEE CHAPTER 4)	
Country Code	+45 (except dependencies)
International Access Code	00
Long-Distance Access Code	none
Typical City Codes	none
Typical number formats	31 26 02 30
Ringing and busy signals	European (see text)

Denmark abolished city codes in 1989. All numbers are now eight digits long. If you have a shorter number, or an eight-digit number beginning with 0, it will no longer work. Mobile phones have numbers starting with 30. Numbers beginning with 80 are special toll-free and other numbers, which you cannot usually call from outside Denmark.

The Danish ringing signal is very short compared with most European countries. The tone is the same length as most busy signals, but the gap between tones is longer. The busy signal is rapid, with evenly spaced tones.

FINLAND

Address Summary

Example of a street address with P.O. Box included:

Jussi[1] Virolainen[2]
OY[3] Kansainvälinen Julkaisija[4] AB[5]
Hämeenkatu[6] 13[7] A[8] 8[9]
Pl[10] 354
00561[11] HELSINKI[12]

Key:

[1] Given name.
[2] Family name.
[3] **OY** signifies a corporation.
[4] Company name.
[5] **AB** signifies a corporation (Swedish-language equivalent of **OY**).
[6] Street name; the suffix **-katu** means "street."
[7] Building number.
[8] Letter designates entrance or staircase.
[9] Room or suite number. *Use this line, not the following line, for freight and courier deliveries.*
[10] **Pl = Postilokero**, meaning "P.O. Box." *Use this line for postal delivery, not the line above.*
[11] Five-digit postcode for the box address (*essential*); may have an **SF-** prefix. *Two spaces must follow the postcode.*
[12] City or delivery-post-office name; *must be capitalized.*

Languages

About 6 percent of the population of Finland speaks Swedish as a first language. Some areas are officially Swedish-speaking and some are officially bilingual. For historical reasons, Swedish-speaking people are probably overrepresented in business management. Refer, however, to the chapter on Sweden for more information and examples on Swedish-language names and addresses. For most practical business purposes, Finland is a Finnish-speaking country.

Address Elements

PERSONAL NAMES

Most Finns identify themselves with a single given name, followed by their family name. They usually do have two given names. Most people use their first

141

one, but a few prefer to use their second one. Also, a few prefer to use their two initials instead of a given name, and occasionally people with common names may use their second initial to distinguish themselves.

There are no translations of "Mr." and "Ms." in current use. Business-people use their given names with each other.

Most women probably still adopt their husbands' family name on marriage. However, many women use both names. Suppose **Hanna Kosonen** marries **Marko Virtanen**. She will become either **Hanna Virtanen** or **Hanna Kosonen-Virtanen**. In either case you should call her **Ms. Virtanen** in formal English and list her under V. On a formal legal document a woman's name may be followed by the abbreviation **o.s.** and her own family name, or the abbreviation **ent.** and a former name.

Academic titles and degrees are rarely used in Finland. You might see **DI** (**Diplomi Insinööri**, an engineering degree) or **Ekon.** (**Ekonomi**, a business de-gree) on a business card, but you are not obliged to reproduce it. You are more likely to see Finnish job titles including or ending in **johtaja** ("director") or **päällikkö** ("manager"). A **pääjohtaja** is a corporation President, and a **toimitus-johtaja** might be the General Manager of a subsidiary or the Chief Operating Officer or an Executive Vice President. Functional prefixes are **talous** (for ex-ample, a **talouspäällikkö** is a financial manager), **myynti** (sales), **markkinointi** (marketing), **tuote** (product), or **tuotanto** (production). Any of these might be abbreviated in various ways.

COMPANY NAMES

Companies doing international business are invariably corporations, designated by the abbreviation **Oy** or **OY** (**Osakeyhtiö**). The corresponding Swedish abbre-viation **AB** or **Ab** is often also included in a company name, in various se-quences: for example, **OY Arabia AB**, **Fiskars OY AB**.

If only one of the abbreviations OY or AB is used in the name, it is possible that the company has both a Finnish-language registered name and a Swedish-language one. Alternatively, it is possible, but less likely, that the single abbre-viation indicates the working language of the company or the language of its original founders.

OFFICES

Smaller offices often have street addresses written in the form **Eteläranta 4 B**, in which the **B**, always separated from the building number by a space, desig-nates an entrance or staircase, or in the form **Joutsentie 9 A 11**, which means room 11 on staircase A. (This is also a typical residential address style, in which case the 11 would signify apartment 11.)

BUILDING NAMES

Building names are not used in postal addresses.

BUILDING NUMBERS

Building numbers are usually quite low, and follow the street name without a comma.

A divided building is indicated by a lowercase letter after the building number, as in **Ulvilantie 8b A 11**. **8b** does not necessarily imply a small building, as it would in many countries. It could very well be a large apartment complex or other building, particularly if the following letters or numbers are high, as in **Teijonkatu 8b G 115**, which probably has at least six entrances.

Combined buildings exist but are rare (**Särkiniementie 11-17**).

STREET NAMES

Street Designator	Explanation
-katu, -tie	Most common designations for a street
-väylä	"Way" (major business street)
-ranta	River bank or lakeshore
-portti	Gate
-tori	Square

-katu and **-tie** are sometimes abbreviated to **-k.** and **-t.**, but the Finnish Post Office would prefer that you avoid abbreviations.

LOCALITY NAMES

Names of localities are not used. All addresses are written in two lines: (1) a street or box, followed by (2) the postcode and city.

CITY NAMES

City names must be written in capital letters. Most international business is done with **Helsinki** (the capital), **Tampere**, and **Turku**. All larger towns in Finland have alternative Swedish names. Helsinki is called **Helsingfors**, Tampere is **Tammerfors**, and Turku is **Åbo**. If you see, for example, **Turku/Åbo**, there is no point in copying both names; use "Turku" alone unless you happen to know you are writing to a Swedish-speaking person.

STATE/PROVINCE/ETC. NAMES

Finland is divided into twelve provinces, but their names are not used in addresses.

POSTCODES

A five-digit postcode is written in front of the city name, separated from it by two spaces. Postcodes are allocated roughly from south to north, starting at Helsinki.

P.O. BOXES

A P.O. Box is called a **Postilokero** in Finnish, abbreviated **Pl**, but the English term **P.O. Box** is also often used. Many businesses have boxes. **PPA** in an address refers to a "Mobile Post Office," which is used in rural areas.

Boxes have their own postcodes, always ending in 1.

P.O. Boxes must not be used for International Express Mail to Finland.

COUNTRY NAME

Finland is called **Suomi** in Finnish. **Finland** is its Swedish and English name. Both names appear on stamps. The postcode is sometimes prefixed with the country code **SF-**.

Letterheads

The following words are often seen on a Finnish letterhead:

Finnish Expression	Meaning
Lvv rek.	Value-Added Tax registration no.
Osoite	Address
Puhelin	Telephone number
Puhelinkeskus	Switchboard number

Dates, Money, Typographical Conventions

DATES AND MONEY	
Date format	Day, Month, Year
Typical date abbreviation	29.2.92
Currency unit	markka
Cents	penni
Domestic currency code	mk
ISO international currency code	FIM
Other international codes	FMK
Decimal separator	comma
Thousands separator	period
Typical currency amount	5.879,50 mk (note one space before *mk*, no period after it)

Even amounts are sometimes written in the form **1.250,— mk**.

Envelopes

You are supposed to leave 15mm (0.6″) left, right, and bottom margins and a 40mm (1.6″) top margin around the address block. Return addresses should be written at the top left.

MESSAGES FOR THE MAILROOM	
English	Finnish
Urgent	Kiireellinen
Please forward	Toimitatko Eteenpäin
Confidential	Luottamuksellinen
Please do not bend	Ei Saa Taittaa
Fragile	Särkyvää
Care of	(use c/o)

Phone Numbers

PHONE SYSTEM INFORMATION (SEE CHAPTER 4)	
Country Code	+358
International Access Code	990
Long-Distance Access Code	9
Typical City Codes	one-digit (only 0 = Helsinki) two-digit (e.g., 31 = Tampere) three-digit in rural areas
Typical number formats	(90) 692 681 (90) 703 6011
Ringing and busy signals	European

The usual rule of "drop the zero" does not apply in Finland. A number given as **(90) 692 681** must be dialed as +358-0-692-681.

In a large organization, if **703 3543** is a direct-dial number, then **703 1** is likely to be the switchboard.

A **(9800)** prefix indicates a toll-free number.

FRANCE

Address Summary

Example of a street address:

> **Madame[1] Pascale[2] RIVIÈRE[3]**
> **Éditions Internationales[4] S.A.[5]**
> **17,[6] rue[7] de l'Église[8]**
> **75016[9] PARIS[10]**

Key:

[1] **Madame** means "Mrs."; do not abbreviate.
[2] Given name.
[3] Family name (not always capitalized).
[4] Company name.
[5] **S.A.** = **Société Anonyme**, meaning a corporation.
[6] Building number, usually followed by a comma.
[7] **rue** is the most common word for "street"; no initial capital.
[8] Street name.
[9] Five-digit postcode (*essential*); may have an **F-** prefix. *One space must follow the postcode.*
[10] City or district name; *must be capitalized*.

Example of a mixed postal and street address, as commonly written on business stationery:

> **Monsieur LEFÈVRE[11] Alain**
> **Éditions Internationales S.A.**
> **Siège Social[12]**
> **Immeuble[13] Le Bonaparte[14]**
> **64–68,[15] av.[16] Galliéni**
> **B.P.[17] 154**
> **93155 LE BLANC MESNIL[18] CEDEX[19]**

Key:

[11] Family name is often written first.
[12] **Siège (Social)** means "head office" (*optional*).
[13] **Immeuble** means "building."
[14] Building name.
[15] Large building occupying positions 64, 66, 68 on the street.

146

[16]**av. = avenue**; no initial capital. *Use this line, not the following line, for freight and courier deliveries.*

[17]**B.P. = Boîte Postale**, meaning "P.O. Box." *Use this line for postal delivery, not the two lines above.*

[18]Three-word suburb name.

[19]**CEDEX** means the postcode is for the P.O. Box.

Address Elements

PERSONAL NAMES

French businesspeople usually write their first given name in full, and then their family name. Sometimes the given name is abbreviated to its initial letter. They may have several other given names, which they never tell you. If they give two initials, it is because they have a double first name, such as **Jean-Marie**, usually abbreviated **J.M.** (punctuation may vary). **Jean-Marie** is addressed as **Dear Jean-Marie**, not **Dear Jean**, when you are on familiar terms with him. Women may also have double given names, such as **Marie-Aude**. However, the French only use each other's given names when they work together on a regular basis.

The family name is often written in capitals, and may be written before the given name or initial—for example, **Monsieur DUPONT Guy**. If nothing is capitalized, assume that the last word of their name is the family name. It is a good idea for foreigners to capitalize their own family names when writing to France.

"Mr.," "Mrs.," and "Miss" are **Monsieur**, **Madame**, and **Mademoiselle** in French. Though these are usually written in full, they can be abbreviated to **M.** (note period), **Mme** (note no period), and **Mlle** (no period). "Mademoiselle" is pronounced *madd-mwah-zell* (many foreigners think wrongly that the *d* is silent). It is safer to address women as "Madame," but some young unmarried women prefer to be called "Mademoiselle." It is a little more polite to address French people in writing as "Monsieur" and "Madame" rather than "Mr." and "Mrs.," but call them "Mr." and "Mrs." when speaking English to them.

There is no simple way of telling men from women by the spelling of their given names. It is not generally true that the letter *e* at the end of the name indicates a woman, but there are a number of pairs of male and female names—**Jean/Jeanne**, **François/Françoise**, etc.—in which the final *e* does indicate the woman.

A **de** or **d'** in a family name is an indication of upper-class status, or at least a desire for it, and must be included in salutations; for example, **Dear Monsieur de la Rivière** or **Dear Monsieur Delacroix de Villeneuve**. (The latter may turn out to prefer to be plain **Monsieur Delacroix**.)

In business, the French do not usually use academic titles or degrees.

The chief executive of a French corporation is the **Président-Directeur-Général**, usually abbreviated **P.-D.-G.** (punctuation may vary). An **Administrateur** is a senior officer of the company. A typical company structure consists of **Départements**, each headed by a **Directeur-Général**, divided into **Directions** ("directorates"), each headed by a **Directeur**, and subdivided into **Divisions**, then **Services**, then **Sections**, managed respectively by a **Chef de Division**, **Chef de Service**, and **Chef de Section**. **Responsable** is a currently fashionable alternative to **Chef**.

COMPANY NAMES

Legal Entities	Abbrev.	Explanation
Société Anonyme	S.A.	Most common designation for a corporation, either publicly traded or privately owned
Société à Responsabilité Limitée	S.A.R.L.	Smaller corporation, privately owned
Compagnie, Entreprise, Établissements, Maison	Cie., Ets.	Older business names; indicates an unincorporated business unless S.A., etc., also stated
Cabinet	Cab.	Implies a small firm of professionals, unincorporated unless S.A., etc., also stated

It is fashionable to name companies with pronounceable acronyms or near-acronyms, with or without capitals and periods:

> **S.C.O.D.** (Société de Conseil et de Développement)
> **Sidercom** (Société Commerciale de Sidérurgie et d'Équipements)
> **TRIGA** (Traitement Industriel de Gadoues)

OFFICES

In a shared building, individual tenants are occasionally indicated by **boîte** ("box"), **étage** ("floor"), or **escalier** ("staircase"). **Rez de chaussée**, abbreviated **RC**, means "street level." "Apartment" in French is **appartement**, abbreviated **appt.**

A mailstop for internal mail distribution in a large company is usually called a **Poste de Courrier**, and would follow the name of the individual or department (e.g., **Mlle REDONET, PC: 3L98**).

None of these notations is common.

BUILDING NAMES

Building names are rather rare. Modern high-rise buildings do sometimes have names, especially in the newer suburban office areas around Paris. Names usually start with **Tour**, **Immeuble**, or **Résidence**, which are somewhat interchangeable in practice: one tenant may write "Tour Continental" and another "Immeuble Le Continental." **Bâtiment** is another general word for building. **Usine** is the usual name for a factory building. Examples:

> **Tour Crédit Lyonnais**
> **Résidence du Parc d'Armeville**
> **Immeuble Valmy**
> **Bâtiment 4**
> **Usine de l'Ondaine**

Technology companies are often located in industrial parks, which are called **zones industrielles, zones artisanales, zones d'aménagement concerté**, and other variations, and also **domaines**. These terms are interchangeable in practice, and are abbreviated in a variety of ways: **Z.A., Z.I., Z.A.C., z.a.**, and so on. For example, **Z.I. de Courtaboeuf** and **Z.A. Courtaboeuf** are the same place. A **ZIRST** is a research park.

BUILDING NUMBERS

A building number is written before the street name, usually separated from it by a comma. It is almost always required. You can only drop it if you are addressing an industrial park location, a factory in a rural area, or someone in a small village.

It is quite common for an office or plant to have expanded along a street and taken over a whole series of street numbers:

> **25-33, avenue Louis Roche**
> **6 et 8, rue du 4 Septembre** (6 and 8)
> **13 à 17, rue de l'Industrie** (13 to 17)

A building may also have been divided, in which case the supplementary addresses are usually written in the form

> **28 bis, rue Barbis**
> **21 ter, bd. de Stalingrad**

which would be "28A" and "21B" in most countries.

STREET NAMES

Street Designator	Abbrev.	Explanation
rue	r.	Most common designation for a street
avenue, boulevard	av., bd.	Major business streets
place, square	pl., sq.	Square
route	rte.	Rural highway or major road out of town
quai		Waterfront or riverside drive
allée, chemin, cours, impasse, passage, villa		Residential areas
cité		Large complex such as an office campus or a public housing project
about 150 others		Rare

Street names are quite complicated, and foreigners need to pay attention to punctuation and capitalization to keep their addresses from looking strange to French eyes. The connective word **de** (**d'** before a vowel), meaning "of," occurs very frequently. It is never capitalized, and it does not count when streets are sorted in an alphabetical index. These are streets named after towns:

> **rue d'Abbeville**
> **rue de Rouen**

When the street is named after something other than a town, different forms of "de" are used:

> **rue des Moines** (Monks' Street)
> **rue de la Monnaie** (Mint Street)
> **pl. de l'Europe** (Europe Square)
> **rue du Foin** (Hay Street)

Occasionally a **Le** or **La** is capitalized because it is part of a proper name: **rue de La Rochefoucauld** would be found under *L* in a street directory.

Streets are very commonly named after people. Their names, including initials and titles, are joined together with hyphens:

rue Claude-Debussy

rue J.-Sébast.-Bach

pl. Colonel-Fabien

sq. Card.-Mercier

rue du Gén.-Blaise

rue Dr.-J.-Clémenceau

rue Saint-Denis or **rue St.-Denis** (male)

rue Sainte-Lucie or **rue Ste.-Lucie** (female).

When streets are named after popes and kings, a Roman numeral is always used (e.g., **bd. Henri-IV**).

Streets may be named after significant dates in history: **rue du 8 mai 1945** will be found in a street directory under *h* for **Huit** (8) if it is not under *m* for **mai**.

In rural areas, a highway may be known as the "road from ———" (e.g., **route d'Angers**) or occasionally by the national highway number, in which case initial capitals are required (e.g., **Route Nationale 7** or **R.N. 7**).

The French Post Office asks that you avoid abbreviations of all kinds unless they are necessary to keep the length of an address line down to 32 characters.

LOCALITY NAMES

Locality names are rarely necessary. Since 1989, fewer than 10 percent of localities in France do not have their own postcode, and the large majority of these are obscure villages. You have to allow for an extra line, but most of the time the locality information you are given is unnecessary. If you want to check a pre-1989 address like

24, rue de la Gare

Lisle

41100 VENDÔME

ask your correspondent if Lisle is a "commune" (see "City Names" below). Since it is, the address should read:

24, rue de la Gare

41100 LISLE

CITY NAMES

City names must be written in capital letters. Strictly speaking, what goes on the last line of the domestic address is not a city but a **commune**, the smallest administrative unit in France. All commune names are supposed to fit into 26 characters (there are approved abbreviations for longer names). If a name is long, unnecessary locality information such as a suburb name may have been added to it.

A slash is often used to abbreviate the word **sur**, meaning "on," usually referring to a river: thus, "**IVRY/SEINE**" is really **IVRY SUR SEINE**. Avoid abbreviations, because automated equipment probably will not read them.

The city name in an address is sometimes followed by the codeword

CEDEX ("Courrier d'Entreprise à Distribution Exceptionnelle," or "Special Delivery of Business Mail"), which means the mail is not delivered by the regular letter carrier for the neighborhood. For example, it is used when a company has its own postcode. When there are multiple postal distribution centers in a city, there may be a number after the word CEDEX. In Paris, Lyon, and Marseille, CEDEX must be followed by the number of the **arrondissement**, an administrative subdivision of the city. Before the five-digit postcode was introduced, the arrondissement number was always used as part of the address, and you may still occasionally see "PARIS 19" or "PARIS 19ème" or "PARIS XIX," which should now all be written **75019 PARIS**. Today the 19 is only required in CEDEX addresses (e.g., **75942 PARIS CEDEX 19**). See "Postcodes" and "P.O. Boxes" below for more on CEDEX.

The following table lists the principal French business cities. To help you to locate businesses, the first digits of the phone numbers and postcodes which are used in the surrounding area are shown.

City	Phone nos. begin:		Postcodes begin:
Amiens	03	22	80
Angers	02	41	49
Bordeaux	05	56	33
Clermont-Ferrand	04	73	63
Dijon	03	80	21
Grenoble	04	7	38
Le Mans	02	43	72
Lille	03	20	59
Limoges	05	55	87
Lyon	04	7	69
Marseille	04	9	13
Metz	03	8	57
Montpellier	04	67	34
Nancy	03	8	54
Nantes	02	40	44
Nice	04	93	06
Nîmes	04	66	30
Orléans	02	38	45
Paris—downtown	01	4	75
Paris—suburbs	01	3, 4, 6	77, 78, 91, 92, 93, 94
Perpignan	04	68	66
Rennes	02	99	35
Rouen	02	35	76
St.-Étienne	04	77	42
Strasbourg	03	88	67
Toulon	04	94	83
Toulouse	05	61	31
Tours	02	47	37

The names Marseille and Lyon should be spelled without any final *s*.

STATE/PROVINCE/ETC. NAMES

France is divided into **départements**, called "departments" or "prefectures" in English. Their names used to be required many years ago, before postcodes were introduced, but not now.

POSTCODES

The postcode is essential to avoid delays in the mail in France.

A five-digit postcode is written in front of the city name. There should be one space—less than 10mm (0.4″)—between the postcode and the city.

The first two digits of the postcode represent the département. The départements are numbered in approximately alphabetical order, so sorting lists by postcode is not very meaningful geographically. The last three digits identify the distributing post office. One post office typically serves a number of communes. In Paris, Lyon, and Marseille, the postcodes show the arrondissement; for example, 75012 is the twelfth arrondissement.

CEDEX postcodes are different from regular geographic postcodes. Regular postcodes usually end in 0 and CEDEX postcodes usually do not. There are detailed rules which allow street addresses to be omitted from certain CEDEX addresses; however, it is always best to include a street address if you know it, unless there is also a P.O. Box in the address.

There is a special use of CEDEX in the important office area just outside Paris called La Défense, shown in this example (AFNOR is the French National Standards Institution):

AFNOR
Tour Europe
CEDEX 7
92080 PARIS LA DÉFENSE

French people do not understand the CEDEX system very well themselves, so do not be surprised to see nonstandard address layouts on business stationery.

P.O. BOXES

Boîte Postale, abbreviated **B.P.**, is French for "P.O. Box" and is always followed by a number. Normally, the name of the city or commune where the box is located will be followed by the word **CEDEX**. You are not supposed to include a street name when you address something to a P.O. Box, but people often do.

Avoid mailing heavier parcels (over about 30 pounds) to box numbers and other CEDEX addresses in France, or at least try to include a street address as well. Otherwise, substantial delays can occur when incoming international parcels fall into the hands of a nonpostal organization called the SERNAM, which does not understand special postal addresses.

COUNTRY NAME

France calls itself **France**. Postage stamps say **R.F.** or **République Française** ("French Republic"). The country prefix **F-** is sometimes written in front of the postcode.

Monaco, the area around the city of **Monte Carlo**, is an independent principality which is important as a financial center. It is integrated into the French postal and phone systems. Its French postcode is **98000**. Some countries recognize **MC-** as a valid country prefix.

Letterheads

Votre référence (plural, **Vos références**) and **Notre référence** (plural, **Nos références**), abbreviated **V/réf.** and **N/réf.**, mean "Your reference" and "Our reference," respectively.

A French letterhead must show a company registration number, which usually appears in a phrase like **RCS Nanterre B 682010228**. Variants of the same number are sometimes identified by the initials **INSEE**, **SIREN**, and **SIRET**. **APE** is an industrial classification number. **TVA** is the French abbreviation for "Value-Added Tax," the European sales tax. Corporations must show their legal capital in a phrase like **S.A. au capital de 13.155.900 F**.

The word **fax** is used in France, but **télécopie** ("fax message") or **télécopieur** ("fax machine") is preferred. A fax cover sheet is often headed **Bordereau de Télécopie**.

A letterhead sometimes shows multiple addresses for different installations of the company: **bureaux** means "offices," as distinguished from **usine**, "factory"; the **siège** is the head office; the **siège social** is the legally registered address; **agences** or **succursales** are branches; and a **filiale** is a subsidiary.

Dates, Money, Typographical Conventions

DATES AND MONEY	
Date format	Day, Month, Year
Typical date abbreviation	29.02.1992
Currency unit	franc
Cents	centimes
Domestic currency codes	F, Fr.
ISO international currency code	FRF
Other international codes	FFR, FFr, FF
Decimal separator	comma
Thousands separator	period
Typical currency amount	5.879,50 F
	(note one space before the F)

The time of day is usually written in the style **20h30** (for 8:30 p.m.).
Quotation marks are often written like «this».
Prices are often quoted **HT**, which means "excluding taxes," or **TTC**, which means "including taxes."

Envelopes

All domestic addresses are supposed to fit into six lines of 32 characters each, including the name and job title and company of the addressee.

You are supposed to leave left, right, and bottom margins of 20mm (0.8″) around the address, and a top margin of 40mm (1.6″). The two last lines of the address (not counting the word FRANCE) must be within 65mm (2.5″) of the bottom edge of the envelope so that automated equipment can read it.

MESSAGES FOR THE MAILROOM	
English	French
Urgent	Urgent
Please forward	Veuillez faire suivre
Confidential	Confidentiel
Please do not bend	Ne pas plier, s.v.p.
Fragile	Fragile
Care of	Aux bons soins de . . . (some people use c/o)

Return addresses are always placed in the top left-hand corner.

Phone Numbers

PHONE SYSTEM INFORMATION (SEE CHAPTER 4)	
Country Code	+33
International Access Code	00
Long-Distance Access Code	None
Typical City Codes	None
Typical number formats	01 53 56 96 00 Numbers are always written (and pronounced) in pairs.
Ringing and busy signals	European

France abolished city codes some years ago. Until October 1996, the country was divided into two telecommunications regions. Eight-digit numbers were used within each region, and the prefix 16 was used to reach the other region. Currently, all regular telephone numbers in France are ten digits long, and now all ten digits are always dialed.

An old eight-digit number in the Paris region printed as (1) 42.42.43.43 is dialed the same way as before in international calls (+33-1-42.42.43.43). To reach an eight-digit provincial number, an extra digit is necessary:

If it begins with	Prefix it with
30, 31, 32, 35, 37–41, 43, 47, 48, 51, 54, 96–99	2
20–29, 44, 60, 80–89	3
42, 50, 66–79, 90–95	4
34, 45, 46, 49, 53, 55–59, 61–65	5
36	8

For example, an old number written as 42.42.43.43 alone or (16) 42.42.43.43 is now dialed 04 42 42 43 43 domestically and +33-4-42 42 43 43 from outside France.

A plus sign after the phone number means that there are multiple incoming lines that roll over, automatically passing the call on to the first line that is not busy.

Numbers prefixed **06** are mobile phones.

Numbers beginning **0 800** are called **numéros verts** ("green numbers") and are toll-free. They cannot usually be dialed from outside France. The prefix 05 was used in the former eight-digit system: try replacing it with 0 800.

Numbers beginning **08 36** provide videotext services designed for "Minitel" terminals. A very wide selection of business information services is available in France on these numbers and can be accessed from overseas through various servers and gateways. For more information, fax France Télécom Intelmatique in New York City at +1-212-399-0129 or in Paris at +33-01.45.82.21.16.

GERMANY

Address Summary

Example of a street address:

> **Herrn**[1]
> **Gerhardt**[2] **Schneider**[3]
> **International Verlag**[4] **GmbH**[5]
> **Schillerstraße**[6] **159**[7]
> **44147**[8] **DORTMUND**[9]

Key:

[1] **Herr** means "Mr.", **Herrn** means "to Mr."; usually on a line by itself.
[2] Given name.
[3] Family name.
[4] Company name.
[5] **GmbH** means "Inc."
[6] Street name; many names end in **-straße**, meaning "street."
[7] Building number.
(In domestic usage, there is a blank line between this line and the following line.)
[8] Five-digit postcode (*required*). *One space must follow the postcode.*
[9] City name or delivery post office; not usually capitalized in domestic usage.

Example of a postal address:

> **Frau**[10]
> **Hannelore Müller**
> **International Verlag AG**[11]
> **Postfach**[12] **10 03 35**[13]
> **10728 BERLIN**

Key:

[10] **Frau** means "Mrs."
[11] **AG** signifies a (larger) corporation.
[12] **Postfach** means "P.O. Box."
[13] Box numbers are always written in pairs.

Address Elements

PERSONAL NAMES

Germans always write one given name or initial followed by their family name. They usually have a second given name, often the given name of a grandparent or godparent, but it is never used except on legal documents. Some men, and a few women, have double names like **Karl-Heinz**, which would be abbreviated **K.-H.**

Most women adopt their husband's names, but a married woman may continue to use her own name, or, more likely, she may use both family names. Currently, her husband's name must follow her own. **Gisela Hallstein Richter** will have been born Gisela Hallstein and is now probably known as **Frau Hallstein Richter**, but she might prefer "Frau Richter." However, German law changed in the 1970s; women who married under the old law still write their own name after their husband's.

"Mr.," "Mrs.," and "Miss" are **Herr**, **Frau**, and **Fräulein** in German. "Fräulein" is obsolete in business, and therefore "Miss" should not be used.

A foreigner cannot be certain from a German given name whether the person is male or female, but many women's names end in -a or -e, and it is very rare for a male name to do so.

The word **von** (note no initial capital) before a family name indicates that the family has or had a claim to higher social status.

Germans are relatively formal. Outside of American companies, only people who work together all the time and know each other well will use their given names with each other, and then only in private.

Academic and other titles are rather common, and should be copied carefully if people use them in correspondence or on their business cards:

Abbreviation	Meaning
Dipl.	Graduate
Dipl.-Ing.	Engineering Graduate
Dipl.-Kfm.	Business Graduate
Dipl.-Vw.	Political Science Graduate
Dir.	Director
Dr.	Doctor
Ing.	Engineer (see text)
Insp.	Inspector (see text)
Kfm.	Sales Representative (see text)
Mag.	Master (see text)

Dr. and **Mag.** are usually followed by an abbreviation indicating the subject of the degree, often in Latin: **iur.** (law), **techn.** (engineering), **rer. comm.** (business studies), **rer. nat.** (science), **rer. pol.** (politics), or **rer. soc. oec.** (economics). **Mag.** is a teaching qualification not seen in business unless a person has changed careers. **Ing.** used to be a lower-level degree than **Dipl.-Ing.**, but is now more likely to be a company title than an academic qualification. **Insp.** is a title more common in the government than in corporations. A title of

Kaufmann (Kfm.) is obtained by studying at a chamber of commerce or similar business organization.

It is usual to put **Herrn** (not "Herr"), **Frau, Fräulein,** or a title like **Dipl.-Ing.** on the first line of an address by itself. **Firma** or **Herren** or **Verlag** is used when an individual executive is not named. You are not obliged to do this for individual letters in English, but it does look more natural and should be taken into account if, for example, you are constructing a multinational mailing list that will be used for Germanlanguage sales materials.

The Chief Executive Officer of a German corporation has the title **Vorstand** (if it is an AG; see "Company Names" below) or **Geschäftsführer** (if it is a GmbH). A **Vorstandsvorsitzender** corresponds to a Chief Operating Officer in the United States. A **Finanzdirektor** is a Chief Financial Officer. The suffixes **-direktor** (a senior manager) or **-leiter** (less senior) may be added to department names (e.g., **EDV-Leiter,** meaning "EDP Manager"). A typical company hierarchy, from top to bottom, consists of units called **Bereich, Hauptabteilung, Abteilung,** and **Gruppe,** headed, respectively, by a **Bereichsleiter,** a **Hauptabteilungsleiter,** an **Abteilungsleiter,** and a **Gruppenleiter.** The last two do not usually have real management authority. Company officers and purchasing agents will sometimes use the title **Prokurist,** showing they have the power to bind the company.

COMPANY NAMES

Legal Entities	Abbrev.	Explanation
Aktiengesellschaft	AG	Large corporation, usually publicly traded
Gesellschaft mit beschränkter Haftung	GmbH	Most common designation of a corporation

GmbH is often reduced to **mbH** when the company considers **Gesellschaft** to be part of its name (e.g., **Software-Entwicklungsgesellschaft mbH,** or Software Development Company, Inc.).

GmbH is the commonest form of incorporation in Germany. A GmbH could very well have a publicly traded parent company, particularly a foreign one.

A **KG** is a form of partnership and is less likely to be doing international business, but you certainly will encounter names like **International Verlag GmbH & Co. KG.** In this case, the GmbH corporation is the general partner in the partnership; the other partners are probably the founders or their family. Other rare forms of unincorporated business exist.

OFFICES

Internal office designations are not very common and are not necessary for postal delivery. You will occasionally see numbers written in the style **Alserbachstraße 18/7,** which probably means the office is on the seventh floor, but could possibly mean a seventh building or a seventh entrance. A residential apartment is sometimes designated in the style **Waldstraße 14 W 182,** where **W** stands for **Wohnung** (dwelling). (See Chapter 7 for information on how to produce the ß character on non-German computers.)

BUILDING NAMES

Building names are never used in postal addresses. You will occasionally see the name of an **Industriegebiet** (industrial park) in an address.

BUILDING NUMBERS

Building numbers, which are usually quite low, follow the street name without a comma. A second entrance to a building may be designated—for example, **Landstraße 7 a** or **Landstraße 7 II**. Like the floor-number example above, this last designation is not standardized and is slightly ambiguous; it could possibly be used to mean the second floor.

Combined buildings are indicated in the style **Waldfriedhofstr. 46-48** or **46/48** or **46 u. 48** (**u. = und**, meaning "and").

STREET NAMES

Street names usually end with a suffix.

Street Designator	Abbrev.	Explanation
-straße	-str.	Most common designation for a street
-weg, -ring, -damm, -allee, -bahn	not used	Major business streets
-platz	-pl.	Square

When a street is named after a person, which is common, the "street" word is not suffixed, but stands alone, with or without a hyphen:

Kurt-Schumacher-Str.
H.-Bunte-Str.
Friedrich-Ebert-Damm
Kaiser-Karl-Ring

In older areas, streets may have more colorful names without any "street" word:

Zum Alten Zollhaus (At the Old Customs House)
An der Schleusse (At the [canal] Lock)
Am Wallgraben (At the Moat)
Lange Wand (Long Wall)

The German Post Office wants you to avoid abbreviations of street names (except **-str.**).

LOCALITY NAMES

Names of localities are not used. The name of a community may occasionally be written above the street line of a rural address. Nothing should come between the street line and the city line in a German postal address.

CITY NAMES

Germans customarily leave a blank line between the street line and the city line, and this is supposed to help their automatic sorting equipment. However, a blank line is contrary to international standards and is therefore not required on incoming international mail. Within Germany, city names need not be written in capital letters.

Germany is highly decentralized. In addition to the cities in the following table, international businesses are found in hundreds of towns, particularly in the heavily industrialized area between Dortmund and Köln. Germans often abbreviate city names in directories and lists of addresses. The abbreviations are recognized by the German Post Office but should not be used in letters or on envelopes.

City	Abbrev.	City	Abbrev.
Berlin	Bln.	Koblenz	Kblz.
Bremen	Brm.	Köln (Cologne)	Kln.
Dortmund	Dtmd.	Leipzig	Lzg.
Dresden	Dsdn.	München (Munich)	Mchn.
Düsseldorf	Dssd.	Münster	Mstr.
Essen	Esn.	Nürnberg (Nuremberg)	Nbg.
Frankfurt	Ffm.	Regensburg	Rgsb.
Hamburg	Hmb.	Saarbrücken	Sbr.
Hannover	Han.	Stuttgart	Stgt.

It is rather common to find superfluous geographical information along with city names, although in introducing the new five-digit postcode system the German Post Office is trying to get people to simplify place-names. Traditionally, these connecting words have been quite common:

Abbrev.	Connective	Meaning
a	am, an, auf	on
b	bei	near
d	dem, der	the
i	in, im	in
v	vor, vorm	near (literally, in front of)

For example, in **Frankfurt am Main, Saal a d Donau**, and **Ingelheim a Rhein**, the appended phrases mean "on the river Main," ". . . Danube," and ". . . Rhine." The river names are part of the traditional name of the town but are not required in a postal address. You will also see unnecessary province or region names:

> Riedlingen/Württ.
> Freiburg i Br.

even though the postcode by itself determines which Riedlingen and which Freiburg the letter will go to. Including nearby cities is also unnecessary:

> Kirchhain (b Marburg/L.)
> Magstadt bei Stuttgart
> Eching b München

Unnecessary suburb names are sometimes added in parentheses:

    Hagen 1 (Oberhagen)

    Siegen (Geisweid)

Before the current postcode system was introduced, all large towns had postal districts, whose numbers were written after the city name (e.g., "FRANKFURT 60"). In a rural area, it used to be occasionally necessary to include a post town name written in the style "Siebeneichhöfe Post Treuchtlingen," but addresses like these are out of date.

Standard abbreviations are defined by the German Post Office for places with long names.

Many German town names begin with prefixes, which it may be useful to recognize:

Prefix	Meaning	Prefix	Meaning
Ober-	Over, Upper	Nord-	North
Unter-	Under, Lower	Süd-	South
Neu-	New	Ost-	East
Alt-	Old	West-	West
Groß-	Large, Greater	St.	Saint
Klein-	Small, Lesser	Bad	Spa
Schwarz-	Black	Wald-	Wood, Woods
Weiß-	White		

    Germany has one small bilingual area, centered on the eastern city of Cottbus, in which the streets and towns have alternative names. **Cottbus** is spelled **Chośebuz** in the local language, which in English is called "Wendish."

STATE/PROVINCE/ETC. NAMES

Germany is divided into states, but their names are never used in postal addresses.

POSTCODES

Since the middle of 1993, Germany has had a five-digit postcode system. The postcode is written in front of the city name, separated from it by one space, and is essential to avoid delays. The postcode is called a **Postleitzahl**, often abbreviated **PLZ**. Postcodes are allocated in an orderly fashion, roughly counterclockwise around the country starting from Dresden.

    Before the reunification of Germany, both East and West Germany used four-digit postcode systems. While the current system was being developed, **W-** (for **West**) was written in front of the former West German postcodes and **O-** (for **Ost**, meaning "East") in front of the former East German postcodes. You may therefore see postcodes like 6000 or W-6000 or D-W-6000 for some time. The old codes do not bear any simple relation to the new ones. Do not confuse an old code such as O–1000 with a new numeric one such as 01000.

P.O. BOXES

Box addresses are written in the form **Postfach 83 45 06**. "Postfach" is sometimes abbreviated to **Pf.** or **Postf.** Every box is numbered, and its digits are always written in pairs, starting from the right.

The German Post Office asks that you not write the street address as well as the P.O. Box address, but if for some reason you must, it is acceptable as long as the street address is above the Postfach line.

COUNTRY NAME

Germany's full name is **Bundesrepublik Deutschland** (Federal Republic of Germany), sometimes abbreviated **BRD**.

The country prefix **D-** is sometimes written in front of the postcode.

Letterheads

There is a national standard layout for letterheads, which is usually observed. You can expect to see most of the following words on a letterhead:

German Expression	Meaning
Ihr(e) Zeichen	Your reference
Unser(e) Zeichen	Our reference
Datum	Date
Betreff	Subject
Ihre Nachricht vom . . .	Your letter of . . . (date)
Postadresse	P.O. Box address
Fernsprecher (older word), Telefon	Telephone
Durchwahl	Direct Dial
Fernschreiber (older word), Telex, Tx.	Telex
Telefax, Fax	Fax
Bildschirmtext, Btx.	Videotext
Bankleitzahl, BLZ	Bank Routing Code
Postkonto, Postgiro, Postgirokonto	Postal banking account no.
Hauptverwaltung	Head office (address)
Büro	Office (address)
Fabrik, Werk, Betrieb	Factory (address)
Gebietsbüro(s)	District office(s) (addresses)
Vertretung(en)	Distributor(s) (addresses)
Stammkapital	Capital
Gleitzeit, Kernzeit	Flextime hours, Core hours
Mehrwertsteuer, MwSt.	Value-Added Tax, the European sales tax

A little telephone symbol ☎ is often used instead of the word "Telefon." The postal address is often written on a horizontal line in small type somewhere on the letterhead.

Companies are not required to show their capital, but a capital figure may be printed voluntarily by large companies to show you how large they are.

It is best to quote a German office's reference back to them in your reply.

Dates, Money, Typographical Conventions

DATES AND MONEY	
Date format	Day, Month, Year
Typical date abbreviation	29.02.1992
Currency unit	mark (deutsche mark)
Cents	pfennig
Domestic currency code	DM
ISO international currency code	DEM
Other international codes	none
Decimal separator	comma
Thousands separator	Space
Typical currency amount	DM 2 300,50 (note one space after DM)

Words like "third" and "fourth" are abbreviated in the form 3. and 4. in German (which Germans are inclined to use in English also).

Even amounts are sometimes written in the style **DM 8,—** or **DM 8,--** rather than **DM 8,00**.

Quotation marks are often written like »this« or „this" as well as like "this" or "this."

Most typed and printed material in Germany uses sans-serif typefaces. Your sales literature may look a little foreign if you use a serif font.

Envelopes

You are supposed to leave left, right, and bottom margins of 15mm (0.6″) and a top margin of 40mm (1.6″).

The address area is supposed to be less than 100mm (4″) wide, and the left edge of the address is supposed to be within 140mm (5.5″) of the right edge of the envelope.

The return address should appear in the top left corner.

MESSAGES FOR THE MAILROOM	
English	**German**
Urgent	Dringend
Please forward	Bitte nachsenden
Confidential	Vertraulich
Please do not bend	Bitte nicht falten
Fragile	Zerbrechlich!
Care of	use c/o

The phrase **zu Händen von** is the equivalent of "Attention," not "c/o."

Phone Numbers

PHONE SYSTEM INFORMATION (SEE CHAPTER 4)	
Country Code	+49
International Access Code	00
Long-Distance Access Code	0
Typical City Codes	two-digit (e.g., 30 = Berlin) three-digit (e.g., 711 = Stuttgart) longer in smaller towns and rural areas
Standard number formats	Prefixes: (01) (021) (02 28) (0 12 34) 15 61 82 27 5 05 56 86 25 35 60 2 12 72 68 85 281
Ringing and busy signals	European

The number formats in the table are German national standards, but Germans do not observe them rigidly. In particular, you will see five- and seven-digit numbers written as **212 72** and **505 56 86**. Also, you will often see prefixes written in the format **08 21/15 50 30**.

Most local numbers are six or seven digits long. However, in most German offices you can dial the internal extension as part of the external number. For example, the switchboard operator may be **4304-0** and an individual extension may be **4304-71**. Any number written with a **-0** or **-1** at the end is probably the switchboard, but not every firm uses that convention. You might see the main number given as **77 46 80** and the fax as **77 46 818**.

Offices may also nominate one extension to receive inquiries, so they might give their "main" number as **493 12 55** when that is in fact extension 55. It is important to be aware of this system. You may be given a number like **Fax: 813 35 16/37 u. 28**; this means they have two fax machines, at 813 35 16 extensions 37 and 28 (**u. = und**, meaning "and"), and if they are both out of paper you can probably dial 813 35 16 0 to complain.

There is a little ambiguity in the presentation of phone numbers. A number such as **440 83-4**, as in most European countries, could indicate a small office with just two lines, 44083 and 44084.

The prefix (**0130**) is used for toll-free numbers.

The country code +37 for the former East Germany is no longer valid, and East German city codes have changed. Call information for current codes, or if you do not know the city name, try replacing +37 with +493. For example, Leipzig's code was +37-41- and is now +49-341.

The following table will help you to identify the location of suburban addresses from either their phone number or their five-digit postcode:

City code	City	Postcodes begin:
201	Essen	45
203	Duisburg	47
211	Düsseldorf	40
221	Köln	50–51
228	Bonn	53
231	Dortmund	44
261	Koblenz	56
30	Berlin	10–13
341	Leipzig	04
351	Dresden	01
381	Rostock	18
40	Hamburg	20–22
421	Bremen	28
431	Kiel	24
451	Lübeck	23
511	Hannover	30–31
521	Bielefeld	33
531	Braunschweig	38
551	Göttingen	37
561	Kassel	34
621	Mannheim	68
681	Saarbrücken	66
69	Frankfurt (Main)	60–61
711	Stuttgart	70–71
721	Karlsruhe	76
761	Freiburg	79
89	München	80–81
931	Würzburg	97

GREECE

Address Summary

Example of a street address:

> **Mr. Petros[1] Mavropoulos[2]**
> **Diethni Ekdotiki[3] A.E.[4]**
> **39[5] Stadiou[6]**
> **105 59[7] ATHENS[8]**

Key:

[1] Given name.
[2] Family name.
[3] Company name.
[4] **A.E.** = **Anonimos Etairia**, signifying a corporation.
[5] Building number.
[6] Street name; the word **odos**, meaning "street," is usually omitted.
[7] Five-digit postcode; *one space is required after the third digit*.
[8] City or delivery-post-office name.

Language

The Greek language uses its traditional alphabet; therefore, anything you see in English has been transliterated. One Greek letter generally corresponds to one Roman letter or a pair of Roman letters. For example, their sigma, written Σ (uppercase) or σ (lowercase), is transliterated as **s**, and their theta, written θ, is transliterated as **th**. However, there is not a strict one-for-one correspondence, and different people will transliterate words somewhat differently. Also, individuals have preferences as to how their names are transliterated; **Hatzis** and **Chandjis** are different ways of spelling the same Greek family name.

Diacritical marks are used in Greek, but they are usually omitted in the transliteration.

Address Elements

PERSONAL NAMES

Greek people usually sign themselves with their single given name and their family name. It used to be common for Greeks to use the English or French equivalent of their given name in international dealings; for example, **Petros** might spell his name **Peter** or **Pierre**. Younger people today tend to keep to the Greek spelling.

166

Men's given names usually end in **-os**, **-es**, **-as**, **-is**, or rarely **-ou** or **-o**. Women's given names usually end in **-a**, **-e**, or **-i**.

Greeks are accustomed to using their given names with Americans, but among themselves, only people who work together regularly and who have approximately the same rank and seniority will use their given names. It is best to address Greeks as **Mr.** and **Ms.** in speech and in writing until you know they expect to be more familiar with you.

"Mr." in Greek is **Kúrio**, abbreviated **K.** or **Ko.**, and "Mrs." or "Ms." is **Kúria**, abbreviated **Ka.** A married woman uses her husband's family name, but the ending changes; for example, the wife of Mr. Angelakis is **Mrs. Angelaki**. Increasingly, married women use both their own family name and their husband's. Usually their own comes first, but some women choose to write their husband's name as a middle name. The Greek title for unmarried women is very rare, and therefore "Miss" should not be used unless you know specifically that the woman prefers it.

Double family names exist; **Iannis Papadopoulos-Hatzis** should be addressed as **Mr. Papadopoulos-Hatzis** until you know his personal preference, which might also be "Mr. Papadopoulos" or "Mr. Hatzis."

In business, Greeks do not use academic degrees or professional titles.

COMPANY NAMES

Greek companies engaged in international business are invariably corporations. In Greek, a corporation's name must include the abbreviation **A.E.** (**Anonimos Etairia**). In international correspondence, they may either leave it as A.E. or translate it as **S.A.** (the French equivalent) or even **Ltd.**

In fact, unless the company is named after its founders, the whole name may be translated into English, so be aware that "Athens Pharmaceuticals Ltd." is not the legal Greek name of the company you are dealing with.

You cannot distinguish a publicly traded company by its name.

OFFICES

Most office buildings are small and there is usually no indication of where an office is located in a building.

BUILDING NAMES

Building names are rare and are not used in addresses.

BUILDING NUMBERS

In Greek, street numbers are written after the street name, but this is almost always reversed in international correspondence.

Multiple street numbers—for example, **33-35 Solonos**—mean that buildings have been combined.

A building with multiple entrances may occasionally have an address like **32a Kapodistriou**.

STREET NAMES

Most streets have simple names. **Odos**, the commonest word for "street," is usually dropped.

15 Mitropoleos
5 Pentelis
16 Kifissou

Major streets are called **Avenue** in English. You also occasionally see a transliterated address. For example, instead of **68 Vas. Sophias Ave.** (usual) someone might write **Leof. Vas. Sophias 68** (rare).

The English word **Square** is used, abbreviated **Sq.** Rarely, the Greek equivalent **Plateia**, abbreviated **Pl.**, is used.

The abbreviations **Vas.**, meaning "King" or "Queen," and **Ag.**, meaning "Saint," occur commonly in street names and place-names. **Prof.** is not "Professor" but a religious title meaning "Prophet."

Addresses are sometimes given as intersections:

12 M. Botsari & Epidavrou
Ag. Annis and 190 Orfeos
46 Makedonias & 8 M. Voda

If you have a correct postcode, this is not strictly necessary, but since many streets have the same or similar names, it is a habit to specify the cross-street to remove ambiguity.

The address of a rural plant is often written by giving the position on a highway. For example,

E. O. Athinon-Lamias (12 km.)
Metamorfossi

means 12 kilometers out from Metamorfossi on the Athens-to-Lamia highway. If "E. O." is translated, as it often is, the first line will read **Athinon-Lamias National Road (12th km.)**.

LOCALITY NAMES

In rural areas, village names are used along with city names. They are often written after the street, on the same line:

Kavari 21, Perdikkas
502 00 PTOLEMAIDA

Small villages do not always have street addresses, in which case the village name stands alone as though it were a street.

The use of locality names was commoner in the past, but now most areas you will deal with in international business will have their own postcodes.

CITY NAMES

The city name must be written in capital letters on the last line of the domestic address. Most international business is done with **Athens (Athinai)** and **Piraeus (Peiraias)**, the port of Athens. Other business cities are **Thessaloniki, Larisa,** and **Patrai**.

STATE/PROVINCE/ETC. NAMES

Greece is divided into about 50 **nomoi**, translated as "prefectures." Their names are not required in addresses. However, people often still use the old forms of address with a prefecture name instead of a postcode. The name you are most likely to encounter is **Attica (Attiki)**, which is the prefecture around Athens.

POSTCODES

Postcodes are not universally used. However, it is highly desirable for foreigners to obtain them and use them to compensate for any errors of spelling and transcription in other parts of the address.

A Greek postcode consists of three digits, a space, and two more digits. The first two digits correspond more or less to a prefecture. The principal exception is that the Athens urban area uses the series **100–189** and the rest of the Attica prefecture uses **190–199**.

Postcodes are allocated in an orderly fashion from south to north on the mainland. The series continues across the islands.

A few dozen high-volume mailers have their own postcodes.

P.O. BOXES

Greeks usually write **P.O. Box** (followed by a number) in English. The Greek abbreviation is **T. Th.**

COUNTRY NAME

Greece calls itself **Ellas** or **Hellas**. The country code prefix **GR-** is sometimes used but is not universally recognized by other postal administrations.

Letterheads

There is no standard letterhead layout or convention. For international correspondence, most companies have a letterhead entirely in English or French.

Dates, Money, Typographical Conventions

DATES AND MONEY	
Date format	Day, Month, Year
Typical date abbreviation	29.02.92
Currency unit	drachma
Cents	not used
Domestic currency code	Drs.
ISO international currency code	GRD
Other international codes	none
Decimal separator	comma
Thousands separator	period
Typical currency amount	1.060 Drs.

Other abbreviations for **drachma** may be seen.

Envelopes

You are supposed to leave an upper margin of 40mm (1.6″) and right and lower margins of 15mm (0.6″). Return addresses are usually written in the top left corner.

	MESSAGES FOR THE MAILROOM	
English	**Greek**	**WordPerfect Code**
Urgent	ΚΑΤΕΠΕΙΓΟΝ	20,0,40,10,32,10,18,6,30,26
Please forward	ΠΑΡΑΚΑΛΩ	32,0,34,0,20,0,22,50,space
	ΓΙΑ	6,18,0,space
	ΠΑΡΑΔΟΣΗ	32,0,34,0,8,30,36,14
Confidential	ΕΜΠΙΣΤΕΥΤΚΟ	10,24,32,18,36,40,10,42,40,20,30
Please do not bend	ΜΗΝ	24,14,26,space
	ΔΙΠΛΩΝΕΤΕ	8,18,32,22,50,26,10,40,10
Fragile	ΕΥΘΡΑΥΣΤΟ	10,42,16,34,0,42,36,40,30,space
	ΠΡΟΣΟΧΗ	32,34,30,36,30,46,14
Care of	C/O is used and understood	

There is a Greek expression for "care of," used in the opposite sequence: [Mr. X] C/O [Mr. Y] is [Mr. Y] ΓΙΑ ΤΟΝ [Mr. X].

The right-hand column in the table above tells you how to reproduce the Greek letters in WordPerfect. Each number is x in the compose sequence CTRL + V,8,COMMA,x,ENTER. Whether this works correctly may depend on your printer and the way your WordPerfect printer driver is set up for character set 8.

To attract the attention of a Greek mailroom, these messages should be written in large letters.

Phone Numbers

PHONE SYSTEM INFORMATION (SEE CHAPTER 4)	
Country Code	+ 30
International Access Code	00
Long-Distance Access Code	0
Typical City Codes	one-digit (1 = Athens and Piraeus)
	two-digit (e.g., 61 = Patrai)
	three-digit in rural areas
Typical number formats	22.806
	285.062
	32.31.010
Ringing and busy signals	European

Local numbers are usually six or seven digits long. There is a lot of variation in the way they are written. Separators are usually periods in Greek, which are sometimes converted to hyphens in English contexts to look more American. City codes, if they are written at all, look like **01-32.31.010**.

If you see a number in the format **3241 811-14**, it means there is more than one incoming line—in this case, 324-1811 through 324-1814.

A **(0800)** prefix indicates a toll-free number, which may not be accessible from outside the country.

HONG KONG

Address Summary

Example of a street address:

Mr. WONG[1] Yat-ming[2]
International Publishing Ltd.[3]
4/F,[4] Island Building[5]
31[6] Repulse Bay Rd.[7]
CENTRAL[8]
HONG KONG[9]

Key:

[1] Family name.
[2] Given names.
[3] **Ltd. = Limited**, signifying a corporation.
[4] **4/F** means 4th floor.
[5] Building name.
[6] Building number.
[7] **Rd. = Road**, the most common word for "street."
[8] District name.
[9] City and country name.

Language

English and Chinese are the official languages of Hong Kong. Chinese names in Hong Kong are transliterated according to Cantonese dialect phonetics, not Pinyin. English-language spelling conventions are British. There are also Indian and Pakistani minorities in Hong Kong, particularly in retail and clothing businesses.

Address Elements

PERSONAL NAMES

Hong Kong Chinese names are usually written with the family name first, often in capitals, followed by two given names, which are usually hyphenated together when typed or printed. Many people now regard the result as a single given name. Traditionally, however, the first given name was the generation name, which was common to all the boys in a family. All the girls of the generation also shared (a feminine) name. The second given name was the name of the individual. However, Chinese given names are only used by family and close

171

friends. People who work together will normally call each other by their family names.

Chinese-speaking people in Hong Kong often adopt an additional Western (British) given name. **Mr. LEUNG Chi-pui** may call himself **William C. P. Leung** in international correspondence. Once you know him, you can call him William and address him as **Dear William**. If he wants to be sure you call him Mr. Leung, he may give you his name British-style as **C. P. Leung**.

Chinese-speaking women do not change their legal names on marrying, but in Hong Kong Mr. Leung's wife is usually known socially as **Mrs. Leung**.

To direct correspondence to a particular individual in a small company, you should write **Attention Mr. Wong** or **Mr. Wong, c/o [company]**. To write a person's name followed immediately by the company name might imply that the person was the owner or president of the company. If that is not the case, the true owner or president may not be pleased.

British businesspeople (and other foreigners) in Hong Kong are usually on short-term assignments and their names should be treated according to the practices of their countries of origin.

COMPANY NAMES

Companies doing international business are likely to be corporations, designated **Ltd.** (**Limited**). You cannot distinguish a publicly traded company by its name.

OFFICES

Offices are usually identified by a floor number, abbreviated in the form **12/F** ("12th floor") and written in front of the building name. This implies that the company occupies the entire floor. Individual offices may also be designated as **Rooms 401-2**, (i.e., 401 and 402 on the fourth floor). Rooms may also be called **Units** or **Suites**.

BUILDING NAMES

Office buildings commonly have names, which may be English or Chinese:

> **Far East Finance Centre**
> **California Tower**
> **Highland Mansion**
> **Sunning Plaza**
> **Sun Hung Kai Centre**
> **Tung Ying Building**

BUILDING NUMBERS

Building numbers are usually quite low, as in Europe. They are written in front of the street name, without a comma:

> **199 Connaught Road West**
> **5 Cleveland Street**

Combined buildings are indicated by hyphenated numbers (**19-21 Nathan Road**) and split buildings by letters (**39A Broadway**).

Street numbers are occasionally omitted when there is a named building in the address.

STREET NAMES

Road is the most common street designator, but **Street** and **Avenue** are also common. **Square**, **Drive**, **Terrace**, and other British-style names are sometimes seen.

Most streets in business areas have British names (**Murray Road, Old Bailey Street**) but a minority have transliterated Chinese names (**Lok Ku Road, Tsuen Nam Road**).

LOCALITY NAMES

After the street line in an urban address, there must be a district name. A home address in a rural area would have a village name as the locality line.

The principal international business district of **Hong Kong Island** is called **Central**. Many trading companies are also located in **Wan Chai**, and **Causeway Bay** is an important commercial area. Other districts on Hong Kong Island are **Aberdeen**, **Happy Valley**, and **Taikoo Shing**.

Kowloon is the tip of the peninsular north of Hong Kong Island. Its tourist and business district is **Tsim Sha Tsui East**. Some of the many other districts of Kowloon are **Ho Man Tin**, **Hung Hom**, **Mong Kok**, **To Kwa Wan**, and **Yau Ma Tei**.

The third area is known as the **New Territories** and is less likely to figure in international business correspondence.

The locality name should be written in capital letters.

CITY NAMES

The last line of the domestic address must be the name (in capitals) of one of the three areas:

> **HONG KONG**
> **KOWLOON**
> **NEW TERRITORIES**

STATE/PROVINCE/ETC. NAMES

Hong Kong has no states or provinces other than the three areas mentioned above.

POSTCODES

There is no postcode system.

P.O. BOXES

Businesses commonly have P.O. Boxes. The locality line should then be the name of the post office where the box is located. The words POST OFFICE are sometimes added:

> **P.O. Box 245871**
> **CAUSEWAY BAY POST OFFICE**
> **HONG KONG**

The abbreviation **GPO Box** means the box is in the **General Post Office**, a main post-office building. There is one GPO on Hong Kong Island and another in Kowloon.

COUNTRY NAME

In July 1997, Hong Kong's official name became **Hong Kong Special Administrative Region (SAR) of the People's Republic of China.** The U.S. Postal Service wants you to write simply **Hong Kong** on envelopes. There is no point in repeating "Hong Kong" if it is part of the domestic address, but an address in Kowloon or the New Territories must be followed by HONG KONG in capitals.

Letterheads

Letterheads are usually printed in English as well as Chinese.

Dates, Money, Typographical Conventions

DATES AND MONEY	
Date format	Day, Month, Year
Typical date abbreviation	29/2/92
Currency unit	dollar
Cents	cents
Domestic currency code	$
ISO international currency code	HKD
Other international codes	HK$
Decimal separator	period
Thousands separator	comma
Typical currency amount	$5,879.50 (note no space after the $)

Envelopes

A 40mm (1.6″) top margin and 15mm (0.6″) lower, right, and left margins are required. Return addresses should be written on the flap of the envelope, but are accepted in the top left corner of the address side.

Phone Numbers

PHONE SYSTEM INFORMATION (SEE CHAPTER 4)	
Country Code	+852
International Access Code	001
Long-Distance Access Code	none
Typical City Codes	none
Typical number formats	28680940
Ringing and busy signals	British

Phone numbers are currently eight digits long. Older seven-digit numbers can usually be prefixed with a 2. Numbers written in the form 5-218363 relate to an obsolete system.

Spaces are sometimes inserted into local numbers at different positions.

HUNGARY

Address Summary

Example of a street address, in international format (in domestic Hungarian use, the sequence is different).

Sándor[1] Csilla[2]
Nemzetközi Kiadó[3] Kft[4]
Rákóczi[5] u.[6] 73[7]
7626[8] PÉCS[9]

Key:

[1] Family name.
[2] Given name (female).
[3] Company name.
[4] **Kft = Kovlátolt felelössegü társaság**, signifying a smaller corporation.
[5] Street name.
[6] **u. = utca**, meaning "street."
[7] Building number.
[8] Four-digit postcode (*required*).
[9] City or delivery-post-office name.

Another example in international format:

Szabó[10] Lászlo[11]
Nemzetközi Kiadó[12] Rt.[13]
Thököly[14] ut.[15] 31[16]
1146[17] BUDAPEST[18]

Key:

[10] Family name.
[11] Given name (male).
[12] Company name.
[13] **Rt. = Részvénytársaság**, signifying a larger corporation.
[14] Street name.
[15] **út**, meaning a larger street.
[16] Building number.
[17] Four-digit postcode.
[18] City or delivery-post-office name.

Address Elements

PERSONAL NAMES

In Hungarian, the family name always precedes the given name, though translators frequently reverse the sequence. Common family names are derived from ancestors' crafts (**Kovács**, "smith," **Szabó**, "tailor," **Varga**, "tanner") or personal appearance (**Fehér**, "white," **Nagy**, "big," **Kiss**, "small") or ethnic origin (**Németh**, "German," **Tóth**, "Slovak," **Horváth**, "Croat").

Hungarians ordinarily employ a single given name. (Multiple given names were discouraged during the Communist regime.) Most given names are recognizable as Christian names if you can see through the spelling variations: for example, **István** (Steven), **Ferenc** (Frank), **János** (John), **Erzsébet** (Elizabeth), **Zsuzsanna** (Susanna), **Katalin** (Katherine). Older given names also continue to be used: for instance, **Örs**, **Árpád**, and **Csaba** (male); and **Boglárka**, **Emőke**, **Gyöngyi**, **Tünde**, and **Virág** (female). About half of all female names end in -a, but very few male names do (the principal exceptions are **Attila**, **Géza**, **Gyula**, **Huba**, and **Miksa**). The diminutive suffixes -ka and -ke may be added to a given name.

Kiss úr means "Mr. Kiss," although you are unlikely to see it. There is no equivalent of "Ms." in common use in a business environment. **Kocsis Júlia Asszony** would be a very formal way of addressing "Ms. Julia Kocsis." **Kisasszony** is an even rarer way of translating "Miss." **Júlia néni** represents another respectful way of addressing women, but inappropriate for business.

Hungarian women almost always change their family name on marriage. A married woman may write her name by adding -né to her husband's name: thus, if **Kiss Eszter** marries **Nagy Péter**, she may list herself as **Nagy Péterné**, "Mrs. Peter Nagy." She is never orally addressed as "Péterné." She has the right to keep her own name or to combine names; for example, **Nagyné Kiss Eszter** is "Mrs. Eszter Kiss Nagy." Children are named at birth after their fathers but may change to their mothers' family names at the age of 18.

Ifjabb, abbreviated **Ifj.**, distinguishes a man from a father of the same name; thus, **Ifj. Takács Imre** is "Imre Takács Jr."

The title **Dr** is commonly used by all types of university graduates in business and should be copied. **Gróf**, **Báró**, and **Vitéz** are old aristocratic titles that used to be in relatively widespread use. Family names ending in -y (**Eszterházy**, **Kazinczy**, **Kólcsey**) also have a connotation of higher social class.

Given names are only used by family and close personal friends. Hungarians often have nicknames that are used among friends. They usually are derived from the real given name or refer to the person's appearance or reputed behavior.

COMPANY NAMES

Hungarian companies have two common legal forms: **Kovlátolt felelössegü társaság** (abbreviated **Kft**), indicating a smaller, privately owned company, and **Részvénytársaság** (**Rt.**), indicating a larger, probably publicly traded company. The abbreviation **Kv** (for **Közös vállalat**) indicates a joint venture.

OFFICES

It is rare to see an internal address inside a building, but **Andrássy ut 12 II em 4** would mean door or office 4 on the 2nd floor ("II em").

BUILDING NAMES

Building names are not used. **Lakó Telep**, abbreviated **LTP**, indicates an apartment complex.

BUILDING NUMBERS

Building numbers are written after the street name. In **Debreceni u. 138/a** the "a" implies an entrance, and **Középpfasor 41-43** implies that two buildings have been combined.

STREET NAMES

Street	Abbrev.	Meaning
utca	u.	Most common word for "street"
út, útja	(none)	Larger street or avenue
körút	krt.	Ring or loop
tér, tere	(none)	Square

    A few other designators are in use in residential or pedestrian areas. The difference between "út" and "útja" is only grammatical. **Győri út** is "Győr Street" (named after a city) and **Bartók Béla út** is "Béla Bartók Street" (named after the composer), but **Felszabadulás útja** means "Street of Freedom." Similarly, **tere** means "square of," as opposed to plain **tér**, "square."

    Names of streets and squares have been changed to eliminate most references to Communist heroes and concepts. For example, **Engels tér** has been renamed **Erzsébet tér** (after a Hungarian queen).

    Streets named after people are commonly abbreviated: thus, **Bartók út**, **Bartók B. út**, and **Bartók Béla út** are all the same street.

    A few streets in suburban Budapest are numbered: **12. u.** means "12th Street."

LOCALITY NAMES

Locality names are rare. In rural areas, if a village lacks its own postcode, its name should appear in parentheses after the name of the post town; for example, **2131 GÖD (Alsógöd)**.

CITY NAMES

The principal cities are **Budapest** (the capital), **Debrecen**, **Győr**, **Miskolc**, **Pécs**, and **Szeged**.

    Budapest (often abbreviated **Bp.** in lists of names and addresses) was divided into 22 postal districts, whose numbers are always written in roman numerals. Although the numbers are no longer used in postal addresses, they remain very much in everyday use. You would be expected to realize that **Bp.VIII** (or just **VIII**) at the beginning of an address means "Budapest 8." The postal district number usually forms part of the postcode.

STATE/PROVINCE/ETC. NAMES

No regional names are used in postal addresses.

POSTCODES

A four-digit postcode system is in general use. People are expected to hand-write postcodes in preprinted boxes on envelopes for private mail. An envelope or a postcard sent from Hungary to another country is supposed to have an X written in the leftmost box. Postcodes are allocated roughly clockwise around the country, starting from 1000 in Budapest. The 22 Budapest postal districts have base postcodes numbered 1010 through 1220, the postal district number being the middle two digits. High-volume mailers have their own postcodes.

See "Words of Warning" regarding the positioning of the postcode.

P.O. BOXES

A P.O. Box is called a **Postafiók** in Hungarian, usually abbreviated to **Pf.** Boxes are numbered; they have their own postcodes, different from those of the street address. Boxes are not universal but are used by businesses with significant volumes of mail. In a list of addresses, the entry **Bp. Pf.: 154, 1475** would mean you should address international mail to

> **Pf. 154**
> **1475 BUDAPEST**

COUNTRY NAME

The Hungarian Republic is called **Magyar Köztársaság**. "Magyar Népköztársaság" was the name of the Communist régime. Stamps and meter labels are marked **Magyar Posta**. The country prefix **H-** in front of a postcode is allowed.

Letterheads

There are no particular conventions or standards for letterhead layouts.

Hungarian term	Meaning
Datum	Date
Tárgy	Subject
Hivatkozási számunk	Our reference
Hivatkozási számuk	Your reference
Kereckedö	Dealer
Áruház	Store
Fiók	Branch
Gyár	Factory
Föhivatal	Home office
Ügyintéző	Contact person

Dates, Money, Typographical Conventions

DATES AND MONEY	
Date format	Year, Month, Day
Typical date abbreviation	96 2 29, 96 II 29
Currency unit	forint
Cents	fillér

Domestic currency codes	Ft
ISO international currency code	HUF
Other international codes	not used
Decimal separator	comma
Thousands separator	period or space
Typical currency amount	180.000 Ft
	(note space before Ft)

The sequence day-month-year is quite likely to be used in international correspondence.

Envelopes

International rules require a 40mm (1.6″) top margin and 15mm (0.6″) bottom, right, and left margins. A return address should be written in the top left corner.

MESSAGES FOR THE MAILROOM	
English	**Hungarian**
Urgent	Sürgős
Fragile	Törékeny
Confidential	Bizalmas
Please do not bend	Kérem, ne hajtsa össze!
Please forward	Kérem, továbbitsa
c/o	use c/o

These translations are not necessarily in conventional domestic use in Hungary.

Phone Numbers

PHONE SYSTEM INFORMATION (SEE CHAPTER 4)	
Country Code	+36
International Access Code	00
Long-Distance Access Code	06
Typical City Codes	two-digit, except 1 = Budapest
Typical number formats	(37) 313-022
	59/361-911
	112-5873
Ringing and busy signals	European

Punctuation of phone numbers is not very standardized. The Budapest city code, 1, is often omitted. If you see a seven-digit number, you may assume it is in Budapest. Six-digit numbers in Budapest are obsolete: a 1 was prefixed to them, so to call an old 125-873 Budapest number you should try +36-1-112-5873.

The Hungarian phone system is expected to undergo extensive renovation in the next few years which may lead to changes in numbering.

Words of Warning!

Domestically, Hungarians still use the old Central European sequence of address elements, in which the city name, usually underlined, precedes the street address. The postcode comes last, on a line by itself. Thus, the sample address at the beginning of the chapter would be written:

> **Szabó Lászlo**
> **Nemzetközi Kiadó Rt.**
> **B u d a p e s t**
> **Thököly ut. 31**
> **1146**

This is quite contrary to current international treaties, and the format at the beginning of the chapter is allowed for incoming international mail. If you were remailing inside Hungary, however, you would be expected to use the domestic format.

The Hungarian phone system was neglected under the Communist régime. International calls can be significantly slower to connect than in most countries. Don't give up after 15 seconds (as advised in Chapter 4); wait 30–45 seconds before redialing.

INDIA

Address Summary

Example of a street address:

> Shyam[1] Lal[2] Gupta[3]
> International Publishing (Pvt.)[4] Ltd.[5]
> 1820[6] Rehaja Centre[7]
> 214,[8] Darussalam[9] Road[10]
> Andheri East[11]
> BOMBAY[12] - 400049[13]

Key:

[1] Given name.
[2] Second given name.
[3] Family name.
[4] (Pvt.) = (Private), meaning the corporation is privately owned.
[5] Ltd. = Limited, signifying a corporation.
[6] Probably office 20 on the 18th floor.
[7] Building name.
[8] Building number.
[9] Street name.
[10] Road is a common alternative to Street.
[11] Suburb name.
[12] City or delivery-post-office name; *should be capitalized. There is usually a hyphen and a few spaces between the city and the postcode.*
[13] Six-digit postcode (*essential*).

Language

A very large number of languages and dialects are spoken in India, but English is widely used as a common business language. Many Indians are educated in English and can be regarded as native English-speakers. In addition to English, the Hindi language is spoken and understood throughout the northern states, and the Tamil language throughout the southern states. Other major regional languages are Bengali, Gujarati, Marathi, and Urdu in the north, and Kannada, Malayalam, and Telugu in the south.

Address Elements

PERSONAL NAMES

India is a secular state in which people of all religions follow their respective religious practices, including conventions of personal names.

Over 80 percent of Indians observe the Hindu religion. A Hindu has two given names, which usually have their origins in Sanskrit names of plants, trees, birds, or animals. Given names often refer to characters or gods in religious and classical literature. Brothers usually have the same middle name, and sisters have a common feminine middle name. The family name is normally written last, so **Chander Prakash Gupta** is **Mr. Gupta**. It is not offensive to call him "Mr. Chander" by mistake, but only his family and close personal friends will call him Chander, without a Mr. or other title. You will see certain variations on the three-name tradition. Many Indians use their initials, British-style (e.g., **C. P. Gupta**), and some adults stop using their middle name.

Hindu women adopt their husband's family name on marriage and traditionally also changed their given names to new ones chosen by their husband's family.

"Mr." and "Mrs." in Hindi are **Shri** and **Shrimati**. However, the English titles **Mr.**, **Mrs.**, and **Miss** are in common use. It would seem odd for a foreigner to address people as "Shri" and "Shrimati" and to do so might give offense if the person addressed was not in fact a Hindu. However, the words "Shri" and "Shrimati" can also be given names. The American title "Ms." may be used by the most westernized Indian women, but ordinarily "Mrs." and "Miss" are used in India strictly according to whether the woman is married or not.

The largest minority community, over 10 percent of the population, consists of Muslims, who speak Urdu and whose names have an Arabic or Persian appearance; for example, **Ahmed Iqbal**, who would be called **Mr. Iqbal**. Men from the Sikh minority community have traditionally had the name **Singh**, and Sikh women have had the name **Kaur**. Singh or Kaur may be either a last name or a middle name in current usage. They are also used by some non-Sikhs.

There is also a Christian minority who have British first names, although their middle names are usually traditional ones. In India, a Western Christian name is almost certainly the person's legal name, whereas Indians living outside India often westernize their names for convenience, without changing their legal names or implying anything about their religious affiliations.

All Indian languages are written in their own alphabets. Differences in transliteration can occur, but they are minor compared with those of other non-Roman alphabets described in this book. In a large list of Indian names, some may appear to be out of order because, for example, **Kuldip** and **Kuldeep** are treated as being the same name.

In business circles, academic titles are unusual, but it is quite common to show degrees after an executive's name on a business card. It is not necessary to copy them.

COMPANY NAMES

Corporations must have the abbreviation **Ltd.** (**Limited**) at the end of their names. (**Pvt.**) **Ltd.** means the corporation is privately owned rather than publicly traded. Indian business names often have some religious or cultural association with wealth or good fortune.

The abbreviation **M/s** is a variation of "Messrs.," the old British plural of "Mr.," and often precedes a company name.

OFFICES

Many companies are located in large buildings, and it is quite usual to give a room or suite number. You would assume that 1001 is on the 10th floor.

BUILDING NAMES

Indian office buildings often have British-style names:

> **Chiranjiv Tower**
> **Hermes House**
> **Allahabad Bank Building**
> **Prahad Chambers**

Industrial parks are sometimes named (e.g., **Mayapuri Industrial Area Phase II**).

BUILDING NUMBERS

Building numbers are written in front of the street name. Numbers are not necessarily allocated in an orderly fashion. Various combinations of letters and numbers commonly identify a particular office or dwelling:

> **6/290 A Rani Ka Ghera**
> **CC 7/324 Parsi Panchayat Street**
> **E-2/27 Nehru Marg**

The exact meaning of building letters and numbers such as these is unpredictable, but the first element (6, CC, E) is usually some kind of block of buildings or a lot that has been subdivided over time.

STREET NAMES

Major streets are usually called **Road**; **Street**, **Avenue**, and **Boulevard** are also used.

Street names are gradually being changed to local equivalents. In Hindi, **Marg** and **Path** may be used instead of "Street"; **Sarak** and **Gali** are used in Muslim areas.

LOCALITY NAMES

The name of a district or suburb may be written after the street name in an urban address, and a village name may be included in a rural address. A **Colony** (**Nagar** in Hindi) is a city neighborhood.

CITY NAMES

India's principal business cities are as follows:

Ahmedabad	Delhi	Lucknow
Bangalore	Hyderabad	Madras
Bombay	Jaipur	Nagpur
Calcutta	Kanpur	Pune (Poona)

Indian city names often end in **-pur** or **-bad**, which are equivalent to *-town* or *-ton* or *-ville* in English.

The Indian postal administration wants city names to be underlined for domestic usage, which is contrary to agreements for international mail standards.

STATE/PROVINCE/ETC. NAMES

India is divided into states, and their names are sometimes included in postal addresses, especially by indiviuals, but their use has been rendered obsolete by the postcode system.

POSTCODES

A six-digit postcode system is in use. The postcode is called a "pin code" and is written after the city name, usually separated from it by a hyphen and a few spaces.

P.O. BOXES

P.O. Boxes are relatively common for businesses. It may be written **P.O. Box**, **P.B.**, **Post Box**, **Post Box No.**, or **GPO Box**. A **GPO** is the central ("general") post office in a city.

COUNTRY NAME

India is the name commonly used for the country, but the full Hindi name is **Bharat Varsha**, usually **Bharat** for short.

Letterheads

Letterheads used for international correspondence are always printed with English transliterations or translations.

Dates, Money, Typographical Conventions

DATES AND MONEY	
Date format	Day, Month, Year
Typical date abbreviation	29/2/92, 29.2.92
Currency unit	rupee
Cents	paise
Domestic currency code	Rs.
ISO international currency code	INR
Other international codes	none
Decimal separator	period
Thousands separator	comma
Typical currency amount	Rs. 1,350.50 (note one space after the Rs.)

A **lakh** is 100,000 rupees and a **crore** is ten million rupees.

Envelopes

International rules apply: top margin, 40mm (1.6″); other margins, 15mm (0.6″).

Phone Numbers

PHONE SYSTEM INFORMATION (SEE CHAPTER 4)	
Country Code	+91
International Access Code	00
Long-Distance Access Code	0
Typical City Codes	two-digit (e.g., 22 = Bombay) three- or four-digit (e.g., 842 = Hyderabad) up to six-digit in rural areas
Typical number formats	52315 635161 (022) 357-3944
Ringing and busy signals	British

City codes are called **STD codes**. Indians often omit to provide their city codes, since long-distance calling is relatively unusual.

INDONESIA

Address Summary

Example of a postal address:

Mr. Bambang[1] Harianto[2]
PT[3] Publikasi Internasional[4]
Jl.[5] Layumenten V[6]/27[7]
JAKARTA[8] 11460[9]

Key:

[1] Given name.
[2] Second given name.
[3] **PT = Perseroan Terbatas**, signifying a corporation.
[4] Company name.
[5] **Jl. = Jalan**, the most common word for "street."
[6] **Layumenten V** is the street name.
[7] **27** is the building number.
[8] City name.
[9] Five-digit postcode *(required)*.

Language

A large number of regional languages and dialects are spoken in Indonesia, and in addition there is an influential minority of ethnic Chinese. The national language, called Bahasa Indonesia, is the medium of instruction in schools and the common language used internally in business and government offices. Bahasa Indonesia contains words from Arabic, Javanese, Malay, Sanskrit, some foreign languages, and various Indonesian dialects. It is written very phonetically in Roman characters with spelling conventions visibly influenced by the Dutch, the former rulers of Indonesia. International communications are expected to be in English.

This chapter focuses on practices and conventions on the island of Java, which may differ in minor respects from those of other regions of Indonesia.

Address Elements

PERSONAL NAMES

Indonesians do not have family names in the Western sense. A child's name is entirely selected by its parents. Most people have two names, but some have only one, and some have three. To have more is very rare, at least on Java. Many names are recognizably Moslem; for example, **Abdul**, **Ibrahim**,

Salim. Others are Javanese: **Budi**, **Sugeng** (male), and **Sugiarti**, **Titik**, **Wiwik** (female). Ethnic Chinese people may have Chinese names disguised by Dutch spelling—for example, **Lie**, **Tjin**, **Tjoeng**—but many Chinese adopt Javanese names. Javanese names may be words you would find in a dictionary, or they may be purely personal names. A name is usually reserved for one gender or the other, but not always, so an Indonesian will not always know whether a particular person is male or female. A foreigner's only chance is to recognize a resemblance to a feminine Arabic name (ending in -a).

People with more than one name are known by their first name, so **Hamid Saleh** is **Mr. Hamid** and is listed under H, and **Saleh Hamid** is **Mr. Saleh**, a different person, listed under S. Longer Javanese names, such as **Darmawan**, **Hartono**, and **Widjaja**, are usually reserved for second names.

Someone with a single name can be difficult to identify uniquely. A schoolteacher may designate two students as **Achmad A** and **Achmad B**. In an office, one may be known informally as "Achmad with the curly hair." A foreigner could add a department name to dispel possible ambiguity: "We spoke to Mr. Achmad from the Controller's office about this last week."

Although an Indonesian with many foreign contacts might adopt a more easily pronounced English name, that is exceptional, and names like **Eddy**, **Emmy**, **Freddy**, and **Jenny** can be assumed to be the true, unabbreviated, names of the individuals. They will usually have a more traditional second name. Indonesians do have nicknames, but they are only used by family and close personal friends.

There is no objection to using the English **Mr.** and **Ms.** However, you should be aware that there are a number of respectful titles in common use, which must not be confused with personal names. To be polite, a man called **Indra Kelana** would be addressed in writing as **Bapak Indra Kelana**, and a woman called **Dyati Kurnia** would be **Ibu Dyati Kurnia**. In speech, these would be shortened to **Pak Indra** and **Bu Dyati**. Socially, a married woman usually uses her husband's name—thus, **Ibu Indra Kelana**—but in business communications she is likely to retain her own name. **Saudara** and **Saudari** are titles for a man and a woman of roughly the same age as the speaker, and **Mas** is a title for a man a little older than the speaker. Abbreviations like **B.R.A.**, **R.A.**, **R.M.**, and **R.T.** are titles implying higher social status, and should be reproduced. As everywhere, devout Muslims who have made a pilgrimage take the title **Haji** (a man) or **Hajah** (a woman), which may be abbreviated to **H**. You should use this title until you discover the person's preference: to write **Ibu Hajah Laila** is unfailingly polite, but she may let you know she prefers to be less formal.

Academic titles are sometimes used in business. **Drs.** and **Dra.** indicate men and women with doctorates (**dr.** would imply a medical doctor). **Ir.** (**Insinyur**) is the European usage of "Engineer," equivalent to a master's in English-speaking countries. **Dpl.** (**Diploma**) is a general title for a graduate. The letters **S.H.** or **Bchk** after a name indicate a lawyer, and **S.E.** indicates an economist or business school graduate.

Tuan and **Nyonya** are approximately equivalent to "sir" and "ma'am" in American English. **Nona** is used in speech to address a woman who is known to be unmarried. These terms are not accompanied by the person's name.

COMPANY NAMES

Most companies doing international business have names that include the abbreviation **PT**, standing for **Perseroan Terbatas,** although it might be translated as "Inc." or "Ltd." A foreign joint venture with a foreign company will usually have the legal form **PMA**, standing for **Penanaman Modal Asing.**

OFFICES

Floor and suite numbers are occasionally added to postal addresses in high-rise buildings. The Indonesian word for "floor" is **Lantai**, abbreviated **Lt.**

The slash / is usually used to separate a building number from a Roman numeral, as explained below under "Street Names." However, you would assume that **Jl. Abdulah Lubis No. 31 A/41** was Room 41 inside "31A, Abdulah Lubis Street."

BUILDING NAMES

Building names are quite common in major business centers:

> **Bank Pacific Building**
> **Pusat Perbelanjaan Glodok Plaza**
> **Siliwangi Plaza**
> **Setiabudi Building 2**

The Indonesian word sometimes used for "building" is **gedung**.

Plants are sometimes grouped in named areas:

> **Kompleks Industri Pasir Jaya Jatiuwung**
> **Komp. Perkantoran Taman Surya**

Any abbreviation beginning with K (**Kb, Kr, Ks, Kt**) in front of a name probably refers to some kind of industrial area

A **Ruko** (short for **Rumah Toko**) is a small shopping center. It is likely to be the address of a retail business.

BUILDING NUMBERS

Buildings in urban areas are numbered. The number follows the street name. The abbreviation **No.** is often inserted for clarity. A **Blok** number or **Kavling** (abbreviated **Kav.**) number may be provided for additional clarity, either on a street or in an industrial area; for example, **Jl. Sunter Karya Utara IV, Blok G 1 No. 17. Blok** and **Kavling** are the adopted Dutch words for "block" and "lot," respectively.

Two buildings could have been merged, as in **Jl. Kelenteng No. 12-14**, or there could be multiple entrances to a building, as in **Jl. Gajah Mada 149 B-C**.

In rural areas, a distance in kilometers may be used instead of a building number, as in **Jalan Raya Bekasi KM.12**.

STREET NAMES

Jalan, abbreviated **Jl.**, or occasionally **Jln.**, is the most common word for "street" seen in business addresses. **Gang** and **Lorong**, abbreviated **Gg.** and **Lr.**, are smaller streets.

Streets are often named in groups. For example, **Jl. Mangga V/10** means "10 Mangga V Street"; in this particular case, there are eight parallel streets called **Jl. Mangga**.

LOCALITY NAMES

The use of locality names has been made obsolete by the postcode system, but you might still see district names of various kinds inserted between the street name and the city name in older publications. You do not need to be concerned in detail with the administrative geography of Indonesia, but you should recognize that certain words are not the names of individual places: a **Kota** is a city, a **Desa** is a village or a small urban neighborhood, and a **Kabupaten** (abbreviated **Kab.**), a **Kecamatan** (**Kec.**), and a **Kelurahan** (**Kel.**) are all administrative subdivisions. **Kodya** and **Kotif** are contractions for different types of municipality.

CITY NAMES

Indonesia, especially Java, is a densely populated country with many urban centers. Most international business is done with the capital, **Jakarta**. The word **Jabotabek** refers to the capital region, being a contraction derived from the names **Jakarta**, **Bogor**, **Tangerang**, and **Bekasi**. **Jakarta** is divided into five municipalities:

Jakarta Barat	West Jakarta
Jakarta Pusat	Central Jakarta
Jakarta Selatan	South Jakarta
Jakarta Timur	East Jakarta
Jakarta Utara	North Jakarta

These five directional words also occur in other contexts and are worth recognizing.

Other major cities on Java are **Bandung**, **Bogor**, **Jogjakarta**, **Malang**, **Semarang**, **Surabaya**, and **Surakarta**.

STATE/PROVINCE/ETC. NAMES

Indonesia is divided into 27 **provinsi** (provinces), but their names never appear in addresses. You should be aware of the other major islands besides **Java**: **Kalimantan** ("Borneo" in English), **Sulawesi** ("Celebes" in English), and **Sumatera** ("Sumatra" in English). Among the thousands of small islands, the resort areas of **Bali** and **Lombok** are well-known internationally.

POSTCODES

A well-structured five-digit postcode system, known as the **SKPI** (**Sistem Kode Pos Indonesia**), is in universal use. Postcodes around Jakarta begin with 1. Apart from those, postcodes are allocated from west to east across the country. Javan postcodes are in the range 10000–19999 and 40000–69999. A postcode ending in 00 designates a post office, and one ending in 09 is reserved for the postal banking system (**giro**). In very rare cases, a single alphabetic character is suffixed to the postcode, which would indicate that mail is routed to or through a mobile post office in a remote area.

P.O. BOXES

P.O. Boxes are used by businesses. A box is called a **Kotak Pos**, but the English expression **P.O. Box** is widely known. The box number is often followed by an abbreviation of the post-office name; for example, **P.O. Box 1123/JKS** is located in the Jakarta Selatan post office.

COUNTRY NAME

The country is always known simply as **Indonesia.**

Letterheads

Letterheads and business stationery for international use are printed in English. Some Indonesian words you may see in advertisements and trade literature are

Kantor	office
Kantor Cabang	branch
Kantor Perwakilan	distributor
Kantor Pusat	head office

Dates, Money, Typographical Conventions

DATES AND MONEY	
Date format	Day, Month, Year
Typical date abbreviation	29/2/1996
Currency unit	rupiah
Cents	not used
Domestic currency codes	Rp
ISO international currency code	IDR
Other international codes	none
Decimal separator	comma
Thousands separator	raised dot
Typical currency amount	Rp 45·000,– (note space after Rp)

There is always some ambiguity in abbreviated dates, because an Indonesian might have used the U.S. sequence in an attempt to be helpful. A period is acceptable instead of a raised dot (ANSI 0183). A period is not usually written after **Rp**, but an amount might be printed as **Rp·45·000,–** on a check or contract to discourage alterations.

Envelopes

A top margin of 40mm (1.6″) and a bottom margin of 20 mm (0.8″) are required by the Indonesian Post Office. International standards require left and right margins of 15mm (0.6″).

Return addresses are usually written at the left side of the envelope on a level with the destination address, but the top left corner is also acceptable.

Phone Numbers

PHONE SYSTEM INFORMATION (SEE CHAPTER 4)	
Country Code	+62
International Access Code	00
Long-Distance Access Code	0
Typical City Codes	two-digit for major cities (21 = Jakarta, 22 = Bandung) three-digit for other areas
Standard number formats	Local numbers are six or seven digits (021) 659-3333 (031) 319-438
Ringing and busy signals	European

The abbreviation **SLJJ** refers to the long distance direct dialing system. The English word **hunting** implies that there is automatic rollover between a number of incoming lines.

"Telephone" is spelled **Telepon** or **Telpon** (abbreviated **Tel.** or **Telp.**), and **Pesawat** (abbreviated **Pes.**) refers to an internal telephone extension number.

IRELAND

Address Summary

Example of a Dublin street address:

Liam[1] MacCarthy[2]
International Publishing Ltd.[3]
87,[4] Parnell Road[5]
DUBLIN[6] 1[7]

Key:

[1] Given name.
[2] Family name.
[3] **Ltd. = Limited**, meaning a corporation.
[4] Building number.
[5] **Road** is at least as common as "Street."
[6] City or delivery-post-office name; *must be capitalized*
[7] Postal district number (Dublin only).

Example of a street address outside Dublin:

Seosamh Ó Catháin
International Publishing Ltd.
Cork House[8]
Cork Street[9]
DUN LAOGHAIRE[10]
Co.[11] Dublin[12]

Key:

[8] **House** means an office building.
[9] **Street** is also used frequently.
[10] City or delivery-post-office name; *must be capitalized*.
[11] **Co. = County**; always required in front of a county name.
[12] County name (Dublin is both a city and a county).

Language and Alphabet

Gaelic and English are both official languages of Ireland, but English is used for all business purposes. Spelling conventions in English are British.

Address Elements

PERSONAL NAMES

Most Irish people are baptized with two given names and acquire a third one (which is never ordinarily used) at a religious confirmation ceremony. Given names are called *Christian names*. People usually use one given name followed by their family name. A minority of individuals (usually men) prefer to use the initials of their two given names, and another minority (both genders) prefer to give a middle initial, particularly if their name is a common one. It is a little more formal to use a middle initial.

Irish businesspeople normally use their given names with each other, except on a first contact with someone outside their organization, when the use of **Mr.** or **Ms.** is expected. Do not use "Mrs." and certainly not "Miss" unless you know it is the woman's preference.

Many family names begin with **O'** or **Mac** or **Mc**. "Mc" is the anglicized version of "Mac." These prefixes must be joined to the rest of the name without an intervening space, and the next letter must be a capital (e.g., **MacCarthy**, **O'Leary**). They all originally meant "son of," but they are now considered as an integral part of the name.

Some married women change to their husband's family name and some retain their own; they are equally divided. A minority use both: someone who gives her name as **Eileen Smythe O'Callaghan** will probably have been born Eileen Smythe and is probably married to a Mr. O'Callaghan. You should address her as **Dear Ms. Smythe O'Callaghan**. You cannot be certain that she is married—her mother might have been Niamh Smythe O'Callaghan.

Many Irish people have given names that can be spelled in either Gaelic or English. For example, **Seán**, **Liam**, and **Máirín** are spelled **John**, **William**, and **Maureen** in English. Traditional Gaelic names with no English equivalent spelling are common—for example, **Cormac** (male) and **Ciara** (female). Family names can also have either anglicized or traditional spelling. Irish people can legally use both forms of their names, and commonly do so. A man who signs himself **Patrick MacGowan** on a contract with a U.S. company might sign his checks **Pádraig Mac Gabhann**. (A gabha was a smith, by the way.) In the Gaelic form of names, **Mac** and **Ó** are both followed by a space.

University degrees (**BA, MA, BSc, MSc**) are occasionally seen after people's names on business cards and letterheads. **ACA** indicates an accountant. Anyone who uses the title **Dr.** in a business context is probably a researcher, except that a senior executive might have received an honorary degree. **Esq.** is used, but rarely, by men only, in its British sense, not in its American sense.

COMPANY NAMES

Legal Entities	Abbrev.	Explanation
Limited	Ltd.	Most common abbreviation for a privately owned corporation
Public Limited Company	plc, PLC	Normally a large, publicly traded corporation

Teoranta, often abbreviated **Teo.** after a company name, is the Gaelic word for "Limited." The words **Company** or **Associates** or their abbreviations **Co.** and **Assocs.** indicate unincorporated businesses, unless **Ltd.** or **plc** is also added to the name.

OFFICES

A floor number or room number may be used to indicate an office in a shared building, but this is usually unnecessary.

BUILDING NAMES

Office buildings are usually called **House** or **Court**, and are often named after the street or the principal tenant. An **Estate** is an industrial park.

BUILDING NUMBERS

A building number is written in front of the street name, with or without a comma. **12A** is an entrance between 12 and 14. A company in a named office building will probably not use its building number. In rural areas, even a residence may have only a name and no number.

STREET NAMES

Road, abbreviated **Rd.**, is the most usual word for well-traveled streets. **Street**, abbreviated **St.**, is also common, and other British-style designators are seen.

LOCALITY NAMES

There is often a locality name above the city name. In Dublin, it is a neighborhood name, such as **Donnybrook** or **Ballsbridge**. It is only required by the Irish Post Office if there are multiple streets with the same name in the city, but people often include it to be safe. In rural areas, the locality is the village, whose name is essential to include in the address.

CITY NAMES

The city name must be written in capital letters on a line by itself. In Dublin, a postal district number is required, e.g. **DUBLIN 4**. Most international business is done with the cities of Dublin and **Cork** and with development areas around Shannon Airport near **Limerick**. Other larger cities are **Galway** and **Waterford**.

STATE/PROVINCE/ETC. NAMES

Ireland is divided into **counties**. The county name must be written, without capitalization, on the next line after the city name, except when the city and county have the same name. Dublin City is in County Dublin, so no county name is required.

The abbreviation **Co.** is always written (e.g., **Co. Clare**, **Co. Limerick**).

POSTCODES

There is no postcode system (except for the postal district numbers in Dublin).

P.O. BOXES

P.O. Boxes exist, but are not common.

COUNTRY NAME

The short name of the Republic of Ireland is **Ireland** in English and **Éire** in Gaelic. Postage stamps are usually marked "Éire."

Letterheads

Irish letterheads are supposed to show a list of directors of the company or a list of the partners or owners of an unincorporated business. The company registration number is also printed in a phrase like **Registered in Dublin No. 98787**. Sometimes, a **Registered Office** address is printed in small type. If it is different from the principal mailing address, ignore it. It is, however, the correct address for the service of legal documents in a dispute.

VAT (**Value-Added Tax**) is the European sales tax.

Government agencies usually repeat their address and other information on the letterhead in Gaelic. For example, the address **O'Connell Street, Dublin 1** is written in Gaelic as **Sráid Uí Chonaill, Baile Átha Cliath 1**. If a private company adds Gaelic translations to its business stationery, which is becoming more common, that is an indication of progressiveness rather than traditionalism.

Dates, Money, Typographical Conventions

DATES AND MONEY	
Date format	Day, Month, Year
Typical date abbreviation	29-2-92
Currency unit	punt, pound
Cents	pence
Domestic currency codes	£
ISO international currency code	IEP
Other international codes	IR£
Decimal separator	period
Thousands separator	comma
Typical currency amount	£5,879.50
	(note no space after the £)

The Irish punt is occasionally referred to as a pound but is not equal to the U.K. pound. Decimal points are often raised, particularly in handwriting, and commas are often omitted in numbers smaller than a million (e.g., **£5879·50**).

Salutations and closings follow British conventions (refer to the United Kingdom chapter), except that some people close a letter with **mise, le meas,** instead of the British equivalents of "Sincerely."

Envelopes

There are no national rules for envelope addresses. By international convention, the top margin is supposed to be 40mm (1.6″) and the other margins 15mm (0.6″).

Phone Numbers

PHONE SYSTEM INFORMATION (SEE CHAPTER 4)	
Country Code	+353
International Access Code	16
Long-Distance Access Code	0
Typical City Codes	one-digit (only 1 = Dublin) two-digit (e.g., 21 = Cork) three-digit in rural areas
Typical number format	01-7233355 045-54145
Ringing and busy signals	British

City codes are called **area codes** and are also often written in parentheses; for example, **(045) 463501**. Local numbers are usually five or six digits long, but overall numbers, local number plus area code, are not all the same length. Dublin numbers have been extended to seven digits. The 01- prefix for Dublin is often omitted. The prefix (**1800**) indicates a toll-free number which cannot normally be used from overseas. **088** is used for mobile and car phones.

The International Access Code changed from 14 to 00 in 1995.

Word of Warning!

Six counties of Ireland—**Antrim**, **Armagh**, **Down**, **Fermanagh**, **Londonderry** (also written **Derry**), and **Tyrone**, including the business cities of **Belfast** and **Londonderry** (or **Derry**)—are politically part of the United Kingdom, not of the Republic of Ireland. Mail to them is not routed through the Republic. Business addresses in this area will include at least one of the following features: (1) the country name **United Kingdom**, (2) the province name **Northern Ireland**, (3) one of the six county names above, or (4) a U.K.-style postcode beginning with **BT** (for "Belfast").

Let me say that again, louder: You must not send mail to "Belfast, Ireland"! And dial +44-232 for Belfast, not +353-232.

ISRAEL

Address Summary

Example of a street address:

Ephraim[1] Ben-Aharon[2]
International Publishers Ltd.[3]
25,[4] Druyanov Street[5]
63143[6] TEL AVIV[7]

Key:

[1] Given name.
[2] Family name.
[3] **Ltd. = Limited**, signifying a corporation.
[4] Building number.
[5] **Street** is the most common word.
[6] Five-digit postcode; *should precede the city name*.
[7] City or delivery-post-office name.

Language and Alphabet

The official languages of Israel are Hebrew and Arabic, although Israelis of different backgrounds speak many languages. Addresses and other commercial conventions are still influenced by the period of British rule.

Hebrew words may be either translated into (British) English equivalents or just transliterated into the Roman alphabet. There is no standard system of transliteration, so you will see a lot of apparent inconsistencies in spelling. For example, *ch*, *kh*, or even *h* or *c* or *k* alone may be used to represent the Hebrew letter *heth*. One sensible convention is to write an apostrophe between the syllables of a transliterated word, which helps foreigners to pronounce it a little more realistically.

Address Elements

PERSONAL NAMES

Most Israelis have a single given name (some have more), which they write in full, followed by their family name. Someone who gives a middle initial may have invented it to look more American.

Israelis are informal and quick to use their given names with strangers, although you should start out using **Mr.** and **Ms. Ms.** is appropriate for all women because there is no difference in the Hebrew form of address for married and unmarried women.

Academic titles and degrees are seldom used by businesspeople. The European-style **Ing.** (Engineer) is used in Hebrew, but people do not usually try to find an English-language equivalent.

The first line of an Israeli address in Hebrew is often the word **Likh'vod**; this is sometimes translated as a superfluous "To:" although it really implies a respectful form of address for which there is no equivalent convention in English (approximately, "To the Honorable").

COMPANY NAMES

Companies doing international business are likely to be corporations, almost always designated British-style as **Ltd.** (**Limited**). You might see alternatives such as **Inc.** or **S.A.** if that is the usage in a particular company's principal market. The Hebrew term is **Be'eravon Moug'bal** ("Limited Liability").

Company names are often translated into English. The true legal name of "International Publishers Ltd." might be **Mo'tsi'im La'or Ben'le'oumi'im B.M.**

OFFICES

There is not usually any indication of where an office is located in a building. Mail is delivered to boxes at the building entrance. Sometimes an entrance will be specified if the building is confusing: for example, **25, Hayarqon Street** (**Entrance C**). The Hebrew word for "Entrance" is **Kni'ssa**.

BUILDING NAMES

Office buildings do have names, but they are not required in postal addresses. If given, they are just for the convenience of visitors. Names begin with **Beit**; **Beit Gibor**, for example, may be translated as **Gibor House** or **Gibor Building**.

BUILDING NUMBERS

In English-language correspondence, street numbers are written in front of the street name, usually with a comma. In Hebrew they follow the street name, so an address might be written differently depending on the country to which the Israelis are writing.

STREET NAMES

Both Hebrew street designators and English translations are used, and translations into other languages might be used by people who deal primarily with non-English-speaking countries.

Street Designator	Translation	Explanation
Re'khov	Street	Most common designation for a street
De'rekh	Road	Major business street
Sde'rot	Avenue, Boulevard	Major business street
Simtat	Lane	Smaller side street
Ki'kar	Square	Square
Ra'tsif	Quay	Waterfront, riverside drive

In Hebrew, or on a map, the word **re'khov** may be omitted; the street is a re'khov unless otherwise specified. Spelling may vary. Street names themselves may be British, Hebrew, Yiddish, or Arabic:

> **Shaul Hamelekh Blvd.**
> **Rehov Ibn-Gvirol**
> **Hazanovitch St.**
> **Wingate Street**
> **Derekh Shalma**

In rural areas, the street line may be replaced with a reference to a Mobile Post Office, usually identified by the abbreviation **D. N. (Do'ar Na)** or sometimes by its English translation, **M. P.** What follows is usually the name of the district where the Mobile Post Office travels:

> **D. N. Hanegev 3**
> **D. N. Emek Izre'el**
> **D. N. Galil Elyon**

LOCALITY NAMES

Names of localities are not used.

CITY NAMES

The city name must be written in capital letters on the last line of the domestic address. Most international business is done with **Tel Aviv** and the adjoining port of **Jaffa**, with **Jerusalem**, or with **Haifa**. These last three names are the anglicized versions of **Yafo**, **Yerushalayim**, and **Kheifa**.

The rural industrial and farming enterprises called **kibbutzes** also engage in international business. They usually have a Mobile Post form of address and may also operate a P.O. Box address in a city.

STATE/PROVINCE/ETC. NAMES

Provincial district names are not used in postal addresses, except when they are part of a Mobile Post address.

POSTCODES

A five-digit postcode system is in use. Though compliance is not by any means universal, foreigners should make an effort to find Israeli correspondents' postcodes because they will protect you against mistakes you might make in other parts of the address.

Israelis are inconsistent about the positioning of the postcode in transliterated addresses. The majority of businesspeople write it after the city name, either because that is where it is in Hebrew or to imitate the position of a U.S. ZIP code. However, the Israeli Post Office wants you to write it in front of the city name. Do not hesitate to move it to the correct position, because the Post Office's automated equipment looks for it at the left-hand end of the line.

P.O. BOXES

P.O. Boxes are commonly used by businesses. "P.O. Box" is usually written **POB**, without spaces. Boxes have different postcodes from street addresses. If a letterhead gives you both addresses, the postcode will be correct for the box.

COUNTRY NAME

The short name of the country is **Israel**. Stamps show the name in English, Hebrew, and Arabic.

Letterheads

There is no standard layout or convention. For international correspondence, most companies have a letterhead entirely in English.

Dates, Money, Typographical Conventions

DATES AND MONEY	
Date format	Day, Month, Year
Typical date abbreviation	29.02.1992
Currency unit	shekel
Cents	agorot
Domestic currency codes	not used
ISO international currency code	ILS
Other international codes	NS, NIS
Decimal separator	period
Thousands separator	comma
Typical currency amount	1,060 shekels

Israel has its own calendar, but Western dates are used in business correspondence. The abbreviation ILS is not common outside banking circles. NS and NIS stand for "New (Israeli) Shekel," referring to a currency change that took place a few years ago.

Envelopes

You are supposed to leave an upper margin of 40mm (1.6″) and right and lower margins of 20mm (0.8″). The top of the address block is supposed to be within 70mm (2.75″) of the lower edge of the envelope.

MESSAGES FOR THE MAILROOM		
English	**Hebrew**	**WordPerfect Code**
Urgent	דחוף	19,5,7,3
Please forward	נא למסור לנמען	15,18,14,16,12 24,5,17,14,12 0,16
Confidential	סודי	9,3,5,17
Please do not bend	לא לקפל	12,30,23,12 0,12
Fragile	שביר	3,9,1,25
Care of	(c/o is used and understood)	

The right-hand column in the table above tells you how to reproduce the Hebrew letters in WordPerfect. Each number is x in the compose sequence CTRL+V,9,COMMA,x,ENTER. Whether this works correctly may depend on your printer and the way your WordPerfect printer driver is set up for character set 9.

To attract the attention of an Israeli mailroom, these messages should be written on a slant in large, red letters.

Phone Numbers

PHONE SYSTEM INFORMATION (SEE CHAPTER 4)	
Country Code	+972
International Access Code	00
Long-Distance Access Code	0
Typical City Codes	one-digit (3 = Tel Aviv) two-digit (e.g., 59 = Eilat)
Typical number formats	(03) 630831 Numbers vary in length at present
Ringing and busy signals	European

Hyphens are sometimes inserted into numbers to Americanize their appearance, but a number like **513313-5** means there are three consecutively numbered lines (i.e., 513313, 513314, and 513315), which may not automatically roll over.

Numbers beginning **177** are for toll-free information and cannot usually be accessed from other countries. Prefix **050** is used for mobile phones and are accessible internationally.

Israel is planning to abolish city codes and change to a national eight-digit numbering system.

ITALY

Address Summary

Example of a street address:

Egr.[1] **Sig.**[2]
Giacomo[3] **Mariotti**[4]
Edizioni Internazionali[5] **S.p.A.**[6]
Via[7] **Terenzio,**[8] **21**[9]
20138[10] **MILANO**[11] **MI**[12]

Key:

[1] Honorific (**Egr.** = **Egregio**).
[2] **Sig.** = **Signor**, meaning "Mr."; not always on a separate line.
[3] Given name.
[4] Family name.
[5] Company name.
[6] **S.p.A.** = **Società per Azioni**, indicating a corporation; probably publicly traded.
[7] **Via** is the most common word for "street."
[8] Street name.
[9] Building number.
[10] Five-digit postcode (*essential*).
[11] City or delivery-post-office name.
[12] Province abbreviation

Address Elements

PERSONAL NAMES

Italian businesspeople usually give their first given name followed by their family name. A first initial is only used if you do not know the addressee's given name, and it is not respectful to write the family name alone.

"Mr.," "Mrs.," and "Miss" are **Signore**, **Signora**, and **Signorina** in Italian, usually abbreviated **Sig.**, **Sig.ra**, and **Sig.na**. The equivalent of "Ms." is **Sig.a**. Women in business are now usually addressed as "Signora," regardless of marital status.

Academic, military, and professional titles are commonly used in business. **Dottore** ("Doctor"), abbreviated **Dott.** or occasionally **Dr.**, is widely used by all levels of male university graduates. If followed immediately by the family name, it is written thus: **Dear Dottor Rossetti**. A woman is called **Dottoressa**, abbreviated **Dott.ssa** or **D.ssa**. Another common title for graduates in many subjects is **Ing.** ("Engineer"). **Avv.** designates a lawyer, **Arch.** an architect.

Cav. (Cavaliere) and **Comm. (Commendatore)** are public-service honors, similar to British knighthoods.

In Italian, it is customary to add an honorific in front of "Mr." or the equivalent. **Egr. (Egregio)** is the most common for men; **Gent. (Gentile)** is the most common for women. **Ill.mo (Illustrissimo)** and **Preg.mo (Pregiatissimo)** are also used for men (e.g., **Ill.mo Dott. Eugenio Damia**), and **Gent.ma (Gentilissima)** is also used for women.

When a letter is addressed to a company without being marked to the attention of any individual, the honorific **Spett.le (Spettabile)** is used in front of a corporation's name, and **Spett.le Ditta** in front of an unincorporated business name, meaning "Respectable (Firm)." Italians sometimes feel that a plain "Mr." is not polite enough in English; you may encounter eccentric attempts to find an English translation for one of these honorifics.

Men's given names generally end in **-o** or **-e**, less frequently in **-i**, rarely in **-a**. Women's generally end in **-a**. Italian women often have double names such as **Maria Giuseppina** or **Anna Paola**. The double name is used in writing. The individual may prefer one or the other or both to be used by her friends and acquaintances. However, it is not safe to use the given names of either men or women until you have met them in person and have a good working relationship with them.

Some family names are preceded by the word **de** ("of"), which indicates higher social status. You would address **Sig. Alessandro Cortese de Bosis** as **Mr. Cortese** in English, not "Mr. Bosis."

COMPANY NAMES

Legal Entities	Abbrev.	Explanation
Società per Azioni	S.p.a., SpA	Larger company, probably publicly traded
Società a responsabilità limitata	S.r.l.	Smaller (private) company

OFFICES

It is not normally necessary to identify an office within a building. You may occasionally see information given to assist visitors: **piano** means "floor," **ingresso** means "entrance," and **interno** means "suite" or "room."

BUILDING NAMES

Office buildings are rarely named, but names can appear in addresses. Words for "Building" are **Edificio**, **Palazzo**, and **Centro**, as in **Palazzo dei Congressi**.

An industrial area is sometimes called a **Zona Industriale**, abbreviated **Z.I.**

BUILDING NUMBERS

A street number is written after the street name, usually preceded by a comma: for example, **Via G. Giusti, 35**.

If there is any possibility of confusion, an **n.** is written between the name of the street and the building number: **Via Statale 12 n. 102** means "102, State Highway 12."

A second entrance to a building is usually written in the form **Via L. da Vinci 35/a**. Further entrances would be labeled **35/b**, **35/c**, etc.; however, **bis** and (rarely) **ter** are also used for the second and third entrances.

Combined buildings are addressed in the form **Viale della Liberazione 16/18**.

STREET NAMES

Street Designator	Abbrev.	Explanation
Via	V. (but not usually abbreviated)	Most common designation for a street
Viale, Corso	V.le	Major business street
Strada		Highway
Piazza	P.zza	Square

Words like **de** ("of") are very common in street names and are not capitalized:

Via dei Fori Imperiali
Via dell'Aprica
Via degli Alfani
Via del Ponte

As you might expect, Roman numerals are quite often used in streets named after historical figures and significant dates:

Corso XXII Marzo
Via Innocenzo III

Streets are often named after historical figures:

Viale F. Crispi
Corso Vittorio Emanuele
Viale Giulio Cesare (Julius Caesar)

Streets are also named after saints; **Sant'** and **Santa** are abbreviated **S.**, as in **Viale S. Rita da Cascia**.

EUR in Roman addresses—for example, **Viale America (EUR)**—refers to the master-planned exhibition area **Esposizione Universale di Roma** in the southern suburbs, constructed in the 1930s.

An address on a National Highway in an urban area takes the form **Strada Statale Emilia, 154**. In a rural area, the address **S.S. 131 Km. 7,250** would mean "¼ km past the 7-km post on National Highway 131." **Strada Provinciale** means "County Road." Kilometer positions are also used for addresses on the ancient Roman roads: for example, **Via Tiburtina Km. 17,800**.

LOCALITY NAMES

Village names may be needed in rural areas, but business addresses are normally written in two lines: (1) street and number, followed by (2) postcode and city.

CITY NAMES

City names must be written in capitals. In the past, they were generally underlined.

English Name	Italian Spelling	English Name	Italian Spelling
Bologna	Bologna	Naples	Napoli
Florence	Firenze	Rome	Roma
Genoa	Genova	Turin	Torino
Milan	Milano	Venice	Venezia

STATE/PROVINCE/ETC. NAMES

Italy is divided into almost a hundred provinces. The two-letter abbreviation of the province is usually written in parentheses after the name of the city, unless the names are the same, which is the case for all the large cities. In a suburban area, the city name will take the form **AGRATE BRIANZA (MI)**. The (MI) tells you the city is near Milan. You would not write MILANO (MI).

POSTCODES

The postcode, called the **CAP (Codice di Avviamento Postale)**, is essential to avoid delays in the mail in Italy.

The postcode is a five-digit number written in front of the city name. The city and region of Rome have postcodes in the range 00000 through 06999, and the island of Sardinia has 07000 through 09999. Otherwise, postcodes are allocated roughly north to south, starting with 10000 in the city and region of Turin.

P.O. BOXES

An Italian P.O. Box is called a **Casella Postale**. They are not commonly used. If a box is given, the street address should not be used.

COUNTRY NAME

The short name of the country is **Italia**. Postage stamps are sometimes marked **Repubblica Italiana**. The country prefix **I-** in front of the postcode is recognized but is rarely used by Italians themselves.

The Vatican City and San Marino are technically independent countries, but are integrated into the Italian postcode and phone systems:

> **00120 CITTA DEL VATICANO**
> **47031 SAN MARINO**

Letterheads

There is no standard layout or convention, except that **Vostro Riferimento (Vs/Rif.)** and **Nostro Riferimento (Ns/Rif.)**, meaning "Your reference" and "Our reference" respectively, are sometimes included. **Oggetto** means "Subject." **IVA** introduces a Value-Added Tax registration number.

Dates, Money, Typographical Conventions

DATES AND MONEY	
Date format	Day, Month, Year
Typical date abbreviation	29.02.92
Currency unit	lira
Cents	not used
Domestic currency codes	L.
ISO international currency code	ITL
Other international codes	LIT, Lit
Decimal separator	comma
Thousands separator	period or space
Typical currency amount	L. 175.879 (note one space after the L.)

The £ sign used to be the Italian currency symbol and is still occasionally seen.

Italians often punctuate English according to the conventions of their own language, breaking a word from one line to the next by underlining the last letter on the first line:

Every company must expand its inter
national business in order to prosper.

They use a period instead of an apostrophe to indicate missing letters, so they tend to write "Int.l" in English instead of "Int'l."

Envelopes

You are supposed to leave right and bottom margins of 15mm (0.6"). You are supposed to be able to write any address in six lines of no more than 32 characters each. Return addresses are always written in the top left corner.

MESSAGES FOR THE MAILROOM	
English	Italian
Urgent	Urgente
Please forward	Pregasi rispedire
Confidential	Riservata
Please do not bend	Non piegare
Fragile	Fragile
Care of	Presso . . . c/o is used and understood

Phone Numbers

PHONE SYSTEM INFORMATION (SEE CHAPTER 4)	
Country Code	+39
International Access Code	00
Long-Distance Access Code	0
Typical City Codes	one-digit (e.g., 2 = Milan) two-digit (e.g., 55 = Florence) three-digit (e.g., 831 = Brindisi)
Typical number formats	(02)6189080 02/6189080
Ringing and busy signals	European

Spaces and periods are occasionally used as separators in phone numbers—for example, **61.89.080** or **618 90 80**. Usually a separator is telling you one of two things. **834621-2-3** or **834621/2/3** means there are three lines with consecutive numbers. **5735-1** or **5735.1** indicates a switchboard; extension numbers can be dialed in place of the 1. Someone in a large office might give you two alternative extensions by writing **5735.4373/4273**.

A **Numero Verde** is a toll-free phone number for domestic use only.

Word of Warning!

Many foreigners are suspicious of Italian mail service because at one time delays of three weeks were commonplace. Service is certainly better than it used to be, but unexpected delays still do occur. It is safer to use air freight and courier services for anything valuable or urgent.

JAPAN

Address Summary

Example of a street address:

Mr. Taro[1] Tanaka[2]
Kokusai Shuppan[3] K.K.[4]
10[5]-23,[6] 5-chome,[7] Minamiazabu[8]
Minato-ku[9]
TOKYO[10] 106[11]

Key:

[1] Given name.
[2] Family name.
[3] Company name.
[4] **K.K.** = **Kabushiki Kaisha**, signifying a corporation.
[5] Lot number 10 (in area 5 of Minamiazabu neighborhood).
[6] Building number (in lot 10).
[7] Area 5 of **Minamiazabu** neighborhood.
[8] Neighborhood name (often ends in **-cho** or **-dori**).
[9] District of the city; indicated by **-ku**, often translated as "ward."
[10] City name.
[11] Three-digit postcode (*recommended*).

Another Tokyo example:

Mr. Masao Yamada
International Publishing Co. Ltd.
2-17-10,[12] Ningyo-cho[13]
Nihonbashi[13]
Chuo-ku
TOKYO 103

Key:

[12] 2-chome, lot 17, building 10.
[13] **Nihonbashi Ningyo** is the full name of the neighborhood.

208

Example of an address in a rural area:

Mr. Yoshio Suzuki
International Publishing Co. Ltd.
2338,[14] Shiokawa[15]
Maruko-machi[16]
Chiisagara-gun[17]
NAGANO-KEN[18] 386-04[19]

Key:

[14] Building number.
[15] **Shiokawa Maruko** is the full name of the neighborhood.
[16] **-machi** is equivalent to **-cho**.
[17] **-gun** indicates a rural part of a prefecture.
[18] Name of the prefecture.
[19] Five-digit extended postcode.

Example of a grid-system address on Hokkaido Island:

Mr. Yutaka Sato
International Publishing Co. Ltd.
6-ban,[20] Kita-10,[21] Nishi-2[22]
Kita-ku[23]
SAPPORO[24] 001

Key:

[20] Building number (**-ban** = no.).
[21] **Kita-10** means "North 10th (Avenue)."
[22] **Nishi-2** means "West 2d (Avenue)."
[23] **Kita-ku** means "North Ward."
[24] City name.

Language and Alphabet

There are several ways of writing the Japanese language. The romanizations in this chapter are entirely suitable for business purposes, even if they do not correspond precisely to any standard romanization system or represent a thorough guide to pronunciation. But bear in mind that different people may transliterate differently; for example, Ota, Ōta, Oota, and Ohta are just different ways of spelling the same name (Ohta is the most current).

It is useful to recognize the following Japanese words in addresses: **Kita** (North), **Minami** (South), **Higashi** (East), **Nishi** (West), and **Chuo** (Central).

Address Elements

PERSONAL NAMES

In dealing with foreigners, Japanese executives will write their given name followed by their family name. In a large organization, it may be necessary to add their title or department name to ensure that correspondence reaches the right person. Businesspeople do not call each other by their given names, except perhaps when working with foreigners from more informal countries. They call themselves by title (e.g., **Tanaka-bucho**, "Director Tanaka"). Here are some titles you may encounter, in descending order of seniority:

Japanese	American Equivalent	Other Conventional Translations
kaicho	Chairman	
shacho	Chief Executive Officer	President
fukushacho	Chief Operating Officer	Vice President
senmu	Executive Vice President	
jomu	Vice President	Managing Director
torishimariyaku (supplementary title)	Officer	Director
bucho	Director	General Manager
kacho	Department Manager	
kakaricho	Section Head	
shunin	Supervisor (shop-floor)	

It is best to establish an executive's Japanese-language title because of the uncertainties in translation. There is usually only one **fukushacho** in a company, and he functions as a deputy to the **shacho**. A **jomu** is a vice president in the usual American sense of a "V.P., Finance" or "V.P., Marketing." A **jomu torishimariyaku** or a **senmu torishimariyaku** is a jomu or a senmu who is also a member of the Board of Directors; the titles usually go together. Because of the different organization of Japanese and American companies, it is more accurate to think of a torishimariyaku as an executive with an officer's authority to commit the corporation rather than as a Board member.

An approximate equivalent of "Mr. Tanaka" is **Tanaka-san**, the form to use when you do not know the person's title. "Tanaka-san" can also mean "Ms. Tanaka." It is more respectful, however, to address people in official correspondence (or on envelopes) as **Tanaka-sama** or **Tanaka-dono**.

A woman's given name often ends in **-ko**, **-e**, or **-mi**; no hyphen is used (e.g., **Masako**).

COMPANY NAMES

All Japanese companies doing international business are corporations, designated in Japanese by at least the word **Kaisha** (pronounced "gaisha") and most often by **Kabushiki Kaisha**, abbreviated **K.K.** The traditional British **Co. Ltd.** is usually used as a translation of "K.K." Alternatively, they may choose "Corp.," "Inc.," or even "S.A." It is also common to translate parts of the company's name; thus, **Aoba Trading Co. Ltd.** will be the same company as **Aoba Boeki K.K.** Be aware that a name like **Electric Power Development Co. Ltd.** is a complete translation and not the legal name of the company.

Most corporations using the abbreviation "K.K." are publicly traded, but not all.

OFFICES

Internal addresses of offices are not common.

In a high-rise building, you may see the floor number written as **4th fl.** or just **4F**, before or after the building name. Room numbers are also sometimes used. See below under "Building Names" for examples.

If there is no building name, room or suite numbers are occasionally added as an extra (large) number after the building number; thus, **7-9-7-702 Akasaka** can be assumed to designate Suite 702, which would be on the seventh floor as in a U.S. building.

BUILDING NAMES

Major office buildings have names. A building is indicated in Japanese by the suffix **-biru**, but **Building** or **Bldg.** is almost always written in postal addresses. However, use of building names such as the following in addresses is not common:

> **Swan Building 9F**
> **3rd fl. Yoei Ginza Bldg.**
> **5th fl. No. 15 Mori Bldg.**
> **Rooms 521/3 Yurakucho Bldg.**

BUILDING NUMBERS

A building is most commonly designated by a series of two or three numbers. Consider as an example the address line **1-4-7 Roppongi**, which can also be written **4-7 Roppongi 1-chome** or **4-7 1-chome Roppongi.**

Roppongi is the name of a particular neighborhood; that is, an area comparable to Mayfair in London, the Marais in Paris, the Campo di Marzo in Rome, the Lower East Side of Manhattan, or one colonia in Mexico City. It will usually contain about a half-dozen subdivisions, each of which is called a **chome**; 10-chome is about the largest number you will see, except on Hokkaido Island, which uses a grid system.

Number 4 in the example represents what is usually called a "block" in English, but not a block in the ordinary Western sense of a group of buildings surrounded by four public streets. In Japanese, this address element is called **4-banchi**, meaning literally "lot no. 4," but neither "banchi" nor a translation is ever used in a postal address. Again, the number is not usually large; a few dozen in a chome is typical, but there are more in some places.

The number 7 in the example is that of the individual house or office building, separated from the banchi number by a hyphen. The suffix **-ban** means "no." in Japanese, and you will occasionally see it identifying a building number.

The numbering system is now more orderly than many foreigners believe. In business districts, 2-chome does adjoin 1-chome; inside 2-chome, its 4-banchi does adjoin its 5-banchi; and building 2-4-6 probably adjoins 2-4-7, although in a crowded area there may be irregularities. Smaller, older towns may have more irregular layouts.

STREET NAMES

As explained above, the Japanese addressing system is based on neighborhoods, not streets. However, a neighborhood is sometimes named after a major street, whose name will end in **-dori** or **-jo**. Thus, **5-5-10 Kitanagasa-dori** is not necessarily an entrance off of Kitanagasa Avenue. The neighborhood is named after the avenue, and divided into several chomes and banchis just as Roppongi was in the previous example.

Unless the neighborhood is named after a street, its name will probably end in either **-cho** or **-machi**. These are two ways of reading the same Japanese character. Not every neighborhood name has the suffix. You cannot choose whether or not to add it: Roppongi is never called Roppongi-cho, and Ningyo-cho is never called Ningyo.

One complication that occurs in Tokyo is that there may appear to be two neighborhood names in the address. Consider this address in the natural Japanese sequence:

103 Tokyo Chuo-ku Nihonbashi Ningyocho 2-17-10

One writer may Westernize it as:

2-17-10 Nihonbashi Ningyocho
Chuo-ku
Tokyo 103

and another may write it as:

2-17-10 Ningyocho
Nihonbashi
Chuo-ku
Tokyo 103

These are two different ways of looking at the same geographical structure. The first writer is regarding "Nihonbashi Ningyo" as the compound name of a -cho. The second writer regards Nihonbashi as an intermediate level between a -cho and a -ku. This is justifiable, because an adjoining area is called "Nihonbashi Hongoku." The second style has the disadvantage of lengthening the address but it is a closer transcription of the original Japanese address.

One more possibility for a neighborhood name suffix is **-mura**, which is a village in a rural area. It is rather rare in business addresses.

In smaller towns, there is often a single number, which may be quite large, to designate the building, and a double neighborhood name:

881 Nagasuna Noguchi-cho
1100 Ohaza Hasedashi
197 Toda Kitagawara

or there may be two numbers, a large banchi number and a smaller building number, as in **578-2 Uwano**.

LOCALITY NAMES

Addresses in all the major cities listed below under "City Names" must include the name of a locality, indicated by the suffix **-ku**, which is usually translated into English as "ward." It is an area comparable in size to a "postal district" as defined in many cities in other countries before postcodes were introduced (e.g., Paris 16, Manchester 3, Oslo 2, Houston 25, Dortmund 12).

Some business areas of Tokyo are **Chuo-ku**, **Minato-ku**, **Ohta-ku**, **Chiyoda-ku**, and **Shinjuku-ku**.

An outer district of a major city may be called **-shi** rather than "-ku." You will know you are dealing with a suburban business location if you see a "-shi" in a Tokyo address.

CITY NAMES

Japan's principal business cities are as follows:

Fukuoka	Kobe	Sapporo
Hiroshima	Kyoto	Sendai
Kawasaki	Nagoya	Tokyo
Kitakyushu	Osaka	Yokohama

In general, town names are distinguished by the suffix -shi in Japanese. It is the one suffix that is likely to be translated. Thus, you may see both **Asahi-kawa City** and **Asahikawa-shi**; in an atlas you would just look for **Asahikawa**.

A -shi is divided into several -chos in the same way as a -ku. Only the 12 major cities listed above are divided into -kus.

In a rural area, what appears on the city line of the address is a name ending in **-gun**, usually translated as "county." A -gun is also divided into -chos. The difference is that a -shi is an urban or suburban population center, with probably at least 30,000 inhabitants, while a -gun is an unincorporated rural area. A -shi is not part of a -gun, or vice versa.

STATE/PROVINCE/ETC. NAMES

Japan is divided into the following administrative districts, which are always called "prefectures" in English.

Aichi	Hyogo	Miyazaki	Shimane
Akita	Ibaraki	Nagano	Shizuoka
Aomori	Ishikawa	Nagasaki	Tochigi
Chiba	Iwate	Nara	Tokushima
Ehime	Kagawa	Niigata	Tokyo
Fukui	Kagoshima	Ohita	Tottori
Fukuoka	Kanagawa	Okayama	Toyama
Fukushima	Kochi	Okinawa	Wakayama
Gifu	Kumamoto	Osaka	Yamagata
Gunma	Kyoto	Saga	Yamaguchi
Hiroshima	Mie	Saitama	Yamanashi
Hokkaido	Miyagi	Shiga	

The Japanese suffix indicating a prefecture is **-ken**, with the exceptions of **Tokyo-to, Osaka-fu, Kyoto-fu,** and **Hokkaido**.

As a general principle, the name of the prefecture is required in a postal address. However, there are two exceptions to the rule which together mean that it is omitted from many business addresses. The first exception is that the prefecture name is normally omitted from addresses in the 12 major business cities listed above. Also, where a prefecture has the same name as its principal city, it is optional to repeat the name: **TOKUSHIMA-SHI**, Tokushima-ken is correct, but **TOKUSHIMA-SHI** (or **TOKUSHIMA CITY**) alone is sufficient.

There is no standard practice for capitalizing either city or prefecture names. For the sake of uniformity in a multinational list or report, you should probably capitalize the city and not the prefecture.

POSTCODES

There are two forms of postcode. A system of three-digit sorting codes, each code corresponding roughly to one post office, is in general use in major cities. A five-digit system applies generally to suburbs, towns, and villages. The additional digits are separated from the sorting code by a hyphen.

The postcode comes at the end of the domestic address. It follows the prefecture name, if there is one; otherwise it follows the city name.

A hundred or so large organizations and high-volume mailers have their own postcodes.

P.O. BOXES

The English phrase **PO Box** is used, usually without punctuation. Boxes are rather rare in postal addresses. If the five-digit postcode is used, it will end in **-91**.

COUNTRY NAME

The Japanese refer to their country as **Nihon** or **Nippon**. "Nippon" appears on postage stamps.

Letterheads

Most Japanese companies use an English-language letterhead for foreign business dealings. There is no standard format or useful information on it.

If you have to photocopy a Japanese-language enclosure, check first whether it is written horizontally or vertically.

You do not have to understand Japanese to recognize easily that, when it is written vertically, there are neat vertical columns of characters with vertical white space between the columns. Horizontally written documents are copied the same way as Western documents (even if they contain small sections of vertical writing, which are probably captions or sidebars). However, if the document is predominantly vertically written, it should be copied from what appears to be back to front, then stapled at the top right. To get loose pages the right way up, remember that our "ragged right" is their "ragged foot"—the top of the columns will all start at more or less the same level.

Dates, Money, Typographical Conventions

DATES AND MONEY	
Date format	Year, Month, Day (see text)
Typical date abbreviation	92-2-29
Currency unit	yen
Cents	not used
Domestic currency codes	¥, yen
ISO international currency code	JPY
Other international codes	none
Decimal separator	period
Thousands separator	no separation
Typical currency amount	¥10250

Japanese dates are abbreviated: for example, **H. 4. 2. 29.**, meaning February 29, 1992, in the 4th year of the Heisei era or reign. Consequently, the Japanese tend to write Western dates in the order 92-2-29; however, both American and European date sequences are used in international dealings.

Envelopes

You must leave a bottom margin of 20mm (0.8″). Roman-alphabet return addresses should be written at the top left. By international convention, you should leave a top margin of 40mm (1.6″) and side margins of 15mm (0.6″).

MESSAGES FOR THE MAILROOM	
English	Japanese
Urgent	Shikyu
Please forward	Tenso
Confidential	Shinten
Please do not bend	(Shashin) Zaichu (= "Pictures Enclosed")
Fragile	Kowaremono, toriatsukaichui
Care of X Co. Ltd.	X onchu
Care of Mr. X	X-sama kata ("c/o" is also used)

Phone Numbers

PHONE SYSTEM INFORMATION (SEE CHAPTER 4)	
Country Code	+81
International Access Code	001
Long-Distance Access Code	0
Typical City Codes	one-digit (3 = Tokyo) two-digit (45 = Yokohama) three-digit (e.g., 958 = Nagasaki)
Typical number formats	(04)438-1662 (04) 438-1662 04-438-1662 (0460)3-6321 0764-24-1481 0566(24)3083 (see text)
Ringing and busy signals	North American

The length of local numbers varies from four to eight digits. One constant is that the last four digits are usually grouped together (with a preceding hyphen). In Japanese text, parentheses often surround the exchange rather than the city code, but this is usually changed by translators to avoid confusing foreigners.

Tokyo numbers have been expanded recently to eight digits. If you have an old seven-digit number, try adding a 3 to the front of it: (03)438-1662 is likely to have changed to +81-3-3438-1662.

Numbers beginning with the prefix (**0120**) are toll-free and cannot usually be dialed from overseas.

Vocabulary of Suffixes

Suffix	Interpretation	Sequence
-ban	number	3
-biru	building	2
-cho	neighborhood, precinct	5
-chome	"block," subdivision of a -cho	4
-domo	person	1
-dori	avenue, alternative to -cho	5
-fu	urban prefecture	9
-gun	county	8
-jo	avenue, alternative to -cho	5
-ken ("Pref.")	prefecture	9
-ku	ward, district	7
-machi	same as -cho	5
-mura	village, alternative to -cho	5
-sama	person	1
-san	person	1
-shi ("City")	town, suburb	8
-to	capital	9
(none)	(unless obviously a city or prefecture)	6

The "sequence" column in this table is a guide (only a guide) to completeness and correct order. Suffixed names, when present, should be in this sequence in a Roman-alphabet address (thus, a -cho should precede a -ku). You should not have two names with the same sequence number (for example, a -dori and a -cho) in the same address. But do not expect to have all nine levels of name in a single address; the examples at the beginning of this chapter are the most usual sequences for business addresses.

KOREA

Address Summary

Example of a street address:

Mr. KIM[1] Chang-ik[2]
International Publishers[3] Ltd.[4]
Room 206,[5] Korea Building[6]
33-4[7] Nonhyon-dong[8]
Kangnam-ku[9]
SEOUL[10] 135-010[11]

Key:

[1] Family name.
[2] Given names, usually hyphenated.
[3] Company name.
[4] **Ltd. = Limited**, signifying a corporation.
[5] Office number inside the building.
[6] Building name.
[7] Area **4** of subdivision **33** of Nonhyon-dong.
[8] **-dong** indicates a city neighborhood name.
[9] **-ku** indicates a subdivision of a city.
[10] City or delivery-post-office name.
[11] Extended postcode.

Example of a rural address:

Mr. KIM Chang-ik
International Publishers Ltd.
631-7 Woonyang-ri[12]
Kimpo-eup[13]
Kimpo-kun[14]
KYONGGI-DO[15] 415-800

Key:

[12] **-ri** indicates a neighborhood name in a smaller town.
[13] **-eup** indicates a small town.
[14] **-kun** indicates a subdivision of a prefecture.
[15] **-do** indicates a prefecture name.

Language

The Korean language is written with its own 24-character alphabet. There are three standard ways of transliterating it into Roman letters. One is used by the Korean government, the second (a simplified form of a system called McCune-Reischauer) in the academic world, and the third by almost everybody else. Therefore, there is no guarantee that two people will transliterate a Korean word in the same way, and you must expect some variation in spelling.

Address Elements

PERSONAL NAMES

A Korean has a family name and one given name. Traditionally, the given name has two parts. Brothers and sisters share one part (either first or second) of the given name as well as the family name. Thus, **Ku Chang-ik** and **Ku Chang-sook** are brother and sister, and **Yu Dai-won** and **Yu Hyo-won** are brothers. Younger families are deviating from the traditional system and giving more creative names with a more Korean and less Chinese flavor.

There are only about 260 family names in Korea, according to the 1985 census. By far the most common are **Kim** (which means "gold"), **Lee** ("plum"), and **Park** ("gourd"). Others are **An, Chae, Cho, Choe, Chong, Han, Ku, Ko, Im, O, No, Shin, Yu**, and **Yun**.

Koreans normally write their family name first. However, in an attempt to be helpful, they may reverse the order when dealing with Westerners. They may also divide their given name in order to offer an American-looking middle initial.

Individual Koreans will usually have a preferred Roman spelling of their names. Thus, **Park** could also be spelled **Pak** or **Bak**. Do not change "Pak" to "Park" to standardize a list of names.

Women do not change their name on marriage, although Mr. Lee may refer to his wife as "Mrs. Lee" to avoid confusing Westerners.

There is no general equivalent of "Mr." The nearest translation would be **si**, spelled **ssi** according to the Government transliteration method, which just indicates that the preceding word is a family name. Various respectful titles are used in the Korean language, which do not get translated into English. The English word "Mr." is used in Korean only to address social inferiors, but there is no objection to foreigners using it as a term of respect in English correspondence.

Among themselves, Korean businesspeople are more likely to address each other by job title, in the same way as Americans address public officials formally as "Senator Gramm" or "Mayor Daley." A President is called a **Sa Jang** and would be addressed as **Moon Sa Jang Nim** ("Mr. President Moon"). **Nim** is an honorific suffix which would be used in oral conversation. In descending order of importance, the president's subordinates would be titled **Pu Jang, Cha Jang, Gua Jang**, and **Gae Jang**. A foreigner's trading contact is mostly likely to be at the Gua Jang level.

COMPANY NAMES

All Korean companies doing international business are corporations, designated in Korean **Jusik Hoesa**. This is most often translated as **Ltd.**, but a few companies prefer **Inc.** or **Corp.**

Most Korean companies use English or partially English names in international business. Their true legal names will normally be in Korean, but the English versions do have some official standing.

You cannot distinguish a publicly traded company by its name.

OFFICES

In large downtown buildings, the address may contain a **Room** number, sometimes called **Suite**.

BUILDING NAMES

Major office buildings have names:

> **Korea Building**
> **Dainong Mapo Building**
> **Marine Center Building**
> **Bong Woo Building**

The names are an essential part of the address.

BUILDING NUMBERS

Koreans do not use a building number as such. The first number on the street line of the address is the area number. If there is a second number, and there usually is, it is the number of a subdivision of the **-dong** neighborhood: **43-9, Bangbae-dong** indicates area 9 in the 43rd subdivision of Bangbae-dong, which is a neighborhood, not a street.

STREET NAMES

As stated above, what you see on the street line of the address is usually a neighborhood name, not a street. In major cities, the neighborhood names always end with **-dong**. In smaller towns, the endings are **-dong** or **-ri**. A -dong or a -ri is divided into a few hundred numbered subdivisions, each of which contains a handful of numbered areas.

> **396-1, Hae Wol-ri**
> **35-2, Sangdaewon-dong**

Alternatively, a -dong may be divided into a larger number of smaller subdivisions, in which case only a single number appears in the address (e.g., **866, Secho-dong**), but this is unusual in major cities.

Street names are sometimes used in addresses. A street may end with **-ro** or **-no** or even **-'o**, depending on the pronunciation. A street is divided into numbered sections called **1-ka**, **2-ka**, and so on. The ending **-ka** can also be spelled **-ga**. Sections are usually numbered from the east end of the street. A true street address has the form **118, 2-ka, Namdaemun-ro**, meaning area 118 on the 2d section of Namdaemun Street. At the end of 2-ka, the area numbers will begin again at 1 (**1, 3-ka**).

It is also quite possible for a -dong to be a length of a single main street on which addresses look like **84, 1-ka, Dongkwang-dong**.

Many -dongs have split. In addition to the original **Myonmok-dong**, there is now **Myonmok 1-dong**, **Myonmok 2-dong**, and so on up to **Myonmok 7-dong**.

LOCALITY NAMES

Addresses normally require a locality name, written on a separate line between the street line and the city line. In major cities, locality names end in **-ku**, also spelled **-gu**, usually translated as "ward." There are about 20 -kus in Seoul and each -ku has a few dozen -dongs, including split ones.

In a rural area, the locality name usually ends in **-myon**, usually translated as "village" or "township." An alternative is **-eup**, also spelled **-up**, usually translated as "town." A -myon is more rural than an -eup.

CITY NAMES

Korea's principal business cities are as follows:

Inchon (Incheon)	Taegu (Daegu, Daeku)
Kwangju	Taejon (Daejon, Daejeon)
Pusan (Busan)	
Seoul	

Smaller towns are distinguished by the suffix **-shi** in Korean, but it is often translated into **-city**, as in **Songnam-city**. Smaller cities are also divided into -dongs.

In a rural area, a name ending in **-kun**, also spelled **-gun**, which is sometimes translated as "county" in English, should follow the name of an -eup or a -myon.

STATE/PROVINCE/ETC. NAMES

Korea is divided into nine administrative districts, identified by the suffix **-do** and called "prefectures" in English. Their names are:

Cheju-do (an offshore island)	Kangwon-do
Chollabuk-do	Kyonggi-do
Chollanam-do	Kyongsangbuk-do
Chungchongbuk-do	Kyongsangnam-do
Chungchongnam-do	

The six major cities listed under "City Names" are each considered to have the same administrative status as a prefecture. Therefore, no prefecture name follows their names. Otherwise, the name of the appropriate prefecture is required in postal addresses.

POSTCODES

A six-digit extended postcode system is in use. The first three digits enable mail to be sorted to the -ku in the six major cities and to the -shi and the -gun in the prefectures. The second group of three digits identifies a local delivery area. The two groups are always separated by a hyphen.

Sorting mailing lists by postcode has some value. The first digit of the postcode indicates the city or prefecture:

	POSTCODE GROUPS	
Postcode Range	**Covers These Prefectures:**	**and These Cities:**
1xx-xxx		Seoul
2xx-xxx	Kangwon-do	
3xx-xxx	Chungchongbuk-do, Chungchongnam-do	Taejon
4xx-xxx	Kyonggi-do	Inchon
5xx-xxx	Chollabuk-do, Chollanam-do	Kwangju
6xx-xxx	Kyongsangnam-do, Cheju-do	Pusan
7xx-xxx	Kyongsangbuk-do	Taegu

The first digit group indicates the -ku in the six major cities, the -shi and the -gun in the nine -dos. The fourth digit is **xxx-0xx** through **xxx-5xx** for a street postcode (in a city -dong), **xxx-6xx** for a P.O. Box, **xxx-7xx** for a large building, **xxx-8xx** or **xxx-9xx** for an -up or a -myon in a rural area.

Three-digit postcodes from an earlier system are still seen in many publications and can still be used if current information is not available.

P.O. BOXES

P.O. Boxes are relatively common. The English term is usually used in international correspondence. In Seoul there are two main groups of boxes: **CPO Box** (Central P.O.), using postcodes in the series **100-6xx**, and **KPO Box** (Kwangwhamun P.O.), using postcodes in the series **110-6xx**.

COUNTRY NAME

South Korea calls itself the **Republic of Korea**. Postage stamps are marked **Korea**. The U.S. Post Office wants you to write **Rep of Korea** in addresses in order to distinguish South Korea from North Korea, which calls itself the "People's Democratic Republic of Korea" and receives comparatively little international mail.

Letterheads

Letterheads used in foreign correspondence are usually printed in English and have no special Korean terms on them.

Dates, Money, Typographical Conventions

DATES AND MONEY	
Date format	Month, Day, Year; also Year, Month, Day
Typical date abbreviation	2/29/92, 1992-02-29
Currency unit	won
Cents	not used
Domestic currency code	₩
ISO international currency code	KRW
Other international codes	not used
Decimal separator	period
Thousands separator	comma
Typical currency amount	₩1,250 (note no space after the ₩)

WordPerfect can produce the won symbol with an overstrike sequence consisting of the eight keystrokes SHIFT + F8,4,5,1,W, = ,F7,F7. If your word processor has no backspace capability, write the amount in the form **1,250 won**.

Envelopes

A 40mm (1.6″) top margin and 15mm (0.6″) bottom, right, and left margins are required. A Roman-alphabet return address must be placed in the top left corner.

MESSAGES FOR THE MAILROOM	
English	**Korean**
Urgent	지급
Confidential	친전
Please do not bend	접지마세요
Fragile	취급주의
Care of	……방

Phone Numbers

PHONE SYSTEM INFORMATION (SEE CHAPTER 4)	
Country Code	+ 82
International Access Code	001
Long-Distance Access Code	0
Typical City Codes	one-digit (only 2 = Seoul)
	two-digit (e.g., 51 = Pusan)
	three-digit (e.g., 331 = Suwan-shi)
Typical number formats	(02) 265-9050
	(032) 83-5401
Ringing and busy signals	North American

A number written in the form **83-5402/6** indicates there are five consecutive lines, 835402 through 835406.

Vocabulary of Suffixes

Suffix	Meaning
-do	prefecture (province)
-dong	city neighborhood, "block"
-eup or -up	small town in a rural area
-ka or -ga	section of a street
-kun or -gun	county in a rural area
-ku or -gu	city district, "ward," in the six major cities
-myon or -myun	rural area (same administrative status as -eup)
-ro or -no	street in a city
-ri	town neighborhood outside the major cities
-shi	city

Sometimes the hyphen is omitted in the transliteration.

To summarize the most frequently encountered Korean administrative divisions:

> The six major cities are divided into *-kus*, which are divided into *-dongs*.
>
> Elsewhere, a *-do* contains some *-shis* (cities), which are divided into *-dongs*.
>
> Outside the *-shis* a *-do* is divided into *-kuns*, which are divided into *-eups* and *-myons*.

LUXEMBOURG

Address Summary

Example of a street address:

> **Monsieur**[1] **Albert**[2] **BUCHLER**[3]
> **Editions Internationales**[4] **S.A.**[5]
> **49,**[6] **rue**[7] **Mathias Kirsch**[8]
> **1859**[9] **LUXEMBOURG**[10]

Key:

[1] **Monsieur** means "Mr."
[2] Given name.
[3] Family name; sometimes precedes given name.
[4] Company name.
[5] **S.A.** = **Société Anonyme**, signifying a corporation.
[6] Building number.
[7] **rue** is the most common word for "street"; no initial capital.
[8] Street name.
[9] Four-digit postcode (*essential*); may have an **L-** prefix.
[10] City or delivery-post-office name; *must be capitalized*. **Luxembourg** is the name of the principal city as well as of the country.

Languages

The official language is Luxemburgisch, the local dialect of German. Written material from business and the government is usually available in French and in standard German. However, Luxembourg is a very cosmopolitan place with many foreign residents. The internal working language of a company may be French or German or even English. Addresses are French in appearance. For practical business purposes, Luxembourg can be treated as a French-speaking country.

Address Elements

PERSONAL NAMES

Businesspeople usually use one given name followed by their family name, which is often written in capitals.

COMPANY NAMES

Most Luxembourg companies engaging in international business are corporations, designated by the abbreviation **S.A.** (**Société Anonyme**). Other corporate forms do exist. You might encounter **S.A.R.L.** (**Société à Responsabilité Limitée**), which signifies a smaller, privately owned company. S.A.s may be either privately owned or publicly traded.

OFFICES

Internal addresses in a building are not usually used in addresses. Individual tenants of a shared building might be indicated by **boîte** ("box") number.

BUILDING NAMES

Building names may be included to guide visitors to well-known buildings, but they are not required in a postal address.

BUILDING NUMBERS

The building number precedes the street name.

STREET NAMES

Street Designator	Abbrev.	Explanation
rue	not used	Most common designation for a street
avenue, boulevard	av., bd.	Major business streets
route	rte.	Highway
place	pl.	Square

Street designators do not have initial capitals. For more detail about street names, refer to the chapter on France.

A very few streets have Luxemburgisch names, which end in **-gaass**, **-strooss**, or **-wee**. Sometimes a street with a Luxemburgisch name also has a French name, which is not a translation. For example, **rue Chimay** in French is **Dräikinneksgaass** in Luxemburgisch.

LOCALITY NAMES

Names of localities are not used.

CITY NAMES

Most international business is done with the city of Luxembourg, sometimes written **Luxembourg Ville** ("Luxembourg City") to distinguish it from the country.

STATE/PROVINCE/ETC. NAMES

Luxembourg is not divided into states or provinces.

POSTCODES

A four-digit postcode is written in front of the city name and is essential to avoid delays in the mail. Postcodes in Luxembourg City are in the 1000–2999 range. Each one approximately identifies a street, and they are allocated in approximately alphabetical order of streets. In the rest of the country, postcodes are allocated roughly from south to north. High-volume mailers have their own postcodes.

P.O. BOXES

P.O. Boxes are used by high-volume mailers. The French term is used: **Boîte Postale**, abbreviated **BP**, without periods. A street address must not be included with a P.O. Box address. Boxes have their own postcodes, which are in the ranges 1010–1050 and 2010–2019 in Luxembourg City.

COUNTRY NAME

The short name of the country is **Luxembourg** in French and English, **Luxemburg** in German.

The country prefix **L-** is often added to the postcode.

Letterheads

A letterhead is usually printed in French and has a line for references and the date. **Objet** means "Subject." A note like **R.C.Lxbg.B3421** is a company registration number. Bank-account numbers are often printed on the letterhead. A P.O. Box address is often identified as an **adresse postale**, and a delivery address as **bureaux** ("offices"). A **CCP** number refers to a postal checking account.

For other possible terms, see the chapter on France.

Dates, Money, Typographical Conventions

DATES AND MONEY	
Date format	Day, Month, Year
Typical date abbreviation	29/02/92, 29-02-92
Currency unit	franc
Cents	not used
Domestic currency code	F
ISO international currency code	LUF
Other international codes	FLux.
Decimal separator	comma
Thousands separator	period
Typical currency amount	F 5.879 (note one space after the F)

Even amounts are often written in the form **F 35,—**. The Luxembourg franc is held equal to the Belgian franc. The ISO codes **LUC** and **LUL**, corresponding to the Belgian franc codes BEC and BEL, refer to Luxembourg francs which trade at slightly different exchange rates for different financial transactions.

Envelopes

You must leave left, right, and bottom margins of 15mm (0.6″), and a top margin of 40mm (1.6″). The return address should be written at the top left.

See the chapter on France for mailroom messages that can be written on envelopes.

Phone Numbers

PHONE SYSTEM INFORMATION (SEE CHAPTER 4)	
Country Code	+352
International Access Code	00
Long-Distance Access Code	none
Typical City Codes	none
Typical number formats	34-79-11
Ringing and busy signals	European

Phone numbers were five digits long until recently.

MALAYSIA

Address Summary

Example of a postal address:

> **Mr. Mustaffa[1] Saleh[2]**
> **International Publishing Sdn. Bhd.[3]**
> **Wisma[4] Damansara[5]**
> **176,[6] Jalan[7] Sultan Ismail[8]**
> **59200[9] KUALA LUMPUR[10]**

Key:

[1] Given name.
[2] Father's name.
[3] **Sdn. Bhd.** = **Sendirian Berhad**, signifying a corporation.
[4] **Wisma** means "Building."
[5] Building name.
[6] Building number.
[7] **Jalan** is the most common word for "street."
[8] Street name.
[9] Five-digit postcode (*required*).
[10] City name.

Example of an address in an industrial area:

> **Siti[11] Nur Azian[12] Said[13]**
> **International Publishing Sdn. Bhd.**
> **Lot 15,[14] Lorong[15] SS 12/2C[16]**
> **Subang Jaya Industrial Estate Phase 2[17]**
> **43200[18] KAJANG[19]**
> **Selangor[20]**

Key:

[11] (Female) title (see text).
[12] Given names.
[13] Father's name.
[14] **Lot** numbers substitute for building numbers.
[15] **Lorong** is a word for a (smaller) street.
[16] Streets in industrial areas are numbered or coded.

228

¹⁷ Name of the industrial development area.
¹⁸ Five-digit postcode *(required)*.
¹⁹ Town or delivery post office name.
²⁰ State name.

Language

The official language of Malaysia is Bahasa Malaysia, a standardized form of Malay. There is a substantial minority of ethnic Chinese people who speak various dialects of Chinese, and a smaller minority of ethnic Indians speak a wide variety of Indian languages, mainly from southern India. The common language of an office will usually be Bahasa Malaysia, with English used for international dealings. Malays are closely related to people in parts of Indonesia, and there is some mutual intelligibility between Bahasa Malaysia and Bahasa Indonesia.

Address Elements

PERSONAL NAMES

Ethnic Malay people are named in the Muslim tradition. Their names therefore have an Arabic appearance although spelling conventions are national.

A man called **Mustaffa bin Ali** is himself named **Mustaffa** and is the son of a man called **Ali**. His sister would be **Norani binti Ali**, "Norani the daughter of Ali." **Binti** is often abbreviated **bt.** Under an older spelling convention it was written **binte**. However, the words **bin** and **binti** are frequently dropped except on formal occasions and on legal documents. People with simple traditional names like these are addressed in English as **Mr. Mustaffa** and **Mrs. Norani**. If there are several people with similar names in a company or workgroup, you can ask for **Mr. Mustaffa Ali** and **Mrs. Norani Ali** to avoid ambiguity.

However, in current usage, many names are longer and it is difficult for a foreigner to avoid foolish mistakes that display ignorance of social and religious conventions. You should at least be aware of how names are constructed, and you should know some common titles so as to distinguish them from given names.

Many Malays, especially younger ones, have two given names. A few have three or even four. **Yusof Omar (bin) Achmad** is probably known as **Mr. Yusof**, but **Mr. Yusof Omar** is safer to use until you know his personal preference. **Muhammad Salim (bin) Ambak** is probably known as **Mr. Salim** because Muhammad is such a common name, but, again, **Mr. Muhammad Salim** is safe. "Mr. Muhammad Salim Ambak" is overly formal. He might also be known informally as **Mr. Mat Salim**, "Mat" being a contracted form of Muhammad. Malays who have three names in total probably have two given names and are descended from a father with a single name, but it is not certain. A Moslem would know that **Hashim Abdul Hamid** was Hashim bin Abdul Hamid and not Hashim Abdul bin Hamid, because the name Abdul customarily does not stand alone. This man would be addressed as **Mr. Hashim** or **Mr. Hashim Abdul Hamid** but never "Mr. Hashim Abdul." The common girl's name **Nur**, meaning "light," is also always followed by another name, which is sometimes joined to it, thus one woman will write **Nur Hayati** and another will prefer **Nurhayati**. **Nur Aini (binti) Ahmad** is therefore **Mrs. Nur Aini**.

Malaysians rarely address each other without a title. Addressing business contacts by their names alone, unless they have invited you to do so, is being excessively familiar. **Mr.** and **Mrs.** are acceptable in English-language business correspondence and conversation. **Madame** is politer than "Mrs." "Ms." is liable to be not understood or misinterpreted. However, it is more courteous to use Malaysian titles if you know them, and it is obviously important not to confuse them with given names. The ordinary title corresponding to "Mr." is **Encik** (pronounced "N-chic"), sometimes abbreviated **En.** "Dear Mr. Encik Hashim" is redundant and wrong. A married woman's title corresponding to "Mrs." or "Madame" is **Puan**, and an unmarried woman uses **Cik**. Do not use "Cik" (or "Miss") to a woman in a position of responsibility unless you happen to know that she is unmarried.

Other titles which you may hear among people who know each other well are **Pak Cik** (to an older man), **Kakak** (to an older woman), **Mak Cik** (to a much older woman), **Adik** (to a younger woman), **Saudara** (to a man of similar age), and **Saudari** (to a woman of similar age). These titles are not safe to use unless you are familiar with the culture. **Tuan**, however, is a title used for men in a position of authority, and you can and should use it if you realize someone is entitled to it.

In addition, there are many local and regional first names that can almost be regarded as titles because they indicate that the person is descended from a distinguished family in the past. Examples are **Siti**, **Sharifah**, **Che'**, and **Dayang** (female); **Sheikh**, **Syed**, and **Tun** (male), and **Wan** and **Nik** (both genders). **Siti** is also a common given name for a woman. **Tengku** is an aristocratic title that some senior officials in business and government are entitled to use. **Haji** (sometimes abbreviated **Hj**) and **Hajjah** (never abbreviated) indicate that a man or a woman has completed the Muslim pilgrimage. You should call them **Tuan Haji** and **Puan Hajjah** (**Hajjah** alone if she is known to be unmarried) until invited to be less formal. However, note that a man called **Hasbullah Haji Ahmad** is "Hasbullah, the son of the pilgrim Ahmad" and not a pilgrim himself.

The academic title **Dr.** is used by some businesspeople, both male and female. A system of public-service honors on the British model exists. The honorific titles you are most likely to encounter are **Dato'** or **Datuk** (male) and **Datin** (female), which should be used in place of "Mr.," "Mrs.," "Encik," or "Puan." Finally, the @ sign in a name on a legal document indicates an assumed name, known in Malaysia as an *alias*. The initials **a.k.a.** ("also known as") are an alternative to the @ sign.

Ethnic Chinese names are explained in more detail in other chapters. In Malaysia as in Singapore, Chinese people write their family name first and do not hyphenate their given names, so **Yap San Lim** is **Mr. Yap**. A few Malaysian Chinese have Muslim or Christian given names.

Ethnic Indians in Malaysia have a variety of cultural and religious backgrounds. An Indian Muslim has a name indistinguishable from that of a Malay. Some Indian names include the English abbreviations **s/o** ("son of") or **d/o** ("daughter of") or the Malay equivalents, which are respectively **a/l** (**anak lelaki**) and **a/p** (**anak perempuan**). Otherwise, it is safe to assume that an ethnic Indian called **Rajagopal Munisamy** is **Mr. Rajagopal**.

COMPANY NAMES

Corporations use the legal identifier **Sendirian Berhad**, abbreviated **Sdn. Bhd.**, or translated as **Private Co. Ltd.**

OFFICES

Floor and room numbers are occasionally added to postal addresses in high-rise buildings.

BUILDING NAMES

Buildings in major business centers sometimes have names, often the name of the owner or principal tenant:

> **Wisma Telekom**
> **Wisma Selangor Dredging**
> **Kompleks Tun Abdul Razak**
> **Kompleks Pejabat Damansara**

Wisma is the most common Malaysian word for "building"; **Bangunan** is another. **Menara** denotes a single high-rise tower. A **kompleks** could be any combination of a shopping center and business offices. **Kompleks Pejabat** means specifically a government center.

Many business addresses in Malaysia relate to plants or offices in recently constructed industrial areas. These are usually described with the British term **Industrial Estate**. The Malay equivalent is **Kawasan Perindustrian**. The words **Persiaran** and **Taman** (as in **Taman Connaught**) indicate a residential subdivision.

BUILDING NUMBERS

Buildings in urban areas are numbered, unless they have names. The number precedes the street name.

The details of addresses in industrial areas are complicated and unlikely to be understood in detail by anyone except local employees and delivery people. A planned area is usually divided into **Sections** (spelled **Seksyen** in Malay) and further subdivided into **Lots**. For example, **Lot 3, 17/6 Jalan Paku** would mean lot 3 in section 17 of an area whose collective street address is **6 Jalan Paku**.

In rural and industrial areas, a distance in kilometers, or more often in miles, is often used instead of a building number. "Miles" can be abbreviated in unexpected ways, as in **4 Ms Jalan Skudai**. The Malay word **Batu** means "miles," as in **Lot No. 1504, Batu 5, Jalan Tebrau**.

STREET NAMES

Jalan is the most common word for "street." A **Lorong**, translated as "alley," is usually a small street leading off a major thoroughfare. Especially in industrial areas, streets are numbered or coded rather than named:

> **Lorong SS 13/3C**
> **Jalan 26/3**

LOCALITY NAMES

Locality names are sometimes used, but what looks like a locality name may turn out to be the name of an industrial area. A **kampung** is a true locality, a village or a city neighborhood.

CITY NAMES

Most international business is done with the capital, **Kuala Lumpur**, and its surrounding industrial areas, and with **Johor Baharu**, bordering on Singapore. Other major cities are **Ipoh**, **Kelang**, **Kota Baharu**, **Kuantan**, **Kuala Terengganu**, **Melaka**, **Pulau Pinang**, **Port Dickson**, **Seremban**, and **Taiping**. Melaka and Pulau Pinang were known in the past as Malacca and Penang.

STATE/PROVINCE/ETC. NAMES

Malaysia is divided into 13 states. In addition, there are two federally administered territories, the federal capital of Kuala Lumpur, and the small island of Labuan, which is being developed as a financial center. A state name is generally written following the city line, unless the state and city names are the same. The full names of the states of Malaysia are

Johor Darul Takzim	**Perlis Indra Kayangan**
Kedah Darul Aman	**Pulau Pinang**
Melaka	**Sabah**
Negeri Sembilan Darul Khusus	**Sarawak**
Pahang Darul Makmur	**Selangor Darul Ehsan**
Perak Darul Ridzuan	**Terengganu Darul Iman**

Sabah and Sarawak are located on the island of Borneo and known as "East Malaysia," as opposed to "peninsular Malaysia." The word **Darul** means "state," so Johor Darul Takzim is often referred to simply as "Johor." **WP** stands for **Wilayah Persekutuan**, meaning the "Federal Territory" where Kuala Lumpur is situated.

POSTCODES

A five-digit postcode system is in use. It precedes the city name, and is therefore not necessarily on the last line of the address. Postcodes are allocated roughly from north to south down peninsular Malaysia.

P.O. BOXES

P.O. Boxes are used by businesses. The Malaysian term is **Peti Surat**, but the English expression **P.O. Box** is widely used. A **G.P.O. Box** is a box in the principal (general) post office of a city. At least in larger cities, boxes have their own postcodes, different from the postcode of the street address of the boxholder.

COUNTRY NAME

Malaysia is the full name of the country.

Letterheads

Letterheads and business stationery are printed in English as well as Bahasa Malaysia.

Dates, Money, Typographical Conventions

DATES AND MONEY	
Date format	Day, Month, Year
Typical date abbreviation	29/2/96
Currency unit	ringgit
Cents	sen
Domestic currency codes	RM
ISO international currency code	MYR
Other international codes	$, M$
Decimal separator	period
Thousands separator	comma
Typical currency amount	RM1,350.50 (note no space after RM)

The words **ringgit** and **sen** are sometimes translated as "dollars" and "cents" in English, hence the use of the $ sign.

Envelopes

International layout standards apply: left, right, and bottom margins of 15mm (0.6″) and a top margin of 40mm (1.6″).

Return addresses are expected in the top left corner or on the flap.

Phone Numbers

PHONE SYSTEM INFORMATION (SEE CHAPTER 4)	
Country Code	+60
International Access Code	007
Long-Distance Access Code	0
Typical City Codes	One-digit for major cities: 3 = Kuala Lumpur Two-digit beginning with 8 for Sabah and Sarawak
Standard number formats	Local numbers have seven digits 03-781 3316
Ringing and busy signals	British

Punctuation of phone numbers tends to follow British conventions but is not standardized. The long-distance dialing system is referred to by the former British name **STD**. Numbers beginning **800** are toll-free. Local numbers have been changed in recent years from six digits to seven digits, but there might still be six-digit numbers in Sabah and Sarawak during the currency of this book.

The Malaysian phone number prefix **02-** is a short-cut to numbers in Singapore. If a Malaysian told you to call 02-223-8565, you would dial **+65-223-8565**.

Fax (sometimes spelled **telefeks**) numbers are often quoted with the country code prefixed, as in (603) 905-7431 even when the corresponding voice numbers are written in domestic format. A phone number cannot begin **+60-60-** or exceed nine digits after the country code.

MEXICO

Address Summary

Example of a street address:

Sr.[1] **Francisco**[2] **Pérez**[3] **Martínez**[4]
Editores Internacionales[5] **S.A.**[6]
Independencia[7] **No.**[8] **322**[9]
Col.[10] **Juárez**[11]
06050[12] **MEXICO**[13] **D.F.**[14]

Key:

[1] **Sr. = Señor**, meaning "Mr."
[2] Given name.
[3] Family name; thus, **Mr. Pérez**, not "Mr. Martínez."
[4] Mother's family name, used as part of the formal legal name.
[5] Company name.
[6] **S.A. = Sociedad Anónima**, signifying a corporation.
[7] Street name; **calle**, meaning "street," is omitted.
[8] **No. = Número**, meaning "number"; can be omitted.
[9] Building number.
[10] **Col. = Colonia**, a district of a city, sometimes omitted.
[11] Locality name.
[12] Five-digit postcode (*required*).
[13] City or delivery-post-office name.
[14] **D.F. = Distrito Federal**, the federal capital.

Address Elements

PERSONAL NAMES

"Mr.," "Mrs.," and "Miss" are **Señor**, **Señora**, and **Señorita** in Spanish, abbreviated **Sr.**, **Sra.**, and **Srta.** In common with most other Spanish-speaking people, Mexicans usually give you three names on their correspondence and business cards: **Ángel Flores Sánchez** must be addressed in English as **Mr. Flores**. Ángel is his given name. His father was Señor Flores. His mother was Señorita Sánchez before she married and became Señora Sánchez de Flores; you would call her **Mrs. Flores** in English.

Some men will give you a final initial instead of their mother's family name; for example, **Ángel Flores S.**, or even **Á. Flores S.**

Double given names exist, such as **José María** (a man) and **María Antonieta** (a woman). Different people have different preferences: he may want to be called José and addressed as **Dear José** in a letter, or he may want to be called José María. If you don't know a person's individual preference, you should not be using his or her given name anyway.

Mexican businesspeople are accustomed to dealing with the United States and will quickly use their first names with English-speaking people. However, it is still best to address strangers as **Mr.** and **Mrs.**

Some Mexicans use academic and professional titles; you should copy them carefully in addresses. **Dr.** (Doctor), **Ing.** (Engineer), and **Lic.** (Graduate) in front of a name are university degrees; "Ing." is particularly common. **Arq.** is a title used by architects.

COMPANY NAMES

Legal Entities	Abbrev.	Explanation
Sociedad Anónima	S.A.	Most common designation for a corporation, either publicly traded or privately owned
Sociedad Anónima de Capital Variable	S.A. de C.V.	Alternative corporate form, not necessarily larger or smaller than an S.A.

OFFICES

It is not common to designate an office inside a shared building, but in large buildings in Mexico City you may see floor numbers included in the address in any of several formats:

Piso 18 (floor 18)
18° Piso (18th floor)
3er Piso (3d floor)
Planta Baja, abbreviated **P.B.** (street level)
P.H. (penthouse)

In an industrial area or shopping center, an address may specify a unit as being **Local 37** or **Loc. 37.**

Despacho, abbreviated **Desp.**, is the usual Mexican translation of the U.S. term "Suite." It is not common. A high number following the building number may be a U.S.-style suite number; for example, **Río Nilo No. 80-501** probably means Suite 501 on the fifth floor of Río Nilo 80.

BUILDING NAMES

Mexican buildings do not usually have names. Exceptionally, you may see **Torre** ("Tower"), as in **Reforma 445 Torre A**, which implies a modern high-rise complex with multiple buildings at the same address.

BUILDING NUMBERS

The building number is written after the street name. It is very common to precede it with **No.** or **N°**, as in **Estocolmo No. 208**, but this is optional, and **Estocolmo 208** is acceptable. A few people use **Núm.** or **#** rather than "No." as an abbreviation for **Número**.

Different entrances to split buildings are quite common; they are either designated by letters, as in **Chihuahua No. 38-A** (followed by **38-B**, etc.), or by numbers, as in **Plateros No. 34-1** (followed by **34-2**, etc.).

In a rural area or on a very short street, buildings may not be numbered. In that case, you will see **s/n** (**sin número**, "unnumbered") after the street name (e.g., **Blvd. San José s/n**).

STREET NAMES

Street Designator	Abbrev.	Explanation
Calle (omitted)		Most common designation for a street
Avenida, Boulevard, Calzada, Paseo	Av., Blvd, Calz.	Major business streets
Plaza		Square
Eje		Major artery in Mexico City

The best-known streets in Mexico City are **Av. Insurgentes Sur**, **Av. Paseo de la Reforma**, and **Av. Chapultepec**, but the word "Avenida" can also be omitted, and in fact **Reforma** alone is sometimes used for that particular street.

There is a kind of grid in Mexico City formed by major arteries with names like **Eje 1 Sur**, **Eje 2 Sur**, **Eje 2A Sur**.

The points of the compass are used occasionally in other addresses as well:

> **Norte** (north)
> **Sur** (South)
> **Oriente** or **Este** (East)
> **Poniente** or **Oeste** (West)

Most streets are named according to standard Spanish conventions, but there are a few exceptions. Take particular care with the spelling of Indian names such as **Netzahualcóyotl**.

A few neighborhoods have numbered streets, written in the form **Calle 56 No. 80**, where for once the word **calle** is required, and **No.** is always written to prevent confusion between, for example, "1 56th St." and "15 6th St." A name like **Poniente 112 No. 99** would be "99 West 112th Street" in the United States or Canada.

Addresses are occasionally given as intersections, particularly for larger buildings:

> **Lázaro Cárdenas y V. Guerrero**
> **Eje Central y Eje 3 Oriente**
> **Sur 122 Esq. Río Tacubaya**

Here, y means "and" and **Esq.** (**esquina**) means "corner."

Plants in rural areas are often identified by their position on a highway: **Carretera Quiroga-Pátzcuaro Km. 6** means near the sixth kilometer post on the highway between Quiroga and Pátzcuaro.

LOCALITY NAMES

In Mexico City and most other large cities, the name of a **colonia** must be included in the address. Colonias are small city neighborhoods. There are several hundred in Mexico City. The main business areas of central Mexico City are

Col. Anzures, Col. Centro, Col. Cuauhtémoc, Col. Federal, Col. Juárez, Col. Polanco Chapultepec, Col. Polanco Reforma, Col. Roma, Col. Tabacalera, and **Col. Zona Centro.**

A few colonias are divided into sections:

> **Col. San Bernabe Núm. 11**
>
> **Col. Providencia, 4ta Sección**

On the locality line of the address, you may see alternatives to the word "colonia" in provincial cities: for example, **Fraccionamiento Las Playas, Zona Centro, Sector Juárez.**

Small towns (called *poblaciones*) do not require a locality in the address.

CITY NAMES

Mexico City is usually just written **México** but can also be called **Ciudad** (abbreviated **Cd.**) **de México,** to distinguish it from the state of the same name, **Estado** (abbreviated **Edo.**) **de México.** Apart from Mexico City, the principal business cities in the interior of the country are **Chihuahua, Monterrey, Puebla,** and **Torreón.** A number of smaller towns on the U.S. border are highly industrialized: **Tijuana, Mexicali, Cd. Juárez, Nuevo Laredo, Reynosa,** and **Matamoros.**

STATE/PROVINCE/ETC. NAMES

Mexico is divided into 31 states plus the **Distrito Federal** (Federal District), where Mexico City is located. An abbreviated state name is always included in an address, even when the city name is the same as the state name.

State	Abbrev.	State	Abbrev.
Aguascalientes	Ags.	Morelos	Mor.
Baja California Norte	B.C.N. or B.C.	Nayarit	Nay.
Baja California Sur	B.C.S.	Nuevo León	N.L.
Campeche	Camp.	Oaxaca	Oax.
Chiapas	Chis.	Puebla	Pue.
Chihuahua	Chih.	Querétaro	Qro.
Coahuila	Coah.	Quintana Roo	Q.R.
Colima	Col.	San Luis Potosí	S.L.P
Distrito Federal	D.F.	Sinaloa	Sin.
Durango	Dgo.	Sonora	Son.
Edo. de México	Edo. Méx.	Tabasco	Tab.
Guanajuato	Gto.	Tamaulipas	Tamps.
Guerrero	Gro.	Tlaxcala	Tlax.
Hidalgo	Hgo.	Veracruz	Ver.
Jalisco	Jal.	Yucatán	Yuc.
Michoacán	Mich.	Zacatecas	Zac.

POSTCODES

The Mexican Post Office requires postcodes, but they are not in universal use.

A five-digit number is written in front of the city name. It is called the **Código Postal,** abbreviated **C.P.** Whenever you see the abbreviation "C.P.," make sure you have a city name! In a directory or a list of addresses, the city name may appear only as a heading or only in the first address, so when you see **López 23, Col. Coloso, C.P. 32394** you are supposed to realize the complete address is

> **López 23**
> **Col. Coloso**
> **32394 CIUDAD JUÁREZ, Chih.**

Another time you will see "C.P." is when it is assumed you know the address is in Mexico City, which it is when the postcode is below 17000. Postcodes of 20000 and above are allocated to the states outside the Federal District, in alphabetical order.

P.O. BOXES

A Mexican P.O. Box address is written in the form **Apartado Postal 752** and the street name is omitted. Boxes are not very common.

COUNTRY NAME

The short name of the country is **México**. You should repeat **MÉXICO** on the last line of an envelope even if the city is **MÉXICO, D.F.**

Letterheads

There is no standard layout or convention.

Dates, Money, Typographical Conventions

DATES AND MONEY	
Date format	Day, Month, Year (see text)
Typical date abbreviation	29-2-92
Currency unit	peso
Cents	centavos
Domestic currency codes	N$, NP
ISO international currency code	MXP
Other international codes	MX$
Decimal separator	period
Thousands separator	comma
Typical currency amount	N$1,879.50 (note no space after the N$)

When writing in English, Mexicans are quite likely to write dates in the order month–day–year.

Envelopes

You are supposed to leave a bottom margin of 20mm (0.8″) below the address. Return addresses are always written in the top left corner of the envelope.

See the chapter on Spain for mailroom messages that can be written on envelopes.

Phone Numbers

PHONE SYSTEM INFORMATION (SEE CHAPTER 4)	
Country Code	+52
International Access Code	98 (see text)
Long-Distance Access Code	91
Typical City Codes	one-digit (only 5 = Mexico City)
	two-digit (e.g., 83 = Monterrey)
	three-digit (e.g., 322 = Puerto Vallarta)
Typical number formats	546-91-40
	15-14-06
	310-03 or 3-10-03
Ringing and busy signals	European

Prefixes 91, 92, 95, 96, 98, and 99 are long-distance and international access codes called LADA codes, all of which should be ignored when dialing from outside Mexico.

If the city code is written—and it often is not—it will be in parentheses, in the form **(14) 16-60-00**. Multiple lines may be written in the form **301-41 y 305-95 al 97** (**y** meaning "and," and **al** meaning "to"); in this case the office has four lines: 301-41, 305-95, 305-96, and 305-97. Calls might not roll over automatically, so if the first one is busy try one of the others.

Be suspicious of any number that has 706 or 905 near the beginning, regardless of how arranged. Parts of Mexico used to have North American System numbers with those area codes. The number 1-70-667-61901 is an example of one that will not work any longer.

Numbers beginning 800 are toll-free within Mexico.

Word of Warning!

The Mexican addressing system is orderly and logical, but unfortunately Mexicans tend to ignore it and give you incomplete or outdated addresses on their business stationery. For almost all business addresses, you need three lines after the company name: (1) a street name and a building number, (2) a colonia name (except in small towns), and (3) a postcode, a city, and a state abbreviation.

Without a postcode, you can run into all kinds of problems and create undeliverable addresses because of duplicate names of streets and colonias and towns. There are other administrative units, such as **delegaciones**, which can be included to make up for the lack of a postcode, but the details of Mexican administrative geography are too complicated for foreigners to master.

NETHERLANDS

Address Summary

Example of a postal address:

> **Jos[1] van Raalten[2]**
> **Internationale Uitgeverij[3] B.V.[4]**
> **Postbus[5] 649[6]**
> **7300[7] AR[8] APELDOORN[9]**

Key:

[1] Given name.
[2] Two-word family name; no initial capital on preliminary words like **van**.
[3] Company name.
[4] **B.V.** signifies a corporation, probably privately owned.
[5] **Postbus** means "P.O. Box"; the English term is also used.
[6] Box number.
[7] Four-digit postcode for sorting; *essential; don't use NL-prefix.*
[8] Two-letter postcode extension for delivery; *essential. Two spaces must follow the extended postcode.*
[9] City or delivery-post-office name; *must be capitalized.*

Example of a mixed postal and street address, as commonly written on business stationery:

> **K. L. F.[10] op het Veld[11]**
> **Internationale Uitgeverij N.V.[12]**
> **Kerkstraat[13] 21[14]**
> **1794[15] AM[16] OOSTEREND[17] NH[18]**
> **PoB[19] 401**
> **1794 ZH[20] OOSTEREND NH**

Key:

[10] Initial letters of multiple given names.
[11] Three-word family name; no initial capitals on preliminary words.
[12] **N.V.** signifies a corporation, probably publicly traded.

[13] Street name; the suffix **-straat** means "street."

[14] Building number. *Use this line and the next one for freight and courier deliveries.*

[15] Four-digit postcode for both street address and postal address (they could have different postcodes).

[16] Postcode extension for street address.

[17] City name for both street address and postal address (they could be different).

[18] Province abbreviation (rare).

[19] **PoB** means "P.O. Box." *Use this line and the next one for postal delivery.*

[20] Postcode extension for box address (always different from street-address extension).

Address Elements

PERSONAL NAMES

Dutch people may give you a given name in full, or one or more initials of their given names, followed by their family name. In these examples, the intermediate names are part of the family name, not given names, and must not be written with initial capitals:

> **Paul van Zutphen**
> **C. het Hof**
> **J. E. van der Weert**
> **F. van de Berg**
> **L. van het Veld**
> **J. van 't Hof**

Van means "from," **op** means "on," and **de**, **der**, **den**, **het**, and **'t** all mean "the."

The Dutch equivalents of "Mr.," "Mrs.," and "Miss" are **De heer**, **Mevrouw**, and **Mejuffrouw**, which are all usually written out in full if they are used at all. "Mejuffrouw" is largely obsolete in business, and therefore "Miss" should not be used unless you know it is the woman's preference. Dutch people who work together regularly use each other's given names. The only titles seen in business are **Dr.** (Doctor), **Mr.** (a lawyer), and **Ir.** (Engineer, equivalent to "Ing." in most European countries).

The abbreviation **t.a.v.** in front of a name means "Attn."

COMPANY NAMES

Most Dutch companies engaging in international business are corporations, designated by **B.V.** or **N.V.** An "N.V." is almost always a larger publicly traded company. A B.V. is always private but can very well be the subsidiary of a publicly traded parent company.

OFFICES

Offices in a shared building are not usually identified separately, but you will sometimes see a floor indicated in Roman numerals for the convenience of visitors, as in **Neptunusstraat 21 II**.

BUILDING NAMES

The Dutch word for "building" is **gebouw**. Although buildings do sometimes have names (e.g., **Gebouw Waterland**), they are only written for the convenience of visitors and are not necessary in addresses.

BUILDING NUMBERS

Building numbers follow the street name in Dutch addresses. When a building has been divided, the second entrance is usually identified by a letter: **Deventerweg 3 a**.

STREET NAMES

Street Designator	Abbrev.	Explanation
-straat	-str	Most common designation for a street
-laan	-ln	
-weg	-w	
-plein	-pl	Square
-haven, -dijk, -kade, -singel, -gracht	(rare)	Streets which follow (or used to follow) water (harbors, levees, canals, rivers)

Many street names do not end in a "street" suffix.

Compass words occur occasionally in street (and town) names: "north," "south," "east," "west" are written **noord**, **zuid**, **oost**, **west**. You will also see them suffixed: **noordzijde**, **zuidzijde**, etc., which are just like "North Side," "South Side," etc., in U.S. cities.

LOCALITY NAMES

Locality names are never used in addresses. All addresses can be written on two lines: (1) a street or box, followed by (2) a postcode and city.

CITY NAMES

City names must be written in capital letters.

The principal business cities in the Netherlands are:

Amsterdam	Eindhoven	Haarlem
Apeldoorn	Groningen	Rotterdam
Arnhem	Den Haag	Utrecht

Some towns with longer names use standard abbreviations: **Alphen aan den Rijn**, meaning "Alphen on the (river) Rhine," is usually written **Alphen a.d. Rijn** or **Alphen a/d Rijn**.

The full name of the capital city, which is called **The Hague** in English, is **'s-Gravenhage**, but it is commonly written **Den Haag**. A small number of other town names begin with 's- or 't-, which are never capitalized (e.g., **'s-Hertogenbosch**, found under H in a directory).

STATE/PROVINCE/ETC. NAMES

The Netherlands is divided into 12 provinces:

Province	Abbrev.	Province	Abbrev.
Drenthe	DR	Noord-Brabant	NB
Flevoland	FLD	Noord-Holland	NH
Friesland	FR	Overijssel	OV
Gelderland	GLD	Utrecht	UT
Groningen	GN	Zeeland	ZLD
Limburg	LB	Zuid-Holland	ZH

Theoretically, the postcode makes province names unnecessary in addresses, but it is customary to include the abbreviations to distinguish between towns of the same name (e.g., **HOORN NH**), and you may see them in other business contexts as well.

POSTCODES

The Dutch postcode has two parts, separated by one space. The first part consists of a four-digit sorting code. The first three of the digits generally represent a mail-sorting center. Codes are allocated roughly counterclockwise around the country, starting from Amsterdam. The second part is a delivery code consisting of two letters. The complete postcode usually represents a small group of houses or a single business. It is written in front of the city name.

P.O. BOXES

P.O. Boxes are very commonly used by businesses. The Dutch word is **Postbus**, but **P.O. Box** and **PoB** are used and accepted. A box address normally has a different postcode from the street address, and it can be in a different town. Horizontal addresses in directories and lists can be confusing, as in the following example:

> Nobelstraat 78, 3262 PM Oud-Beyerland, Postbus 3542, 3264 ZG Nieuw-Beyerland

which actually consists of two addresses, one immediately following the other, separated only by a comma.

COUNTRY NAME

The Netherlands calls itself **Nederland**. "Holland" and its translations are not correct. The U.S. Postal Service wants Americans to write **NETHERLANDS**, without "The."

The postcode is sometimes seen prefixed with the country code **NL-**, but this should not be used.

Letterheads

You can expect to see most of the following words on a letterhead:

Dutch Expression	Meaning
Uw kenmerk	Your reference
Ons kenmerk	Our reference
Datum	Date
Onderwerp	Subject
Uw brief van . . .	Your letter of . . . (date)
Correspondentieadres	Postal address
Telefoon	Telephone
KvK reg nr.	Chamber of Commerce registration no.
Postgiro	Postal banking account no.
BTW	Value-Added Tax registration no.

Dates, Money, Typographical Conventions

DATES AND MONEY	
Date format	Day, Month, Year
Typical date abbreviation	29.02.1992
Currency unit	guilder
Cents	cents
Domestic currency code	f
ISO international currency code	NLG
Other international codes	none
Decimal separator	comma
Thousands separator	period
Typical currency amount	f 5.879,50 (note one space after the f)

The currency units are usually called "guilders" in English, or sometimes "florins" (an older term). In Dutch they are spelled **gulden**. Even amounts are usually written **f 167,—**. The script *f* that is present on many computer printers is an obsolete convention and should not be used.

Sans-serif typefaces are most common for business purposes in the Netherlands.

Envelopes

International margin rules apply: 40mm (1.6″) top, 15mm (0.6″) left, right, and bottom. Return addresses are usually printed in the top left corner.

MESSAGES FOR THE MAILROOM	
English	**Dutch**
Urgent	Dringend
Please forward	Gelieve door te zenden
Confidential	Vertrouwelijk
Please do not bend	Niet vouwen a.u.b.
Fragile	Breekbaar
Care of	Per adres . . . (or p.a.)

Phone Numbers

PHONE SYSTEM INFORMATION (SEE CHAPTER 4)	
Country Code	+31
International Access Code	09
Long-Distance Access Code	0
Typical City Codes	two-digit (e.g., 20 = Amsterdam) longer in rural areas
Typical number formats	(040) 45 71 77 (010) 429 81 99
Ringing and busy signals	European

Phone numbers are sometimes written other ways, e.g., 079-51 00 59 or 079-510059. Prefixes **060** and **064** are toll-free numbers called **groene nummero** ("green numbers"). **063, 068,** and **069** are prefixes for chargeable information numbers, like U.S. 900 numbers. **065** is a mobile-phone prefix.

The International Access Code is expected to change to 00 during the currency of this edition.

NEW ZEALAND

Address Summary

Example of a street address:

David[1] Green[2]
International Publishing Ltd.[3]
5-201[4] Neilson[5] Street[6]
Te Papapa[7]
AUCKLAND[8] 1106[9]

Key:

[1] Given name.
[2] Family name.
[3] **Ltd. = Limited**, signifying a corporation.
[4] Unit **5** in building no. **201**.
[5] Street name.
[6] **Street** is the usual word.
[7] Neighborhood.
[8] City name, *in capitals*.
[9] Four-digit postcode.

Address Elements

PERSONAL NAMES

New Zealanders have traditionally followed the British convention of giving two initials followed by their family name. But businesspeople are now more likely to use their first given name in full, and then their family name. It is safer to call strangers **Mr.** or **Mrs.** ("Ms." is understood but not widely used) on first contact, but New Zealanders are informal and expect you to use their given names.

Academic degrees are sometimes listed after a person's name.

COMPANY NAMES

Companies doing international business are invariably corporations, designated **Ltd.** ("Limited").

OFFICES

An office in a shared building may be identified by a **Floor** number or by a **Unit** number or letter. The American term **Suite** and the Australian term **Level** are used occasionally. However, internal addresses are not always necessary: most office buildings are small.

The office number, when there is one, is often prefixed to the building number. The following are different ways of writing the same thing:

Unit 2, 173 Smith Street
2/173 Smith Street
2-173 Smith Street *(preferred)*

The New Zealand Post Office wants you to use the last of these. If the office is designated by letter, the Post Office asks that it be addressed in the form **173-B Smith Street**. Compliance with the Post Office's requirements is still rather low, however.

BUILDING NAMES

Building names are rare but becoming more popular. The New Zealand Post Office does not want them in addresses.

BUILDING NUMBERS

The street number precedes the street name, with or preferably without a comma. **101-103 Watt Street** indicates that two buildings have been merged. The New Zealand Post Office would like people to stop writing addresses like this and just use the first number.

STREET NAMES

Street and **Road** are about equally common in business addresses. **Avenue** is used for major streets. Residential streets are often called **Place**. A number of other British terms are used, plus **Grove**.

In rural areas, you may see addresses written in the form **R D 3**, meaning "Rural Delivery Route 3," instead of a street name.

LOCALITY NAMES

There is often a locality name above the city name. Locality names may be prosaic English, like **Blockhouse Bay**, or more exotic Maori, like **Papatoetoe** and **Otahuhu**.

CITY NAMES

City names should be written in capital letters. **Auckland, Christchurch**, and **Wellington** were divided into postal districts which have traditionally appeared as numbers after the city name (e.g., **CHRISTCHURCH 3**). This system is being replaced by postcodes, but it is still the addressing style most commonly used by individuals and businesses.

Other business cities are **Dunedin, Hamilton**, and **Invercargill**.

STATE/PROVINCE/ETC. NAMES

New Zealand is divided into counties and other administrative districts, but they should not appear in postal addresses.

POSTCODES

The New Zealand Post Office is trying to introduce a four-digit postcode system. Postcodes are allocated in an orderly fashion from north to south. So far, compliance by New Zealanders is low, except for high-volume mailers. However, foreigners should always use a postcode if they know it, because it protects against errors in the address. Here are the ones you are most likely to need:

City	Streets	Boxes	Bags
AUCKLAND 1	1001	1000	1020
AUCKLAND 2	1002	1000	1020
AUCKLAND 3	1003	1000	1020
AUCKLAND 4	1004	1000	1020
AUCKLAND 5	1105	1130	1130
AUCKLAND 6	1106	1130	1130
AUCKLAND 7	1207	1230	1230
AUCKLAND 8	1208	1230	1230
CHRISTCHURCH x	800x	8000	8020
DUNEDIN	9001	9000	9020
HAMILTON	2001	2000	2020
INVERCARGILL	9501	9500	9520
WELLINGTON x	600x	6000	6020

P.O. BOXES

P.O. Boxes are commonly used by businesses. The standard abbreviation is **P O Box**; the national post office prefers that you not use periods.

A **Private Bag** is a P.O. Box used by a higher-volume mailer.

COUNTRY NAME

New Zealand is the full name of the country.

Letterheads

There are no standard conventions or legal requirements for letterheads.

Dates, Money, Typographical Conventions

DATES AND MONEY	
Date format	Day, Month, Year
Typical date abbreviation	29/2/92
Currency unit	dollar
Cents	cents
Domestic currency code	$
ISO international currency code	NZD
Other international codes	NZ$, $NZ
Decimal separator	period
Thousands separator	comma
Typical currency amount	$5,879.50 (note no space after the $)

British spelling conventions are used.

Envelopes

You are supposed to leave 15mm (0.6″) left, right, and bottom margins and a 40mm (1.6″) top margin. Return addresses should be written at the top left, but are often omitted.

"Care of" is usually written **C/-**.

Phone Numbers

PHONE SYSTEM INFORMATION (SEE CHAPTER 4)	
Country Code	+64
International Access Code	00
Long-Distance Access Code	0
Typical City Codes	See text
Typical number formats	(04) 496 4473
Ringing and busy signals	British

The phone system is in the process of changing to an eight-digit national numbering system without city codes. In the past, city codes were one to five digits long, and local numbers were four to seven digits long. There is currently an intermediate system in use, in which most phone numbers are seven digits long and most city codes are one or two digits long.

(0800) is a prefix for toll-free numbers, and **(025)** and **(026)** are for mobile phones and pagers.

NIGERIA

Address Summary

Example of a postal address in a major city:

Mr. Emeka[1] Ejiogu[2]
International Publishing[3] Ltd.[4]
68, Nnamdi Azikiwe Street[5]
P.O. Box[6] 60831
Ikeja[7]
LAGOS[8]

Key:

[1] Given name.
[2] Family name (see text).
[3] Company name.
[4] **Ltd. = Limited**, signifying a corporation.
[5] "Street" and "Road" are equally common.
[6] "P.M.B." is another common abbreviation for a type of P.O. Box.
[7] Locality name.
[8] City name (states' names only follow smaller towns).

Language

English is the official language of Nigeria and the one most commonly used in large-scale business. Nigerians belong to three major ethnic and linguistic groups: The Hausa and Fulani peoples inhabit the northern part of the country, Yorubas the western part, and Ibos the eastern part. Hausa, Yoruba, and Ibo are understood throughout their respective regions, but hundreds of local languages are used by small minorities, with some degree of mutual intelligibility between close neighbors.

Ibos in particular hold positions of responsibility outside their home region, and so do the other groups to a lesser extent.

Address Elements

PERSONAL NAMES

Nigerians have at least two names and usually three. A child's names are normally chosen by its paternal grandfather, with other grandparents potentially contributing additional names. It is customary, though not mandatory, to pass

250

the last name down from father to child. The last name is therefore referred to in this chapter as a family name.

Examples of Ibo traditional names are **Nkwocha, Okorie, Amaefula, Okorocha** (male), and **Adanma, Chinyere, Ugochi** (female). Although some names are common to both men and women, Nigerians will usually know the gender of a correspondent, at least one from the same culture. Names do have meaning; for example, **Okorie** means a man born on a certain market day, and **Adanma** means "first daughter." Longer traditional names may carry some meaning that is felt to be a personal statement about the family's hopes for the child. For example, the Ibo name **Ejereonyeoku** is built from syllables implying "who to go out [and gather wealth] for." Any male name may, in principle, appear as either a given name or a family name, but there are preferences, and given names tend to be shorter. The family name is always the last name and is always inherited from a male ancestor.

Foreigners cannot expect to distinguish Ibo and Yoruba names, although Nigerians can. Almost all the Hausas and Fulanis, some Yorubas, and a very few Ibos are Muslims, and their names are recognizably Arabic; for example, **Mohammed Abubakar**. The Hausa words **dan**, meaning "son of," and **mai**, simply meaning "of," are equivalent to the Arabic *bin*. In the Hausa-Fulani group, people have also adopted the names of towns, villages, clans, and occupations as family names.

The way a person is addressed depends primarily on the relative age of the speakers, as is common throughout Africa. The older person is more often than not addressed with a title and family name. A younger person is addressed by first name. In a Westernized company where managers may sometimes be younger than subordinates, practice may vary, but age is likely to be more important than position in the company. Some people adopt nicknames, or are given them, in which case they may be flattering or unflattering. Foreigners should avoid using Nigerians' nicknames unless they understand the social situation fully.

Titles, however, are important to Nigerians and therefore worth some effort to understand and use. In the Nigerian languages, elaborate systems of titles exist, for which the generic English translation is **Chief**. Common titles are **Eze, Nze, Oba,** and **Obi**. The Ibo titles **Dede** and **Mazi** (male) and **Nda** (usually female, although local usage could vary) are widely used for people who rank below chiefs in the social hierarchy. **Nwoko** (male) and **Nwanyi** or **Mata** (female) denote non-chiefs. The Yoruba word **Oga**, meaning "boss," is used throughout Nigeria. If you know someone's correct Nigerian title, it is polite to use it. Still, "Chief" and **Mr.** are commonly used by foreigners who are in doubt about a Nigerian's status. **Mrs.** and **Miss** are used and understood, but "Ms." is likely to be misinterpreted. Women in positions of responsibility, or who are older than you are, are more customarily and safely addressed in English as **Madam**.

The title **Alhaji** indicates a (male) Muslim who has made a pilgrimage to Mecca. A woman pilgrim takes the title **Alhaja**. **Mallam**, meaning "teacher," is a respectful title for a devout Muslim who has not made a pilgrimage. All Nigerian titles, even **Alhaji**, are occasionally bestowed as given names.

It is rather common for Nigerians to write their names in the British manner, abbreviating their given names to initial letters; for example, **A. O.**

Ogunlana (a Yoruba). Some Christians have British given names in addition to their traditional names and may prefer to use them in international business dealings.

COMPANY NAMES

Nigerian corporations are called **Limited Companies**, always abbreviated to **Ltd.** Following British and European practice, publicly traded companies are labeled **PLC.**

OFFICES

Internal office identification is rarely necessary. Occasionally, a floor number in a large building is included in an address.

BUILDING NAMES

High-rise buildings in major business centers are named:

> **Afrijet House**
> **Ramadan House**
> **IMB Plaza**
> **Unity House**

Smaller commercial buildings may also carry names.

Industrial plants are sometimes grouped in named areas:

> **Trans Amadi Industrial Layout**
> **Ilupeju Industrial Scheme**
> **Challawa Industrial Estate**

BUILDING NUMBERS

Buildings are usually numbered, unless the address is in a remote area, or the company is very well-known, or the building is better known by its name. Building numbers are written in front of the street name, usually followed by a comma. A street address such as **8/10, Broad Street** indicates that two buildings or plots have been combined; an address such as **34A, Ojuelegba Street** indicates that the building has multiple entrances. The word **Plot** in front of a building number probably indicates that it is located in a planned industrial area.

In rural areas, a distance in miles or kilometers may be used to indicate the position of a plant:

> **Km. 23, Badagry Express Road**
> **Mile 41, Ijoko Road**

STREET NAMES

Most streets are called **Street** or **Road**. **Way** and **Causeway** indicate major thoroughfares. An **Expressway** is a federal highway, but not necessarily a limited-access highway in the American sense. A **Dual Carriageway** is a divided highway. A **Round-About** is a rotary or traffic circle. Other names following British practice are found, mainly in residential addresses.

It is quite common to see directions included in a postal address, even when the address appears complete, as in **13, Kayode Street, off Morocco Road**. A **B/Stop** is a bus stop. Leave these directions in if you have room.

LOCALITY NAMES

Locality names are sometimes used in major urban areas. Many business addresses in Lagos are located in the areas **Ikeja**, **Ojota**, or **Victoria Island**. The locality may be a distinct municipality (**Ikeja** is one), or simply a neighborhood or subdivision. The abbreviation **LGA** ("Local Government Area") denotes a municipality. **GRA** ("Government Reserved Area") indicates a residential subdivision, probably a prosperous one.

CITY NAMES

By international convention, city names should be written in capital letters. The principal business cities of Nigeria are **Ibadan**, **Kano**, **Lagos**, and **Port Harcourt**. **Abuja**, in a centrally located Federal District, is the new official capital of Nigeria. Other major cities are **Abeokuta**, **Benin City**, **Calabar**, **Enugu**, **Ilorin**, **Kaduna**, **Ogbomosho**, and **Oshogbo**.

STATE/PROVINCE/ETC. NAMES

Nigeria is divided into 30 states (in addition to the Federal Capital Territory), whose names are

Abia	**Imo**	**Ogun**
Adamawa	**Jigawa**	**Ondo**
Akwa Ibom	**Kaduna**	**Osun**
Anambra	**Kano**	**Oyo**
Bauchi	**Katsina**	**Plateau**
Benue	**Kebbi**	**Rivers**
Borno	**Kogi**	**Sokoto**
Cross River	**Kwara**	**Taraba**
Delta	**Lagos**	**Yobe**
Edo	**Niger**	
Enugu		

A state name should follow the name of a smaller town:

    Agbara
    OGUN STATE

In domestic usage a name may be repeated, since many states are named after their principal city (e.g. **Kano, Kano State**). For computer database purposes, two address lines will ordinarily accommodate either a locality and a city, or a town and a state.

POSTCODES

There is currently no postcode system in Nigeria, but one is in the planning stages.

P.O. BOXES

P.O. Boxes are very commonly used by businesses. The street name is usually included in an address as well as the box number.

A **GPO Box** is a P.O. Box in a central post office, and **P.M.B.** stands for "Private Mail Bag," which implies a higher-volume mailer. Both of these are numbered in the same way as regular P.O. Boxes.

COUNTRY NAME

The **Federal Republic of Nigeria** is called **Nigeria** for short.

Letterheads

Letterheads and business stationery are printed in English.

Dates, Money, Typographical Conventions

DATES AND MONEY	
Date format	Day, Month, Year
Typical date abbreviation	29-2-96
Currency unit	naira
Cents	kobo
Domestic currency codes	N or ₦
ISO international currency code	NGN
Other international codes	none
Decimal separator	period
Thousands separator	comma
Typical currency amount	N 15,000.00

If you cannot produce the Nigerian currency symbol with an "N, BACK-SPACE, =" sequence, use an N alone, or write "15,000.00 naira" in full. The naira symbol is included in the Unicode as U + 20A6.

Envelopes

International layout standards apply: left, right, and bottom margins of 15mm (0.6″) and a top margin of 40mm (1.6″).

Return addresses are usually written on the flap.

Phone Numbers

PHONE SYSTEM INFORMATION (SEE CHAPTER 4)	
Country Code	+234
International Access Code	009
Long-Distance Access Code	0
Typical City Codes	1 = Lagos, 9 = Abuja Others are two digits: e.g., 64 = Kano, 84 = Port Harcourt
Standard number formats	Local numbers are five or six digits: 01-634660
Ringing and busy signals	European

Signals from older equipment may sound British rather than European.

Words of Warning!

The northern (Hausa-Fulani) part of Nigeria is predominantly Muslim, and business there is restricted during the lunar month of Ramadan.

The Nigerian phone system is improving, but the postal system is often unreliable and subject to pilferage. It is advisable to use air courier systems for anything you care about.

In recent years, Nigeria has become famous as the origin of unsolicited business propositions of a manifestly fraudulent nature. Faxes offering incredible profits should be treated with great suspicion, even if they appear to come from government agencies or well-known companies. Before you get too indignant with these crooks, recall that many of the money-laundering techniques they propose were learned from Americans and Europeans during the oil-boom years. We are only reaping what some of us sowed.

NORWAY

Address Summary

Example of a postal address (domestically, addressee's name normally is written below company name):

Bjørg[1] Grøndahl[2]
Internasjonalt Forlag[3] A/S[4]
Postboks[5] 19[6] - Sentrum[7]
0101[8] OSLO[9] 1[10]

Key:

[1] Given name.
[2] Family name.
[3] Company name.
[4] **A/S = Aksjeselskap**, signifying a corporation.
[5] **Postboks** means "P.O. Box"; sometimes written in English.
[6] Box number.
[7] Name of the post office where the box is located.
[8] Four-digit postcode *(essential)*; sometimes has an **N-** prefix. *Two spaces must follow the postcode.*
[9] City or delivery-post-office name; *must be capitalized.*
[10] Oslo postal-district number (no longer required, but still commonly used).

Example of a mixed postal and street address, as commonly written on business stationery:

Kjell Fredriksen
Internasjonalt Forlag A/S
Nygata[11] 4[12]
Pb[13] 1266 - Vika
0111[14] OSLO

Key:

[11] Street name; the suffix **-gata** means "street."
[12] Building number. *Use this line for freight and courier deliveries.*
[13] **Pb = Postboks**, meaning "P.O. Box." *Use this line for postal delivery.*
[14] Postcode ending in 1 is for the P.O. Box. *Two spaces must follow the postcode.*

Address Elements

PERSONAL NAMES

Norwegian businesspeople usually write their (only) given name followed by their family name. Translations of "Mr." and "Ms." are not used, but you may see the professional titles **Ing.** (Engineer), **Adv.** (Lawyer), and **Øk.** (Economist). **Siv. Ing.** or **Siv. Øk.** is a more prestigious qualification than "Ing." or "Øk." (A "Siv. Ing." is not a civil engineer as it is understood in English-speaking countries.) All these titles are quite likely to be used by women as well as men.

A married Norwegian woman may keep her own family name, adopt her husband's, or use both. A woman called **Unni Hoff Simonsen** was probably originally Unni Hoff and married a Mr. Simonsen; she should be addressed formally as **Dear Ms. Simonsen** unless you know that she prefers something else.

A foreigner often cannot tell from a Norwegian name whether the person is male or female. If you think you may be dealing with a woman, you have the option to omit the salutation altogether. There is no equivalent of "Dear . . . " in Norwegian-language business correspondence, so the recipient will not think it is odd.

An "attention" line is normally written below the company name.

COMPANY NAMES

Norwegian companies engaging in international business are invariably corporations, designated by the abbreviation **A/S**, usually after the name but sometimes in front of it. There is also a rare legal form for smaller businesses abbreviated **K/S**. There is no way of identifying a publicly traded company by its name.

OFFICES

Office suites are not identified. Shared office buildings (and residential apartment complexes) have boxes for each tenant.

BUILDING NAMES

Building names do not normally appear in addresses.

BUILDING NUMBERS

The building number is written after the street name, without a comma. When a building has been divided, or a lot has been split, the addresses look like **Sandakerveien 50 A**, **Sandakerveien 50 B**, and so on.

STREET NAMES

Street Designator	Abbrev.	Explanation
gate, -gata, -gaten	-gt.	Most common designation for a street
vei, -veien	v., -vn.	Major business streets
plass	pl.	Square
allé, alle, alleen		Major street (tree-lined)

Street words like **gate** and **vei** are usually suffixed to the street name, and often abbreviated:

> Tollbugata 6
>
> Stenersgt. 20
>
> Gladengvn. 14

(The suffixes **-en** and **-et** are just the equivalent of "the" in English.) The street word is written separately when the street is named after a person:

> **Professor Dahls gate 17**
>
> **Niels Hansens vei 2**

In some towns, "vei" is spelled **veg**:

> **Holtermanns veg 15**
>
> **Granåsvegen 41**

If a street has more than one word, apart from "gate" or an equivalent, it is almost certainly named after a person, unless it begins with one of these words:

> **Øvre** (Upper)
>
> **Nedre** (Lower)
>
> **Nordre** (North)
>
> **Søre** (South)
>
> **Østre** (East)
>
> **Vestre** (West)

LOCALITY NAMES

Locality names are not used. All postal addresses consist of two lines: (1) the street or the box, and (2) the postcode and the city. If an address appears to be longer, it probably consists of a mixture of geographical (street) and postal (box) address elements, as in the second example under "Address Summary" above.

CITY NAMES

City names must be written in capital letters. The principal cities of Norway are: **Ålesund, Bergen, Drammen, Kristiansand, Oslo, Stavanger,** and **Trondheim.**

Until 1991, Oslo addresses had to include the postal district number, even though it normally repeated the first two digits of the postcode (e.g., 1273 OSLO 12). This number is no longer required but is still in common use.

The city of Kristiansand is always written **Kristiansand S** (South) to distinguish it from **Kristiansund N** (North), even though they are spelled differently. In a town name like **Lyngdal i Numedal,** "i" means "in," and distinguishes this Lyngdal from another one somewhere else in the country.

STATE/PROVINCE/ETC. NAMES

No regional names are used in postal addresses.

POSTCODES

The postcode is a four-digit number written in front of the city name. The Post Office wants two spaces between the postcode and the city name. A postcode is generally for a post town and the surrounding area, but the seven cities listed above under "City Names" have multiple postcodes for different neighborhoods.

A town of any size has two postcodes, one ending in 0 for street addresses and one ending in 1 for P.O. Boxes.

A few high-volume mailers have their own postcodes.

P.O. BOXES

P.O. Boxes are very common in business use. The Norwegian spelling is **Post-boks**, abbreviated **Pb**, but **P.O. Box** is sometimes written in English.

In Oslo, there are P.O. Boxes in at least a dozen different postal centers, whose names are always added after the P.O. Box number. The names seen most often on business correspondence are **Sentrum** (the central post office), **Rodeløkka**, and **Vika**. The Norwegian Post Office may drop the requirement to write these names in the future.

A box address usually has a different postcode from the street address and occasionally is located in a different town.

The Norwegian Post Office does not want you to write the street address as well as a box address.

COUNTRY NAME

Norway calls itself **Norge**, sometimes spelled **Noreg**. The postcode is often prefixed with the country code **N-**.

Letterheads

Norwegian letterheads often show two addresses: a **Postadresse** for mail (the P.O. Box and its town and postcode), and a **Besøksadresse** (literally, "address for visitors") for deliveries. They may omit the postcode from the delivery address. If the P.O. Box postcode ends in 1, change it to 0 for courier and airfreight labels; otherwise, use it unchanged.

Letterheads and invoices usually show "Postgiro" and "Bankgiro" account numbers for making electronic funds transfers. You may also see **Vår referanse** and **Deres referanse**, or obvious abbreviations, for "Our reference" and "Your reference," respectively.

Dates, Money, Typographical Conventions

DATES AND MONEY	
Date format	Day, Month, Year
Typical date abbreviations	29.02.1992, 29/2/92
Currency unit	krone
Cents	øre
Domestic currency code	Kr
ISO international currency code	NOK
Other international codes	NKR
Decimal separator	comma
Thousands separator	space or period
Typical currency amount	Kr5 879,50 (note no space after Kr)

Envelopes

MESSAGES FOR THE MAILROOM	
English	**Norwegian**
Urgent	Haster
Please forward	Vennligst videresend
Confidential	Privat
Please do not bend	Må ikke brettes!
Fragile	Forsiktig
Care of	(use c/o)

Return addresses are always placed in the top left-hand corner of the envelope.

Phone Numbers

PHONE SYSTEM INFORMATION (SEE CHAPTER 4)	
Country Code	+47
International Access Code	095
Long-Distance Access Code	0
Typical City Codes	none (see text)
Typical number formats	67 14 56 90
Ringing and busy signals	European

Norway abolished city codes during the year 1993, changing to a national eight-digit system. High numbers are in the north. Before then, all numbers dialed from outside the country had seven digits (after the country code) and looked like: 02-19 78 19 or (055) 1 11 57.

Numbers beginning **80** (formerly 050) are toll-free. Numbers beginning **82** (formerly 020) are extra-cost information services, like U.S. 900 numbers. Numbers beginning with **9** (formerly a variety of prefixes) are mobile telephones or pagers, or belong to the phone company.

THE PHILIPPINES

Address Summary

Example of a postal address in a business area of the Manila conurbation:

Mr. Mañuel[1] N.[2] Santiago[3]
International Publishing[4] Inc.[5]
Roxas Building[6]
145[7] Recoletos[8] St.,[9] Urdaneta,[10] Makati[11]
1225[12] METRO MANILA[13]

Key:

[1] Given name.
[2] Initial of mother's family name.
[3] Family name.
[4] Company name.
[5] **Inc. = Incorporated**, signifying a corporation.
[6] Building name.
[7] Building number.
[8] Street name.
[9] **St. = Street**, the usual word.
[10] District name.
[11] City name.
[12] Postcode (of the district).
[13] Equivalent of a province name.

Example of a postal address in central Manila:

Mrs. Lydia[14] Fajardo[15]-Galvez[16]
International Publishing Inc.
1650 Taft Avenue,[17] Malate[18]
1004[19] MANILA[20]

Key:

[14] Given name.
[15] (Father's) family name.
[16] (Husband's) family name.
[17] **Avenue** indicates a major business street.
[18] District name.
[19] Postcode (of the district).
[20] City name.

Example of a provincial postal address:

> **Mr. Ernesto D. Macapagal**
> **International Publishing Inc.**
> **220 Rizal Blvd.,[21] Lanang,[22] Davao[23] City[24]**
> **8000[25] DAVAO DEL SUR[26]**

Key:

[21] **Boulevard** indicates a major business street.
[22] District name.
[23] City name.
[24] **City** is usually added when the province name is similar.
[25] Postcode (of the city).
[26] Province name (often omitted).

Language

English is the language of international business in the Philippines. Most public notices and printed material are in English, and Filipinos in responsible positions will have been educated in English since grade school. The "national language" of the Philippines is officially Filipino, also spelled Pilipino. In practice, Filipino is synonymous with Tagalog (pronounced T'*gah*-log), the language of the Manila region, which is the most widely understood indigenous Philippine language.

Address Elements

PERSONAL NAMES

Outside the ethnic Chinese minority, almost all personal names in the Philippines appear Spanish. A few family names, such as **Katigbak**, **Macalinao**, **Macapagal**, **Manalang**, **Manansala**, **Masangkay**, and **Panglinan**, are Tagalog in origin. Younger Filipinos are more likely to have American given names. Double names (such as **Mary Grace** and **Dianne Karen**) are currently fashionable, especially for women.

A middle initial normally represents the family name of the person's mother, and should not be omitted in an address or a list of names.

The abbreviation **Jr.** ("Junior") after a name distinguishes a son who has the same names as his father.

Ethnic Chinese Filipinos are about equally likely to have Chinese, Spanish, or American given names: for example, **Kheng Hua Lo**, **Nieves Ong**, **Sally Hung**. The last name will be the person's family name.

The use of **Mr.** and **Mrs.** is customary for written or respectful forms of address. **Ms.** may be preferred by younger professional women. Most married women hyphenate their own and their husband's family names: thus, **Miss Isabel Reyes** marries **Mr. Carlos Cruz** and becomes **Mrs. Isabel Reyes-Cruz** in full, or **Mrs. Cruz** for short. Among business people of approximately equal seniority, it is customary to use given names on the first personal contact. Office staff should address executives as Mr. or Mrs. until invited to be less formal.

Nicknames are very common and do not necessarily follow Spanish practice. **Ime**, **Jo**, **Eloy**, **Lulu**, and **Lito** are common nicknames for **Imelda**, **Juliet**,

Eloisa, **Lourdes**, and **Rizalito**. Nicknames such as **Baby** (female) or **Bong** (male) should not be assumed by foreigners to be childish or reserved for family. The full given name should be used in writing, except in friendly salutations. For example, if a man called **Rolando** signs himself **Randy**, you should address a letter or fax to the attention of **Mr. Rolando G. Castillo**, but you can begin it **Dear Randy**.

The title **Atty.** (Attorney) is used by lawyers (e.g., **Atty. Oscar R. Mendoza**) of both genders. University degrees are not used by businesspeople. **Dr.** (**Dra.** in the case of a woman) would imply that the person is a researcher or academic consultant.

COMPANY NAMES

All companies, public or private, are designated **Inc.** or **Corp.**

OFFICES

Floor numbers are occasionally added to a building name, but otherwise internal office addresses are not necessary. **G/Flr** means "ground floor" (street level).

BUILDING NAMES

High-rise buildings in developed parts of Manila are usually named:

> **Legaspi Towers**
> **Don Pablo Building**
> **United Group Building**
> **PLDT Business Center**

BUILDING NUMBERS

All buildings in urban areas are numbered. The number precedes the street name. A lot number—e.g. **Lot No. 152-B-1**—may be substituted for a building number, or provided for additional precision, in an industrial area.

In rural areas, a distance in kilometers is occasionally used instead of a building number, as in **Km. 14 South Superhighway**.

STREET NAMES

Most street names are Spanish, although a few commemorate U.S. personalities. The English word **Street** is used, together with **Avenue** and **Boulevard** for major thoroughfares. An **Alley** is a small street leading off another street in older areas. These are not translations: street signs and maps use the English words.

EDSA is the commonly used abbreviation for **Epifanio de los Santos Avenue**, a major artery in Metro Manila.

Cross-streets are sometimes specified by **corner,** abbreviated **cor.**:

> **Duterte cor. Ilustre Sts.**
> **Queblar St. cor Enriquez St.**

You may drop the name of the cross-street only if you know the building number on the principal street.

LOCALITY NAMES

Major cities are divided into districts. A district is called a **barangay** in Tagalog. A district name is usually written after the street name, on the same line of the address. A district name is informative if the street is a long major artery; for example, **930 Aurora Boulevard, Cubao, Quezon City**.

Some district names in central Manila should be recognized: **Ermita** (the former tourist and entertainment area), **Intramuros** (the historic Spanish colonial center), **Malate** (universities and hospitals), and **Quiapo** (an older business and trading district).

The words **Village** and **Subdivision** imply a modern residential development, such as **Dasmariñas Village**, a well-known prosperous enclave. The word **Project** implies a residential district at the other end of the social scale. In postal addresses, these districts can encompass more than the purely residential area, so a business or institutional address which includes a project or village name is not necessarily being operated out of a residence.

CITY NAMES

The city of **Manila** is surrounded by a number of separately administered cities. Together, these constitute the conurbation **Metro Manila**, frequently abbreviated **M.M.** Of the surrounding cities, **Quezon City** is the country's capital, and **Makati**, **Mandaluyong**, and **Pasay City** are important, modern, rapidly developing business areas, more so than Manila itself. Industrial development is occurring in many parts of South Luzon island around Metro Manila.

The second city of the Philippines is **Cebu City** on the central island of Cebu. The word **City** is sometimes included to distinguish a city from the province of the same or a similar name, such as **Iloilo City** in **Iloilo Province.** The expression "Iloilo proper" in Filipino English would designate the city as opposed to the province.

Except for the city of Manila itself, the city name is commonly written after the street name, and after the district name, if there is one, all on the same line. However, the layout of a postal address is not precisely defined and so practice varies. The name "Manila" is always the last line of an address and is not followed by "M.M." or a province name.

STATE/PROVINCE/ETC. NAMES

The Philippines is divided into almost 80 provinces. The provinces of the rapidly industrializing area surrounding Manila are called **Batangas**, **Bulacan**, **Cavite**, **Laguna**, **Pampanga**, and **Rizal**. The island of **Cebu** is also a province and the sugar-producing island of Negros is divided into eastern and western provinces, **Negros Oriental** and **Negros Occidental**.

Outside the city of Manila, the province is supposed to be the last line of the postal address. This is widely disregarded. A district, city, and province name are often run together:

> **Dolores, San Fernando, Pampanga**
> **Pamplona, Las Piñas, M.M.**

The province name is omitted if there is felt to be no ambiguity, as in **Carmen, Cagayan de Oro City.**

POSTCODES

There is a four-digit postcode, which is called a **ZIP Code**. The Philippine Postal Corporation wants it written in front of the province name, on the last line of the address, as in the examples at the beginning of the chapter. However, this requirement is widely disregarded. If the postcode is included at all on business stationery, it is just as likely to be written "**1600 Pasig, Metro Manila**," "**Pasig 1600**," or "**Pasig, Metro Manila 1600.**"

Postcodes beginning 1 are in Metro Manila, and a given postcode relates roughly to a district. Postcodes beginning 0 are allocated to bulk mailers in Metro Manila. Outside Metro Manila, the first two digits of the postcode represent the province, and the second two specify the city or town. Provincial postcodes are allocated in very approximate sequence from north to south.

P.O. BOXES

P.O. Boxes are used by businesses. The English expression **P.O. Box** is always used, and the box number is usually followed by the name of the post office where it is located; for example, **P.O. Box 1526, Ortigas Center**. Each group of boxes in Metro Manila has its own postcode, which will always be different from the postcode of the street address of the boxholder.

COUNTRY NAME

The full name of the country is **Republika ng Pilipinas**, or, in English, "Republic of the Philippines." The abbreviation (**Phils.**) is sometimes used in the names of subsidiary companies of foreign parents; for example, **International Publishing (Phils.) Inc.**

Letterheads

Letterheads and business stationery are printed in English. A **TIN** is a Tax Identification Number, and **VAT** is a Valued-Added Tax registration number.

Dates, Money, Typographical Conventions

DATES AND MONEY	
Date format	Month, Day, Year (see text)
Typical date abbreviation	12/25/95
Currency unit	piso (see text)
Cents	sentimos (see text)
Domestic currency codes	P
ISO international currency code	PHP
Other international codes	none
Decimal separator	period
Thousands separator	comma
Typical currency amount	P 1,350.50 (note space after P)

The names of the currency units are usually translated as **pesos** and **centavos** in international dealings, even with English-speaking countries.

The sequence month–day–year is usually used by individuals, but business equipment and computer software of non-American origin may print the sequence day–month–year.

Envelopes

International layout standards apply: left, right, and bottom margins of 15mm (0.6″) and a top margin of 40mm (1.6″).

Return addresses are supposed to be written in the top left corner, but are sometimes found on the flap.

Phone Numbers

PHONE SYSTEM INFORMATION (SEE CHAPTER 4)	
Country Code	+63
International Access Code	00
Long-Distance Access Code	0
Typical City Codes	2 = Metro Manila, 32 = Cebu City Longer in rural areas
Standard number formats	Local numbers are five, six, or seven digits 711-7863 or 711-78-63 (08521) 77-16-90
Ringing and busy signals	North American

A number without a city code can be assumed to be in Metro Manila.

Prefixes such as (125), (141), (150), and (155) are used to access pagers.

Businesses frequently have a series of consecutive numbers. You cannot assume that calls roll over automatically. If you get a busy signal, dial another number in the series. The word **local** means "extension."

The Philippine phone system, at least in business areas, is now reasonably reliable. Frequent power failures in the past gave it a bad reputation among foreigners which is no longer justified.

Metro Manila phone numbers are being changed gradually from six to seven digits, and there is no easy correlation between the old and the new. If you cannot reach a six-digit number, you must inquire.

It is common to see Metro Manila fax numbers written in the form (632) 436-4348 as though 632 was an area code, even when a different convention is used for the voice line. What is meant is clearly +63-2-436-4348.

POLAND

Address Summary

Example of a postal address:

Krzysztof[1] Kowalski[2]
Wydawnictwo Międzynarodowe[3] S. A.[4]
ul.[5] Chałubinskiego[6] 12[7]
00-613[8] WARSZAWA[9]

Key:

[1] Given name.
[2] Family name.
[3] Company name.
[4] **S.A.** = **Spółka Akcyjna**, indicating a (larger) corporation.
[5] **ul.** = **ulica**, the standard word for "street."
[6] Street name.
[7] Building number.
[8] Five-digit postcode *(required);* a dash must follow the second digit;
   sometimes preceded by the country prefix **PL-**.
[9] Name of the city or post office.

Address Elements

PERSONAL NAMES

Poles usually write a single given name followed by their family name. However, it is currently fashionable to add the initial of a second given name, if the person has one. Given names are only used among family and close friends.

Women's given names generally end in -a, and men's generally do not. Women's family names often have characteristic endings, following two different rules of Polish grammar. The common ending -ski is masculine, and -ska is the corresponding feminine form. Thus, the wife and daughters of **Janusz Malinowski** will be called **Malinowska**. Other family names do not change in the same way. For example, **Halina**, the wife of **Mieczysław Nowak** will usually be called **Halina Nowak**. However, depending on the social situation, she may emphasize her position as a spouse by calling herself **Halina Nowakowa**. She might very well call herself Nowak at work and Nowakowa in her private life. Much more rarely, their daughter might call herself **Zofia Nowakówna** to emphasize that she is the daughter of a Mr. Nowak. The endings -owa and -ówna can be added to any family name other than those already ending in -ski and -ska; for example, **Urbanowicz** becomes **Urbanowiczowa** or **Urbanowiczówna**.

Pan and **Pani** are not given names but rather translations of "Mr." and "Mrs." **Panna**, the equivalent of "Miss," is rarely used in modern Poland, so it is advisable to call all Polish women **Ms.** in English.

These comments refer to Polish names as they would be written after a signature or on a list of employees. In continuous prose or speech, name endings can vary according to a number of grammatical rules.

Businesspeople sometimes use the academic titles **Dr.** (**Doktór**), **Mgr.** (**Magister**), and **Inż.** (**Inżynier**), which should be retained.

COMPANY NAMES

Poland has adopted the two-level corporate structure of Western Europe. Companies are identified by the abbreviations **S.A.** (**Spółka Akcyjna**) and **Sp. z o. o.** (**Spółka z ograniczoną odpowiednialnością**). The former is the "larger" type of European corporation, and the latter is the "smaller," although you cannot read too much into the distinction.

OFFICES

It is rare to see a room number or office number in a Polish address; however, **ul. Wilcza 25/2** would probably imply office no. 2 at 25 Wilcza Street. The abbreviation **m.** (**mieszkanie**) means "apartment," and is commonly used in residential addresses; for example, **ul. Lazurowa 125 m. 35**. The word **apartament** in a business address would imply a suite of offices with several rooms. The abbreviation **kl.** (**klatka**) is occasionally used to designate an entrance or a staircase. **Pokój,** (abbreviated **pok.**) means "room" or "office," **piętro** (abbreviated **p.**) means "floor," **parter** means "street level," and a **pawillon** (abbreviated **paw.**) is a small building or warehouse unit.

BUILDING NAMES

Buildings are not normally named.

BUILDING NUMBERS

The building number follows the street name, without an intervening comma. A suffixed letter, as in **17b** or **17B**, distinguishes between multiple entrances to a building. Consecutive numbers, as in **ul. Rakowiecka 35/37**, mean that buildings have been combined (these are rather common).

STREET NAMES

The most common equivalent of the word "street" is **ulica**. Its abbreviation, **ul.**, is always included in a postal address, without an initial capital, but it is often omitted in directories or lists of addresses. A street is understood to be an "ulica" unless otherwise specified. The only common alternative is **Aleja** (abbreviated **Al.**), which indicates a major business street (for example, **Al. Jerozolimskie 101**). The word **Plac** (abbreviated **Pl.**) means "square." Other designators exist but are rarely used.

Street names often end in -ego, expressing the Polish genitive. Thus, **ul. Tadeusza Kotarbińskiego** means "the street of (Mr.) Tadeusz Kotarbinski," and you would find it listed under the letter K in a street directory.

Streets are sometimes named after saints (for example, **ul. św. Barbary** is "Saint Barbara Street") or after royal personages from the past (**Króla Artura,**

"King Arthur," **Królowej Aldony**, "Queen Aldona," **Księcia Janusza**, "Prince Janusz," **Księżnej Anny**, "Princess Anna").

LOCALITIES

The name of a village may be necessary in an address when one delivery post office serves several villages. Locality names are rare in business addresses.

CITY NAMES

The Polish Post Office requires city names to be spelled in Polish in postal addresses. Polish cities almost all have alternative names in German or other languages.

Poland's principal business cities are:

Bydgoszcz	**Łódź**
Gdańsk	**Poznań**
Gdynia	**Szczecin**
Katowice	**Warszawa (Warsaw)**
Kraków	**Wrocław**
Lublin	

Warszawa is frequently abbreviated **W-wa**, but this abbreviation is not allowed in postal addresses. In a list of branch offices you may well see **w Warszawie**, which just means "in Warsaw."

In advertisements and brochures, the name of the city sometimes precedes the name of the street. In the past, addresses in Germany and all over Central Europe were written in this sequence, and the habit still lingers.

STATE/PROVINCE/ETC. NAMES

An administrative subdivision of Poland is called a **województwo** (abbreviated **woj.**), approximating to a county in an American state. Poles invent the English word "voivodeship" and equivalents in other European languages (such as "voïvodie" in French). Most of these regions have the same name as their principal town. The names are rarely used in postal addresses, but lists of companies and customers are often sorted by "voivodeship."

POSTCODES

Polish postcodes have five digits and precede the name of the city or delivery post office. There must always be a dash between the second and third digits. The Polish Post Office has allocated postcodes approximately clockwise around the country, starting from 00- in Warsaw.

P.O. BOXES

P.O. Box addresses are not widely used. There are two kinds of box. The more usual is called a **skrytka pocztowa**, which may be written out in full or abbreviated in various nonstandard ways, as in **skr. poczt. 35**. The other kind of box is called a **przegródka pocztowa**; "przegródka pocztowa 35" would simply be written **P-35**.

Box addresses have different postcodes from street addresses.

COUNTRY NAME

The full name of Poland is **Polska Rzeczpospolita** ("the Polish Republic"). The term "Polska Rzeczpospolita Ludowa" described the former Communist regime and is obsolete. The single word **Polska** appears on stamps and postage-meter impressions. The country code **PL-** is sometimes added in front of the postcode.

Letterheads

Here are a few Polish phrases commonly seen on company letterheads:

Polish	English
Panskie Wasze referencje	Your reference
Nasze referencje	Our reference
Data	Date
Osoba do skontaktownia	Person to contact
Numer konta bankowego	Bank account no.
Numer konta pocztowego	Postal checking account no.

Dates, Money, Typographical Conventions

DATES AND MONEY	
Date format	Day, Month, Year
	Year, Month, Day also used
Typical date abbreviation	29.2.1996
Currency unit	złoty
Cents	groszy
Domestic currency codes	zł.
ISO international currency code	PLN
Other international codes	none
Decimal separator	comma
Thousands separator	period
Typical currency amount	112,55 zł.

The currency name is often spelled "zloty" rather than "złoty" in international dealings. In Polish handwriting, the letter ł often appears like an l with an acute accent, and the letter Ż looks like Ƶ.

Envelopes

International regulations require a top margin of 40mm (1.6″) and other margins of 15mm (0.6″). The return address is expected to be written on the flap, but the top left corner of the address side is accepted.

MESSAGES FOR THE MAILROOM	
English	**Polish**
Urgent	Pilny
Please forward	Proszę przesłać dalej
Confidential	Poufny
Please do not bend	Nie zginać
Fragile	Ostroźnie
Care of...	(use c/o)

Phone Numbers

PHONE SYSTEM INFORMATION (SEE CHAPTER 4)	
Country Code	+48
International Access Code	00
Long-Distance Access Code	0 or 8
City Codes	two-digit (e.g. 91 = Szczecin) except 3 = Katowice longer for small towns and rural areas
Typical number formats	(0-41) 431-35 (852) 26-05-57 (02) 633-96-77
Ringing and busy signals	European

The abbreviation **w.** or **wew.** indicates an internal extension.

There are two national systems for long-distance calls; depending on which system is being used, you must remove either an initial 0 or an initial 8. A dash is often written after the 0, because inside Poland you should hear a second dial tone after dialing it. Polish business literature sometimes provides misleading phone prefixes, in the mistaken belief that other countries' systems are similar to Poland's. A number given as (0-04822) 624-69-04, for example, should be dialed as **+48-22-624-69-04**.

The city code for Warsaw is now always **22**. (There has been confusion in the past about when to use 2 and when 22.)

The prefix **90** is used by mobile telephones.

PORTUGAL

Address Summary

Example of a street address with P.O. Box included:

Exmo.[1] **Senhor**[2]
Luis[3] **Martins Rodrigues**[4]
Internacional Edição S.A.[5]
Rua[6] **de S. Bento,**[7] **39**[8] **- 4.º**[9] **B**[10]
Apartado[11] **2574**
1114[12] **LISBOA**[13] **CODEX**[14]

Key:

[1] Honorific.
[2] **Senhor** means "Mr."; not usually abbreviated.
[3] First given name.
[4] Family names; probably addressed as **Mr. Rodrigues**.
 (In domestic usage these two lines are more likely to be written
 as a single "attention" line under the following line.)
[5] **S.A.** = **Sociedade Anônima**, meaning a corporation, probably publicly
 traded.
[6] **Rua** is the most common word for "street."
[7] Street name.
[8] Building number.
[9] Fourth floor.
[10] Office **B**. *Use this line, not the following line, for freight and courier
 deliveries.*
[11] **Apartado** means "P.O. Box." *Use this line for postal delivery,
 not the line above.*
[12] Four-digit postcode (*essential*).
[13] City name.
[14] **CODEX** means the postcode relates to the P.O. Box.

Address Elements

PERSONAL NAMES

Portuguese businesspeople usually give their first given name followed by one
or two family names. **Mr. Luis Martins Rodrigues** is the son of Mr. Rodrigues,
who married Miss Martins. It is safe to address him as **Mr. Rodrigues**, but an
individual may prefer to be called **Mr. Martins Rodrigues**. Women's names are
constructed in the same way.

Family names are sometimes connected with the words **e** ("and") or **de** or

do ("of"), not capitalized. These are just connectives and do not usually indicate any claim to social status. You don't use them in a salutation: **José Correia de Oliveira** would be addressed as **Mr. Oliveira** in English until you found out he preferred something different.

Portuguese people may have additional names that are used for formal, legal purposes, but they are not usually visible in business dealings.

"Mr.," "Mrs.," and "Miss" are **Senhor, Senhora**, and **Senhorita** in Portuguese. The abbreviations are **Sr., Sra.**, and **Srta.** but are not often used. The titles **Dr.** (Doctor), **Eng.** (Engineer), and **Arq.** (Architect) are seen in business. Women in business are now usually addressed as "**Senhora**," regardless of marital status. The honorific **Exmo.** is commonly used in front of "Senhor," and **Exma.** in front of "Senhora."

Many women's names end in **-a**, but a foreigner cannot tell reliably whether a name belongs to a man or a woman. Compound given names are rather common in Portugal, especially for women. **Maria do Céu, Maria de Fatima, Maria Rosa**, etc., are complete compound names, and it is inaccurate and somewhat impolite to abbreviate them to "Maria" as foreigners often do.

The letters **A/c** stand for **Ao cuidado**, meaning "Attn.:". An individual's name is usually written as an attention line underneath the company name.

COMPANY NAMES

Legal Entities	Abbrev.	Explanation
Sociedade Anônima	S.A.	Larger company, almost certainly publicly traded
Sociedade por quotas de responsabilidade limitada	Lda.	Smaller (private) company

OFFICES

An office in a shared building is usually identified by its floor number and a letter. The internal address follows the building number, separated from it by a dash: for example, **Rua da Bandeira, 35 - 1º D** means Suite D on the first floor. There are many variations, of which the most common are listed below:

Office Designator	Explanation
- 1º D	Suite D on first floor
- 1º sala D	same (rarer)
- 1º D sala 15	Room 15 in a (large) Suite D
- 2º	Addressee occupies entire 2d floor
- 2º andar	same
- 113 8º s/807	Probably a modern building with suites numbered American-style; thus, 8th floor, Suite 807
- r/c E	Suite E at street level
- 3º Esq.	3d floor, on the left
- 3º Dto.	3d floor, on the right
- 3º Fte.	3d floor, at the front
- cv E	Suite E below street level

BUILDING NAMES

Building names are not usually used in postal addresses, though the name of a well-known building may appear in an address to guide visitors. The Portuguese words **Edifício** ("Building") and **Torre** ("Tower") are used.

Plants are often located in planned industrial areas, with names like **Zona Industrial Cruz de Barro**, followed sometimes by position references such as **Sector 7**, **Lote 111**, or **Loja E-8**.

BUILDING NUMBERS

A street number is written after the street name, preceded by a comma, as in **Rua Alexandre Herculano, 39**. Combined buildings are written in the form **Rua 15 de Agosto, 51-55**, and a second entrance to a building is indicated by a letter, as in **Rua Infante de Sagres, 29A**.

STREET NAMES

Street Designator	Abbrev.	Explanation
Rua	R.	Most common designation for a street
Avenida	Av.	Major business street
Estrada	Estr.	Highway
Praça	Pç.	Square
Travessa, Largo, Praceta, Calçada	Tv., Lg., Pt., Cç.	Small streets and squares

The words **de**, **da**, **dos**, and **das** ("of") are common in street names and are not capitalized. Streets are usually named after people (especially religious figures), places, and dates:

> **Rua General José Celestino da Silva**
> **Rua de São Francisco Xavier**
> **Av. João XXIII**
> **Rua do Funchal**
> **Praça 25 de Abril**

Santo and **São** both mean "saint."

LOCALITY NAMES

Village names are required in rural areas, but business addresses are normally expressed in two lines: (1) street and number, followed by (2) postcode and city.

CITY NAMES

City names must be written in capitals. Most international business is done with Lisbon, spelled **Lisboa**, and **Porto**.

STATE/PROVINCE/ETC. NAMES

Regional names are not used in postal addresses.

POSTCODES

The postcode, called the **Código Postal**, is a four-digit number written before the city name. Postcodes are allocated clockwise around the country, starting at 1000 in Lisbon.

Postcodes ending in 0 or 5 are for street addresses:

3000 COIMBRA
3360 PENSACOVA
3365 SÃO PEDRO DE ALVA

which are respectively a regional center, a post town, and a village. Only Lisbon and Porto have multiple postcodes for different parts of town.

The word **CODEX** (Código Excepcional, "Special Code") indicates that the postcode is not a geographical code but one allocated to a high-volume mailer, a group of high-volume mailers, or a group of P.O. Boxes. A CODEX code always resembles the corresponding geographic code, but does not end in 0 or 5.

P.O. BOXES

P.O. Boxes are used by businesses. The Portuguese term is **Apartado**, abbreviated **Apart.** Except in small towns, box addresses have CODEX postcodes.

COUNTRY NAME

The short name of the country is **Portugal**, which is used on postage stamps. The postcode prefix **P-** is rarely used.

Letterheads

There is no standard layout or convention. The word **Escritórios** may introduce a P.O. Box address, and **Armazéns** may introduce the delivery (street) address.

Dates, Money, Typographical Conventions

DATES AND MONEY	
Date format	Day, Month, Year
Typical date abbreviation	29/2/92
Currency unit	escudo
Cents	not used
Domestic currency code	$
ISO international currency code	PTE
Other international code	ESC
Decimal separator	comma
Thousands separator	space
Typical currency amount	2 235 $ (note one space before the $)

Envelopes

You are supposed to leave a top margin of 40mm (1.6″) and side and bottom margins of 20mm (0.8″). Return addresses are always written in the top left corner of the envelope.

MESSAGES FOR THE MAILROOM	
English	**Portuguese**
Urgent	Urgente
Please forward	Por favor, remete (see text)
Confidential	Confidencial
Please do not bend	Por favor, não dobrar
Fragile	Frágil
Care of	Aos cuidados de (abbreviated C/do) (see text)

We have forced a translation of "please forward" and "c/o" where the Portuguese would probably just use an "attention" line (**a/c**).

Phone Numbers

PHONE SYSTEM INFORMATION (SEE CHAPTER 4)	
Country Code	+351
International Access Code	00
Long-Distance Access Code	0
Typical City Codes	one-digit (only 1 = Lisbon area, 2 = Porto) two-digit (all other areas)
Typical number formats	(01) 244 3619 (034) 31 20 45 (041) 2 29 28
Ringing and busy signals	European

A local number written in the form **2 68 96/7/8** means there are three lines: 26896, 26897, 26898.

RUSSIA

Address Summary

Example of a postal address:

> **Natalya[1] Konstantinova[2]**
> **Mezhdunarodnoye Izdatel'stvo[3] TOO[4]**
> **Ulitsa[5] Plekhanova[6] 6[7]**
> **MOSCOW[8] 115201[9]**

Key:

[1] Given name (female).
[2] Family name (female).
[3] Company name.
[4] **TOO = Tovarishchestvo s Ogranichennoy Otvetstvennost'yu**, signifying a (smaller) corporation.
[5] **Ulitsa** is the most common word for "street."
[6] Street name.
[7] Building number.
[8] City name.
[9] Six-digit postcode.

Language

The Russian language is written in the Cyrillic alphabet, which resembles Greek. Different people may transliterate the same Russian word differently into the Roman alphabet; for example, "Dmitrii Charlamow" and "Dmitry Tcharlamov" are two different ways of transliterating the same Russian name. A system of transliteration for English-speaking people approved by the Library of Congress is used in this chapter. Transliterations in other countries will vary to suit local pronunciation. See the section on "Postcodes" for more information about Cyrillic-alphabet addresses.

Address Elements

PERSONAL NAMES

Many Russian given names are familiar to foreigners and are not easily confused with family names: **Alexandr, Alexei, Andrei, Dmitry, Igor, Nikolai, Oleg, Petr, Sergei,** and **Vladimir** are common male names. **Anna, Ekaterina, Elena, Galina, Lyudmila, Maria, Marina, Natalya, Olga,** and **Svetlana** are some common female ones. Women's given names almost always end in -a (**Lyubov'** is a common exception) and men's generally do not, except in the case of their nicknames.

There is a nickname corresponding to most Russian given names, and occasionally there is a choice of several. For example, **Vova** is **Vladimir**, **Kostya** is for **Konstantin**, **Pasha** is for **Pavel**. Feminine nicknames are sometimes more familiar in other countries than the full Russian name: **Nadya** is for **Nadezhda**, **Natasha** is for **Natalya**, **Tanya** is for **Tatyana**. Note that most men's nicknames end in -a and most women's in -ya (or -ia). Nicknames are not reserved for family and friends; they are also commonly used among people who work together regularly, depending on the character of the individuals and on the corporate culture. Russians who do not work together regularly, but are of a similar age and status, will call each other by their full given name. Like other European languages, Russian has both familiar and formal ways of saying "you," but it is exceptional in that a Russian may call you by your given name without using the informal "you."

To show more respect—for example, to supervisors or to older people—Russians use both a given name and a patronymic. The patronymic is a second name, which is derived from the person's father's given name. Thus **Sergei Gennadyevich** is **Sergei**, the son of **Gennady**. **Marina Grigoryevna** is **Marina**, the daughter of **Grigory**. The endings -yevich and -yevna unambiguously indicate a man and a woman, respectively. In international correspondence, Russians may well use the first letter of their patronymic to give a more American appearance to their names; for example, **Andrei K. Petrov**.

The use of a family name in speech is relatively rare. Russians will introduce each other formally by a given name and a family name, possibly inserting the patronymic, but there are few social or business situations where the family name would be necessary. It is used in lists of employees and meeting attendees and in an address block on an envelope or in a letter, and it will be typed under a Russian's signature.

Family names are usually derived from given names (**Petrov** is derived from **Petr**, just as Peterson is derived from Peter in English) or from medieval occupations (**Kuznetsov** is Smith) or from physical features (**Gorbachev** comes from the word for "hump"). Women's family names are always grammatically feminine, so the wife or daughter of **Nikolai Tsvetkov** will use the family name **Tsvetkova**. Most feminine names end in -a, but some names, like **Vladimirsky**, have the form of adjectives, and change to **Vladimirskaya**.

Names ending in -o, and especially -enko, such as **Griko** and **Ivchenko**, are of Ukrainian origin, although some of them are quite common in Russia. They do not have a different feminine form, nor do names of Belarussian origin such as **Dzhikovich**.

Most women adopt their husband's family name, although it is not a legal requirement, and on a second marriage it is quite possible that a woman will want to keep a name in common with her children from the first marriage.

There is no commonly used equivalent of "Mr." and "Ms." as a respectful title. **Gospodin** is used as a translation of "Mr." or "sir," and **Gospozha** for "Ms." or "ma'am." There is no distinction in Russian corresponding to "Mrs." and "Miss," and therefore **Ms.** is appropriate in English for all Russian women. **Tovarishch** ("Comrade"), the universal form of address in Communist days, is no longer used except in jest.

Russian executives may list their degrees on their business cards, but it is not necessary to reproduce them in correspondence. The title **Dr.** is used by some business executives who may have qualifications in economics, finance, or accountancy as well as technical and scientific disciplines. People with **Kandidat** degrees (which results in abbreviations like **K.T.H.**) may use the title "Dr." in English since it is comparable to an American Ph.D. As in most of Western Europe, the **Inzhener** ("engineer") degree is equivalent to an American master's.

COMPANY NAMES

Following the Western European model, there are two types of corporation: the smaller ones are called **Tovarishchestvo s Ogranichennoy Otvetstvennost'yu** (abbreviated **TOO**), and the larger ones are called **Aktsionernoye Obshchectvo** (abbreviated **AO**).

OFFICES

Internal designations of offices are rare. The word **kvartira**, abbreviated **Kv.**, usually refers to a residential apartment. **Komnata** is a general word for "room." Either of these words could be used as a translation of "suite."

Department names are usually necessary for the internal mail systems of large organizations. A large organization, public or private, is usually called an "enterprise" in English, translating the Russian word **predpriyatiye**. A division of an enterprise is called an **otdeleniye**, which is divided into a number of **otdel**s, which are finally divided into **sektor**s.

BUILDING NAMES

Buildings are normally identified by number, not by name. Representative offices of foreign corporations sometimes occupy hotel suites, in which case a line of the address will name the hotel.

Offices and plants, and also residential buildings, are often arranged as a group of parallel buildings which all have the same street address. An individual building in the group is called a **korpus**, abbreviated **k.**, and its number or letter then becomes an essential part of the address, to ensure delivery of freight and correspondence.

BUILDING NUMBERS

Buildings are invariably numbered, and the number follows the street name.

STREET NAMES

The most common word for "street" is **Ulitsa** (abbreviated **Ul.**). Rarer alternatives for average streets are **Alleya** (abbreviated **Al.**) and **Val**. A **Prospekt** is a wide avenue, probably with a median. The French words "Boulevard" and "Chaussée" are also used for major thoroughfares: if transliterated from the Russian, they are spelled **Bulvar** (abbreviated **B-r.**) and **Shosse** (**Sh.**) respectively. A street called a **Naberezhnaya** (**Nab.**) would run alongside a river or lake. A square is a **Ploshchad** (**Pl.**). Smaller streets are called **Pereulok** (**Per.**) or **Proyezd** (**Pr.**). A **Tupik** (**Tup.**) is a dead end.

When a street is named after a historical personage, which is common, the name that follows "ulitsa" or its equivalent is grammatically genitive. Thus, **Prospekt Yuriya Gagarina** is "Yuri Gagarin Boulevard" ("Boulevard of Yuri Gagarin"), and **Ulitsa Professora Popova** is "Professor Popov Street." These are not to be confused with feminine endings. An example of a street named after a woman is **Ulitsa Sof'i Perovskoi**.

Streets may also be named after cities and other places. These names have the form of adjectives, and precede "Ulitsa" or its equivalent:

> **Minskoye Shosse** (Minsk Highway)
> **Sofiyskaya Ulitsa** (Sofia Street)

Streets may also be named after important historical dates or references:

> **Ulitsa 1905 Goda** (Street of the Year 1905)
> **Ulitsa 26 Bakinskikh Komissarov** (Street of the 26 Commissars from Baku)

Words for "street" are sometimes translated out of a desire to be helpful to foreigners. Do not be surprised to see English, French, or German words in a transliterated address.

In Moscow, street names which had Communist associations have mostly reverted to their prerevolutionary names, and the same process is also occurring elsewhere. Address information from USSR days is therefore unreliable.

LOCALITY NAMES

Locality names are not used in Russian postal addresses. The only additional word that might be seen is **Tsentr** ("center"), used to emphasize a downtown address.

CITY NAMES

By international convention, city names should be written in capital letters. Most international business is done with **Moskva** (Moscow) and **St. Petersburg** (**Leningrad** during the Communist era), but there are many large, heavily industrialized provincial cities in Russia.

Two unnecessary abbreviations sometimes accompany city names. **G. Moskva** just means "City of Moscow." **Moskva K-112** is an example of an older system of postal-district numbering; the "K" number refers to a particular post office and will usually appear as the last three digits of the postcode.

It is useful to recognize the following Russian words in city names and other place-names:

Bolshoy	large
Maly	small
Novy	new
Stary	old
Sredny	middle
Nizhny	lower
Verkhny	upper
Severny	northern
Yuzhny	southern
Vostochny	eastern
Zapadny	western

The endings of these words will vary in different contexts.

STATE/PROVINCE/ETC. NAMES

Russia is currently divided into 89 Autonomous Regions, which are further subdivided into **oblast**s. Although the postcode distinguishes between towns of the same name, people do add the name of the oblast when they feel extra precision is called for, particularly when the town is small.

POSTCODES

A six-digit postcode system is in universal use. The postcode is commonly known as the "index." The system is inherited from the USSR and therefore postcodes in Russia do not duplicate those in the neighboring republics. The postcode is usually written after the city name in a transliterated address, although sometimes it is written ahead of the city name in the Western European manner.

It follows the city name because the entire sequence of the Russian address is being reversed to accommodate to international convention. The proper order of a Cyrillic-alphabet address is:

> line 1: index, followed by city
> line 2: street name, followed by building number
> line 3: apartment or office number
> line 4: company name
> line 5: individual (family name first)
> line 6: "RUSSIA" (for the benefit of the foreign post office)

Providing a correct Cyrillic address on an envelope will improve its chances of prompt delivery, but it must *be* correct. Do not attempt amateur transliteration. If you are in regular communication with a Russian office, send them some labels and ask for the address to be printed on them, or get a well-printed copy of the Cyrillic address and make a rubber stamp out of it.

P.O. BOXES

P.O. Boxes are not very common and are faintly suspect. There are two types, **Pochtovy Yashchik** (postal boxes) and **Abonentsky Yashchik** (subscriber boxes). The numbers are written immediately after the city name in the Russian sequence (e.g., **117418 MOSKVA P/YA 177**), which you might see retained in catalogs and on business stationery.

COUNTRY NAME

The **Russian Federation**, commonly known simply as **Russia**, is nominally part of the **Commonwealth of Independent States** (**CIS**), the successor to the **Union of Soviet Socialist Republics** (**USSR**). Postage stamps say **Rossiya** in Roman letters. The postal and telephone systems of the former Soviet Union still present a uniform appearance. Postcodes and telephone city codes are the former Union codes.

Letterheads

Larger organizations doing business internationally will have bilingual letterheads and business stationery in English and Russian. English translations are printed on the backs of business cards.

Dates, Money, Typographical Conventions

DATES AND MONEY	
Date format	Day, Month, Year
Typical date abbreviation	25.12.96
Currency unit	ruble
Cents	See text
Domestic currency codes	rub.
ISO international currency code	RUR
Other international codes	none
Decimal separator	comma
Thousands separator	period
Typical currency amount	10.000 rub.

The ruble is nominally divided into 100 **kopek**s. Kopeks may occasionally appear in formal financial documents, but as a practical matter they are too small to be meaningful at the time of writing. Prices are sometimes quoted in U.S. dollars, written in the form **10$**, for future conversion at the prevailing exchange rate.

Envelopes

International layout standards apply: left, right, and bottom margins of 15mm (0.6″) and a top margin of 40mm (1.6″).

You should write return addresses at the top left of the envelope. Russian correspondents may have different preferences, including putting it at the bottom right, which is liable to cause misunderstanding and delay in other countries.

MESSAGES FOR THE MAILROOM	
English	**Russian**
Urgent	СРОЧНО
Fragile	ОСТОРОЖНО, ХРУПКО!
Confidential	ЛИЧНО
Please do not bend	ОСТОРОЖНО, НЕ СГИБАТЬ!
Please forward	ПЕРЕСЛАТЬ АДРЕСАТУ
c/o	X ДЛЯ ПЕРЕДАЧИ Y

Phone Numbers

PHONE SYSTEM INFORMATION (SEE CHAPTER 4)	
Country Code	+7
International Access Code	8~10 (tone after the 8)
Long-Distance Access Code	8
Typical City Codes	three or four digits in cities, longer in rural areas 095 = Moscow 812 = St. Petersburg 381, 3812 = Omsk
Standard number formats	Local numbers in cities are six or seven digits long (095) 229 6536
Ringing and busy signals	European

Domestic phone numbers are always ten digits long, including the city code.

Phone numbers are sometimes quoted confusingly. An initial 7 means they are giving you the country code. An initial 8 or 810 is probably a mistake; they could be assuming that you dial 810 to obtain an international line out of your country. Quite a number of city codes do begin with a 0, which you must dial: Ivanovo (0932), Kaliningrad (01122), Krasnodar (0422), Smolensk (081), Tver (08222).

A three-digit prefix in the 500 series indicates that the phone is connected to one of the several satellite systems. Dial it as +7-501- followed by a seven-digit number. City codes are not used after one of these prefixes, and you cannot tell where the phone is located, although most of them seem to be in Moscow. The prefix (096) is a mobile telephone system; you would dial +7-096-.

The countries of Kazakhstan and Tajikistan are still using the +7 country code inherited from the former USSR. The others have received new country codes, and isolated changes have been made to their city codes. From inside Russia, all the countries of the former USSR, including the Baltics, are dialed as though they were still domestic long-distance calls, so Russians are not always aware of how you should dial the "near abroad" countries from outside the area.

Words of Warning!

Telephone service out of Russia is unreliable, although switching equipment is being modernized. Calls may have to be booked hours in advance. Some organizations have access to the former military telecommunications infrastructure, which is much more reliable. Internet service, where it exists, is more reliable. However, incoming international calls to major urban centers work quite well. It is therefore more courteous and efficient for you to keep calling your Russian trading partners than to leave messages asking them to return your call.

Mail service to and from Russia is slow and subject to both official inspection and delays and unofficial inspection and pilferage. If you can address a letter correctly in the Cyrillic alphabet, it will probably be delivered a bit more quickly. Anything you care about should be sent by air courier; however, even express air services can take five to eight days.

Foreign visitors may be subject to visa requirements and internal travel restrictions. Business travelers may be required to produce invitations from the organization they are visiting as well as confirmation of hotel reservations, and to send their passports to a Russian consulate to obtain travel documents.

Foreigners frequently rearrange Russians' names into bizarre sequences. **Alexander Petrovich Razumov** would be addressed "Dear Mr. Razumov," although you might call him "Alexander Petrovich" on the phone if you knew him a little.

SAUDI ARABIA

Address Summary

Example of a postal address:

Ahmad[1] Faraj[2] Al Ghamdi[3]
International Publishing Ltd.[4]
P.O. Box 4732[5]
RIYADH[6] 11491[7]

Key:

[1] Given name.
[2] Father's name.
[3] Family name.
[4] **Ltd. = Limited**, signifying a corporation.
[5] P.O. Boxes are universally used.
[6] City or delivery-post-office name; *should be capitalized.*
[7] Five-digit postcode.

Language

Arabic is the language of Saudi Arabia, but American English is very widely used in international business. The romanization of Arab names can vary without being incorrect, since the Arabic letters are the only ones that really matter to the Saudis. In particular, Arab names tend to be transliterated differently in French and English sources; for example, the city of Jeddah will be written "Djeddah" by French-speakers.

Address Elements

PERSONAL NAMES

Almost all Saudi Arabians have three names: the first is their given name, the second is their father's given name, and the final one is their family name. There is not necessarily a distinction in the Arabic language between given names and family names. In a name like **Shamsaddin Shokri Khaled**, Khaled is the family name, but in **Khaled Saleh Ramadhan** it is a given name. Equally, there will be people whose family names are Shamsaddin, Shokri, and Saleh. It is possible for people to have repeated names like **Hussein Saad Hussein** or **Mohammed Ismail Mohammed**.

The article **Al** ("the") is commonly part of a family name; thus, **Hamoud Hammad Al Lagany** will be called **Mr. Al Lagany** but will be found under L in an alphabetical list. Until you know an individual's preference, you can address him as "Mr." followed by either his complete name or just his last name.

285

Sheikh or Shaikh is used in Saudi Arabia (usage in other Arab countries is different) as a general respectful term for senior executives and business owners. **Salahaddin Mousa Mohammed** might be referred to as **Sheikh Salahaddin** or, in English, **Mr. Salahaddin** rather than **Mr. Mohammed**. Do not be surprised if they refer to you as, say, "Mr. Eric." Note, however, that it is unacceptable for non-Arabs to use the title "Sheikh" for themselves or each other.

The particle **bin** is the traditional way of expressing "son of," and **bint** means "daughter of." Most women's given names end in -a and few men's names do; however, this does not apply to names beginning with **I**.

COMPANY NAMES

The word **Limited**, abbreviated **Ltd.**, is usually used to designate a corporation.

OFFICES

Internal office designations are not usually given or necessary. (See also the comments under "Street Names.")

BUILDING NAMES

Building names are not used in addresses. (See also the comments under "Street Names.")

BUILDING NUMBERS

Building numbers are written in front of the street name, with or without a comma following. (See also the comments under "Street Names.")

STREET NAMES

It is extremely rare to see street addresses at all in dealings with Saudi Arabia from outside the country. There is no postal delivery to street addresses; all businesses have P.O. Boxes.

The English word **Street** is regularly used; its Arabic equivalent, **Sharia**, is less common. Many major streets are named after religious or royal personalities; for example, **Al-Imam Abdul Aziz Ibn Mohammed Street**. An **Imam** is a religious leader, an **Amir** is a provincial governor, and **Al-Malek** means "King."

A few streets in the Dhahran area are numbered (e.g., **28th Street**).

LOCALITY NAMES

Names of localities are not used in addresses.

CITY NAMES

The three principal business areas are **Riyadh** (the capital), **Jeddah**, and **Dhahran** with its close neighbors, **Dammam** and **Alkhobar** (also known as **Khobar**). **Jubail** and **Yanbu** are showpiece industrial cities.

The religious centers Al-Makkah Al-Mukarramah ("Mecca the Revered") and Al-Medinah Al-Munawarah ("Medina the Radiant"), although large cities, are closed to non-Muslims.

STATE/PROVINCE/ETC. NAMES

Regional names are not used in addresses.

POSTCODES

There is a five-digit postcode system in use. The postcode should be written after the city name in an address.

Riyadh's postcodes begin with 1; Jeddah's with 2; Dhahran's, Dammam's, Alkhobar's, and Jubail's with 3; and Yanbu's with 4.

P.O. BOXES

Use of P.O. Boxes by businesses is universal. The English term is always used.

COUNTRY NAME

The full English name of the country is **Royal Kingdom of Saudi Arabia**, sometimes abbreviated as **KSA**. The U.S. Post Office wants you to write **Saudi Arabia** on envelopes.

Letterheads

Letterheads used for international correspondence are always printed in English.

Dates, Money, Typographical Conventions

DATES AND MONEY	
Date format	Day, Month, Year (see text)
Typical date abbreviation	29/02/92 (see text)
Currency unit	riyal
Cents	hallalah(s)
Domestic currency code	SR, S.R.
ISO international currency code	SAR
Other international codes	none
Decimal separator	period
Thousands separator	comma
Typical currency amount	SR 3,325.50 (note one space after SR)

Saudi Arabia uses the Muslim calendar, and therefore there is always a risk of misunderstanding abbreviated dates. **27/04/93 H** is a date in the Hejira year 1393, not the 1993 of the Western calendar. The Hejira year 1420 begins about April 17, 1999. The Muslim (lunar) year is 11 days shorter than the Western (solar) year.

Envelopes

International rules apply: top margin, 40mm (1.6″); other margins, 15mm (0.6″).

Phone Numbers

PHONE SYSTEM INFORMATION (SEE CHAPTER 4)	
Country Code	+966
International Access Code	00

Long-Distance Access Code	0
Typical City Codes	one-digit (1 = Riyadh)
Typical number formats	(01) 392-0523
Ringing and busy signals	European

The city code is called a **zone code**, since the country is actually divided into six zones. Riyadh's zone code is 1; Jeddah's is 2; Dhahran's, Dammam's, Alkhobar's, and Jubail's are all 3; and Yanbu's is 4.

The prefix **800** is used for toll-free numbers.

Word of Warning!

Businesses in Saudi Arabia are closed on Fridays, and often on Thursday afternoons also. Business hours are shortened (irregularly from business to business) during the month of Ramadan, which lasts 29 or 30 days. Ramadan begins about December 9, 1999, and November 27, 2000; it moves back 11 days per Western year.

Travel arrangements to Saudi Arabia require advance planning. Almost everyone requires a visa, and you cannot just apply cold to an embassy or consulate for it; business travelers have to be sponsored by an individual or organization in Saudi Arabia. Visas are not issued to tourists; except for visitors on religious pilgrimage, the only way around this is to get a Saudi family to be the sponsor.

A woman traveler is subject to a number of legal restrictions in Saudi Arabia, unless she is constantly accompanied by her husband. You should consult your Saudi business partners about the organization of any trips involving female engineers or executives.

SINGAPORE

Address Summary

Example of a street address:

Tan[1] Ming Ho[2]
International Publishing (Pte.)[3] Ltd.[4]
Shing Kwan House[5]
215,[6] Outram[7] Road,[8] #06-09[9]
SINGAPORE[10] 169037[11]

Key:

[1] Family name.
[2] Given names.
[3] (**Pte.**) = **Private**, meaning the corporation is privately owned.
[4] **Ltd.** = **Limited**, signifying a corporation.
[5] Building name.
[6] Building number.
[7] Street name.
[8] Most common word for "street."
[9] Office 9 on the sixth floor.
[10] City.
[11] Six-digit extended postcode.

Language

Although Malay is the national language of Singapore, English is the language of business and government, and over three-quarters of the population is of Chinese origin. In addition to ethnic Malay people, there are also Tamil and other Indian minorities.

Address Elements

PERSONAL NAMES

Chinese names consist of three characters, one of which is the family name and the other two are given names. Any of the thousands of Chinese characters can form part of a name. You cannot say that a particular character is a given name or a family name. In Singapore, the family name is written first, followed by the given names, without hyphens. The second character is usually a name which is common to all the men (and sometimes the women) of one generation in a family. In a few families, the generation name is the third character rather than the second. The traditional system of generation names is still strong in Singapore but is no longer universal.

289

Many Chinese in Singapore, both men and women, have adopted an English-language given name and use it in business dealings. Often, it is an unofficial name and will not be used on formal legal documents. However, some Chinese-speaking Singaporeans are Christians and are baptized with a Western name. A Western name is written first and may or may not be followed by Chinese given names:

Danny Tan
Danny Tan Ming Ho

A Chinese-speaking person may sometimes choose to use British-style initials—for example, **M. H. Tan**.

In Singapore, the ethnic Chinese speak a half-dozen different dialects. They usually transliterate their name according to the phonetics of their family dialect. However, the use of Mandarin Chinese and its Pinyin system of transliteration is officially encouraged. There can therefore be two ways of spelling the same name in Roman letters: **Chua Kok Huat** (dialect phonetics version) and **Cai Guo Fa** (Pinyin version) are the same name. Younger people are somewhat more likely to use Pinyin, so even a father's family name and his children's family name may appear to be different.

Chinese women do not change their name on marriage. A married woman was traditionally addressed as **Madam Tan**, when Tan was her father's family name. **Ms. Tan** is more appropriate for businesswomen now. To Westerners, a married woman may call herself **Mrs. Chan**, using her husband's family name. Businesswomen may hyphenate the two names; **Jennifer Chan-Lee Bee Leng** is Ms. Lee, married to Mr. Chan, known to her family as Leng and to Western colleagues as Jennifer. You should address her as **Mrs. Chan** if you have never met her.

Ethnic Malay people are Muslims with Arabic-style personal names. Use the complete name until you know the individual's preference. **Abdul Ismail** should therefore be addressed as **Mr. Abdul Ismail**, unless you find out he is known as "Mr. Abdul" or "Mr. Ismail."

In business circles, academic titles are unusual, but it is quite common to show degrees after an executive's name on a business card. It is not necessary to copy them.

COMPANY NAMES

Corporations must have the abbreviation **Ltd.** (**Limited**) at the end of their names. (**Pte.**) **Ltd.** means it is a privately owned corporation.

OFFICES

Many companies are located in high-rise buildings. It is usual to give an internal address consisting of the floor and room numbers, usually written in the style **Chin Swee Road, #03-71**, meaning office or room 71 on the third floor. A floor is called a **storey** in Singapore.

BUILDING NAMES

High-rise buildings in Singapore have names, which are usually included in addresses. They end in a variety of British and American terms such as **Building**, **Court**, **Plaza**, **Park**, **Complex**, **Centre**, **Tower**, and **Mansion**.

Plant names end in **Factory** or **Warehouse**, and plants are often located in an **Industrial Estate**.

Building and plant names should be written before the street name, but the sequence is not always observed.

BUILDING NUMBERS

Building numbers are written in front of the street name, usually with a comma following. To identify a large building complex, a **block number** is sometimes used instead of a building number: for example, **Blk. 12 Chai Chee Road, #02-13**.

When an older building is divided for multiple occupation, the second address is written in the style **47A, North Canal Road**. A combined building may appear as **221/222, Victoria Street**.

An address on a long road may include a kilometer distance as a guide, as in **617, Pasir Panjang Road 5 km**.

STREET NAMES

Most streets have either English names such as **Shenton Way** and **Robinson Road**, or transliterated Chinese names such as **Chin Swee Road**. Major streets are usually called **Road**; **Street**, **Avenue**, and **Boulevard** are also used.

Some streets have Malay names, which may use the Malay word **Lorong** (abbreviated **Lor**) or **Jalan**, both meaning "street":

> **Lorong Tukang Tiga**
> **Jalan Bukit Merah**

Toa Payoh Lorong 1 is "First Street" in a neighborhood called Toa Payoh.

LOCALITY NAMES

Names of localities are not used.

CITY NAMES

The only city is **Singapore**, which must be written in capitals.

STATE/PROVINCE/ETC. NAMES

Singapore is not divided into states or provinces.

POSTCODES

There is a new six-digit extended postcode system in use. The postcode, called a *postal code* in Singapore, is written after the city name. Postcodes beginning with 9 are for P.O. Boxes. An inquiry form on the Web, at http://www. singpost.com.sg/pc6d/, will provide the new postcode for any address.

P.O. BOXES

P.O. Boxes are relatively common for businesses. The English term is used. The name of the post office where the box is located is often written first, on the same line:

> **Orchard Point P.O. Box 401**
> **Bedok Central P.O. Box 112**

COUNTRY NAME

The short name of the country is **Singapore**, which appears on postage stamps.

Letterheads

Letterheads are always printed in English.

Dates, Money, Typographical Conventions

DATES AND MONEY	
Date format	Day, Month, Year
Typical date abbreviation	29/2/92
Currency unit	dollar
Cents	cents
Domestic currency code	$
ISO international currency code	SGD
Other international codes	S$
Decimal separator	period
Thousands separator	comma
Typical currency amount	$1,350.50 (note no space after the $)

Envelopes

International margin rules apply: 40mm (1.6″) top margin and 15mm (0.6″) bottom, right, and left margins. The Singapore postal administration wants the return address to be either on the flap of the envelope or in the lower left-hand corner of the address side.

Messages on an envelope should be written in English.

Phone Numbers

PHONE SYSTEM INFORMATION (SEE CHAPTER 4)	
Country Code	+65
International Access Code	005
Long-Distance Access Code	none
Typical City Codes	none
Typical number formats	223 85 65 2238565
Ringing and busy signals	British

Numbers are always seven digits long after the country code.

SLOVENIA

Address Summary

Example of a postal address:

Mr. Janez[1] Mihelič[2]
Mednarodna Založba[3] d. o. o.[4]
Črtomirova[5] 8[6]
61000[7] LJUBLJANA[8]

Key:

[1] Given name.
[2] Family name.
[3] Company name.
[4] **d. o. o. = družba z omejeno odgovornostjo**, signifying a (smaller) corporation.
[5] Street name. The word **ulica**, meaning "street," is omitted.
[6] Building number.
[7] Five-digit postcode *(required)*.
[8] Name of the city or delivery post office.

Another example:

Mrs. Tatjana Debeljak
Mednarodna Založba d. d.[9]
Zaloška cesta[10] 29
61000 LJUBLANA

Key:

[9] **d. d. = delniška družba**, signifying a (larger) corporation.
[10] **c. = cesta**, meaning a larger street, or avenue.

Language

The Slovenian language is distinct from Serbo-Croatian, although there is a good deal of mutual intelligibility. A minority of Slovenes speak Italian as a first language, and names and addresses in coastal areas may have an Italian appearance. In business, Slovenes speak English, French, German, and Italian.

Address Elements

PERSONAL NAMES

Slovenes usually write a single given name, followed by their family name, but the sequence is sometimes reversed. If one name is written in capitals, it is certainly the family name.

People who work together regularly and have approximately the same level of responsibility will call each other by their given names. If there is an age difference, it is up to the older person to initiate a more informal mode of address.

Traditionally, women's given names ended in -a and very few men's names did. However, it has been fashionable for some time to give girls nontraditional names of obvious foreign origin, especially Italian and Spanish, although the spelling may be modified (for example, **Karmen**).

Slovene wives adopt their husbands' family names, but some women continue to write their former name followed by their married name. This is more common in university circles than in business. **Cvetka Babnik Marolt** would be called **Mrs. Marolt** by an English-speaker.

Gospod (abbreviated **g.**), **gospa** (abbreviated **ga.**), and **gospodična** (abbreviated **gdč**) correspond to "Mr.," "Mrs.," and "Miss," respectively. The usage of "gospa" and "gospodična" relates strictly to whether the woman is married or not.

Use of academic titles is widespread in Slovenia, the result of Austrian influence in the past. **Dipl.**, **Ing.**, **Mgr.**, and **Dr.** are the usual titles, in order of increasing length of study. Subjects are often added; thus, **Dr. iur. Zajc** will be an attorney, a "doctor of law." Other subject abbreviations seen in the business world are **oec.** (economics), **ark.** (architecture), **org. d.** (business administration), and **phil.** (philosophy).

The abbreviation **ml.** after a name (e.g., **Slavko Pirc ml.**) indicates that the man is named after his father. The father might add **st.** to his name. This largely rural custom is much less common than the use of "Jr." and "Sr." in the United States.

COMPANY NAMES

Most Slovenian businesses are corporations of the type known as **d. o. o.** (**družba z omejeno odgovornostjo**), which is the "smaller" of the two-tiered Western European types of corporation. A few larger companies are the other type, denoted by **d. d.**, standing for **delniška družba**.

The abbreviation **p.e.**, which can look like a label for another type of incorporation, just stands for **poslovna enota**, "branch."

OFFICES

Offices inside a building are never separately identified in addresses. The word **hala** is occasionally seen and implies a unit number, as in a factory or warehouse complex.

BUILDING NAMES

Buildings do not have names in Slovenia.

BUILDING NUMBERS

The building number follows the street name, without an intervening comma. Numbers are usually simple. Occasionally a letter follows the number to designate a second entrance to a building; for example, **Prešernova 51 a**.

STREET NAMES

The most common equivalent of the word "street" is **ulica**. A major thoroughfare is often called a **cesta** (abbreviated **c.**); **Celovška cesta** means "the route to Klagenfurt." A true "avenue," bordered by trees, is instead called a **drevored**. **Trg** means "square," and **nabrežje** means "quai." Small businesses may be located on a **prehod** ("alley") or a **podhod** (an underground pedestrian area of a type common all over Central Europe).

Street names are often feminine adjectives modifying "ulica," which is understood and not written; thus, **Cigaletova** means "Cigale Street," and **Mariborska** means "Maribor Street." A few street names do require "ulica"; for example, **Ulica Borcev za Severno Mejo**, "the street of the Northern Frontier Veterans."

A very few streets have (Roman) numbers instead of names; thus, **C. II/12** would be "12 2nd Street" in the United States.

LOCALITY NAMES

No locality name is ever necessary between the street name and the city or delivery-post-office name.

CITY NAMES

The principal business cities are **Ljubljana** (the capital), **Maribor**, **Kranj**, and the port of **Koper**. Koper is in the bilingual region and is called **Capodistria** in Italian.

Suburban areas, especially around Ljubljana, are sometimes written joined to the name of the conurbation (e.g., **Lj.-Šentvid**).

Some Slovenian prepositions that occur often in the names of towns are:

na	in
pri	beside
v	at
nad	above, (upper)
ob	on

and you should also recognize the word **vas**, "village."

STATE/PROVINCE/ETC. NAMES

No regional names appear in addresses.

POSTCODES

A five-digit postcode must precede the city name. It is called the **poštna številka**. All Slovenian postcodes start with 6, as the system was established by the former Yugoslav postal authority.

P.O. BOXES

Few businesses use P.O. Boxes. They are called **poštni predal** (abbreviated **p.p.**), which means literally "P.O. Drawer."

COUNTRY NAME

The name of the country is spelled **Slovenija** locally. Slovenia was formerly the northernmost republic of the Yugoslav Federation. It must not be confused with either Slovakia, the eastern part of Czechoslovakia, or Slavonia, a disputed region of the former Yugoslavia held by Croatia at the time of writing.

The Slovene authorities are encouraging the use of the ISO abbreviation **SI** to designate the country in all contexts. You may see it written as a postcode prefix, but it is not officially recognized by other European post offices. Many Slovenes use the abbreviation SLO, which has no official standing anywhere.

Letterheads

Slovenian businesspeople have an extremely international outlook, and there is no expectation that foreigners will understand the Slovenian language. Companies have letterheads printed in English or other Western European languages according to where they feel their markets are.

Dates, Money, Typographical Conventions

DATES AND MONEY	
Date format	Day, Month, Year
Typical date abbreviation	29.02.1996
Currency unit	tolar
Cents	stotin
Domestic currency codes	SIT
ISO international currency code	SIT
Other international codes	none
Decimal separator	comma
Thousands separator	period or space
Typical currency amount	2 500,- SIT

Envelopes

International convention requires a top margin of 40mm (1.6″) and other margins of 15mm (0.6″). The distance between the left side of the envelope and the address block should not exceed 140mm (5.5″). The return address should be in the top left corner but is also acceptable on the flap.

MESSAGES FOR THE MAILROOM	
English	**Slovenian**
Urgent	Nujno
Please forward	Prosim predajte
Confidential	Zaupno
Please do not bend	Prosim ne pregibajte
Fragile	Lomljivo
(Visitor) c/o (employee)	(Employee) za (visitor)

Phone Numbers

PHONE SYSTEM INFORMATION (SEE CHAPTER 4)	
Country Code	+386
International Access Code	00
Long-Distance Access Code	0
City Codes	two-digit, 61-69 (61 = Ljubljana); also 601, 602, 608
Typical number format	061/145-8528
Ringing and busy signals	European

Local numbers usually have five or six digits. After the three-digit city codes, they only have five. Since 1993 many numbers have changed to seven digits in Ljubljana, usually keeping the five last digits of the old number.

The word **interna številka**, abbreviated **int.**, means "extension number."

You might still see references to the former IAC, which was 99 before Slovenia adopted the European standard **00**.

The country code of the former Yugoslavia was +38. Over most of the country, to convert an old phone number you can usually insert a 6; for example, 063/851-609, which was formerly +38-63-851-609, is now **+386-63-851-609**. Unfortunately, this conversion rule may not work in Ljubljana because of other changes to the phone numbers as described above.

All Slovene city codes begin with **6**, because the system is inherited from the former Yugoslavia.

In most cases, the first two digits of the city code of a business will match those of the postcode.

The prefix **0609** is reserved for mobile phones, and the prefix **0800** is for toll-free numbers.

SOUTH AFRICA

Address Summary

Example of an English-language postal address:

> **Mr. Mandla[1] Ntuli[2]**
> **International Publishing (Pty.)[3] Ltd.[4]**
> **Private Bag[5] X2581[6]**
> **JOHANNESBURG[7] 2000[8]**

Key:

[1] Given name.

[2] Family name.

[3] **Pty.** = **Proprietary**; indicates a smaller corporation, probably privately owned.

[4] **Ltd.** = **Limited**, signifying a corporation.

[5] **Private Bag** means a (large) P.O. Box.

[6] Letters as well as numbers are common for boxes.

[7] City or delivery-post-office name.

[8] Four-digit postcode (*required*); can also be written before the city name or on the next line.

Example of a mixed postal and street address, as commonly printed on business stationery:

> **Mr. P. C. Palmer**
> **International Publishing Ltd.[9]**
> **4th floor, Express House[10]**
> **256[11] Market Road[12]**
> **Sandton[13] 2199[14]**
> **P.O. Box[15] 1162**
> **GALLO MANOR[16] 2052[17]**

Key:

[9] **Ltd.** without **(Pty.)** probably indicates a larger publicly traded corporation.

[10] Building name.

[11] Building number.

[12] **Road** and **Street** are equally common.

[13] City or delivery-post-office name for the street address.

298

[14] Postcode for the street address (often omitted). *Use this line and the two above for freight and courier deliveries.*

[15] *Use this line and the next one for postal delivery.*

[16] City or delivery-post-office name for the postal address.

[17] Postcode for the postal address *(required)*.

Example of an Afrikaans-language mixed postal and street address, as commonly printed on business stationery:

Mnr.[18] **W. A. B. R.**[19] **van der Spuy**[20]
Internasionale Publikasies (Edms.)[21] **Bpk.**[22]
Volkskasgebou,[23] **4de Vl.**[24]
Rietspruitstraat[25] **125**[26]
Pretoria[27] **0002**[28]
Posbus[29] **125, Pretoria**[30] **0001**[31]

Key:

[18] **Mnr.** = **Meneer**, meaning "Mr."

[19] Initials for multiple given names.

[20] Three-word family name; no initial capital on **van** and **der**.

[21] **(Edms.)** is equivalent to **(Pty.)**; see first example.

[22] **Bpk.** is equivalent to **Ltd.**; see first example.

[23] **-gebou** means "Building."

[24] **4de Vl.** means "4th floor."

[25] Street name; the suffix **-straat** means "street."

[26] Building number.

[27] City or delivery-post-office name for the street address.

[28] Postcode for the street address.

[29] **Posbus** means "P.O. Box."

[30] City or delivery-post-office name for the postal address.

[31] Postcode for the postal address.

Languages

The official languages of South Africa are Zulu, Xhosa, Afrikaans, Sepedi, English, Tswana, Sesotho, Xitsonga, Siswati, Tschivenda, and Ndebele. Afrikaans resembles Dutch. You cannot be sure from a person's name which his or her first language is. About 60 percent of the white population speaks Afrikaans as a first language, but a high proportion of business executives are English-speaking or bilingual.

Black South Africans speak many languages and dialects, primarily from the Xhosa and Zulu language groups. Any black person in a position of responsibility is likely to have been educated in English from childhood. Afrikaans is the native language of "Coloured" South Africans, a recognized ethnic group consisting of people of mixed descent living mainly in the Cape region. There is also a substantial community of people of Indian origin, living mainly in Natal, who usually speak English as well as Indian languages.

English-language spelling and vocabulary are British with many local idioms.

Address Elements

PERSONAL NAMES

English-speaking people usually follow the British convention of giving you the two initials of their given names followed by their family name.

Afrikaners often have more than two given names (a child is given its own first name and then other given names, usually those of close relatives). Some family names are prefixed with **van**, **van der**, or **de** (all meaning "of"), which are not written with initial capitals:

> de Wet
>
> van Vuuren
>
> van der Merwe

A man whose full name for legal documents is **J.C.M. Viljoen van Drummelin** usually chooses to be **Mr. van Drummelin** in ordinary business dealings. Occasionally you will see a name with two "of" particles: for example, **D. de V. van Rensburg**.

A substantial number of South Africans are of French descent. Names like **le Roux** and **du Plessis** are common. Pronounce them the French way until you are corrected.

Nonwhite people have not occupied positions of responsibility in corporations and government in the past, but a substantial nonwhite middle class of professionals and small-business owners has existed for some time. Black South Africans are expected to play a rapidly increasing part in international business in the future. A black South African may have a British or biblical given name as well as a traditional given name and a family name from his or her own ethnic group. Only a specialist can identify individuals' ethnic backgrounds from their family names. **Dladla, Khumalo, Kunene, Nyembezi,** and **Vilakazi** are Zulu families; **Gama, Khosa, Mabuza, Mriba,** and **Tamsanqua** are Xhosa names; **Lekeba, Lentsoane, Maphike, Matlosa,** and **Ntsane** are from the Sotho group; and so on. Traditional given names are no longer strongly associated with language groups. **Jabu, Khela, Mohale,** and **Zuko** are common male names, and **Funeka, Leleti,** and **Lulama** are common female names.

South Africans usually address strangers in writing as **Mr.** or **Mrs.** The Afrikaans equivalents are **Meneer** (abbreviated **Mnr.**) and **Mevrou** (abbreviated **Mev.**). Avoid "Miss" and its Afrikaans equivalent, "Mejuffrou" (abbreviated "Mej."). Business is becoming less formal, and the use of given names is increasing.

Academic degrees or titles are not common in business, but if anyone does use **Dr.**, make sure you use it too.

COMPANY NAMES

The name of a corporation must include the abbreviation **Ltd.** ("Limited"), or the Afrikaans equivalent **Bpk.** Many companies have **(Pty.) Ltd.**, or the Afrikaans equivalent **(Edms.) Bpk.** This "Proprietary Limited" form is usually a smaller company and is always privately owned. However, it could also be a wholly owned subsidiary of a public company. A name with "Ltd." alone can be either privately owned or publicly traded, but is likely to be public or to be set up with the intention of going public.

There is also a relatively new and rare form of incorporation for smaller companies known as a **Close Corporation**, abbreviated **C.C.**

OFFICES

Offices in a shared building are usually identified by **floor**. In Afrikaans, the words **vloer** and **verdieping** are both used for "floor." Afrikaans abbreviations like **1ste Vdp** ("1st floor") are common.

BUILDING NAMES

Major buildings have names, which are included in letterhead addresses. Buildings are called **Building** or **House** in English, **Gebou** or **Huis** in Afrikaans.

BUILDING NUMBERS

The building number precedes the street name in English-language addresses and follows it in Afrikaans addresses. Commas are not usually written.

An entrance between **76 Broadway** and **78 Broadway** will be called **76a Broadway**.

STREET NAMES

Street designator (English/Afrikaans)	Abbrev. (Eng./Afr.)	Explanation
Road, Street/ -weg, -straat	Rd., St./ -weg, -str.	Most common designations for a street
Avenue, Drive/ -laan	Ave., Dr./-ln.	Major business streets

South African street names themselves are not usually translated from one language to the other, because they are usually named after people and places, but a generic name like **Main Street** or **Church Street** will be translated (to **Hoofweg** and **Kerkstraat**) in an Afrikaans version of the address.

A few streets have numbers instead of names; these are written with a hyphen to avoid confusion:

> **251-4th St.**
> **25-14th St.**

If you are given an address in both languages on a letterhead or in a directory, there is no point in copying both versions.

LOCALITY NAMES

Locality names, such as the name of a suburb, are not required by the Post Office, provided that you have the postcode correct. However, they do help courier deliveries. Many streets in Johannesburg, for example, run through a number of suburbs with different postcodes, so it helps to distinguish between Livonia Road, Sandown, and Livonia Road, Sandton.

Some areas have names qualified by the word **extension** or **uitbreiding** or an abbreviation:

> **Sunderland Ridge Ext. 2**
> **Sunderlandrif uitbr. 2**

The extensions here are successive additions to the original Sunderland Ridge area. The extension number must be included in a delivery address.

CITY NAMES

City names are not always written in capital letters in South African domestic mail.

Principal business cities are listed under "P.O. Boxes" below.

South Africa differs from other bilingual countries in this book in that it is not possible to say which city speaks which language. **Bloemfontein** is predominantly Afrikaans-speaking, but the other major cities are completely bilingual.

Cape Town is the only place you are likely to encounter that has a significantly different name in Afrikaans (**Kaapstad**). Usually, differences are caused by the words **noord**, **suid**, **oos**, **wes** (north, south, east, west). Otherwise, it is usually obvious that, for example, **Camps Bay** and **Kampsbaai** are the same place.

STATE/PROVINCE/ETC. NAMES

There are nine provinces in South Africa. Their names are not used in postal addresses, but you should recognize them in company names or organization charts:

Eastern Cape	**Free State (formerly Orange Free State)**
Gauteng	**KwaZulu-Natal**
Mpumalanga	**Northern**
Northern Cape	**North-West**
Western Cape	

POSTCODES

A four-digit postcode is used. Postcodes are allocated roughly clockwise around the country, starting with 0001 in Pretoria, the administrative capital.

South African Post Office regulations say the postcode can be written in front of the city name or alone on the next line. However, South Africans usually write the postcode after the city name, often on the same line.

The South African Post Office wants incoming mail to look like this:

> **Springs**
> **1560 Republic of South Africa**

or

> **Springs**
> **Republic of South Africa**
> **1560**

These styles may contravene other countries' regulations for outgoing mail. Follow the regulations of the country of mailing; if in doubt, imitate the examples at the beginning of the chapter.

P.O. BOXES

P.O. Boxes are almost universally used by businesses. Terms in use are **P.O. Box**, **Private Box**, and **Private Bag**, written **Posbus**, **Privaatbus**, and **Privaat-**

sak, respectively, in Afrikaans. Boxes are often identified by a mixture of letters and numbers. They have their own postcodes in the larger cities.

City	Postcode for Boxes	Postcode for Streets
Bloemfontein	9300	9301
Cape Town/Kaapstad	8000	8001
Durban	4000	4001
Germiston	1400	1401
Johannesburg	2000–2199 except:	2001, 2090–99, 2190–99
Port Elizabeth	6000	6001
Pretoria	0001–0199 except:	0002, 0080–89, 0180–89
Springs	1560	1559

This information is provided to help you to disentangle postal addresses from delivery addresses on confusing letterheads.

COUNTRY NAME

The short name of the country is **South Africa** in English and **Suid-Afrika** in Afrikaans. Postage stamps say **RSA** (i.e., Republic of South Africa). The term "Union of South Africa" is obsolete and must never be used.

Letterheads

Letterheads must list the company's registration number, but there are no other letterhead requirements. Postal addresses are frequently mixed in with delivery addresses in ways that confuse foreigners. A small envelope symbol ✉ is sometimes used instead of "P.O. Box" or an equivalent. Addresses are sometimes repeated in both languages; however, bilingual business cards are more common than bilingual letterheads.

Dates, Money, Typographical Conventions

DATES AND MONEY	
Date format	Day, Month, Year (see text)
Typical date abbreviation	29/2/92, 1992-02-29
Currency unit	rand
Cents	cents
Domestic currency code	R
ISO international currency code	ZAR (see text)
Other international code	SAR
Decimal separator	comma
Thousands separator	space
Typical currency amount	R 5 879,50 (note one space after the R)

Dates are usually written in the order day-month-year, but Afrikaans-speaking people sometimes write month-day-year. Government agencies generally use a year-month-day sequence.

South African regulations require that some currency transactions employ a different exchange rate in **financial rands**, for which the international code is **ZAL**.

Envelopes

International margin rules apply: 40mm (1.6″) top, 15mm (0.6″) left, right, and bottom. Return addresses are usually printed at the top left.

MESSAGES FOR THE MAILROOM	
English	**Afrikaans**
Urgent	Dringend
Please forward	Stuur asb. aan
Confidential	Vertroulik
Please do not bend	Moenie vou nie
Fragile	Breekbaar
Care of	Per adres

Phone Numbers

PHONE SYSTEM INFORMATION (SEE CHAPTER 4)	
Country Code	+27
International Access Code	09
Long-Distance Access Code	0
Typical City Codes	two-digit (e.g., 11 = Johannesburg) up to five-digit in rural areas
Typical number formats	(011) 804 7609 (0153) 47 3974 sometimes (011) 804-7609
Ringing and busy signals	British

An **(0800)** prefix indicates a toll-free number, which may not be accessible from outside the country.

Word of Warning!

When you send regular mail to South Africa, it is essential to use postal addresses (boxes) rather than delivery addresses (streets).

However, you must, as usual, give the street address to air freight and air courier companies. (Not all these companies serve South Africa; DHL has done so for a long time.) If you do not have the postcode for the street address, use the one for the box. Be careful to give the air freight company a good phone number on the air waybill, because they routinely have to call for directions.

Transit and customs delays are quite common, even for express services.

SPAIN

Address Summary

Example of a street address:

> **Sr.**[1] **Don**[2]
> **Alberto**[3] **López**[4] **Cisneros**[5]
> **Editores Internacionales**[6] **S.A.**[7]
> **Calle**[8] **San Bernardo,**[9] **15**[10] **- 3º**[11] **- C**[12]
> **28015**[13] **MADRID**[14]

Key:

[1] **Sr.** = **Señor**, meaning "Mr."; usually written on a separate line.
[2] **Don** is a respectful additional title.
[3] Given name.
[4] Family name; thus, **Mr. López**, *not* "Mr. Cisneros."
[5] Mother's family name, used as part of the formal legal name.
[6] Company name.
[7] **S.A.** = **Sociedad Anónima**, signifying a corporation.
[8] **Calle** is the most common word for "street."
[9] Street name.
[10] Building number.
[11] 3rd floor.
[12] Suite C.
[13] Five-digit postcode *(required)*.
[14] City or delivery-post-office name.

Language

Castilian Spanish is the official and principal language of Spain. However, people in the important business city of Barcelona and its surrounding region ordinarily speak the Catalan language among themselves, and its visibility in business is increasing. Catalan versions of street names are often used, and more and more written Catalan is seen. If you are familiar with the appearance of Spanish, you can distinguish Catalan words by their use of the letter x and the combinations ny, tg, ts, tx, and tz. Words that end in -ción and -dad in Spanish end in -cio and -tat in Catalan. Catalan street and place-names often end in -t, -eig, and -eu.

Address Elements

PERSONAL NAMES

Spanish people usually give you three names on their correspondence and business cards: **Frumencio Hernández Aldaca** must be addressed in English as **Mr. Hernández**. Frumencio is his given name. His father was Señor Hernández and his mother was Señorita Aldaca before she married, and you would have called her **Miss** or **Ms. Aldaca** in English. After she married his father, she became Señora Aldaca de Hernández, and you would call her **Mrs.** or **Ms. Hernández** in English.

"Mr.," "Mrs.," and "Miss" are **Señor, Señora,** and **Señorita** in Spanish, usually abbreviated **Sr., Sra.,** and **Srta.** Catalan spellings are **Senyor, Senyora,** and **Senyoreta,** with the same abbreviations. In writing, it is customary to add the respectful titles **Don** and **Doña** for men and women respectively; thus, **Señor Don Luis Fernández Rodríguez** (but **Dear Señor Fernández**). Spanish-speaking people usually prefer to be addressed in writing as "Señor" rather than "Mr.," even when you are writing to them in English.

Double given names exist, such as **José María** (a man) and **María Antonieta** (a woman). Different people have different preferences: he may want to be called José and addressed **Dear José** in a letter, or he may want to be José María. If you don't know their individual preferences, you should not be calling them by their given names anyway.

Spanish businesspeople are relatively formal and do not necessarily use their given names even with people they work with every day.

A man's name may include the word **de** ("of," "from"), which usually indicates higher social status in Spain. Aristocratic family names may have hyphenated or connected words; for example, **Antonio de Luna-Quadra y de la Hoz** (who is **Mr. de Luna-Quadra y de la Hoz**), or **Luis Ángel de la Villa y Sangriz** (who is **Mr. de la Villa y Sangriz**, since Luis Ángel is a double given name).

A few men will give you a final initial instead of their mother's family name—for example, "Frumencio Hernández A.," or even "F. Hernández A."—but this is less common in Spain than in Latin America.

Academic degrees and professional titles are not usually used in business.

COMPANY NAMES

Legal Entities	Abbrev.	Explanation
Sociedad Anónima	S.A.	Most common designation for a corporation, publicly traded or privately owned
Sociedad Limitada	S.L.	Smaller (private) company

The word **Compañía**, abbreviated **C., Cía.,** or **Compª.**, is often used in company names. **S.R.L.** is an older variant of **S.L.**

You cannot distinguish a publicly traded company by its name.

OFFICES

Complex designations of offices inside a building are common. The most common format is **Calle Virgen de Iciar, 5 - 1º - B**, meaning the office marked B on the first floor of building no. 5 on Calle Virgen de Iciar. Less often, an office has a number instead of a letter: **Calle del Duque de Sesto, 17, 2º, 3ª** means the third office (3ª is the feminine form of the Spanish word for "third") on the second floor (2º is the masculine form) of no. 17.

Internal descriptions contain a variety of words and abbreviations:

Office Location	Abbrev.	Meaning
piso	p.	floor
planta	p.	floor
centro	cen.	center
derecha	der., dcha.	right
izquierda	izq., izqda.	left
planta baja	p.b.	1st floor (street level)
alto	a.	top floor
entresuelo	entlo.	mezzanine
ático	átº	attic
sobre ático	s.átº	penthouse
puerta	pta.	door
apartamento	ap.	apartment (or office)

BUILDING NAMES

Office buildings are rarely named, but names can appear in addresses. The general word for "building" is **Edificio** (e.g., **Edificio Montecarlo**).

An industrial area is sometimes called a **Polígono Industrial**. You will see this frequently in factory addresses, often abbreviated in various ways; for example, **Políg. Ind. Fuente del Jarro, Nave 19**.

Nave means building. A location within the area may also be described as a **Parcela** (lot), **Esquina** (corner), or **Fábrica** (factory), or it may have a designation like **Sector C, calle F**, meaning F Street in C Sector.

BUILDING NUMBERS

A street number is written after the street name, usually preceded by a comma, as in **Calle Cristóbal Colón, 15**.

Different entrances to split buildings are not common. When they occur they are usually designated by **bis** and **ter** instead of A and B; for example, **Calle Galileo, 38 bis**.

Combined buildings are much commoner:

Calle Galileo, 14-16

Calle Galileo, 49 al 53 (meaning 49 through 53)

In a rural area or on a short street, buildings may not be numbered. In that case, **s/n** (**sin número**, "without number") is written in place of the number, as in **Calle Monturiol s/n**.

STREET NAMES

Street Designator	Abbrev.	Explanation
Calle	C/	Most common designation for a street
Avenida, Paseo	Av., Pº	Major business street
Callejón		Small street
Plaza		Square

The street designator is sometimes omitted from well-known major streets; for example, in Madrid people write **Alcalá** rather than "Calle de Alcalá" or "C/ Alcalá," and in Barcelona people write **Diagonal** rather than "Avenida Diagonal." One well-known street in Barcelona is called **Las Ramblas**: a "rambla" is a street with a sidewalk down the median.

Words like **de** ("of") and **el, la, los, las** ("the") are common in street names and must not be capitalized:

> **Avenida de José Antonio**
> **Paseo de las Acacias**
> **Plaza de la Cibeles**

A **Carretera** is a major highway. Rural plants are often addressed in the following manner:

> **Crta. Valencia Km 21**
> **Ctra. Nal. II Km. 26,700**

The second example means "0.7 km past the 26-km post on National Highway 2."

In Barcelona, street names have both Spanish and Catalan spellings, with increasing use of the Catalan version. The common Catalan word for "street" is **carrer**, a larger avenue is called an **avinguda**, the word for "paseo" is **passeig**, and a square is a **plaça**. Differences in spelling are usually minor.

> **Plaza de España** (Spanish)
> **Plaça de Espanya** (Catalan)
>
> **Calle Cruz Cubierta** (Spanish)
> **Carrer Creu Coberta** (Catalan)

LOCALITY NAMES

Locality names are no longer needed now that postcodes are required, but some people still give them.

CITY NAMES

City names are usually written in capitals. In the past, they were generally underlined, but this is now contrary to international standards. Most international business is done with Madrid and Barcelona, but all the following cities are important:

Almería	La Coruña	Santander
Badajoz	Granada	Sevilla
Barcelona	Madrid	Valencia
Bilbao	Málaga	Vitoria
Burgos	Murcia	Zaragoza
Cartagena	San Sebastián	

STATE/PROVINCE/ETC. NAMES

Spain is divided into about 50 provinces. Most of the provinces are named after the provincial capital. When the two names are different, the province name is written after the city name in parentheses. Of the principal business cities listed above, only five need a province name:

BILBAO (Vizcaya)
CARTAGENA (Murcia)
SAN SEBASTIÁN (Guipúzcoa)
SANTANDER (Cantabria)
VITORIA (Álava)

There are no standard abbreviations in common use.

POSTCODES

Postcodes are essential for prompt and accurate delivery.

A five-digit number, called the *Código Postal*, is written in front of the city name. The first two digits show the province; these were allocated in alphabetical order of province name, although there have been changes since the system was introduced. Sorting a mailing list by postcode is not very meaningful.

Postcodes ending in **071** are allocated to government agencies, and **070** is reserved for the Spanish Postal Service.

P.O. BOXES

The Spanish term for "P.O. Box" is **Apartado de Correos**, usually abbreviated to **Apartado**, **Aptdo.**, or **Apdo.**

If you use a box, the street line must not be included. Boxes have their own postcodes, ending in **080**.

COUNTRY NAME

The short name of the country is **España**, which is what appears on stamps. The postcode is sometimes prefixed with the country code **E-**.

Letterheads

There is no standard layout or convention.

Su referencia and **Nuestra referencia** (abbreviated **S/ref.** and **N/ref.**), which sometimes appear, mean "Your reference" and "Our reference" respectively.

A P.O. Box address is sometimes labeled **Dirección Postal** to distinguish it from the delivery address.

N.I.F. or **C.I.F.** (**Número** or **Código de Identificación Fiscal**) is a Spanish tax number, which appears on all business stationery. **IVA** is the Spanish abbreviation for Value-Added Tax, the European sales tax.

Larger companies often print their **capital social**, an indication of their financial strength.

Dates, Money, Typographical Conventions

DATES AND MONEY	
Date format	Day, Month, Year
Typical date abbreviation	29/2/92
Currency unit	peseta
Cents	not used
Domestic currency codes	ptas., Pts.
ISO international currency code	ESP

Other international codes	none
Decimal separator	comma
Thousands separator	period
Typical currency amount	5.879 ptas.
	(note one space before the ptas.)

Money amounts are occasionally written **Pts. 30.000** instead of **30.000 ptas.**, but the digraph Pt which is included on many computer printers is unnecessary. **ESB** is the ISO code for pesetas in convertible accounts.

Envelopes

You are supposed to have a bottom margin of 20mm (0.8″) below the address. Return addresses are always written on the flap.

MESSAGES FOR THE MAILROOM	
English	**Spanish**
Urgent	Urgente
Please forward	A reexpedir
Confidential	Confidencial
Please do not bend	No doblar por favor
Fragile	Frágil
Care of	Use c/o (see text)

"C/o" may not be understood, and there is no standard Spanish equivalent. If you must make it absolutely clear to a mailroom that you are addressing, for example, Mr. Tomlinson who is visiting Mr. Martínez, write out the two phrases:

> **A la atención del Señor Martínez**
> **Destinatario final Mr. Tomlinson**

If women were involved, "del" would become **de la** and "Destinatario" would become **Destinataria**.

Phone Numbers

PHONE SYSTEM INFORMATION (SEE CHAPTER 4)	
Country Code	+34
International Access Code	07
Long-Distance Access Code	9
Typical City Codes	one-digit (e.g., 1 = Madrid)
	two-digit (e.g., 76 = Zaragoza)
Typical number formats	(928) 74 21 80
	(91) 351 67 50
Ringing and busy signals	European

Don't forget that the usual rule of "drop the zero" does not apply to Spanish phone numbers: **(91) 351 67 50** is dialed from another country as +34-1-351-6750.

All Spanish phone numbers are eight digits long after the country code.

SWEDEN

Address Summary

Example of a postal address:

> **Stig[1] Svensson[2]**
> **Internationellt Förlags[3] AB[4]**
> **Box[5] 92**
> **631 02[6] ESKILSTUNA[7]**

Key:

[1] Given name.
[2] Family name.
[3] Company name.
[4] **AB** signifies a corporation.
[5] **Box** means "P.O. Box."
[6] Five-digit postcode *(essential) with one space after third digit;* may have an S- prefix.
[7] City or delivery-post-office name; *must be capitalized.*

Example of a street address:

> **Siv Nordström**
> **Internationellt Förlags AB**
> **Vågögatan[8] 6[9]**
> **123 51 FARSTA**

Key:

[8] Street name; the suffix **-gatan** means "street."
[9] Building number.

Address Elements

PERSONAL NAMES

Swedish businesspeople usually write their (only) given name followed by their family name. They expect to use their given name with everybody. Translations of "Mr." and "Ms." are not normally used.

There are no spelling rules in Swedish that reliably distinguish male and female given names, but a name ending in **-a** is probably a woman's (e.g., **Maria, Britta, Birgitta**).

Many family names end in **-sson** (e.g., **Svensson, Persson, Andersson,**

Eriksson). A family name preceded by **af** or **von** (as in **Anders af Petersén** or **Tor von Matern**) implies that the person comes from an old or aristocratic family, but no special courtesy is necessary.

When a Swedish woman marries, anything may happen to her name. She may keep her family name, change to her husband's, or use both in either order. A man usually keeps his own family name, but some men change to their wives'. If somebody has two family names, use both—address **Anna Berg Andersson** formally as **Dear Ms. Berg Andersson**.

Academic titles such as **Dr.** (Doctor) and **Ing.** (Engineer) exist but are rarely used.

COMPANY NAMES

Swedish companies engaging in international business are invariably corporations, designated by the abbreviation **AB**, usually after the name but sometimes in front of it. Both privately owned and publicly traded companies use this designation.

OFFICES

Office suites are not identified. Shared office buildings (and residential apartment complexes) have boxes for each tenant.

BUILDING NAMES

Buildings do not have names. The only additional identification you may see is the name of an **industriområdet**, or industrial park.

BUILDING NUMBERS

A single number is written after the street name, without a comma. Numbers are usually quite low.

STREET NAMES

Street Designator	Abbrev.	Explanation
-gatan	-g	Most common designation for a street
-vägen	-v	Major business streets
-planen, -torget	-pl, -t	Square
avenyn, esplanaden, promenaden	ave, espl, prom	Rarer names for major streets
-backen, -brinken, -gränden, -stigen	-b, -br, -gr, -st	hill, bank, alley, path

There is usually no period after the above abbreviations:

Nordmarksv 3

Exportg 23

The suffixes **-en**, **-n**, and **-et** at the end of a Swedish word are just the equivalent of "the" in English. The "street" word is written separately when the street is named after a person:

Johan Banérs gatan 16

Johan Banérs g 16

If a street has more than one word, apart from "gatan" or an equivalent, it is almost certainly named after a person, unless it begins with one of these words or abbreviations:

First Word	Abbrev.	Meaning
Gamla	G	old
Stora	ST	big, greater
Lilla	L	small, lesser
Norra	N	north
Södra	S	south
Västra	V	west
Östra	Ö	east
Sankta	S:T	Saint

For example, **V Stationsv 8** means **Västra Stationsvägen 8**, "8 West Station Way."

LOCALITY NAMES

Names of localities are not used. All postal addresses consist of two lines: (1) the street or the box, and (2) the postcode and the city.

CITY NAMES

City names must be written in capital letters. The principal business cities of Sweden are **Stockholm**, **Göteborg** (sometimes spelled "Gothenburg" in English), and **Malmö**. Smaller cities are **Hälsingborg**, **Norrköping**, **Uppsala**, **Västerås**, and **Örebro**.

STATE/PROVINCE/ETC. NAMES

No regional names are used in postal addresses.

POSTCODES

The postcode is a five-digit number written in front of the city name. There should always be a space between the third and fourth digits. Postcodes are allocated from south to north, except that the Stockholm area has postcodes in the range 100 00 through 199 99. The first three digits represent the post office, and the last two are the delivery route. There are different postcodes for P.O. Boxes, and about a thousand high-volume mailers have their own postcodes.

There have been revisions to the postcode numbering system, so information older than about 1992 may contain errors.

P.O. BOXES

P.O. Boxes are very common in business use. The word **Box** alone is usually used, followed by a number.

COUNTRY NAME

Sweden calls itself **Sverige**, which appears on postage stamps. The country prefix **S-** is often added to the postcode.

Letterheads

Swedish letterheads often show two addresses: a **Postadress** for mail (the P.O. Box and its town and postcode), and a **Besöksadress** (literally, "address for visitors") for deliveries.

Swedish Expression	Meaning
Er beteckning	Your reference
Vår beteckning	Our reference
Datum	Date
Kontaktperson	Contact person
Bankgiro	Bank-account number
Postgiro	Postal checking account

Dates, Money, Typographical Conventions

DATES AND MONEY	
Date format	Year, Month, Day
Typical date abbreviation	1992-02-29
Currency unit	krona
Cents	öre
Domestic currency code	Kr
ISO international currency code	SEK
Other international codes	SKR
Decimal separator	comma
Thousands separator	period
Typical currency amount	Kr 5.879,50 (note one space after the Kr)

A colon is often used as the decimal separator in money amounts. The thousands separator is often dropped in numbers smaller than a million. Even amounts are usually written **Kr 1000:—** or **Kr 1000,—**. The currency abbreviation **SEK** is widely used in both domestic and international business.

It is standard and customary to avoid unnecessary punctuation in Swedish. For example, periods are never written in any abbreviations.

Envelopes

MESSAGES FOR THE MAILROOM	
English	Swedish
Urgent	Brådskande
Please forward	Eftersändes
Confidential	Konfidentiell
Please do not bend	Vikes ej
Fragile	Ömtåligt
Care of	(use c/o)

Return addresses are always placed in the top left-hand corner of the envelope. All addresses are supposed to be able to be written in five lines of 35 characters each (excluding the country name).

Phone Numbers

PHONE SYSTEM INFORMATION (SEE CHAPTER 4)	
Country Code	+46
International Access Code	009
Long-Distance Access Code	0
Typical City Codes	one-digit (only 8 = Stockholm) two-digit (e.g., 31 = Göteborg) three-digit in rural areas
Typical number formats	08-781 10 00 042-89 01 75 0470-485 15
Ringing and busy signals	European

Hyphens are sometimes used instead of spaces to separate the digits of a local phone number.

A number written in the form **0371-157 95, 166 00** means that there are two lines whose local numbers are 15795 and 16600.

SWITZERLAND

Address Summary

Example of a French-language street address, with P.O. Box included:

Monsieur[1] **Jacques**[2] **Lenoir**[3]
Éditions Internationales S.A.[4]
Rue[5] **de la Muse 14**[6]
Case Postale[7]
1211[8] **GENÈVE**[9] **11**[10]

Key:

[1] **Monsieur** means "Mr."; sometimes appears by itself on the line above.
[2] First given name.
[3] Family name.
[4] **S.A. = Société Anonyme**, signifying a corporation.
[5] **Rue** is the most common word for "street."
[6] Building number.
[7] **Case Postale** means "P.O. Box"; not always followed by a number.
[8] Four-digit postcode, *required*.
[9] City or delivery-post-office name; not usually capitalized in domestic use.
[10] Postal district number.

Example of a German-language address:

Frau[11] **Gisela**[12] **Bauer**[13]
International Verlag AG[14]
Birchstrasse[15] **185**[16]
Postfach[17]
8050 ZÜRICH 12

Key:

[11] **Frau** means "Ms." (**Herrn** would mean "To Mr."); sometimes appears by itself on the line above.
[12] First given name.
[13] Family name.
[14] **AG = Aktiengesellschaft**, signifying a corporation.
[15] Street name; the suffix **-strasse** means "street."
[16] Building number.
[17] **Postfach** means "P.O. Box"; not always followed by a number.

Example of an Italian-language address:

Sig.[18] **Giuseppe**[19] **Moretti**[20]
Edizioni Internazionali S.A.[21]
Via[22] **Ronchetto 15**[23]
Casella postale[24]
6904 LUGANO

Key:

[18] **Sig.** = **Signor**, meaning "Mr."; sometimes appears by itself on the line above.

[19] First given name.

[20] Family name.

[21] **S.A.** = **Società Anonima**, signifying a corporation.

[22] **Via** is the most common word for "street."

[23] Building number.

[24] **Casella postale** means "P.O. Box"; not always followed by a number.

Languages

Switzerland has four national languages, of which three are encountered in business correspondence. About 75 percent of the Swiss speak German dialects, 20 percent French, and 5 percent Italian. (In German, **ss** is usually written in place of the **ß** character used in Germany and Austria.)

Each major business city has one predominant language. If you are enclosing translated material, it is essential to use the correct language. You cannot send German sales literature to a company in French-speaking Switzerland and expect to get any results; in fact, you may give offense. Local languages are listed below under "City Names."

Address Elements

PERSONAL NAMES

Swiss businesspeople usually give their first given name and their family name. "Mr.," "Mrs.," and "Miss" are **Monsieur, Madame,** and **Mademoiselle** in French, **Herr, Frau,** and **Fräulein** in German, and **Signor, Signora,** and **Signorina** in Italian. Academic titles, particularly **Dr.** and **Ing.** (in all three languages), are used. Sometimes degrees are included after a name; if encountered, they should be copied carefully.

The Swiss are relatively formal and do not expect to use their given names until they know each other personally.

See the chapters on France, Germany, and Italy for more information about personal names.

COMPANY NAMES

Most Swiss companies engaging in international business are corporations, designated by the abbreviations **AG** in German (**Aktiengesellschaft**) and **S.A.** in French (**Société Anonyme**) and Italian (**Società Anonima**). Both abbreviations are sometimes included with the company name. AG does not imply a publicly traded company, as it does in Germany.

It is quite common for a Swiss company to translate its name in all company literature. For example, the bank that calls itself in English the **Union Bank of Switzerland** prints its names as:

> **Union de Banques Suisses**
> **Schweizerische Bankgesellschaft**
> **Unione di Banche Svizzere**

and its logo combines the abbreviations UBS and SBG.

OFFICES

Exceptionally, you will see a floor number or apartment number written after the building number: for example, **Rundstrasse 12/2** means the second floor of Rundstrasse 12. Generally, however, every occupant must provide an individually named mailbox in a shared building.

BUILDING NAMES

Building names are never used in postal addresses.

BUILDING NUMBERS

The building number should follow the street name, without a comma. French-speaking people sometimes write the building number in front of the street name. Both combined (**12-16**) and split (**12A, 12B**) building numbers are seen.

STREET NAMES

Street Designator (French/German/Italian)	Explanation
Rue/-strasse/Via	Most common designation for a street
Avenue, Route/-allee, -ring/ Viale, Corso	Probably major business streets
Quai/-kai/Riva	Major street running along a lake or river
Place/-platz/Piazza	Square

Abbreviations and other designators will be found in the chapters on France, Germany, and Italy; however, they are not common in Switzerland. Small side streets are often called **chemin**, **chemine**, **ruelle**, or **chaussée** in French-speaking Switzerland and **-gasse**, **-gässlein**, **-graben**, or **-weg** in German.

LOCALITY NAMES

Names of localities are not used in addresses.

CITY NAMES

Domestically, city names are not usually capitalized, but there is no objection to doing so. In the past, the Swiss used to underline the last line of the address and space the letters out, but this convention is obsolete and incompatible with current automated processing equipment (and international agreements).

In the large cities, a postal district is often shown after the city name; for example, **1000 Lausanne 17**.

The principal business cities are: French-speaking **Genève** ("Geneva" in English) and **Lausanne**, German-speaking **Basel**, **Bern** (often spelled "Berne" in English), **Vaduz** (see "Country Name"), and **Zürich**, and Italian-speaking **Lugano**. You should use these local spellings.

A few small areas are bilingual. Three towns you may encounter in business are called **Bienne**, **Fribourg**, and **Neuchâtel** in French and **Biel**, **Freiburg**, and **Neuenburg**, respectively, in German.

STATE/PROVINCE/ETC. NAMES

Switzerland is divided into 26 *cantons*, but neither their names nor their two-letter abbreviations are needed in postal addresses. In a trade directory, you might see the abbreviation written in parentheses after the name of the city or village: for example, "Sion (VS)."

POSTCODES

The postcode is essential in Swiss addresses.

A four-digit postcode is written in front of the city, town, or village name. There should be a single space between the postcode and the following name. Postcodes are allocated in a zigzag fashion from west to east.

P.O. BOXES

A P.O. Box is called a **Case postale** in French, a **Postfach** in German, and a **Casella postale** in Italian. Businesses often have boxes.

Switzerland is unique among the countries in this book in that a box number is not required. It is quite common to omit it, especially for larger organizations. The Swiss Post Office will figure it out for you, but include it if you know it.

If you use the street address for a business that in fact has a P.O. Box, your mail may be delayed. However, there is no objection to writing both the street address and the P.O. Box as long as the box line comes second, directly above the city line.

COUNTRY NAME

The short name of Switzerland is **(la) Suisse** in French, **(die) Schweiz** in German, and **(la) Svizzera** in Italian. "La" and "die" mean "the." Postage stamps use **Helvetia**, which is the Latin name. The prefix **CH-** is sometimes written in front of the postcode, and in fact is a very commonly used abbreviation for Switzerland. It stands for **Confederatio Helvetica**, which means "the Swiss Confederation" in Latin.

The city of **Vaduz**, an international financial center, is actually part of the separate country called **Liechtenstein**, which is, however, integrated into the Swiss monetary, postcode, and telecommunications systems. Some postal administrations recognize the postcode prefix **FL-** for it.

Letterheads

There is a Swiss national standard governing the information on a business letterhead, but it is not followed rigidly. There are usually date and reference lines; for further details, see the chapters on France, Germany, and Italy. Note, however, that "Subject" in Swiss German is usually written **Gegenstand**, not **Betreff**.

You should look carefully for a postal address, such as **Postfach, 9001 St. Gallen 1**, which may be printed in small type separately from the street address. It may be labeled **Adresse postale**, **Postadresse**, or **Indirizzo postale**.

A letterhead usually shows postal checking account numbers to facilitate a system of electronic funds transfers that is very widely used by both businesses and individuals in Switzerland.

Dates, Money, Typographical Conventions

DATES AND MONEY	
Date format	Day, Month, Year
Typical date abbreviation	29.02.1992
Currency unit	franc
Cents	centimes
Domestic currency codes	Fr., fr.
ISO international currency code	CHF
Other international codes	SFR, FS, SF, SFr, FrS, etc.
Decimal separator	period
Thousands separator	apostrophe
Typical currency amount	Fr. 5'879.50 (note one space after Fr.) 5'879.50 fr.

Even amounts are written **Fr. 1'800.—**.

Sans-serif typefaces are most common for all business purposes in Switzerland.

Envelopes

You are supposed to leave a left margin of 20mm (0.8″), right and bottom margins of 15mm (0.6″), and a top margin of 48mm (1.9″). Return addresses are acceptable in the top left or center left, or on the flap of the envelope.

See the chapters on France, Germany, and Italy for mailroom messages that can be written on envelopes.

Phone Numbers

PHONE SYSTEM INFORMATION (SEE CHAPTER 4)	
Country Code	+41
International Access Code	00
Long-Distance Access Code	0
Typical City Codes	one-digit (1 = Zürich, only) two-digit (e.g., 31 = Bern)
Typical number formats	(01) 462 28 21 (022) 47 88 16 (085) 9 13 15
Ringing and busy signals	European

TAIWAN

Address Summary

Example of a street address:

Mr. Martin[1] Wu[2]
International Publishing Co. Ltd.[3]
519-5,[4] Sec. 3,[5] Ching Tao E.[6] Rd.[7]
TAIPEI[8] 10552[9]

Key:

[1] Adopted Western given name.
[2] Family name.
[3] **Co. Ltd.** = **Company Limited**, signifying a corporation.
[4] Office **5** in building no. **519**.
[5] **Sec.** = **Section**, a length of a major street.
[6] **Ching Tao East** is the street name.
[7] **Rd.** = **Road**, the most common word for "street."
[8] City or delivery-post-office name.
[9] Five-digit extended postcode.

Example of an address in an older area:

Mr. Yu-ching[10] Wang
International Publishing Co. Ltd.
7F,[11] No. 19[12] Alley 83[13] Lane 630[14]
Hwa Cheng Road
SHIN CHUANG[15] 24221
Taipei Hsien[16]

Key:

[10] Chinese given names.
[11] **7F** = **7th floor**.
[12] Building number.
[13] **Alley 83** is a small street leading off **Lane 630**.
[14] **Lane 630** is a small street leading off **Hwa Cheng Road**.
[15] Smaller town (note postcode follows town name).
[16] **Hsien** means "County"; this line required for smaller towns.

Example of a rural address:

Mr. Anthony Chiang
International Publishing Co. Ltd.
4 Lane 50
Chung Chen Road
Yi Chia Chun[17]
JEN TEH[18] **HSIANG**[19] **717**[20]
Tainan Hsien

Key:

[17] **Chun** means "Village."
[18] **Jen Teh** is the delivery post office for **Yi Chia** village.
[19] **Hsiang** means "Town."
[20] Three-digit postcode (older system).

Address Elements

PERSONAL NAMES

Chinese names consist of three characters, one being the family name and the other two being given names. The Taiwanese, unlike other Chinese-speaking people, usually write their given names first and their family name last when dealing with foreigners. The names hyphenated together are the given names and the single word is the family name. Traditionally, the middle character of a Chinese name was common to all the members of a generation of a family, but the traditional system of generation names is not always used by younger people in Taiwan.

Many Chinese businesspeople in Taiwan, both men and women, have adopted an English-language given name and use it in all dealings with foreigners. Their English names are unofficial and will not be used on formal legal documents. However, they are more than just nicknames: a person will choose a name in English class in middle school and retain it. Everybody in an office will know who Ralph and Amy are. They are free to change their adopted names whenever they like, but since all their friends and colleagues will need to be told the new one, it is rare to go to the trouble.

In business circles, it is unusual to see titles or academic degrees unless they are from a foreign university. Doctors, engineers, and accountants may instead show their profession on their business cards in a form that also implies their license to practice.

COMPANY NAMES

Although there are several types of legal entity in Taiwan, as a practical matter, all companies engaged in international business are corporations. They most commonly use the traditional British abbreviation **Co. Ltd.**, although a few choose **Corporation** and other variations. It is common practice to describe the type of company by including a description like **Industrial Co.**, **Mining Co.**, or **Electronics Co.** in the name. Bear in mind that any English words in the company name are almost certainly a translation and not part of its legal name.

OFFICES

A company in a shared office building will usually indicate its location on the seventh floor by writing **7th fl.** or more commonly **7F** or **7FL**.

An office number, preceded by a hyphen, is sometimes added to the building number, as in **236-3, Sec. 4, Chung King N. Road**.

You will occasionally see the terms **Suite**, **Unit**, **Room**, or **Flat** in large buildings.

BUILDING NAMES

High-rise buildings in Taipei have names, but they are not normally used in postal addresses.

BUILDING NUMBERS

Building numbers are usually quite low, as in Europe. They are written in front of the street name, occasionally preceded by **No.**

STREET NAMES

Not all streets are named, by any means. Major streets are usually called **Road** in English. The word **Street** is also used; a Street is probably smaller than a Road. In Taipei, most Road names include the words **North**, **South**, **East**, or **West**. **Chungshan North Road** is the northern extension of **Chungshan South Road**. Long Roads are divided into a few **Sections**, usually abbreviated to **Sec**. The building numbers return to 1 at the beginning of a new Section.

The Section number is written either before or after the Road name. To imitate the Chinese-language sequence, it is more natural to write it between the building number and the Road name.

In older districts, streets leading off a Road are called **Lanes**, and a street leading off a Lane is called an **Alley**. Lanes and Alleys are numbered, not named. A complete address in an older area requires a building number, possibly an Alley number, a Lane number, and a Road name.

In the city of **Kaohsiung**, Roads are partitioned differently, written in English in the forms **Second Wu Fu Road** or **Wu Fu 2 Road**.

LOCALITY NAMES

Neighborhood names are sometimes used and required in cities. The word **Chun** after a name means "Village."

CITY NAMES

Most international business is done by companies in **Taipei**, the capital. Other major cities are **Kaohsiung**, **Keelung**, **Taichung**, and **Tainan**. The word **Hsiang** indicates a smaller town and is sometimes translated as "City."

STATE/PROVINCE/ETC. NAMES

Taiwan is divided into administrative units called **Hsien**, which is sometimes translated as "County." Cities and counties may have the same name, so if an address ends in **Taipei Hsien** it is not in the city of Taipei but in the town whose name is on the previous line.

POSTCODES

Postcodes are not widely used by businesses or individuals. A three-digit system has existed for some time and has recently been extended to five digits. The first three digits show the town or post office, and the two new digits denote a delivery route.

The national post office wants the postcode to follow the city name, not the county name, but you will see all kinds of variations in practice.

Even though your business correspondents may think it is unnecessary, ask them for their postcodes; a postcode may rescue you if you make mistakes in other parts of the address.

P.O. BOXES

P.O. Boxes exist in Taiwan, but it is unusual to use them in international correspondence. People there feel that it is more respectable to give a street address. You might bear this in mind if you are writing from a country where you want them to use your P.O. Box, and reassure them that you do have a street address. People often write box numbers with a dash (e.g., 7-287 or 42-97), but it is not required.

The five-digit postcode for a P.O. Box address should end in 00.

COUNTRY NAME

Taiwan calls itself the **Republic of China**, abbreviated to **R.O.C.** However, because of conflicting territorial claims between the government in Taiwan and the government of mainland China, the U.S. Postal Service and other Postal Administrations overseas want you to write **TAIWAN** as the last line of the address.

Letterheads

Apart from addresses and phone numbers, the only other information you may see on a letterhead from Taiwan is a post-office account number to which you can make payments, equivalent to the "postgiro" systems in Europe.

If you have to photocopy Chinese-language enclosures, remember that Chinese is usually printed vertically and is read from top to bottom, starting with the rightmost column on the page. Photocopy a brochure from what appears to be back to front, then staple it at the top right. To get loose pages the right way up, remember that our "ragged right" is their "ragged foot"—the top of the columns will all start at more or less the same level, except that a heading will stick up above the top of most columns. Western numerals provide another clue: a single numeral will probably be the right way up, but longer numbers will be lying on their right-hand side (with their tops to the right) in the vertical column.

Dates, Money, Typographical Conventions

DATES AND MONEY	
Date format	Day, Month, Year
Typical date abbreviation	29-2-92
Currency unit	dollar
Cents	cents
Domestic currency code	$

ISO international currency code	TWD (see text)
Other international codes	NT\$, NTD
Decimal separator	period
Thousands separator	comma
Typical currency amount	\$5,879
	(note no space after the \$)

The currency is really called the **yuan**, always translated as **dollar**. The international code TWD is unknown outside banking circles, and not well accepted because it resembles the abbreviation of an older currency. NTD stands for "New Taiwanese Dollar."

Envelopes

A 40mm (1.6″) top margin and 15mm (0.6″) bottom, right, and left margins are required. A Roman-alphabet return address must be placed in the top left corner.

In Chinese, the return address is written at the bottom right of a horizontally written envelope and the top right of a vertically written one. The postcode and other numbers must be written in Western numerals, not Chinese.

MESSAGES FOR THE MAILROOM	
English	**Chinese**
Urgent	緊急
Express	快遞
Please forward	請轉寄
Confidential	機密
Please do not bend	易碎
Fragile	請勿轉寄
Care of	請勿折疊

Phone Numbers

PHONE SYSTEM INFORMATION (SEE CHAPTER 4)	
Country Code	+886
International Access Code	002
Long-Distance Access Code	0
Typical City Codes	one-digit (2 = Taipei)
	two-digit (37 = Chulan)
Typical number formats	(02)503-0902
	02-7855171
Ringing and busy signals	North American

A number written in the form **7855172-3** means there are two lines, 7855172 and 7855173.

Numbers are always eight digits long after the country code.

THAILAND

Address Summary

Example of a postal address:

> **Mr. Pradit[1] Suwanasophon[2]**
> **International Publishing[3] Co. Ltd.[4]**
> **459/3[5] Soi[6] Saengsuk[7]**
> **Sadhupradist Road[8]**
> **Yannawa[9]**
> **BANGKOK[10] 10120[11]**

Key:

[1] Given name.
[2] Family name.
[3] Company name.
[4] **Co. Ltd.** = **Company Limited**, signifying a corporation.
[5] Building number.
[6] **Soi** is sometimes translated as "Lane."
[7] Lane leading off a principal street.
[8] **Road** is the most commonly used translation.
[9] District name.
[10] City name.
[11] Postcode (can also be on a line by itself).

Language

The Thai language is written in its own alphabet, and there is no standard way of transliterating it into Roman letters. There are two schools of thought: some try to romanize Thai words letter by letter as far as possible, and others pay more attention to phonetics. A street and locality translated letter by letter might read **Sri-Ayudhya Road, Ajthevi**, and the same address written more phonetically might instead be spelled **Si Ayuthaya Road, Ratheve**.

Address Elements

PERSONAL NAMES

Thai names are very distinctive. Family names are often four or five syllables long, and very frequently begin with S, P, or Ch. Some examples are: **Chamsamritsakul, Chongprasertsak, Jirathammaporn, Patarachinda**, and **Viwatana**.

People of ethnic Chinese origin sometimes retain Chinese names, as described in other chapters, but many of them have adopted names of Thai appearance. When they do this, they are required to create a new name that does not match that of any Thai family. Ethnic Chinese names therefore tend to be particularly long, and you may be able to see a Chinese name in them; for example, **Chinporncharoenpong** contains the common Chinese family name Chin.

Women customarily adopt their husband's name on marriage. A rich or famous woman may write her family name before her husband's, but if you see a hyphenated name in business dealings (**Chiam-vimonvat**, for example), the hyphen has probably been inserted as an aid to pronunciation, not as an indication of a double name.

A Thai has a single given name, which is a meaningful word that you would find in a Thai dictionary. Therefore, encountering two people with the same given name is much rarer in Thailand than in countries with Catholic or Muslim traditions. Some words are felt to be more suitable for boys and some for girls, but there are many names (perhaps one in five) that a Thai cannot identify as male or female. It is impossible for anyone not brought up in the culture to know whether a Thai name refers to a man or a woman.

In addition to a legal given name, a Thai invariably has a nickname, which is not derived in any way from the given name. Family, friends, and people who work together on a regular basis will use each other's nicknames. Supervisors and their staffs will use nicknames regardless of differences in age and gender. Nicknames are not written down or printed on letters or business cards, so it is important for a foreigner to note them in order to correlate spoken and written names.

Outside the workgroup or other social group, people are addressed by their given names, possibly with a respectful prefix, of which there are a large number. A widely used prefix is **Khun**, as in **Khun-Narong**. An older person might be addressed as **Pee-Surat** and a younger one as **Nong-Pranee**. **Narong**, **Surat**, and **Pranee** are given names, the first two male and the third female. Prefixes for official purposes are **Nai-Prasith** (a man) and **Nang-Nitaya** (a woman). **Nang-Soa-Anee** is less common and would indicate a woman who was known to be unmarried. All these prefixes, and others, are always attached to the given name, which may be followed by the family name in the most formal circumstances. Thais will use their family names on legal documents, in formal introductions, and on lists of employees or meeting attendees, but rarely in speech and never alone. It is therefore appropriate to address a Thai in written English as **Mr.** or **Ms.** followed by the full given name and family name. You would address a letter or fax to **Mr. Chainarong Patarachinda**, use the salutation **Dear Chainarong** (unless he was a complete stranger), and use his nickname in speech if you had worked as part of his group. If you are aware of someone's nickname, it is probably correct to use it, but only in informal discussions. Some women actively prefer to be called by their nicknames, feeling it is more friendly.

It is rather common for Thai businesspeople to list their academic qualifications on a business card, especially if they have studied overseas, and many have adopted the British habit of adding the abbreviated name of the university they attended in parentheses after their degree. You are not obliged to reproduce these details.

COMPANY NAMES

A corporation is indicated by the Thai words **Borisat Jamkad**, meaning "Limited Company." When company names are translated into English, which is common, the old British abbreviation **Co. Ltd.** is invariably used. A name that includes **Public Co. Ltd.** would imply that the company was publicly traded.

The legal form of a **Limited Partnership**, indicated by the abbreviation **L.P.**, may imply a joint venture with a foreign company.

OFFICES

Floors are commonly specified in modern office buildings; "19th floor" would usually be written **19/F**. Otherwise, offices are not usually numbered within a building. However, refer to the discussion of building numbers below.

BUILDING NAMES

High-rise office buildings in Bangkok often have names:

> **CCT Building**
> **Prakanong Center**
> **Sino-Thai Tower**
> **Sathorn Thani 2 Bldg.**

BUILDING NUMBERS

A building number always precedes the street or lane name. A two-part number is very common and is somewhat ambiguous. The residential address **36/1 Prachasamosorn Road** could indicate a house that had been built between numbers 36 and 37, or it could indicate Apartment 1 in a multi-occupancy dwelling. There is a similar ambiguity in business addresses. You can guess that a low suffixed number is part of the building number and that a high number, such as **600/61 Phetkasem Road**, refers to Room or Suite 61 within the building numbered 600, but there is inherent uncertainty.

STREET NAMES

The Thai word **Thanon** is usually translated into English as "Road," but occasionally as "Street." Thais may tend to think of a "street" as being larger than a "road."

A **Soi** is a small alley leading off a through street in an older area. "Soi" is sometimes translated as "Lane." A soi can have a name or a number or both. Successive alleys on one side of a street may be called **Soi 5**, **Soi 7**, **Soi 9**, etc. Intermediate alleys may be constructed with names like **Soi 7/1**, **Soi 7/2**, and **Soi 7/3**. The address line **Soi 3 (Soi Nana Nua)** implies that "Soi 3" is the official name but the alley is better known as "Soi Nana Nua" to taxi drivers and people in the area.

Alleys may also be known by the name of the major street off which they lead. The address **1070/1 Sukhumvit 101/3 (Soi Wachirathammasathit)** means building 1070/1 on alley 101/3 leading off Sukhumvit Road, a well-known thoroughfare.

The word **Moo** (occasionally spelled **Mu**), meaning "group," refers to a small area adjoining a major urban street. Thus, **135 Moo 14, Teparak Road** means building 135 somewhere in a section 14 off Teparak Road, where it is not necessary to specify a particular alley. In a rural area, a "Moo" would be just a section of a village, without reference to a street.

It may be useful to recognize the Thai words **Nua** (North), **Tai** (South), **Tawan-ork** (East; literally, "sunrise"), and **Tawantok** (West; literally, "sunset") in addresses.

LOCALITY NAMES

Locality names are included in city addresses; in rural areas, village names are included. The principal type of administrative district is called an **amphoe**. In an urban area, a second level of locality, called a **tambol**, might be included in an address; for example, **1977 Phaholyothin Road, Ladyao, Bangkhen, Bangkok 10900**, or **1977 Phaholyothin Road, Tambol Ladyao, Amphoe Bangkhen, Bangkok 10900**, in which **Bangkhen** is in fact the delivery post office. One locality name is common, two less so. If you need to shorten addresses, the locality names are usually redundant if you have the correct postcode.

CITY NAMES

By international convention, city names should be written in capital letters. Most international business is done with **Krung Thep**, the capital, which is called **Bangkok** by foreigners. Provincial cities are **Chantaburi**, **Chiang Mai**, **Chon Buri**, **Haad Yai**, **Khon Kean**, **Lam Plai Mat**, **Lampang**, **Mae Sai**, **Maha Sarakham**, **Nakhon Phanom**, **Nan**, **Pak Chong**, **Phra-In Racha**, **Phuket**, **Roi Et**, **Si Sa Ket**, **Songkhla**, and **Udon Thani**.

STATE/PROVINCE/ETC. NAMES

Thailand is divided into 73 provinces. Each is named after the principal city that is its administrative center. The word **muang** distinguishes the city from the province: **Muang Nong Khai** is the city Nong Khai, the capital of Nong Khai province. Strictly speaking, the last three lines of the postal address should be the amphoe name, the province name, and the postcode. In practice, the last line of an urban address usually contains the city name followed by the postcode.

POSTCODES

A five-digit postcode system is in general use. The Communications Authority of Thailand wants the postcode written on a line by itself, but this is widely disregarded, at least in Roman-alphabet addresses, even by the CAT itself. The postcode is customarily written after the city or province name. The first two digits correspond to the province. Postcodes between 10000 and 29999 refer to the central region around Bangkok; postcodes from 30000 up are allocated starting from the northeast of the country and progressing toward the south. Most postcodes end in 0 and direct the letter to one particular delivery post office.

P.O. BOXES

P.O. Boxes are relatively new in Thailand and are rarely seen in postal addresses. The English expression **P.O. Box** is always used. Boxes have the postcode of the delivery post office, which is normally the same as the postcode for the street address.

COUNTRY NAME

The full name of the country is **Prathet Thai**.

Letterheads

Letterheads and business stationery for international use are printed in English. Business cards usually have an English translation, sometimes on the back.

Dates, Money, Typographical Conventions

DATES AND MONEY	
Date format	Day, Month, Year (see text)
Typical date abbreviation	29.2.1996
Currency unit	baht
Cents	satang
Domestic currency codes	not used (see text)
ISO international currency code	THB
Other international codes	none
Decimal separator	period
Thousands separator	comma
Typical currency amount	4,096 baht

Dates in the Thai language are written in day–month–year sequence. 1996 is the Thai year 2539. In English, dates may be abbreviated in either European or American sequence and it is advisable to check the meaning.

The word **baht** is normally written out in full in both Thai and English. Alternatively, a capital B with or without an oblique slash may be used as an abbreviation before or after the number. A Thai baht symbol is included in the Unicode as U + 03EF.

Envelopes

International layout standards apply: left, right, and bottom margins of 15mm (0.6″) and a top margin of 40mm (1.6″). The return address is written in the top left corner.

Phone Numbers

PHONE SYSTEM INFORMATION (SEE CHAPTER 4)	
Country Code	66
International Access Code	001
Long-Distance Access Code	0
Typical City Codes	2 = Bangkok
Standard number formats	Local numbers have seven digits in Bangkok, six elsewhere (02) 659-3333 (034) 319438
Ringing and busy signals	European

Thai phone numbers normally consist of nine digits including the initial 0. Hyphens in the numbers are completely optional. It is common to see fax numbers printed with an initial 662 (the country code and Bangkok city code) even if the voice line is presented differently. Numbers beginning (09) are in Malaysia, and must be dialed with the appropriate Malaysian prefixes from other countries. The city code is referred to in English as the **area code**, and long-distance calls are sometimes referred to by the former British abbreviation as **STD** calls.

Mobile phones are widely used. There are two mobile systems in use, with domestic prefixes **01-** and **08-**. It is not always clear which system a subscriber belongs to. Try **+66-1** first; if it does not work, try **+66-8**.

Words of Warning!

Outside of Bangkok, it may not be possible to dial international calls, so to avoid causing expense and delay it is more courteous for you to keep calling rather than leave messages to return your call.

It may be counterproductive to mark correspondence as "private" or "confidential," which could be interpreted by staff in a traditional Thai office as "extra interesting." This comment does not apply to larger companies with more Americanized corporate cultures. Business executives in traditional environments often print their home addresses on their business cards. You can send confidential correspondence to their homes.

TURKEY

Address Summary

Example of a street address:

> **Mr. Mehmet[1] Savaş[2]**
> **Uluslararası Yayınevi[3] A. Ş.[4]**
> **Kemeraltı[5] Cad.[6] Saroğlu[7] Apt.[8] No:57[9] K:2[10] D:3[11]**
> **Tophane[12]**
> **80020[13] İSTANBUL[14]**

Key:

[1] Given name.
[2] Family name.
[3] Company name.
[4] **A. Ş. = Anonim Şirket**, signifying a corporation.
[5] Street name.
[6] **Cad. = Caddesi**, meaning "street."
[7] Building name.
[8] **Apt. = Apartmanı**, meaning "building."
[9] Building number.
[10] Floor number.
[11] Room number.
[12] Locality name.
[13] Five-digit postcode.
[14] City or delivery-post-office name.

Another example of a street address, probably a smaller company in an older area:

> **Ms. Leyla Demir**
> **Uluslararası Yayınevi Ltd.[15]**
> **Yeşilce[16] Mah.[17] Dostluk[18] Sok.[19] No:57**
> **4. Levent[20]**
> **80660 İSTANBUL**

Key:

[15] **Ltd. = Limited**, signifying a smaller corporation.
[16] Neighborhood name.

[17] **Mah.** = **Mahallesi**, meaning "neighborhood."
[18] Street name.
[19] **Sok.** = **Sokağı**, meaning "(small) street."
[20] Locality name (**4.** = 4th).

Address Elements

PERSONAL NAMES

Turks traditionally have three names. The first is only used on formal legal documents. It usually honors a grandparent or other relative. The second name is the person's given name, and the third is a family name inherited from the father. Most family names in current use date only from a 1934 reform. The common endings -oğlu and -gil are equivalent to "-son" in English.

Businesspeople usually write their second and third names; therefore **Ahmet Sönmez** would usually be addressed as **Mr. Sönmez** in English. In Turkish, his colleagues would normally refer to him in speech as **Ahmet Bey**. A woman who writes her name as **Zeynep Şengün** would be **Ms. Şengün** in English and **Zeynep Hanım** in Turkish. **Bey** and **Hanım** are respectful titles analogous to "Mr." and "Ms." in English. Given names alone would only be used by co-workers who knew each other well and who had approximately the same rank and seniority, and then only in private. In an open meeting, they would revert to "Bey" and "Hanım."

Women invariably change to their husband's family name on marriage. A woman who is well-known in a company might continue to write her former name in parentheses; for example, **Lale (Dirin) Öztürk** or **Lale Öztürk (Dirin)**. You should address her as **Ms. Öztürk**. Ms. is appropriate for all Turkish women, since the unmarried form of "Hanım" is obsolete.

Another respectful title you may see in writing is **Sayın**, abbreviated **Sn.**, written in front of the names of both men and women; for example, **Sayın Hasan Turan**. Academic titles and degrees are rarely used by businesspeople.

Most Turks in positions of responsibility will have traditional names as described above. However, in the last 25 years or so, customs have been changing, especially in the major cities and among better-educated people. Younger staff in an office will probably have a single given name with a more Turkish, more European, less Arabic flavor. For example, many young women's names are derived from the Turkish names for plants and flowers.

COMPANY NAMES

Turkish companies doing international business are invariably corporations, of which there are two types, an **Anonim Şirket** (abbreviated **A. Ş.**) and a **Limited Şirket** (abbreviated **Ltd. Ş.** or just **Ltd.**) When it follows a company name, "Şirket" becomes **Şirketi** and is therefore sometimes abbreviated **Şti.** instead of "Ş." You would assume that a "Ltd." company is smaller and privately owned.

It is common to include the activities of a company in its name. In particular, many companies have names ending in **San. ve Tic. A. Ş.**, which stands for **Sanayi ve Ticaret Anonim Şirket**, meaning "Industrial and Trading, Inc." Other descriptive words are **İnşaat** (Construction), **Mimarlık** (Architecture), **Tesisat** (Installation), **Tekstil** (Textile), and **Turizm** (Tourism).

An effort is being made to translate American computer terminology. The company name **Ulukom Bilgisayar Yazılım Donanım Danışmanlık ve Tic. Ltd. Şti.** means "Ulukom Computer Software Hardware Consultancy and Trading, Inc."

OFFICES

Many offices are located in shared buildings, and it is quite usual to specify a floor (**Kat**, abbreviated **K:**) number and an office or apartment number (**Daire**, abbreviated **D:**); for example, **Soğanlık Cad. No:83 D:7 K:2.** More simply, the office number is often written after the building number, as in **Soğanlık Cad. No:83/7.**

BUILDING NAMES

It is quite common for buildings to be named after the builder, the owner, the street, or the principal tenant. The word **Apartman** refers to an entire building, not an individual apartment. **Han** is another common word for "building," often compounded, as in **İşhanı** ("business building") and **Teknohan** ("technology building"). **Merkez** ("Center") and **Plaza** are sometimes used. All these words have a final letter -i when they follow the building name, as in **Karaahmetoğlu İş Merkezi**, meaning "Karaahmetoğlu (a person's name) Business Center."

Building names are written between the street name and the building number. Building names may not be logically necessary but are very frequently included if they exist. In modern business areas of Turkish cities, buildings are clearly numbered in an orderly fashion, but there may be irregularities in older areas.

An industrial park is called a **Sanayi Sitesi**, and its name will appear right after the company name.

BUILDING NUMBERS

Building numbers are written after the street name and after the building name, if any. As explained above, **Apt. No. 83** means "Building No. 83," not "Apartment No. 83." A building number in the form **22/B** implies a second entrance.

STREET NAMES

Dictionary form	Address form	Abbrev.	Meaning
Cadde	Caddesi	Cad.	Most usual word for "street"
Sokak	Sokağı	Sok.	Smaller street
Bulvar	Bulvarı	Bul.	Major business street
Meydan	Meydanı	Mey.	Square
Mahalle	Mahallesi	Mah.	Neighborhood (see text)
Yol	Yolu	Yol	Highway
Çıkmaz	Çıkmazı	Çık.	Dead-end street

The second column shows how the word appears when spelled out in an address.

A "Mahalle" is not strictly a street but a small area of a city; however, it participates in addresses as the first element of the street line. For example, **Fulya**

Mah. Akıncı Bayırı Sok. Yıldız Apt. No: 17/1 means Room 1 in the Yıldız Building, located at 17 Akıncı Bayırı Street, in the Fulya neighborhood.

It is quite common to find two streets mentioned in an address. **Cumhuriyet Cad. Kayahatun Sok. No: 15**, for example, implies that Kayahatun Sokağı leads off Cumhuriyet Caddesi.

Some streets in Ankara and other cities are numbered (for example, **Ege Mah. 151. Sok.**, or **Demetevler 7. Cad.**).

A very long street address in which the words are not interspersed with street designators from the table above probably contains directions for visitors and is not a proper postal address.

Rural addresses may not have street names at all, but they occur infrequently in business addresses. The address of a rural plant may include a highway kilometer post; for example, **Esenboğa Yolu 15km. 06381 Ankara.**

LOCALITY NAMES

Locality names are frequently included in the major cities. They should be written on the line above the postcode and city, but are sometimes prefixed to the city name, as in:

> **81030 Feneryolu-İSTANBUL**
> **80270 Okmeydanı-İSTANBUL**
> **35210 Çankaya/İZMİR**

As localities are quite small, two locality names are sometimes joined together to add precision; for example, **Yakacık-Kartal** or **Kartal-Maltepe**.

CITY NAMES

The principal cities of Turkey are **Ankara** (the capital), **İstanbul** (the major business city), and **İzmir**.

STATE/PROVINCE/ETC. NAMES

Turkey is divided into about 80 areas called **il**. Since each one is named after its principal town, they are not used in postal addresses.

POSTCODES

A five-digit postcode system has been in existence for a number of years, but it is by no means universally used even by businesses. It has not been well publicized, and many Turks will not know the postcode of either their home or office. It should precede the city name on the line following the locality name.

Postcodes are allocated in approximately alphabetical order of the names of the "il" townships, so a geographical sort is not very meaningful. Codes for Ankara begin **06**, codes for western (European) İstanbul begin **34**, codes for the central business district of İstanbul begin **80**, codes for eastern (Asian) İstanbul begin **81**, and codes for İzmir begin **35**.

P.O. BOXES

The Turkish term for "P.O. Box" is **Posta Abone Kutusu**, abbreviated **P.K.** P.O. Boxes are always numbered.

Boxes are often rented for some specific short-term purpose rather than for the general reception of mail. Box numbers should be used with caution, and the street address should not be omitted unless you specifically know that it is safe to do so.

COUNTRY NAME

Turkey is spelled **Türkiye** in Turkish. **Türkiye Cumhuriyeti** appears on postage stamps and means "Republic of Turkey."

Some foreign postal administrations may recognize the country prefix **TR-**, but its use inside Turkey is rare.

Letterheads

Turkish term	Meaning
Tarih	Date
Sayı	Subject
Konu	Subject
İlgi	Subject
Referansımız	Our reference
Referansınız	Your reference
Bilgi	Copies to
Bayi	Dealer
Mağaza	Store
Şube	Branch
Fabrika	Factory
Merkez	Home office
İrtibat Bürosu	Contact person

Dates, Money, Typographical Conventions

DATES AND MONEY	
Date format	Day, Month, Year
Typical date abbreviation	29.02.1996
Currency unit	lira (dictionary form) lirası (usual spelling)
Cents	not used
Domestic currency codes	TL, T.L., occasionally L.
ISO international currency code	TRL
Other international codes	not used
Decimal separator	comma
Thousands separator	period
Typical currency amount	25.000 TL (note space before TL)

Even amounts are often written in the form **25.000,-**. Because of inflation, prices are often quoted in foreign currency, leaving the Turkish lira exchange rate to be determined when payment is made. By analogy with the domestic convention, U.S. dollar amounts may be written in the form **1.776,- $**.

A period follows ordinal numbers; for example, **7.** means "7th."

Envelopes

You are supposed to leave margins of 40mm at the top, and 20mm at the right and at the foot. Return addresses should be written in the top left corner, although some Turks, especially in private correspondence, write them on the flap.

MESSAGES FOR THE MAILROOM	
English	Turkish
Urgent	Acil
Fragile	Kırılacak Eşya
Confidential	Gizli
Please do not bend	Katlamayınız
Please forward (to X)	Lütfen X 'e iletiniz
X c/o Y	X (Y eliyle)

These translations are not necessarily in conventional domestic use in Turkey.

Phone Numbers

PHONE SYSTEM INFORMATION (SEE CHAPTER 4)	
Country Code	+90
International Access Code	00
Long-Distance Access Code	0
Typical City Codes	three-digit; e.g., 312 = Ankara
Typical number format	(212) 223 27 00
Ringing and busy signals	European

The Turkish phone system changed extensively in 1993, and phone numbers now resemble the North American format. All local numbers now have seven digits, and all area codes have three digits. The Long-Distance Access Code is not written in front of the area code. Area code **800** is used for free information services, **900** for chargeable information services, **512** for pagers, and **522** for mobile phones.

There is no simple general rule for converting old number formats into new ones. The city code for İstanbul used to be 1, and the Long-Distance Access Code used to be 9. If the seven-digit number following the 1 began with 2, 5, or 6, try changing the 1 or 91 to 212. If it began with 3 or 4, try changing the 1 or 91 to 216. If you have a seven-digit number with the city code 4 for Ankara, try using 312 instead of the 4 or 94.

An expression in the form **4Hat** means four lines that roll over.

UNITED KINGDOM

Address Summary

Example of a London street address:

> **Mr. G. R.**[1] **Robinson**[2]
> **International Publishing plc**[3]
> **Publishing House**[4]
> **17**[5] **Swiss Cottage Road**[6]
> **LONDON**[7]   **NW3 4TP**[8]

Key:

[1] Initials of two given names.

[2] Family name.

[3] **plc** = **Public Limited Company**, signifying a corporation, probably publicly traded.

[4] Building named after the owner or principal tenant.

[5] Building number.

[6] **Road** is at least as common as "street."

[7] City or delivery-post-office name; *must be capitalized.*

[8] Extended postcode; *one space required between the two parts. City name should be followed by six spaces.*

Example of a suburban or provincial business address:

> **Mr. N. J. Lancaster**
> **International Publishing Ltd.**[9]
> **Kingsbury House**[10]
> **12 Kingsbury Road**
> **EDGWARE**[11]
> **Middlesex**[12]
> **HA8 9XG**[13]

Key:

[9] **Ltd.** = **Limited**, signifying the most common form of corporation, privately owned.

[10] Building named after the street.

[11] City or delivery-post-office name; *must be capitalized.*

[12] County name; *must not be capitalized.*

[13] Extended postcode; could also be written on the county line, *after six spaces.*

Language

In individual correspondence, there is no need to adapt to the spelling conventions or vocabulary of British English, but if you are writing sales literature or other materials which are going to circulate widely, it is not usually in your interests to present a foreign appearance.

Most lists of British/American vocabulary differences are of doubtful accuracy and are for amusement only. Very few words cause real misunderstandings in business.

Word to Avoid	U.S. Meaning	U.K. Meaning
to table	to postpone discussion of an issue	to add an issue to the agenda for discussion
a scheme	pejorative; means a plan whose honesty or legality is suspect	used neutrally in many phrases to describe plans or government programs, as in "pension scheme" (but the verb "to scheme" is pejorative in the U.K. also)
turnover	usually refers to staff departures, so a company with high turnover is bad	the ordinary term for a company's revenues, so a company with high turnover is good

For historical reasons, British and American spelling has also diverged, in minor but often consistent ways.

U.S.	U.K.	U.S.	U.K.
words like authorize	authorise	a license	a licence (the verb is "to license")
words like liter	litre	maneuver	manœuvre
words like color	colour	mold, balk	mould, baulk
words like catalog	catalogue	program	programme (except a computer program)
(bank) check	cheque		
defense, offense	defence, offence	words like totaling	totalling
draft	draught	words like skillful	skilful

The above table is just a warning. You must add a British spell checker to your word processor if you are going to produce materials for other English-speaking countries.

Address Elements

PERSONAL NAMES

Most British people have two given names (which they call their *Christian names*) and a family name (which they call their *surname*). Most people write the initials of their two given names, but some choose to write their first name in full, and some use the U.S. convention of writing their first name in full and their middle initial. A more formal and old-fashioned alternative to **Mr. W. R. Baker** is **W. R. Baker, Esq.** ("Esquire"). British women must never be addressed as "Esq."

The use of three or more initials (e.g., **P. C. P. Jackson**) or the use of two surnames joined by a hyphen (e.g., **R. G. Harmon-Young**) traditionally indicated a claim to higher social status in the British class system. The latter is always addressed as **Mr. Harmon-Young**, not "Mr. Young." Younger people in all walks of life may now have three or more initials, and a few women choose to prefix their family name to their husband's.

Women are usually addressed as **Miss** (if unmarried) or **Mrs.** (if married). A few prefer to be addressed American-style as **Ms.** A few use both their previous family name and their current husband's name. A woman who was well known in a company before marrying, or a woman who wants to keep a name in common with her children from a previous marriage, might be likely to use a double surname. **Emma Lester Richardson**, with no hyphen, would be called **Mrs. Richardson**. If a British woman uses her initials, she traditionally adds "(Miss)" or "(Mrs.)" after her typed name to show that she is a woman: **C. R. Taylor (Mrs.)**. Call British women "Mrs." unless you know their preference.

People who work together usually call each other by their given names, but corporate cultures vary. Enough people would prefer to be called "Mr." and "Mrs." that you have to be careful. Notice whether they sign their names with their given name or their initials. Also listen to how they announce themselves on the phone: a man who answers "Edwards" had better be called "Mr. Edwards."

The title **Dr.** (doctor) is only used in business by researchers or by executives who are deliberately emphasizing their scientific pasts. Executives sometimes list their university degrees on business cards. Most British graduates have a **B.A.** ("Bachelor of Arts") or **B.Sc.** ("Bachelor of Science") degree. A university is sometimes indicated in parentheses after the degree; of these, you should recognize **M.A. (Oxon.)** and **M.A. (Cantab.)** as indicating the high-status universities of Oxford and Cambridge, respectively. Some people add a long list of memberships in professional institutions. You are under no obligation to reproduce any degrees except the title "Dr."

However, you do need to notice and reproduce abbreviations after a name that show the person has received a public-service honor. The two most common honors are abbreviated **M.B.E.** ("Member of the Order of the British Empire") and **O.B.E.** ("Officer of the Order of the British Empire").

You are most unlikely to deal with titled British people in business. The only exception is that knighthoods are routinely given to senior government officials and occasionally to the heads of major private corporations. A knight is referred to as, for example, **Sir Robert Watson**. He is addressed as **Dear Sir Robert** in a letter, and as **Sir Robert** in speech, pronounced with emphasis on the "Robert," not the "Sir." "Sir Watson," used by many foreigners, sounds ridiculous to the British.

Do not address someone as "sir," "madam," or "ma'am" in speech unless you are a store clerk speaking to a rich customer.

COMPANY NAMES

Legal Entities	Abbrev.	Explanation
Public Limited Company	PLC, plc	Large corporation, usually publicly traded
Limited	Ltd.	Most common designation of a corporation

Various old forms of names are still in rare use. For example, unincorporated partnerships used to have names like **Messrs. Brown and Smith** (short for the French "Messieurs," but pronounced "messes"). **Messrs.** is still sometimes used as a respectful prefix, e.g., **Messrs. General Motors**.

OFFICES

Internal office designations are not common. You sometimes see a **floor** number in a shared building, or a **room** number in a government agency or large corporate office. Modern office buildings designed to appeal to American companies may have **suite** numbers, but they are usually numbered sequentially, with no relationship to the floor number.

A **unit** number implies a warehouse or small industrial plant. **Flat** is the British word for "apartment."

BUILDING NAMES

Office buildings, even small ones, usually have names. The name usually relates to the street name, the owner, or the principal tenant, or contains some historical reference. Most buildings are called "Something **House**," but a highrise building may be called a **Tower** and small buildings may be called **Chambers**. Individuals often name private houses, usually with a rural or historical flavor.

Plants are usually called **Factory** or **Works**. An industrial area is called an **Industrial Estate** or **Trading Estate**. Its name should precede the street name, but usage is inconsistent.

As long as you have a building number, you can drop a "house" name if you need to reduce the number of lines in a British address to fit your space constraints.

BUILDING NUMBERS

The British Post Office tries to make everyone use building numbers, but there is some popular resistance. Many British individuals and businesses would rather use a building name and a street name, without a number. The post office is winning, but it is still quite usual to find building numbers missing from both business and private addresses.

A building number of **12A** indicates that a building, or at least an entrance, has been created between 12 and 14. **12B** lies between 12A and 14. A number like **163/166** or **163-166** indicates that buildings or lots have been combined, which is common.

STREET NAMES

Street Designator	Abbrev.	Explanation
Road	Rd.	Most common designation for a well-traveled street
Street	St.	Major business street
Hill, Way	none	Major business streets
Bypass	none	Highway avoiding a town center
Close, Court, Crescent, Drive, Gardens, Lane, and about 200 others	Cl., Ct., Cres., Dr., Gdns., Ln.	Residential streets
Avenue	Ave.	Usually a residential street but sometimes a (newer) major business street
Terrace	Terr.	Usually a residential street but sometimes a strip shopping center

In older areas, it is possible to have two street names in the address: for example,

9 Lion and Lamb Yard
West Street

implies that the first street is small and leads off the second. There is unlikely to be a building name as well, and so this practice does not lengthen addresses.

In older areas, such as the "City" financial district of London, streets do not always have a "street" word (e.g., **Crutched Friars**).

LOCALITY NAMES

It is quite common to see locality names in an address, most of them unnecessary. The British Post Office publishes detailed schedules of required locality names, but British people are not familiar with the requirements. They are inclined to include all possible geographical information in their addresses, regardless of what the post office wants.

In a city, a locality is the name of a neighborhood, smaller than any political subdivision, and is usually unnecessary. In rural areas it is the name of a village, and you should include it.

In fact, in a rural area two localities are allowed, written on separate lines. Fortunately, in practice, this does not mean you have to anticipate an extra line in all addresses: if there are two localities, the area is probably so remote that it does not have street names.

As long as you have a good postcode, you can drop locality names if you need to reduce the number of lines in a British address.

CITY NAMES

The city name must be written in capital letters on a line by itself (except possibly for the postcode; see below).

In residential addresses, the words **by** or **near** are sometimes used to separate the locality and the name of the post town, as in:

Chobham (the locality)
near WOKING (the post town)

The British Post Office tries to discourage this, but does accept **VIA WOKING** as legitimate.

Before postcodes were introduced, a system of postal districts existed in five major cities, written in the form "LONDON S.E. 1." or "SHEFFIELD 3." These districts are obsolete but are still used when people don't know their postcodes.

The principal business cities are as follows:

Aberdeen	Coventry	Lincoln	Portsmouth
Bath	Croydon	Liverpool	Reading
Bedford	Dartford	London	Redhill
Belfast	Derby	Luton	Romford
Birmingham	Dundee	Manchester	Salford
Bournemouth	Edinburgh	Milton Keynes	Sheffield
Brighton	Exeter	Newcastle	Slough
Bristol	Glasgow	Northampton	Southampton
Bromley	Gloucester	Norwich	Twickenham
Cambridge	Hertford	Nottingham	Warwick
Cardiff	Hounslow	Oldham	Watford
Chelmsford	Ipswich	Oxford	Wolverhampton
Chester	Leeds	Peterborough	Worcester
Colchester	Leicester	Plymouth	York

STATE/PROVINCE/ETC. NAMES

The United Kingdom is divided into **counties**. The county name is often required in postal addresses. If present, it must be written on the line after the city name, without capitalization.

Foreigners often confuse city names with county names and abbreviations, creating undeliverable addresses (like "15 High Street, Berkshire," in which there is no town) or foolish-looking lists (like "European sales offices: Eschborn, Nanterre, and Beds.," which specifies particular suburbs in France and Germany and then a relatively large area in the United Kingdom that contains many towns).

You do not need a county name when writing to the cities in the table of principal business centers above. Also, you do not need the county name if it repeats the name of the city—for example, "Selkirk, Selkirkshire." The suffix **-shire**, which always indicates a county name, is pronounced "shuh," not "shyer."

ENGLISH (NOT SCOTTISH, WELSH, IRISH) COUNTIES			
County	Abbrev.	County	Abbrev.
Avon		Cleveland	
Bedfordshire	Beds	Cornwall	
Berkshire	Berks	County Durham	Co. Durham
Buckinghamshire	Bucks	Cumbria	
Cambridgeshire	Cambs	Derbyshire	
Cheshire		Devon	

County	Abbrev.	County	Abbrev.
Dorset		North Yorkshire	N Yorks
East Sussex	E Sussex	Nottinghamshire	Notts
Essex		Oxfordshire	Oxon
Gloucestershire	Glos	Shropshire	Salop
Hampshire	Hants	Somerset	
Herefordshire		South Humberside	S Humberside
Hertfordshire	Herts	South Yorkshire	S Yorks
Kent		Staffordshire	Staffs
Lancashire	Lancs	Suffolk	
Leicestershire	Leics	Surrey	
Lincolnshire	Lincs	Tyne & Wear	
Merseyside		Warwickshire	Warks
Middlesex	Middx	West Midlands	W Midlands
Norfolk		West Sussex	W Sussex
Northamptonshire	Northants	West Yorkshire	W Yorks
North Humberside	N Humberside	Wiltshire	Wilts
Northumberland	Northd	Worcestershire	Worcs

The county in a U.K. postal address is not necessarily the correct county of residence of a business for the purposes of litigation or taxation.

POSTCODES

Postcodes are universally used by businesses, but compliance by individuals in their personal correspondence is rather low. Letters are delivered promptly without them. However, correct postcodes are particularly important for you as a foreigner because they can rescue you from most other errors you might make.

U.K. postcodes are very frequently miscopied by foreigners. You cannot trust postcodes in, for example, any list of U.K. branch offices printed in another country. Even the British regularly confuse the digits 0 and 1 with the letters O and I.

There is no standard format of postcode that could be easily validated by a computer. The postcode consists of two parts, separated by one space. The first part identifies the destination post office, for sorting purposes. The second part identifies the delivery area down to a group of about 15 houses in a residential area, or down to a single business.

The format of the first part varies. Outside of five major cities, it consists of a two-letter code derived from the name of the regional sorting center, followed by a one- or two-digit number. In the five major cities listed first in the following table, the postcodes are based on the older system of postal districts; for example, Sheffield 2 became **S2**, and London E.C.2. became **EC2x**, where x is an additional letter.

The following table gives the letter-number format of the first part of U.K. postcodes. The second part, after one space, always consists of number-letter-letter.

Location	"Postcode Area"	Format of first part of postcode
London	E = East, N = North, W = West	X9, X99, or X9X (e.g., E9, E18, E2A)
	EC = East Central, NW = Northwest, SE = Southeast, SW = Southwest, WC = West Central	XX9, XX99, or XX9X (e.g., SW7, SW19, SW1A, but SW16A is impossible)
Provincial cities	B = Birmingham, G = Glasgow, L = Liverpool, S = Sheffield	X9, X99, or X9X (e.g., L8, B42, B4A)
London suburbs	BR = Bromley, CR = Croydon, DA = Dartford, EN = Enfield, HA = Harrow, IG = Ilford, KT = Kingston, RM = Romford, SM = Sutton, TW = Twickenham, UB = Uxbridge, WD = Watford	XX9, XX99 (e.g., SL6, KT12)
Towns around London	AL = St. Albans, BN = Brighton, CM = Chelmsford, CT = Canterbury, GU = Guildford, HP = Hemel Hempstead, LU = Luton, ME = Maidstone, MK = Milton Keynes, OX = Oxford, RG = Reading, RH = Redhill, SG = Stevenage, TN = Tonbridge	

The British Post Office wants the postcode to be the last element of the address. It is often written on a separate line by itself. However, it is permissible to put it on the last line of the address, at the end, separated by two to six spaces (preferably six) from the city or county name.

The British Post Office would like the postcode to follow the country name on mail from overseas, but this conflicts with the requirements of some other countries' post offices (including the United States'). Obey the rules of the country of mailing.

P.O. BOXES

Boxes are used by some businesses with very high volumes of mail but are not common. They have their own postcodes, different from the business's street-address postcode.

COUNTRY NAME

Mail should be addressed to **UNITED KINGDOM** or the equivalent in the language of the sender's country. The United Kingdom is composed of England, Scotland, Wales, and Northern Ireland. Great Britain (or simply Britain) consists of England, Scotland, and Wales only. It is not necessary or correct to use "England" and the other regional names in either domestic or international mail. An unofficial reason to use UNITED KINGDOM is that you will give offense if you get the region wrong: "Cardiff, England" looks foolish in England and annoys the Welsh.

The country prefix GB- is sometimes written in addresses by mailers in other European countries, but it is not authorized by any postal administration or international agreement.

"The British Isles" is a geographical term describing Great Britain together with all of Ireland and a number of small offshore islands. The **Isle of Man** and the islands of **Jersey** and **Guernsey** are important as financial centers. They are not part of the United Kingdom, but international mail reaches them through it and they are integrated into the U.K. phone system. Only Jersey has post-codes, which have the U.K. format, beginning **JE**.

The postal and phone systems of the Republic of Ireland are completely separate from those of the United Kingdom. Refer to the chapter on Ireland for help in distinguishing addresses in Northern Ireland from those in the Republic.

Letterheads

British company letterheads must show a list of directors of the company, or the partners or owners of an unincorporated business. Foreign directors are supposed to be identified by printing their nationalities (not their countries of residence) in parentheses after their names; for example, **Y. L. Leblicq (Belgium)**.

A company registration number is always printed with a phrase such as **Registered in England No. 1658196**. Often, a **Registered Office** address is printed in small type. Do not ever use this address for commercial correspondence if it is different from the prominently printed address; it is only for the formal service of legal notices.

The **VAT** (**Value-Added Tax**, the European sales tax) registration number is often shown on a letterhead as well as on invoices.

Dates, Money, Typographical Conventions

DATES AND MONEY	
Date format	Day, Month, Year
Typical date abbreviation	29/2/96
Currency unit	pound ("pound sterling")
Cents	pence
Domestic currency code	£
ISO international currency code	GBP
Other international codes	UKL, UK£
Decimal separator	period
Thousands separator	comma
Typical currency amount	£5,879.50 (note no space after the £)

The decimal point is sometimes raised up: **1·5 kg**. A hyphen is often used in money amounts; for example, **£40-56** means forty pounds and fifty-six pence.

American salutations are recognized in the United Kingdom and do not give offense, but they are never used by British writers. The following traditional conventions are not rigidly followed anymore but are safe to use in all circumstances:

Addressee (attention lines do not count)	Traditional Opening (note comma used in place of colon)	Traditional Closing
A company	Dear Sirs,	Yours faithfully,
An individual by title	Dear Sir, ("Dear Madam," if you know the titleholder is a woman)	Yours faithfully,
An individual by name	Dear Mr. Edwards, Dear John,	Yours sincerely,
A friend	Dear John,	Yours,

Officials in the British government and other large, conservative organizations sometimes write the salutation and the closing by hand. This is intended as a courteous personalization. You must not assume that they are correcting a mistake or sending you a form letter.

A woman should type (**Ms.**) after her name at the end of a letter unless she has a traditionally feminine English given name.

The letters **P.T.O.** ("Please Turn Over") at the foot of a sheet of paper mean the text is continued on the back.

Sans-serif typefaces are commonly used in business materials.

Envelopes

The British Post Office prefers that the return address be written on the flap of the envelope, but accepts it positioned in the top left corner of the address side. In practice, British people rarely write return addresses anywhere, even on international mail.

Address lines are supposed to be limited to 32 typed characters. The address block is supposed to be 42mm (1.65″) high by 115mm (4.5″) wide, above a bottom margin of 18mm (0.7″).

Unless you omit some information or combine lines, a British address can easily be ten lines long: addressee/title/company/"House"/ street/locality/city/county/postcode/country.

Phone Numbers

PHONE SYSTEM INFORMATION (SEE CHAPTER 4)	
Country Code	+44
International Access Code	010
Long-Distance Access Code	0
Typical City Codes	1x1 (largest cities) (e.g., 171 = Inner London) 1xxx (most other areas) (e.g., 1222 = Cardiff) Longer in rural areas
Standard number formats	Major cities: 0171-504 5564 Other areas: 01628 23954 But often written (0171) 504 5564 etc.
Ringing and busy signals	British

A large number of special prefixes are used for numbers that may or may not be accessible from overseas: **0800** and **0500** are toll-free numbers; **0345** and **0645** are used for a system for making long-distance calls at the cost of a local call; **0336**, **0338**, **0660**, **08364**, **0839**, **0891**, and **0898** are for premium services (like U.S. 900); and **0370**, **0374**, **0385**, **0802**, **0831**, **0836**, **0850**, **0860**, **0881**, **0956**, and **0973** are for mobile phones.

In 1995 a 1 was added to almost all city codes, so central London numbers changed from 071- to 0171-. 01- is an even older prefix (try either +44-171 or +44-181 instead). There were five exceptions for cities that changed their codes completely (and lengthened their local numbers from six to seven digits at the same time):

Bristol: 0272 is now	**+44-1179**
Leeds: 0532 is now	**+44-1132**
Leicester: 0533 is now	**+44-1162**
Nottingham: 0602 is now	**+44-1159**
Sheffield: 0742 is now	**+44-1142**

followed in each case by the old six-digit number.

"STD code" is an old term for the city code, currently called "dialling code."

Numbers prefixed (**07000**) are "personal" numbers. Calls to them are redirected to whichever regular number the subscriber provides. They may be redirected by time of day or day of the week.

Yet more changes to British area codes are expected to be announced soon, probably including an 020 code for all of London and an 029 code for all of Northern Ireland.

UNITED STATES

(This chapter is intended for foreigners dealing with the United States.)

Address Summary

Example of a street address:

Dale[1] C.[2] Benedetto[3]
International Publishing, Inc.[4]
16850[5] S.[6] Union[7] St.,[8] Suite 2250[9]
LAKEWOOD[10] CO[11]   80028[12]-4892[13]

Key:

[1] Given name; could be male or female.
[2] Initial of second given name.
[3] Family name.
[4] **Inc. = Incorporated.**
[5] Building number (168 blocks from the grid origin).
[6] **S. = South** (of the grid origin).
[7] Street name.
[8] **St. = Street.**
[9] A **Suite** is an office in a shared building; **2250** is probably half of the 22nd floor.
[10] City or delivery-post-office name; not usually capitalized in domestic use.
[11] Two-letter state abbreviation *(essential)*.
   One or two spaces must follow the state abbreviation.
[12] Five-digit postcode *(essential)*.
[13] Four-digit postcode extension for delivery *(optional); hyphen required between the postcode and the postcode extension.*
   These last four elements should be on the same line.

Example of a mixed postal and street address, as commonly printed on business stationery:

Ellen[14] Krueger[15] Murphy[16]
International Publishing Corp.[17]
3100[18] Two[19] First National Plaza[20]
3650[21] West Madison St.
P.O. Box 3567[22]
HOUSTON TX   77269-3567[23]

Key:

[14] Given name (female).
[15] Probably the family name she was born with.
[16] Her current family name; thus, **Ms. Murphy**.

349

[17] Corp. = **Corporation**; same as "Inc."

[18] Office suite number, probably the entire 31st floor.

[19] The second tower in a building complex.

[20] Building name (First National is a typical bank name).

[21] Building number. *Use this line and the line above for freight and courier deliveries.*

[22] P.O. Box *(must come just above the city line). Use this line for postal delivery, not the two lines above.*

[23] Extended postcode for the box; usually repeats the box number.

Address Elements

PERSONAL NAMES

A large majority of Americans are addressed in writing by their first name, middle initial, and family name (e.g., **Bruce W. Kuan**). A minority prefer first initial, middle name, family name (e.g., **J. Robert Braun**). A few people use their two initials only, which may mean that they are addressed like that in speech (e.g., **K. C. Womack**, pronounced "Casey," and addressed as **Dear K.C.**). A significant number of businesswomen use their initials like this.

Women will sometimes give you three names in full. It is most likely that **Rebecca Finlay Hoffman** was born Rebecca Finlay and has since been married to someone whose family name is Hoffman. She is addressed as **Dear Rebecca** or, formally, as **Dear Ms. Hoffman**. Alternatively, particularly in the South, a woman may have a double given name (e.g., **Mary Beth Collins**, who is addressed as **Dear Mary Beth**). "Mrs." and "Miss" are hardly used in business contexts today.

Americans normally use their given names with each other, except when particular respect is felt to be necessary. At a first business contact with someone outside your own organization, particularly if you are selling something, it is still safer to say or write "Mr." and "Ms.," but expect to change quickly to given names. The social risk is that foreigners appear distant and unfriendly if they hesitate to use given names in the United States.

In fact, Americans and other English-speaking people commonly have nicknames, and even the use of someone's full given name in the United States may appear overly formal. In many cases, the nickname is just the first part of the given name (e.g., **Chris** for **Christopher** or **Christine**, **Ron** for **Ronald**, **Ray** for **Raymond**). The following table lists common nicknames which are not close to the full name.

Given Name	Nicknames	Given Name	Nicknames
Andrew	Andy, Drew	Harold	Hal, Harry
Anthony	Tony	James	Jim, Jimmy
Charles	Chuck	John	Jack
Edward	Ted	Richard	Dick, Rick
Elizabeth	Beth, Betty, Liz	Robert	Bob, Bobby
Eugene	Gene	William	Bill
Francis	Frank		

(Note that **Wm.** and **Chas.** are abbreviations for "William" and "Charles," not nicknames.)

In speech, every individual has a definite preference. A Robert who is known as Bob does not want to be called Rob, and not every Robert wants to use a nickname. Don't use a nickname until you are sure you have it right, but don't hesitate to ask people for their preference.

In writing, some individuals will direct you to use their nickname at all times by printing something like **R. W. (Bob) Gartner** on their business cards and under their signatures. More often, a person will sign **Bob** and print **Robert W. Gartner** underneath, in which case you should use the full name everywhere except in salutations (**Dear Bob**) and in speech.

Jr. ("Junior") or **II** following a man's name (e.g., **Craig R. Wilson, Jr.**) indicates that he has the same given names as his father. The third- or fourth-generation man of the same name would use **III** (occasionally **3d**) or **IV** (**4th**). The father might add **Sr.** ("Senior"). You must include these generation indicators when you write their names in full, but not in speech, and they are all just **Dear Mr. Wilson** in salutations.

Foreigners need to take special care to avoid assuming that American executives are men. Many common given names (e.g., **Dale, Lee, Leslie, Lynn**) and nicknames (e.g., **Alex, Sam, Terry**) are used by both genders. Also, many younger women in business have nontraditional given names which even foreigners from English-speaking countries may not recognize (e.g., **Blake, Kimberley**). Don't hesitate to call a receptionist and ask: "Hello, I'm calling from France. Is your Leslie O'Brien a man or a woman?" If you address a letter to an individual by title, the salutation should be **Dear Sir or Madam**; if you address a company, use **Ladies and Gentlemen**. Salutations are followed by a colon in the United States, not a comma. **Sincerely**, followed by a comma, can be used to close all correspondence to the United States, but **Regards** is more common for informal memos and faxes to people you know.

Professionals sometimes mention a degree or accreditation after their name. **J.D.** indicates a lawyer, **C.P.A.** an accountant, and **P.E.** an engineer. Lawyers, both men and women, often add **Esq.** after their names. Retired military officers in business often continue to use their abbreviated ranks: **Gen., Adm., Col., Maj.** Retired naval and air force officers may add **USN (Ret.)** and **USAF (Ret.)** after their names.

COMPANY NAMES

Registered names of companies must include the word **Incorporated** or **Corporation** (or its abbreviation, **Inc.** or **Corp.**). A rare alternative is **Limited**, abbreviated **Ltd.** There is no distinction between the names of public companies and private ones, but a company may indicate on a letterhead that it is publicly traded by mentioning a stock exchange, usually **NYSE, ASE,** or **NASDAQ**.

Some states have special forms of legal incorporation for doctors, dentists, and lawyers, usually indicated by the abbreviation **P.C.** ("Professional Corporation"). In some industries, partnerships are commonly created for tax benefits and are indicated by the word **Partners** or the abbreviation **L.P.** ("Limited Partnership"). Federally regulated banks use **N.A.** ("National Association").

Corporations are chartered by the individual states and have to take specific steps to protect their names in the other states, so it is quite possible to have two companies with the same or similar names.

The word **Company** or **Associates** (or its abbreviation, **Co.** or **Assocs.**) unaccompanied by one of the above abbreviations indicates unincorporated individuals.

OFFICES

Many office buildings in the United States are large and are shared by many companies. Tenants relocate more frequently than in other countries. The same is even more true of residential apartment complexes. It is essential to specify a **Suite** number unless a company is very large. **Apt.** ("apartment") is the abbreviation for a residential unit. The number sign **#** is also frequently used: **2929 Greenbriar Drive #1010**.

You can guess quite a lot about the size of the company from a suite number. **Suite 2200** is a large office on the 22d floor of a high-rise, probably the whole floor. **Suite 2250** is probably half the floor. **Suite 2235** is probably small. **Suite G** or **Suite G-4** is probably a unit in an office/warehouse complex. **Suite 1510-W** is probably in the west wing of a large twin-tower complex. **Suite 236** is probably a small office in a less prestigious low-rise building.

Floor numbers, abbreviated in the form **3rd fl.**, are also sometimes used. In most of the country, that implies that the company occupies the whole floor, but in the older areas of an Eastern city, it might be a small building whose offices are not individually numbered.

In a large plant or office campus belonging to a single company, an internal mail code may be required, variously called a **Mail Station** or **Maildrop** (abbreviated **MS, M/S, MD**, etc.). Other offices, particularly government ones, use **Room** numbers. If your correspondents give you a room number or mail station, be sure to use it, because internal mail services are not always efficient.

BUILDING NAMES

High-rise office buildings are commonly named **Tower, Plaza, Center,** or **Building**. Building names may include a number themselves, usually written as a word: **1900 Five Greenway Plaza** means the 19th floor of Building 5 in the Greenway Plaza complex.

Companies often use the building name in their address, which is unnecessary for mailing purposes but does help visitors to find them:

> **2250 Dresser Tower**
> **601 Jefferson**
> **HOUSTON TX   77002**

is the same as

> **601 Jefferson, Suite 2250**
> **HOUSTON TX   77002**

In practice, mail will be delivered to major buildings without the street address, especially if you have the nine-digit extended postcode, but it is safer to include the street address as well.

BUILDING NUMBERS

Except for the oldest-established areas of Eastern cities, most urban areas in the United States have building numbers assigned on a grid system. At the end of each block, or street intersection, the numbers jump to the next hundred, so **13150 Katy Freeway** will be 20 blocks from 11150 Katy Freeway. Half-numbers, such as **1620 1/2 (1620½) Castle Court** (never 1620.5), usually indicate a garage apartment or other subsidiary residential dwelling.

Do not write commas in street numbers (i.e., use 13150, not 13,150). It is not usual to write a comma after the street number.

STREET NAMES

Street Designator	Abbrev.	Explanation
Street	St.	Most common designation for a street
Avenue, Belt, Boulevard, Drive, Highway, Loop, Parkway, Road	Ave., Blvd., Dr., Pkwy., Rd.	Major business streets
Circle, Court, Lane, Place, Way, many others		Residential streets

In Southwestern states, the word **Street** is customarily omitted (e.g., **4604 Main**), although the U.S. Post Office would prefer that it be included.

Compass directions (**North, South, East, West**) or abbreviations (**N., S., E., W., N.E., N.W., S.E., S.W.**) are very common in addresses and are essential. For example, if a grid is defined by a **Main Street** running east/west and by a **Broadway** running north/south, then **500 South Broadway** will be five blocks south of Main, and **1000 West Main** will be ten blocks west of Broadway. If you look at a street directory, **West Main** will usually be under M, not W. If there are multiple compass directions, the order is important—**West Loop South** is different from **South Loop West**.

Major streets in city grids are frequently numbered rather than named (e.g., **1015 34th St.**). Addresses are sometimes written with a hyphen to distinguish more clearly between, for example, **1133 - 124th St.** and **11331 - 24th St.** Low-numbered streets are sometimes written out (e.g., **515 Fifth Avenue**). (Please remember your English lessons—you will be lucky if "Twoth Street" is recognized as 2nd St.) Half-streets are possible: **10 1/2 (10½) Street** (note no "th") will lie between 10th Street and 11th Street.

Local variations occur. Major business arteries in west suburban Detroit are one mile apart and are called **Nine Mile Road, Ten Mile Road**, and so on. Major roads in Washington, D.C., are designated by letters (e.g., **2017 K St.**), and **I Street** is often written **Eye Street**.

Almost every city has major streets named after John F. Kennedy and Martin Luther King, whose names are often abbreviated to **JFK** and **MLK**.

In urban areas highways usually have names, but in rural areas the federal or state number may be used. These are usually expressed in the form **Highway**

288, but all kinds of abbreviations are possible, specifying the exact type of highway: **Interstate 10, I-10, I.H.10,** or **IH-10; U.S. 59; S.H.** ("State Highway") **260** or **Texas 260**; and so on. Some local variations occur, which Americans are often not aware of themselves outside their home state. For example, **F.M.** ("Farm-to-Market") is common in Texas, as in **5900 F.M. 1960 E.**, and some rural addresses in Wisconsin are expressed as coordinates, as in **W330 N9065 Route 1**.

In rural areas, and sometimes in cities, where a street number may not be available or appropriate, an address is given as the intersection of two roads (e.g., **Highway 52 and N.W. 37th St.**). The words and symbols **and, at, &,** and **@** are all used to show intersections. In remote country areas, residential addresses often take the form **RR 3 Box 271D**, where "RR" stands for "Rural Route" (a rarer alternative is **HC**, "Highway Contract Route"), and the "Box" in this case is a box at the edge of the addressee's property. These are U.S. Post Office routes, not roads you would find on a map, and cannot be used for courier or freight deliveries. Companies in remote areas invariably have regular P.O. Boxes as described below.

LOCALITY NAMES

Locality names are not used in addresses. In fact, all addresses can theoretically be written in two lines.

CITY NAMES

By international convention, and to assist automated mail processing, the city name (strictly speaking, the name of the delivery post office) is supposed to be written in capitals, without punctuation, on envelopes. Domestically, Americans usually type the last line of the address in the form **Chicago, IL 60606**.

The principal business cities (with common abbreviations of their names) are as follows:

Atlanta, GA	Minneapolis (Mpls.), MN
Baltimore (Balto.), MD	New Orleans, LA
Boston, MA	New York (N.Y., N.Y.C.), NY
Cincinnati (Cinc.), OH	Oklahoma City, OK
Cleveland, OH	Philadelphia (Phila.), PA
Dallas, TX	Phoenix, AZ
Denver, CO	Pittsburgh, PA
Detroit, MI	St. Louis, MO
Houston, TX	Salt Lake City, UT
Kansas City, MO	San Francisco, CA
Los Angeles (L.A.), CA	Seattle, WA
Miami, FL	Washington (Wash.), DC
Milwaukee, WI	

In addition to the older abbreviations in the table above, most business travelers are familiar with the three-letter IATA airport codes and use them extensively in business correspondence (**ATL, BOS, SFO**, etc.).

Spanish-language place-names are common in the Southwest. Except for those of the largest cities (e.g., Los Angeles), they are pronounced in more or less a Spanish way; for example, **La Jolla** and **El Cajon** are pronounced "lahoya" and "elkahone."

A place called **Fort** ———— is not necessarily a current military base; it may just have once been a frontier post.

All city and equivalent names can be shortened to 13 positions according to a U.S. Post Office list of approved abbreviations.

STATE/PROVINCE/ETC. NAMES

A two-letter code is essential to designate the state or other territory of the address. Americans occasionally make mistakes with the codes, particularly those beginning with M in the following table (which does not include every associated territory of the United States). It is conventional to include the state name or abbreviation whenever you mention a city: "Our V.P./International is planning to visit Austin, Texas, and Boulder, Colorado, on this trip" (note the commas).

STATES AND TERRITORIES			
Full Name	**Code**	**Full Name**	**Code**
Alabama	AL	Montana	MT
Alaska	AK	Nebraska	NE
Arizona	AZ	Nevada	NV
Arkansas	AR	New Hampshire	NH
California	CA	New Jersey	NJ
Colorado	CO	New Mexico	NM
Connecticut	CT	New York	NY
Delaware	DE	North Carolina	NC
District of Columbia	DC	North Dakota	ND
Florida	FL	Ohio	OH
Georgia	GA	Oklahoma	OK
Hawaii	HI	Oregon	OR
Idaho	ID	Pennsylvania	PA
Illinois	IL	Puerto Rico	PR
Indiana	IN	Rhode Island	RI
Iowa	IA	South Carolina	SC
Kansas	KS	South Dakota	SD
Kentucky	KY	Tennessee	TN
Louisiana	LA	Texas	TX
Maine	ME	Utah	UT
Maryland	MD	Vermont	VT
Massachusetts	MA	Virginia	VA
Michigan	MI	Washington	WA
Minnesota	MN	West Virginia	WV
Mississippi	MS	Wisconsin	WI
Missouri	MO	Wyoming	WY

If you want to write out the name of the state in full, it still goes on the same line as the city name. Many Americans continue to use an older system of state abbreviations (e.g., "Oklahoma City, Okla.") which automated equipment does not understand.

POSTCODES

Postcodes are officially called **ZIP codes**, often reduced to **zipcode** or just **zip**.

On an envelope, the ZIP code is supposed to follow the state abbreviation on the same line after one or two spaces at least as wide as one M. This facilitates reading by automatic scanning equipment.

There is a five-digit system in universal use. Codes are allocated across the country roughly from east to west, so that the lowest ZIP codes are in the northeast and the highest are in Alaska. One five-digit ZIP code corresponds roughly to one local post office building. Mailing lists are frequently sorted by ZIP code.

In the extended nine-digit system, officially called **ZIP + 4**, the code designates a very small area, such as one side of one block of a residential street, or one apartment complex, or one floor of an office building. Most companies that have any significant volume of mail have their own nine-digit ZIP code. The extra four digits are optional but they enable mail to be sorted faster, so you should use them if you know them.

Mail without a ZIP code is handled manually and is subject to delays. If you write addresses by hand, print the digits carefully. European handwritten crossed 7s, or 1s with upstrokes, may be misunderstood.

P.O. BOXES

The use of P.O. Boxes is rather common, because businesses can usually collect their box mail early, whereas mail may not be delivered to a street address until late in the day.

In large cities, the boxes in a particular post office usually have their own five-digit ZIP code. The last four digits of the box number are usually added to the five-digit box ZIP code to form the extended nine-digit ZIP code, which is then unique to the box.

If you put both a street address and a P.O. Box in an address, U.S. Post Office policy is to deliver to whichever immediately precedes the city/state/ZIP line. However, while this may be true when mail is sorted manually, automated equipment seems to go by the ZIP code. In any event, the ZIP code on the city line should be correct for whichever address is on the preceding line.

A service industry has developed to offer private mailboxes. The client's box number is then sometimes disguised as a suite number following the street address of the box rental store, so an address like **P.O. Box 66189, Suite 234** may indicate that intermediaries are collecting the mail from the P.O. Box and distributing it to their clients' boxes.

A **P.O. Drawer** is just a big P.O. Box. It might have a letter instead of a number.

The abbreviations **POB** and **Box** are common. In Puerto Rico, a box is called an **Apartado**, abbreviated **Apdo.**

COUNTRY NAME

The **United States of America** is associated with a number of island territories, of which the only one of business importance is the Commonwealth of **Puerto Rico**. Puerto Rico is integrated into the U.S. postcode and phone system, but its street addresses are always in Spanish. However, businesses and industrial plants invariably have P.O. Box addresses. For information on Puerto Rican Spanish conventions, refer to the chapter on Mexico.

Letterheads

There are no requirements for any particular information to be printed on business stationery, and it is rare to see anything that would help you to legally identify a corporation.

Dates, Money, Typographical Conventions

DATES AND MONEY	
Date format	Month, Day, Year
Typical date abbreviation	2/29/96
Currency unit	dollar
Cents	cents
Domestic currency code	$
ISO international currency code	USD
Other international codes	US$
Decimal separator	period
Thousands separator	comma
Typical currency amount	$10,253.19 (note no space after $)

Most business correspondence and printed material use serif typefaces.

Envelopes

You must leave a bottom margin of ⅝″ (16mm), and left and right margins of ½″ (13mm). The top of the address (or at least the city/state/ZIP line) is supposed to be within 2¾″ (70mm) of the bottom of the envelope. The return address must be written in the top left corner.

Phone Numbers

PHONE SYSTEM INFORMATION (SEE CHAPTER 4)	
Country Code	+1
International Access Code	011
Long-Distance Access Code	1
Typical City Codes	All three-digit (e.g., 312 = Downtown Chicago)
Typical number formats	(310) 869-8792 310/869-8792 310-869-8792 1-310-869-8792
Ringing and busy signals	North American

Area codes are always three digits long, and local numbers are always seven digits long. An area code may cover an area ranging in size from the downtown area of a major city up to one entire state. Area codes subdivide at the rate of about one per year over the entire country. Directory information for any given area code is obtained by dialing the area code followed by 555-1212, which can be called directly from overseas.

There are several special area codes: (**800**) and (**888**) numbers are toll-free, and an **(877)** will appear during the currency of this edition. **(900)** numbers are extra-charge information numbers, and **(700)** provides access to a conferencing system. The accessibility of these numbers varies; usually, they cannot be dialed from outside the United States.

However, if you see an alternative phone number on a letterhead or business cards labeled **Metro**, you can use it. It means the company has set up a local line in a neighboring city so that people there can call in without incurring long-distance charges. Business cards of executives in large organizations often specify an internal telephone extension (**ext.** or **xt.**) or a direct-dial number (**dd**), as well as the switchboard number. Executives with international responsibility often print their home number (as **Res.**, for "Residence").

American telephones have letters, which are used to create easily remembered "numbers." The translation is ABC=2, DEF=3, GHI=4, JKL=5, MNO=6, PQRS=7, TUV=8, WXYZ=9. So 713/MYSTERY is dialed +1-713-697-8379 from overseas.

Words of Warning!

Paper Sizes: There are two sizes of business stationery in the United States. The most common size measures 8½″ × 11″ (216 × 280mm), called **letter-size** (**quarto** in British English). The less common is called **legal-size** (**foolscap** in British English). In addition to looking "foreign," European A4 paper has two practical disadvantages. American photocopiers will usually cut off the top or bottom 20mm, so do not fill the page or print vital information at the foot. Also, A4 will not fit comfortably into letter-size filing systems and filing cabinets.

Business Cards: American business cards are invariably 3½″ × 2″, close enough to 9 × 5cm. Other sizes will not fit into people's boxes and wallets.

Correspondence vs. Telephoning: Foreigners often write to U.S. companies thinking that a letter will have more impact than a phone call. The reverse is usually the case. Compared with most countries, employees in the United States usually make a considerable effort to answer phones promptly and to find someone who can help the caller. Mail just does not have the same priority. Anything difficult to deliver or understand is likely to go astray inside a company.

Nonsexist Language: All professional and technical writers, and all larger American organizations, public and private, have adjusted their vocabulary over the last few years to avoid the appearance of excluding women. It is important in correspondence and sales materials to avoid words like "businessmen" (say "executives") and statements like "The customer will find all *his* requirements met" (use the plural: "Customers will find all *their* requirements met").

VENEZUELA

Address Summary

Example of a street address:

Sr.[1] **José**[2] **González**[3]
Editores Internacionales[4] **C.A.**[5]
Edif.[6] **Bolívar,**[7] **Piso**[8] **7, Of.**[9] **3-A**
Av.[10] **Madrid**[11] **No.**[12] **322**[13]
Urb.[14] **Las Mercedes**[15]
CARACAS[16] **1060,**[17] **D.F.**[18]

Key:

[1] **Sr.** = **Señor**, meaning "Mr."
[2] Given name.
[3] Family name.
[4] Company name.
[5] **C.A.** = **Compañía Anónima**, signifying a corporation.
[6] **Edif.** = **Edificio**, meaning "Building."
[7] Building name.
[8] **Piso** means "floor."
[9] **Of.** = **Oficina**, meaning "Suite."
[10] **Av.** = **Avenida**, meaning "Avenue."
[11] Street name.
[12] **No.** = **Número**, meaning "number."
[13] Building number.
[14] **Urb.** = **Urbanización**, a city district.
[15] Locality name.
[16] City name.
[17] Four-digit postcode.
[18] **D.F.** = **Distrito Federal**, meaning "Federal District."

Example of a grid street address in Maracaibo:

Sr. Pedro López
Editores Internacionales S.A.[19]
Calle 89,[20] **14A**[21]**-22**[22]
MARACAIBO 4001, Edo.[23] **Zulia**[24]

Key:

[19] **S.A.** = **Sociedad Anónima**, signifying a corporation.
[20] **Calle 89**, meaning "89th Street."
[21] **14A** = **Avenida 14A**, the cross-street.
[22] Building number or position.
[23] **Edo.** = **Estado**, meaning "State."
[24] State name.

Address Elements

PERSONAL NAMES

Venezuelans' full legal names usually follow the custom of Spain, in which a given name is followed by the father's family name and then the mother's family name. However, in practice, most businesspeople will either drop their mother's name or reduce it to its initial; for example, **José González Hernández** (**Mr. González**) is likely to write his name as **José González** or **José González H.** If he writes his name in full, he probably wants to be called **Mr. González Hernández**. When the family names are hyphenated or joined with **de** ("of"), you are expected to use both: **Pedro Muñoz-Tebar** and **Augusto Pérez de Márquez** would be addressed as **Mr. Muñoz-Tebar** and **Mr. Pérez de Márquez** in English.

Double given names also exist; **José-María Ortiz Acuña** should be addressed as **Dear José-María** if you are on first-name terms. Cosmopolitan Venezuelans will quickly use their first names, at least with English-speaking people, but it is still best to address strangers as "Mr."

"Mr.," "Mrs.," and "Miss" are **Señor**, **Señora**, and **Señorita** in Spanish, abbreviated **Sr.**, **Sra.**, and **Srta.** Women in business should be addressed as "Señora" regardless of marital status. Professional women increasingly keep their own family names after marriage. Academic and professional titles are quite common, especially **Dr.** (Doctor), **Ing.** (Engineer), and **Lic.** (Graduate). People do call themselves "Dr." without always having a doctorate as it would be understood in other countries.

COMPANY NAMES

Legal Entities	Abbrev.	Explanation
Sociedad Anónima, Compañía Anónima	S.A., C.A.	Most common designation for a corporation, publicly traded or privately owned
Sociedad de Responsabilidad Limitada	S.R.L.	Smaller corporation, privately owned

OFFICES

An office in a shared building is usually called an **Oficina**, abbreviated **Of.**, but **Of. 64**, **Local 64**, and **Loc. 64** all mean the same thing.

In addition, or instead, it is common to give the floor number: **Edificio Aves, Piso 7**.

BUILDING NAMES

High-rise buildings usually have names, which are included in postal addresses. Office-building names usually begin with **Edificio** ("Building") or **Torre** ("Tower"). **Residencia** implies a condominium or apartment complex but could include offices.

Businesses may also be located in houses or low-rise buildings, which have names beginning with **Casa** or **Quinta**.

BUILDING NUMBERS

A building number is written after the street name. It is very common to precede it with **No.** or **#** (**Av. Luis Roche No. 208**, **Ave. Luis Roche #208**), but this is optional, and **Av. Luis Roche 208** is acceptable. When a high-rise building name is included in the address, it is not necessary to put a number after the street name. Occasionally you will see **s/n** (**sin número**) after the street name, which means that the street really is unnumbered.

STREET NAMES

Major streets in Caracas are called "avenues." The Spanish spelling is **Avenida**, abbreviated **Av.** or **Ave.** A smaller street is called a **Calle**. The word "calle" is usually omitted, except when the street has a number instead of a name.

The downtown area of Caracas is laid out on a grid system. The central north–south street is called **Avenida Norte** in the northern half and **Avenida Sur** in the southern half. Parallel streets to the east have odd numbers: **Avenida Norte 1**, **Avenida Norte 3**, etc. Parallel streets to the west have even numbers. East–west streets have names, not numbers, and change their names every few blocks.

Consequently, many addresses are given as intersections—for example, **Hoyo a Santa Rosalía**, which is not an exact address, or **Pilita a Glorieta No. 126**, which means **Pilita 126**. The Spanish words **a** ("at"), **y** ("and"), and **con** ("with") are used interchangeably.

It is common to add directions for visitors—for example, **Entre 5ª y 6ª transversal**, meaning "between the 5th and 6th cross-street," or **Cruz Verde a Velásquez**, meaning "at' the intersection of Verde and Velásquez Streets." These instructions are not needed in a postal address if you already have the street name and building name or number.

The cities of Maracaibo and Valencia are planned on grid systems, and addresses commonly include a cross-street. For example, **Av. 6, #94-24** means the building is on **Avenida 6** ("Sixth Avenue") close to the intersection with **Calle 94** ("94th Street"). The building number, **24**, is based on the position relative to that intersection. Streets and avenues have letters as well as numbers—for example, **Av. 3H, 76-A-209**, which refers to the intersection of **Avenida 3H** and **Calle 76A**.

Plants in rural areas are often identified by their position on a highway; for example, **Carretera Panamericana Km. 6** means near the sixth kilometer post on the Pan-American Highway.

LOCALITY NAMES

A district of Caracas or of other large cities is called an **Urbanización** (abbreviated **Urb.**) or a **Barrio**. Business addresses are likely to be in an Urbanización.

The name of the district (with or without an "Urb.") is written between the street and the city. Examples of locality names in Caracas include **Urb. Bella Vista**, **La Candelaria**, and **Parque Central**.

CITY NAMES

The city name is written in capitals at the beginning of the last line of the domestic address. The principal cities are listed in the next section.

STATE/PROVINCE/ETC. NAMES

Venezuela is divided into 22 states and territories, plus the Federal District where Caracas is located. Collectively, these are referred to as **Entidades** ("administrative entities"). The state (or other entity) name is written after both the city and the postcode. The principal business cities and their states are:

> **CARACAS 1010, D.F.**
> **MARACAIBO 4001, Zulia**
> **BARQUISIMETO 3001, Lara**
> **MARACAY 2103, Aragua**
> **VALENCIA 2006, Carabobo**
> **SAN CRISTÓBAL 5001, Táchira**
> **PORLAMAR 6301, Nueva Esparta**
> **PUERTO ORDAZ 8015, Bolívar**

(The postcodes in the list above are examples, not valid for all addresses.) **D.F.** is often omitted from Caracas addresses.

The word **Estado** ("State") or its abbreviation **Edo.** is often included, without the usual Spanish possessive, "de": **MARACAIBO 4001, Estado Zulia**.

POSTCODES

There is a four-digit postcode system. The postcode must follow the city name. Postcodes are not universally used by Venezuelans, and it is quite usual to be given an address without a postcode. Business stationery also still often shows three-digit postcodes, which are obsolete, but are better than nothing.

P.O. BOXES

P.O. Boxes are used by businesses. A box is called an **Apartado Postal**, usually abbreviated to **Apartado** or **Apdo.**, as in **Apdo. 5.314**. The street address and the box number should not be used together.

COUNTRY NAME

The short name of the country, as it appears on stamps, is simply **Venezuela**.

Letterheads

There is no standard layout or convention. **Su referencia** and **Nuestra referencia**, abbreviated **S/ref.** and **N/ref.**, mean "Your reference" and "Our reference" respectively, but are not very common.

Dates, Money, Typographical Conventions

DATES AND MONEY	
Date format	Day, Month, Year
Typical date abbreviation	29-2-96
Currency unit	bolívar
Cents	céntimos
Domestic currency code	Bs.
ISO international currency code	VEB
Other international codes	none
Decimal separator	comma
Thousands separator	period
Typical currency amount	Bs. 5.879,50
	(note one space after Bs.)

Even money amounts are often written with small zeros, as in **Bs. 30,00**.

Envelopes

There are no national rules. By international convention, the top margin is supposed to be 40mm (1.6″) and the other margins 15mm (0.6″).

See the chapter on Spain for mailroom messages that can be written on envelopes.

Phone Numbers

PHONE SYSTEM INFORMATION (SEE CHAPTER 4)	
Country Code	+58
International Access Code	00
Long-Distance Access Code	0
Typical City Codes	one-digit (only 2 = Caracas)
	two-digit (e.g., 61 = Maracaibo)
Typical number formats	(02) 462.6227
	(02) 77.21.83
	(046) 31.451
Ringing and busy signals	European

Word of Warning!

Mail service to Venezuela is slow and letters sometimes go astray. It is advisable to use certified or insured mail for anything you care about, or to use one of the major air courier services for anything urgent or valuable.

Editorial

When comparing information about any two countries, one is not surprised to find differences in their postal and telecommunication systems, for which there are obviously historical and perhaps cultural reasons. However, when dealing simultaneously with business contacts in a dozen or more countries, the differences become hard to remember, and it is natural to ask whether more standardization or cooperation would be possible. To take a telecommunications example: Why are "home-direct" (USA Direct, France Direct, etc.) numbers different everywhere? Travelers obviously need consistency, and no local residents care what is chosen.

In this chapter, some ideas are presented for improving white-collar productivity and making office workers' lives a little easier. Some of the problems are being worked on, some are not. In all cases, better channels of communication between users and their vendors and regulators would be very welcome.

Dear Phone Companies:

MESSAGES AND SIGNALS

The most urgent problem facing the ordinary international caller is the proliferation of recorded messages in local languages. These may be very convenient for local calls, but they are frustrating for international callers. You have to be quite fluent to follow a recording in another language. If you must call several times to try and figure out what the message says, you are wasting phone system resources as well as your own time, so more effort to coordinate international practice would seem to be in everybody's best interests.

The only message that *needs* to be spoken is one that tells you to dial a different number—for example, because the customer has relocated. Ideally, the destination country's phone system should send a digital message to the originating country's phone system, so that callers could hear the new number spoken in their own language. I am told that this is technically difficult. It would be better if (1) the numbers (just the numbers) could be repeated in English, and also (2) calls originating outside the country could be intercepted by operators, who could dial the new number even if they could not communicate with the caller.

The other two common spoken messages are for "number-unobtainable" and "congestion" conditions. The difference is critical: in the first case there is no point in redialing, but in the second case redialing will probably succeed. The customer wants above all to know whether to redial or not, and the phone company does not want customers to tie up channels with futile redials. A local-language message could be played once for the convenience of local callers, but should be followed by a distinctive standardized signal for the benefit of international callers.

Phone System Condition	Suggested International Standard Signal
Ringing	Local option of U.S., British, or European ringing signal, as presently defined; silence between tones should be noticeably longer than the tones themselves (which is the case for almost all countries already).
Busy	Local option of frequency, recommended range 400–450Hz, and duration, recommended range 0.25–0.5 sec.; silence between tones should be equal to the duration of one tone (which is the case for almost all countries already).
Congestion	Same as local busy signal, but every other tone should be raised 50–100Hz higher.
Nonexistent number	Same as local busy signal, but silence should be replaced with four beeps. (A video-game "bomb" or "raspberry" sound would be ideal.)
Number out of order	Same as a local busy signal, but silence should be replaced by one low-frequency click.

There should be some automatic detection of an "out-of-order" condition, for the benefit of domestic as well as international callers. For example, if every call to a number has failed (with a busy signal) over the last 24 hours, then, on the face of it, the phone is unplugged or there is some equipment failure. The phone system should still try to complete every call, but the "busy" signal should be replaced by the "out-of-order" signal so that the caller does not waste time and resources redialing.

OTHER IMPROVEMENTS

It is amazing that countries around the world are rapidly introducing mobile phones, home-direct services, toll-free numbers, and extra-charge information (U.S. 900) numbers without more cooperation. International travelers and businesses would obviously prefer these numbers to look the same everywhere, and want to see at a glance which ones can be dialed from another country.

It would be good to have some encouragement over the long term for fixed-length phone numbers, so that our local phone-company equipment and our own computers could validate foreign numbers better. Also, all equipment should recognize some "enter" code (#) that ends a variable-length number.

National organizations should be encouraged to adopt the international access code 00 (this is finally happening in Europe) and a long-distance access code of 0 or 1, and be discouraged from allocating city codes that begin with 0.

It would be helpful for business customers if there were a way of finding fax numbers automatically, 24 hours a day. For example, a phone company should offer a service line that would forward calls: when it answered, you would enter a voice number and your call would be forwarded to the corresponding fax machine. The same logic could be used for other purposes, such as finding the operator of a fax machine, or the switchboard corresponding to a direct-dial number.

Dear Fax Manufacturers:

Nobody wants telexes back. However, we have somehow lost one very useful feature of the old telex network. Telexes usually gave us a sensible alphabetic answerback that served to confirm visually that we had reached the right machine.

To reduce the need for wasteful cover sheets, fax machines should transmit a more helpful header from memory, consisting of the name, address, and phone number of their owners, together with an alternative fax number, if possible.

Fax machines should not go off-line and cause busy signals unless there is some desperately serious fault. If they are just out of paper, they should transmit "NO PAPER" in English and Japanese, along with their improved header.

A fax that is on a line with a call-forwarding facility (more and more countries are introducing an equivalent of the long-established U.S. 72# sequence, and in other countries PBX equipment can sometimes forward calls to other extensions) should reroute its calls to an alternative number if it cannot accept messages.

Fax machines should be able to detect paper-feeding irregularities at both ends of the transmission, particularly the sending end.

Dear Voice-Mail Manufacturers:

We need some standardization of basic operating techniques for outside callers. There should be some consistent way of giving the following commands to a voice-mail system:

"Skip to the beep."
"Stop talking and just give me extension X."
"Stop talking and give me the switchboard operator."
"Connect me to an alternative mailbox" (e.g., dept. secretary).
"Connect me to the corresponding fax number."
"Give the corresponding fax number."
"Give your street address."
"Give your mailing address."
"Give directions to your office."
"Give your office hours."
"Give contact names/departments" (e.g., purchasing).

Another common question that callers ask receptionists is whether some particular person, the owner of a particular extension number, is in the office today.

The most urgent need in the next few years will be to create a standard way to change language. We do not want all European companies to present us with a tedious and costly introduction saying, "If you understand English, enter 1; if you. . . ." We need to be able to enter a standard code, based on the country code, so that *33 changes the system to French and *81 changes it to Japanese.

Dear Computer Industry:

Could we have an international keyboard with at least three dead keys on it? Three keys would give us six marks, with the ability to cover most of the Western European languages from any country.

Could we have a standard "compose sequence," so that something easy to remember like COMPOSE,A,O gets us an Å on *any* computer, regardless of its internal workings? (And maybe a keycap that says "Overstrike" or "Accent" or "Eur" or "Dead" rather than "Compose," which is a word that only a software engineer could love?)

Dear Postal Authorities:

You are investing heavily in automated sorting equipment, and we need to cooperate with you. We want our mail to be sorted as efficiently as possible. We would cooperate more if we understood the rules better (I hope this book helps). At the same time, you have to understand that mailers are automating too, and it is very hard for us to keep a mailing list according to dozens of sets of rules for dozens of different countries.

Various proposals have been made over the years for standardizing address formats, at least for international business mail. A suggestion advocated in previous editions of this book was to use a three-line German-style address with a distinctive mark on the last line, followed by the ISO country code, a precise postcode, and the city name:

>US-75001-3463 DALLAS
>FR-75001-3463 PARIS

However, considering recent advances in geographic positioning systems, the obvious postcode of the future would now seem to be the addressee's latitude and longitude coordinates, suitably abbreviated.

In any event, European regulators should either make a reality of the system of country prefixes (F-75001, CH-8021, B-1070, etc.) or abandon it. Every administration publishes a slightly different list of authorized codes; most countries still ask for the destination to be written in full; the codes do not conform to the ISO standard; and business mailers often use codes like GB that no national post office officially recognizes.

Business mailers have an interest in postcode systems for their own internal purposes, regardless of post-office needs. They would like postcodes to be allocated in some rational geographic order, so that they could sort a mailing list by postcode into the territories of their salespeople or distributors or retailers or service engineers. Some countries have adopted systems that make this difficult to achieve. Surely there should be enough accumulated experience by now so that recommendations could be made, at least to countries that have not yet adopted postcode systems.

Conclusion

The general problem is that the globalization of business is proceeding much faster than the globalization of government. Governments and national organizations like post offices, phone companies, and standards organizations still feel free to pass any regulations they like, without much regard for what their neighbors are doing. The intergovernmental organizations that appear on paper to be in a position to coordinate different countries' regulations seem unable to do more than achieve the lowest level of technical cooperation. And yet international correspondence is not the exceptional event it was 50 years ago. To many businesses, all the industrially developed countries are already just states of the global economy, and all business is moving in that same direction.

World Table

The following table lists every nation in the world (in 1996) not discussed in one of the preceding country chapters, along with a number of colonies, territories, and other possessions. The information contained in each column is described in the paragraphs below.

Country & Country Code: For every country or territory that uses a country code, the code appears in parentheses next to its name. If no code is shown, the country cannot be dialed direct. If the initials A.C. precede the code, it may be dialed exactly like an area code within the United States. The parent country of a dependency is shown in square brackets after the latter's name.

Cities & City Codes: The capital city or administrative center is listed first, occasionally followed by other important cities. The appropriate city code (if any) follows each city's name. Whenever a capital city is not the site of a U.S. embassy or consulate, the embassy site is specified.

Time Differentials: Most entries in this column refer the reader to another country with the same time differentials. If the name of the latter country is preceded by a bullet (•), it will be found in the two tables on pages 39–41 (as will the entry "Other Europe"); if there is no bullet, it is listed in this table. For countries that do not share a time zone with a country in those tables, the summer (May–August) and winter (November–February) differentials are given here. All differentials are calculated with respect to Chicago (Central) time.

Languages: Each entry lists, in descending order by number of speakers, the language or languages predominantly spoken in the country. However, the official language (if any) is listed first regardless of the number of speakers.

Currency: The country's official currency is listed. Several currency names— in particular, *franc, peso, rial, dinar, pound, rupee, shilling,* and *dollar*—are used in more than one country for currencies that are not in fact identical. Except where indicated, the currency is that of the individual country only. However, the CFA franc (CFA stands for *Communauté Financière Africaine,* or African Financial Community) and the EC dollar (EC stands for *Eastern Caribbean*) are genuinely international currencies.

Religions: The country's predominant religions are listed in order of the number of adherents within the country. (This column can be helpful in suggesting which of the holidays in the table on page 38 will likely be observed in the country listed here, since the latter can be compared with other countries of similar religious makeup whose holidays are specifically shown.) The major subdivisions of Christianity are indicated by the abbreviations *C* (for *Catholic*), *P* (*Protestant*), and *O* (*Orthodox*); these too are listed in descending order of importance within the country.

Country & Country Code	Cities & City Codes	Time Differentials (with Chicago time)	Languages	Currency	Religions
Afghanistan	Kabul	Summer: 9½ ahead Winter: 10½	Pashto, Dari Persian	Afghani	Muslim
Albania (355)	Tiranë (42)	see •Other Europe	Albanian, Greek	Lek	Muslim, Christian (O)
Algeria (213)	Algiers	see •Nigeria	Arabic, French	Dinar	Muslim
American Samoa [U.S.] (684)	Pago Pago	see Tonga	English, Samoan	U.S. Dollar	Christian (P,C)
Andorra (376)	Andorra la Vella; embassy: Barcelona, Spain	see •Other Europe	Catalan, Spanish, French	Fr. Franc, Sp. Peseta	Christian (C)
Angola (244)	Luanda (2)	see •Nigeria	Portuguese	Kwanza	indigenous, Christian (C, P)
Antigua and Barbuda (A.C. 268)	St. John's	see •Venezuela	English	EC Dollar	Christian (P)
Armenia (374)	Yerevan (2)	see •Russia	Armenian, Russian	Dram	Christian (O)
Aruba (297)	Oranjestad (8)	see •Venezuela	Dutch, English	Florin	Christian (C)
Azerbaijan (994)	Baku (12)	Summer: 9 ahead Winter: 10	Azerbaijani, Russian	Manat	Muslim, Christian (O)
Azores [Port.] (351)	Ponta Delgada (96)	Summer: 5 ahead Winter: 5	Portuguese	Port. Escudo	Christian (C)
Bahamas (A.C. 242)	Nassau	Summer: 1 ahead Winter: 1	English	Dollar	Christian (P, C)
Bahrain (973)	Manama	see •Saudi Arabia	Arabic, English	Dinar	Muslim
Bangladesh (880)	Dhaka (2)	Summer: 11 ahead Winter: 12	Bengali, English	Taka	Muslim, Hindu
Barbados (A.C. 246)	Bridgetown	see •Venezuela	English	Dollar	Christian (P)
Belarus (375)	Minsk (17)	see •Israel	Belorussian, Russian	Rubel	Christian (O, C)
Belize (501)	Belmopan (8), Belize City (2)	see •Mexico	English, Spanish	Dollar	Christian (C, P)

Country & Country Code	Cities & City Codes	Time Differentials (with Chicago time)	Languages	Currency	Religions
Benin (229)	Porto-Novo, Cotonou	see •Nigeria	French	CFA Franc	indigenous, Christian, Muslim
Bermuda [U.K.] (A.C. 441)	Hamilton	Summer: 2 ahead Winter: 2	English	Dollar	Christian (P, C)
Bhutan (975)	Thimphu	see Bangladesh	Dzongkha, Nepali, English	Ngultrum	Buddhist, Hindu
Bolivia (591)	La Paz (2)	see •Venezuela	Spanish, Quechua, Aymara	Boliviano	Christian (C)
Bosnia and Herzegovina (387)	Sarajevo (71)	see •Other Europe	Serbo-Croatian	Dinar	Muslim, Christian (O, C)
Botswana (267)	Gaborone (31)	see •South Africa	English, Tswana	Pula	indigenous, Christian
Brunei (673)	Bandar Seri Begawan (2)	see •Malaysia	Malay, English, Chinese	Dollar	Muslim, Buddhist
Bulgaria (359)	Sofia (2)	see •Israel	Bulgarian	Lev	Christian (O), Muslim
Burkina Faso (226)	Ouagadou-gou	see Ghana	French	CFA Franc	indigenous, Muslim
Burma—see Myanmar					
Burundi (257)	Bujumbura	see •South Africa	French, Kirundi	Franc	Christian (C), indigenous
Cambodia (855)	Phnom Penh (23)	see •Indonesia	Khmer, French	Riel	Buddhist
Cameroon (237)	Yaoundé, Douala	see •Nigeria	English, French	CFA Franc	indigenous, Christian, Muslim
Cape Verde (238)	Praia	Summer: 4 ahead Winter: 5	Portuguese	Escudo	Christian (C)
Central African Republic (236)	Bangui	see •Nigeria	French, Sango	CFA Franc	Christian (C, P), indigenous, Muslim
Chad (235)	N'Djamena (51)	see •Nigeria	French, Arabic	CFA Franc	Muslim, Christian, indigenous
Colombia (57)	Bogotá (1), Barranquilla (58)	Summer: 0 ahead Winter: 1	Spanish	Peso	Christian (C)

Country & Country Code	Cities & City Codes	Time Differentials (with Chicago time)	Languages	Currency	Religions
Comoros (269)	Moroni	see •Saudi Arabia	Arabic, French, Comoran	Franc	Muslim, Christian (C)
Congo, Dem. Rep. of (243)	Kinshasa (12)	see •Nigeria	French	Zaire	Christian (C, P.)
Congo, Rep. of (242)	Brazzaville	see •Nigeria	French	CFA Franc	Christian, indigenous
Costa Rica (506)	San José	see •Mexico	Spanish	Colón	Christian (C)
Côte d'Ivoire —see Ivory Coast					
Croatia (385)	Zagreb (41)	see •Other Europe	Croatian	Kuna	Christian (C, O)
Cuba (53)	Havana (7)	see Bahamas	Spanish	Peso	Christian (C)
Cyprus (357)	Nicosia (2)	see •Greece	Greek, Turkish, English	Pound	Christian (O), Muslim
Djibouti (253)	Djibouti	see •Saudi Arabia	French, Arabic	Franc	Muslim
Dominica (A.C. 767)	Roseau; embassy: Bridgetown, Barbados	see •Venezuela	English	EC Dollar	Christian (C, P)
Dominican Republic (A.C. 809)	Santo Domingo	see •Venezuela	Spanish	Peso	Christian (C)
Ecuador (593)	Quito (2), Guayaquil (4)	see Colombia	Spanish, Quechua	Sucre	Christian (C)
Egypt (20)	Cairo (2), Alexandria (3)	see •Israel	Arabic	Pound	Muslim
El Salvador (503)	San Salvador	see •Mexico	Spanish	Colón	Christian (C, P)
Equatorial Guinea (240)	Malabo (9)	see •Nigeria	Spanish	CFA Franc	Christian (C)
Eritrea (291)	Asmara (4)	see •Saudi Arabia	Tigrinya, Arabic	Ethiopian Birr	Muslim, Christian
Estonia (372)	Tallinn (2)	see •Finland	Estonian, Russian	Kroon	Christian (P, O)
Ethiopia (251)	Addis Ababa (1)	see •Saudi Arabia	Amharic	Birr	Muslim, Christian, indigenous

Country & Country Code	Cities & City Codes	Time Differentials (with Chicago time)	Languages	Currency	Religions
Fiji (679)	Suva	Summer: 17 ahead Winter: 18	English, Fijian	Dollar	Christian (P)
French Guiana [Fr.] (594)	Cayenne; consulate: Fort-de-France, Martinique	see •Argentina	French	Fr. Franc	Christian (C)
Gabon (241)	Libreville	see •Nigeria	French	CFA Franc	Christian, indigenous
Gambia (220)	Banjul	see Ghana	English	Dalasi	Muslim
Georgia (995)	Tbilisi (32)	see •Russia	Georgian, Russian	Lari	Christian (O), Muslim
Ghana (233)	Accra (21)	Summer: 5 ahead Winter: 6	English	Cedi	indigenous, Muslim, Christian
Gibraltar [U.K.] (350)	Gibraltar	see •Other Europe	English	Pound	Christian (C)
Greenland [Denm.] (299)	Nuuk [Godthaab] (2)	see •Brazil	Danish, Greenlandic	Dan. Krone	Christian (P)
Grenada (A.C. 473)	St. George's	see •Venezuela	English	EC Dollar	Christian (C, P)
Guadeloupe [Fr.] (590)	Basse-Terre	see •Venezuela	French	Fr. Franc	Christian (C)
Guam [U.S.] (671)	Agaña	see Papua New Guinea	English, Chamorro	U.S. Dollar	Christian (C)
Guatemala (502)	Guatemala City (2)	see •Mexico	Spanish	Quetzal	Christian (C, P), Mayan
Guinea (224)	Conakry (4)	see Ghana	French	Franc	Muslim
Guinea-Bissau (245)	Bissau	see Ghana	Portuguese	CFA Franc	Muslim, indigenous
Guyana (592)	Georgetown (2)	see •Venezuela	English	Dollar	Christian (P, C), Hindu
Haiti (509)	Port-au-Prince	see Bahamas	French, Creole	Gourde	Christian (C, P)
Honduras (504)	Tegucigalpa	see •Mexico	Spanish	Lempira	Christian (C)
Iceland (354)	Reykjavik (1)	see Ghana	Icelandic	Króna	Christian (P)
Iran (98)	Tehran (21)	Summer: 8½ ahead Winter: 9½	Persian	Rial	Muslim

Country & Country Code	Cities & City Codes	Time Differentials (with Chicago time)	Languages	Currency	Religions
Iraq (964)	Baghdad (1)	see •Russia	Arabic	Dinar	Muslim
Ivory Coast (225)	Abidjan, Yamoussoukro	see Ghana	French	CFA Franc	indigenous, Muslim, Christian
Jamaica (A.C. 876)	Kingston	see Colombia	English	Dollar	Christian (P)
Jordan (962)	Amman (6)	see •Israel	Arabic, English	Dinar	Muslim
Kazakhstan (7)	Aqmola, Alma-Ata	Summer: 12 ahead Winter: 12	Kazakh, Russian	Tenge	Muslim, Christian (O)
Kenya (254)	Nairobi (2)	see •Saudi Arabia	Swahili, English	Shilling	Christian (P, C), indigenous
Kiribati (686)	Tarawa	see Fiji	English, Gilbertese	Australian Dollar	Christian (C, P)
Kuwait (965)	Kuwait	see •Saudi Arabia	Arabic, English	Dinar	Muslim
Kyrgyzstan (7)	Bishkek (3312)	Summer: 11 ahead Winter: 11	Kirghiz, Russian	Som	Muslim, Christian (O)
Laos (856)	Vientiane (21)	see •Thailand	Lao, French, English	Kip	Buddhist
Latvia (371)	Riga (2)	see •Finland	Latvian, Russian	Lats	Christian (P, C)
Lebanon (961)	Beirut (1)	see •Israel	Arabic, French	Pound	Muslim, Christian (C)
Lesotho (266)	Maseru	see •South Africa	English, Sesotho	Loti (pl Maloti)	Christian, indigenous
Liberia (231)	Monrovia	see Ghana	English	Dollar	indigenous, Muslim
Libya (218)	Tripoli (21)	see •South Africa	Arabic	Dinar	Muslim
Liechtenstein (41)	Vaduz (75); embassy: Zurich, Switzerland	see •Other Europe	German	Swiss Franc	Christian (C)
Lithuania (370)	Vilnius (2)	see •Finland	Lithuanian, Russian	Litas	Christian (C)
Macao [Port.] (853)	Macao	see •Taiwan	Portuguese, Chinese	Pataca	Buddhist
Macedonia (389)	Skopje (91)	see •Other Europe	Macedonian	Denar	Christian (O), Muslim

Country & Country Code	Cities & City Codes	Time Differentials (with Chicago time)	Languages	Currency	Religions
Madagascar (261)	Antananarivo (2)	see •Saudi Arabia	Malagasy, French	Franc	indigenous, Christian
Malawi (265)	Lilongwe, Blantyre	see •South Africa	English, Chichewa	Kwacha	Christian (P, C), Muslim
Maldives (960)	Malé; embassy: Colombo, Sri Lanka	see Pakistan	Dhivehi	Rufiyaa	Muslim
Mali (223)	Bamako	see Ghana	French, Bambara	CFA Franc	Muslim
Malta (356)	Valletta, Birkirkara	see •Other Europe	Maltese, English, Italian	Lira	Christian (C)
Marshall Islands (692)	Majuro (9)	see •New Zealand	Marshallese, English	U.S. Dollar	Christian (P)
Martinique [Fr.] (596)	Fort-de-France	see •Venezuela	French	Fr. Franc	Christian (C)
Mauritania (222)	Nouakchott (2)	see Ghana	Arabic	Ouguiya	Muslim
Mauritius (230)	Port Louis	see Azerbaijan	English, French	Rupee	Hindu, Christian (C), Muslim
Micronesia (691)	Palikir, Kolonia	see •Australia	English	U.S. Dollar	Christian (C, P)
Moldova (373)	Chişinău [Kishinev] (2)	see •Finland	Romanian, Russian	Leu	Christian (O)
Monaco (377)	Monaco (93); consulate: Marseille, France	see •Other Europe	French	Fr. Franc	Christian (C)
Mongolia (976)	Ulaanbaatar [Ulan Bator] (1)	Summer: 14 ahead Winter: 14	Mongolian	Tugrik	Buddhist
Morocco (212)	Rabat (77), Casablanca (2)	see Ghana	Arabic, French	Dirham	Muslim
Mozambique (258)	Maputo (1)	see •South Africa	Portugùese	Metical	indigenous, Christian
Myanmar (95)	Yangon [Rangoon] (1)	Summer: 11½ ahead Winter: 12½	Burmese	Kyat	Buddhist
Namibia (264)	Windhoek (61)	see •Other Europe	English, Afrikaans	Dollar	Christian, indigenous

Country & Country Code	Cities & City Codes	Time Differentials (with Chicago time)	Languages	Currency	Religions
Nauru (674)	Yaren; embassy: Canberra, Australia	see Fiji	Nauruan, English	Austral. Dollar	Christian (P, C)
Nepal (977)	Kathmandu (1)	see •India	Nepali	Rupee	Hindu
Netherlands Antilles [Neth.] (599)	Willemstad (9)	see •Venezuela	Dutch	Guilder	Christian (C)
Nicaragua (505)	Managua (2)	see •Mexico	Spanish	Cordoba	Christian (C)
Niger (227)	Niamey	see •Nigeria	French, Hausa	CFA Franc	Muslim
No. Mariana Isls. [U.S.] (670)	Saipan	see Papua New Guinea	English	U.S. Dollar	Christian (C)
North Korea (850)	Pyongyang (2)	see •Korea	Korean	Won	Buddhist, Confucian
Oman (968)	Masqat [Muscat]	see Azerbaijan	Arabic, English	Rial	Muslim
Pakistan (92)	Islamabad (51), Karachi (21), Lahore (42)	Summer: 10 ahead Winter: 11	Urdu, English	Rupee	Muslim
Palau [U.S.] (680)	Koror	see •Japan	Palauan, English	U.S. Dollar	Christian (C)
Panama (507)	Panama City	see Colombia	Spanish, English	Balboa	Christian (C)
Papua New Guinea (675)	Port Moresby	Summer: 15 ahead Winter: 16	English, Tok Pisin, Hiri Motu	Kina	Christian (P, C), indigenous
Paraguay (595)	Asunción (21)	see •Chile	Spanish, Guaraní	Guaraní	Christian (C), indigenous
Peru (51)	Lima (14)	see Bahamas	Spanish, Quechua, Aymara	Sol	Christian (C)
Puerto Rico [U.S.] (A.C. 787)	San Juan	see •Venezuela	Spanish, English	U.S. Dollar	Christian (C)
Qatar (974)	Doha	see •Saudi Arabia	Arabic, English	Riyal	Muslim
Réunion [Fr.] (262)	St.-Denis	see •Russia	French	Fr. Franc	Christian (C)
Romania (40)	Bucharest (0)	see •Israel	Romanian, Hungarian, German	Leu	Christian (O)

Country & Country Code	Cities & City Codes	Time Differentials (with Chicago time)	Languages	Currency	Religions
Rwanda (250)	Kigali	see •South Africa	Rwanda, French, English	Franc	Christian (C, P), indigenous
St. Kitts-Nevis (A.C. 869)	Basseterre; embassy: Bridgetown, Barbados	see •Venezuela	English	EC Dollar	Christian (P)
St. Lucia (A.C. 758)	Castries; embassy: Bridgetown, Barbados	see •Venezuela	English	EC Dollar	Christian (C)
St. Vincent and the Grenadines (A.C. 784)	Kingstown	see •Venezuela	English	EC Dollar	Christian (P, C)
Samoa (685)	Apia	see Tonga	Samoan, English	Tala	Christian (P)
San Marino (39)	San Marino; consulate: Florence, Italy	see •Other Europe	Italian	It. Lira	Christian (C)
São Tomé and Príncipe (239)	São Tomé; embassy: Libreville, Gabon	see Ghana	Portuguese	Dobra	Christian (C, P)
Senegal (221)	Dakar	see Ghana	French	CFA Franc	Muslim
Serbia—see Yugoslavia					
Seychelles (248)	Victoria	see Azerbaijan	Creole, English, French	Rupee	Christian (C)
Sierra Leone (232)	Freetown (22)	see Ghana	English	Leone	Muslim, indigenous
Slovakia (421)	Bratislava (7)	see •Other Europe	Slovak	Koruna	Christian (C, P)
Solomon Islands (677)	Honiara	see Vanuatu	English	Dollar	Christian (P, C)
Somalia (252)	Mogadishu	see •Saudi Arabia	Somali, Arabic	Shilling	Muslim
Sri Lanka (94)	Colombo (1)	see •India	Sinhalese, Tamil, English	Rupee	Buddhist, Hindu, Muslim
Sudan (249)	Khartoum (11)	see •South Africa	Arabic, English	Dinar	Muslim, indigenous
Suriname (597)	Paramaribo	see •Argentina	Dutch, Sranan, English	Guilder	Christian (P, C), Hindu, Muslim

Country & Country Code	Cities & City Codes	Time Differentials (with Chicago time)	Languages	Currency	Religions
Swaziland (268)	Mbabane	see •South Africa	Swazi, English	Lilangeni (*pl*. Ema-langeni)	Christian, indigenous
Syria (963)	Damascus (11)	see •South Africa	Arabic	Pound	Muslim
Tajikistan (7)	Dushanbe (3772)	see Pakistan	Tajiki, Russian	Ruble	Muslim
Tanzania (255)	Dar es Salaam (51)	see •Saudi Arabia	Swahili, English	Shilling	indigenous, Muslim, Christian
Togo (228)	Lomé	see Ghana	French, Ewe	CFA Franc	indigenous, Christian
Tonga (676)	Nuku'alofa; embassy: Suva, Fiji	Summer: 6 behind Winter: 5	Tongan, English	Pa'anga	Christian (P, C)
Trinidad and Tobago (A.C. 868)	Port of Spain	see •Venezuela	English	Dollar	Christian (C, P), Hindu
Tunisia (216)	Tunis (1)	see •Nigeria	Arabic, French	Dinar	Muslim
Turkmenistan (993)	Ashkhabad	see Pakistan	Turkmen, Russian	Manat	Muslim
Tuvalu (688)	Funafuti	see •New Zealand	Tuvaluan, English	Austral. Dollar	Christian (P)
Uganda (256)	Kampala (41)	see •Saudi Arabia	English, Swahili	Shilling	Christian (C, P), Muslim, indigenous
Ukraine (380)	Kiev (44)	see •Russia	Ukrainian, Russian	Hryvna	Christian (O)
United Arab Emirates (971)	Abu Dhabi (2), Dubai (4)	see Azerbaijan	Arabic, Persian, English	Dirham	Muslim
Uruguay (598)	Montevideo (2)	see •Argentina	Spanish	Peso	Christian (C)
U.S. Virgin Islands [U.S.] (A.C. 340)	Charlotte Amalie	see •Venezuela	English	U.S. Dollar	Christian (P, C)
Uzbekistan (7)	Tashkent (3712)	See Tajikistan	Uzbek, Russian	Sum	Muslim

Country & Country Code	Cities & City Codes	Time Differentials (with Chicago time)	Languages	Currency	Religions
Vanuatu (678)	Vila; embassy: Port Moresby, Papua New Guinea	Summer: 16 ahead Winter: 17	Bislama, French, English	Vatu	Christian (P, C)
Vatican City (39)	Vatican City (6)	see •Other Europe	Italian, Latin	It. Lira	Christian (C)
Vietnam (84)	Hanoi (4), Ho Chi Minh City [Saigon] (8)	see •Thailand	Vietnamese, French, English	Dong	Buddhist
Yemen (967)	San'a (1)	see •Saudi Arabia	Arabic	Rial	Muslim
Yugoslavia (381)	Belgrade (11)	see •Other Europe	Serbo-Croatian	Dinar	Christian (O), Muslim
Zambia (260)	Lusaka (1)	see •South Africa	English	Kwacha	Christian
Zimbabwe (263)	Harare (4)	see •South Africa	English	Dollar	Christian, indigenous

Glossary

Terminology

TELEPHONE TERMINOLOGY	
Term	**Meaning**
+ Format	A convention for writing international phone numbers, in which the + sign is written in front of the country code.
Area Code, City Code	The digit or digits dialed after the LDAC to select a particular city or area.
Busy Signal	A sound which means that the call cannot be completed because the called party's equipment is in use.
Called Party	The person being called.
Calling Party	The person making a call.
Chargeable Information Numbers	Numbers that cost extra to call. The fee is divided between the phone company and the called party.
Congestion Signal	A sound which means that the call cannot be completed because the system (lines, satellites, switching equipment) is overloaded.
Country Code	The digit or digits dialed after the IAC to select the particular country.
International Access Code, IAC	The digit or digits dialed at the beginning of a number to signal that the number will be outside the country.
Local Number	A short phone number used for calls within a city or area. (When the number is called from outside the city or area, it must be prefixed with a city code.)
Long-Distance Access Code, LDAC	The digit or digits dialed at the beginning of a number to signal that the call will not be local.
Mobile Phone	A phone in a vehicle.
National Numbering System	A national system in which no city codes are used.
Number-Unobtainable Signal	A sound which means that the call cannot be completed because the system does not understand the dialed number.
Roll over	To automatically switch an incoming call to another internal number when the first number called is not answered.
Toll-free Number	A number that costs the caller nothing, since the called party pays for the call.

POSTAL TERMINOLOGY

Term	Meaning
Address block	A complete name and address as it would appear on an envelope.
Address element	One part of an address block: the name of a person, company, street, locality, city, state or other region, or country; a building number, street number, or postcode.
OCR	Optical Character Recognition; describes equipment that reads envelopes automatically as part of the mail sorting process.
Locality	Whatever needs to be specified between a street name and a city or delivery-post-office name—usually a district of a city or the name of a village in a rural area. (This U.K. Post Office term is used since no U.S. equivalent is in common use.)
Building number	The number that identifies the location of a building on the street (also called "house number" when it refers to residential buildings).
Postcode	A geographical numbering system that speeds the sorting of mail.
Extended postcode	A postcode precise enough to indicate a building or block within the delivery post office's area.
Delivery post office	The local post office responsible for the final delivery of a letter.
Street designator	A word like "Street" or "Road" which identifies the name as a street.

OTHER TERMINOLOGY

Term	Meaning
Foreigner	A person unfamiliar with the practices of the country being discussed.
ISO	International Standards Organization
Grid system	A system of city planning in which the streets are laid out at right angles to each other and building numbers are related to street intersections and sometimes also to street names (e.g., no. 2100 is close to 21st St.).
Publicly traded	Describes a company whose shares are traded on a stock exchange.
Roman alphabet	The alphabet used in English.
Romanization	Transliteration into the Roman alphabet.
Diacritical mark	A mark near or through a letter to indicate a change in phonetic value.
Accent	A diacritical mark over a vowel that usually changes its pitch, stress, or phonetic value.

AMERICAN TERMINOLOGY

Term	Meaning
Domestic(ally)	Refers to calls or correspondence taking place exclusively within one country.
Phone Company	The organization responsible for providing telephone service. Known as the PTT in many countries.
Busy	"Engaged" in British English.
Directory Assistance	"(Directory) Enquiries" in British English.
Precinct	The area around one polling station.
Given name	"Christian name" in British English.
Letter carrier	A person who delivers mail.

Country Identification

How to Use the Keyword Index

The main purpose of the following Keyword Index, which lists words and abbreviations that commonly appear on foreign correspondence, is to help you to identify where mysterious documents have come from. It should also help you to find information in the book.

The left-hand column in the index is the word or abbreviation itself, in American alphabetical order (e.g., Å counts as A).

The second column is either the ISO abbreviation for a country where the word is used, or the name of a language; see the following three tables.

ISO ABBREVIATIONS			
Abbrev.	Country	Abbrev.	Country
AR	Argentina	JP	Japan
AT	Austria	KR	Korea
AU	Australia	LU	Luxembourg
BE	Belgium	MX	Mexico
BR	Brazil	MY	Malaysia
CA	Canada	NG	Nigeria
CH	Switzerland	NL	Netherlands
CL	Chile	NO	Norway
CN	China	NZ	New Zealand
CS	Czech Republic	PH	Philippines
DE	Germany	PL	Poland
DK	Denmark	PT	Portugal
ES	Spain	RU	Russia
FI	Finland	SA	Saudi Arabia
FR	France	SE	Sweden
GB	United Kingdom	SG	Singapore
GR	Greece	SI	Slovenia
HK	Hong Kong	TH	Thailand
HU	Hungary	TR	Turkey
ID	Indonesia	TW	Taiwan
IE	Ireland	US	United States
IL	Israel	VE	Venzuela
IN	India	ZA	South Africa
IT	Italy		

ISO ABBREVIATIONS SORTED BY COUNTRY NAME

Country	Abbrev.	Country	Abbrev.
Argentina	AR	Malaysia	MY
Australia	AU	Mexico	MX
Austria	AT	Netherlands	NL
Belgium	BE	New Zealand	NZ
Brazil	BR	Nigeria	NG
Canada	CA	Norway	NO
Chile	CL	Philippines	PH
China	CN	Poland	PL
Czech Republic	CS	Portugal	PT
Denmark	DK	Russia	RU
Finland	FI	Saudi Arabia	SA
France	FR	Singapore	SG
Germany	DE	Slovenia	SI
Greece	GR	South Africa	ZA
Hong Kong	HK	Spain	ES
Hungary	HU	Sweden	SE
India	IN	Switzerland	CH
Indonesia	ID	Taiwan	TW
Ireland	IE	Thailand	TH
Israel	IL	Turkey	TR
Italy	IT	United Kingdom	GB
Japan	JP	United States	US
Korea	KR	Venezuela	VE
Luxembourg	LU		

LANGUAGE ABBREVIATIONS

Abbrev.	Language	Where Spoken
du	Dutch	BE, NL
fr	French	BE, CA, CH, FR, LU
ge	German	AT, (BE), CH, DE, (IT), (LU)
it	Italian	CH, IT
pt	Portuguese	BR, PT
sp	Spanish	AR, CL, ES, MX, VE

The right-hand column in the index lists (1) English translations of foreign terms, and (2) references to chapter sections for further information. The latter references appear in parentheses, and occasionally in brackets. See the following table.

	REFERENCES	
Reference	**Chapter Section to Consult**	
(boxes)	P.O. Boxes	
(city)	City Names	
(company)	Company Names	
(country)	Country Name	
(county)	State/Province/etc.	
(currency)	Dates, Money, etc.	
(degree)	Personal Names	
(honorific)	Personal Names	
(letterhead)	Letterheads	
(locality)	Locality Names	
(names)	Personal Names	
(offices)	Offices Building Names Building Numbers	
(phones)	Phone Numbers	
(postcodes)	Postcodes	
(prefecture)	State/Province/etc.	
(province)	State/Province/etc.	
(state)	State/Province/etc.	
(street)	Street Names	
(title)	Personal Names	

The following examples will illustrate. An entry like:

    Postleitzahl   ge   Postcode

is translating a German word that could be used in any German-speaking country.

    An entry like:

    bolívar   VE   (currency)

refers you to the "Dates, Money, Typographical Conventions" section of the chapter on Venezuela.

    When brackets are used instead of parentheses in an entry like:

    cho   JP   [street]

it is to warn you that a cho is not really a street, but that information will be found in the "Street Names" section.

Language Identification

This section and the next are intended to help you identify languages and countries. The table on page 385 shows you which marked (accented) characters are used by which languages.

The following table indicates which accented and special characters occur in each language (rows = characters, columns = languages).

Char.	Catalan	Czech	Danish	Finnish	French	German	Hungarian	Italian	Norwegian	Polish	Portuguese	Slovenian	Spanish	Swedish	Turkish
à	•				•			•			•				
á	•	•					•				•		•		
â					•						•				•
ã											•				
ä				•		•								•	
å			•	•					•					•	
æ			•						•						
ą										•					
ç	•				•						•				•
č		•										•			
ď		•													
è	•				•			•							
é	•	•			•		•				•	•	•		
ê					•						•				
ě		•													
ę										•					
ğ															•
ì								•							
í	•	•					•				•		•		
î					•										•
ı															•
ł										•					
ń										•					
ñ													•		
ň		•													
ò	•							•							
ó	•	•					•			•	•		•		
ô					•						•				
ö				•		•	•							•	•
õ											•				
ø			•						•						
ő							•								
ß						•									
ř		•													
š		•										•			
ś										•					
ş															•
ť		•													
ù					•			•							
ú	•	•					•				•		•		
û					•										•
ü	•				•	•	•						•		•
ů		•													
ű							•								
ý		•													
ž		•										•			
ż										•					

In addition to the national characters shown here, several other characters— the dieresis mark on vowels (as in ë), the digraphs æ and œ, and the letter é— all occur on rare occasions in most European languages, including British English. Catalan also has the characteristic sequence l·l (in uppercase, L·L).

Postcode Identification

The next table summarizes the appearance of postcodes in the countries covered in the book. In the left-hand column, the numerals 1 and 0 and the letters A and B stand for numerals and letters in the basic postcode that identifies a delivery post office. The numeral 2 and the letter C represent numerals and letters in extended postcodes used to sort mail by delivery route. X's represent state or province abbreviations.

	POSTCODE FORM	
Postcode	Countries	Prefix
1010 CITY	Argentina	
	Austria	A-
	Belgium	B-
	Denmark	DK-
	Germany (old system)	D-
	Hungary	H-
	Luxembourg	L-
	Norway	N-
	Philippines	
	Portugal	P-
	South Africa (official system)	
	Switzerland	CH-
1010 CC CITY	Netherlands	NL-
10101 CITY	Brazil (old system)	
	Finland	SF-
	France	F-
	Germany	D-
	Israel (official system)	
	Italy	I-
	Malaysia	
	Mexico	
	Slovenia	SI-
	Spain	E-
	Turkey	TR-
10-101 CITY	Poland	PL-
101 22 CITY	Czech Republic	CS-
	Greece	GR-
	Sweden	S-
10101-222	Brazil	
CITY 101	Japan (old system, still used)	
	Korea (old system, still used)	
	Taiwan (old system, still used)	
	Venezuela (old system, still used)	

Postcode	POSTCODE FORM Countries	Prefix
CITY 1010	New Zealand Singapore South Africa (commonly used) Venezuela	
CITY XX 1010	Australia	
CITY 10101	Indonesia Israel (sometimes used) Saudi Arabia Taiwan Thailand	
CITY XX 10101	United States (old system, still used)	
CITY 101-22	Japan (complete system)	
CITY 101010	China India Russia	
CITY 101-222	Korea (complete system)	
CITY XX 10101-2222	United States (complete system)	
CITY XX A1B 2C2	Canada	
CITY AB1 2CC and numerous variations	United Kingdom	
No postcodes	Chile Ireland Hong Kong Nigeria	

Keyword Index

To use this index, see instructions on pages 298–300.

Alphabetization here follows the letter-by-letter principle; that is, it ignores word breaks, capitalization, and punctuation (except commas), as in the following sequence of entries: Stavanger, STD, sterling, St. Étienne, Stgt.

Angers	FR	(city)
Anhui	CN	(province)
Ankara	TR	(city)
Anônima	pt	(company)
Anónima	sp	(company)
Anonimos	GR	(company)
Anonyme	fr	(company)
Antwerp	BE	Antwerpen
Antwerpen	BE	(city)
AO	RU	(company)
Ao cuidado	pt	attn.
Aomori	JP	(prefecture)
ap	ES	(offices)
AP	BR	(state)
a/p	MY	(names)
Apart.	PT	P.O.Box
Apartado	PT	P.O.Box
Apartado de Correos	sp	P.O.Box
Apartado (Postal)	sp	P.O.Box
apartamento	ES	(offices)
Apartman	TR	(offices)
Apeldoorn	NL	(city)
appartement	fr	apartment
appt.	fr	apartment
ApS	DK	(company)
AR	US	(state)
Aragua	VE	(state)
Arch.	IT	architect
Århus	DK	(city)
Arizona	US	(state)
Arkansas	US	(state)
Armazéns	PT	delivery address
Arnhem	NL	(city)
Arq.	sp,pt	architect
ARS	AR	(currency)
A/S,a/s	DK,NO	(company)
a.s.	CS	(company)
A.Ş.	TR	(company)
ASE	US	(company)
át	ES	(offices)
Athens	GR	Athinai
Athinai	GR	(city)
ático	ES	(offices)
Atlanta	US	(city)
Attica	GR	(province)
Attiki	GR	(province)
Auckland	NZ	(city)
AUD	AU	(currency)
Auderghem	BE	(city)
austral	AR	(currency)
Autriche	AT	Austria
Av.	fr,pt, sp	Avenue
Avenida	pt,sp	Avenue
avenyn	SE	(street)
Avinguda	ES	(street)
Avon	GB	(county)
Avv.	IT	lawyer
AZ	US	(state)
B–	BE	(country)
BA	AR	Buenos Aires
BA	BR	(state)
backen	SE	(street)
Bad	ge	spa
Badajoz	ES	(city)
Bahia	BR	(state)
Bahía Blanca	AR	(city)
bahn	AT,CH, DE	(street)
baht	TH	(currency)
Baja California Norte	MX	(state)
Baja California Sur	MX	(state)
Bâle	CH	Basel
Bali	ID	(province)
Baltimore	US	(city)
Balto.	US	(city)
ban	JP	number
Bandung	ID	(city)
Bangunan	MY	(building)
Bangalore	IN	(city)
Bapak	ID	(names)
Barat	ID	west
Barcelona	ES	(city)
Barquisimeto	VE	(city)
Barrio	AR,VE	(locality)
Basel	CH	(city)
Basle	CH	Basel
Batangas	PH	(province)
Bath	GB	(city)
Bâtiment	fr	Building
Batu	MY	(offices)
Bauchi	NG	(state)
BC	CA	(province)
BC	MX	(state)
Bchk	ID	(names)
BÇN	MX	(state)
BCS	MX	(state)
BEC	BE	(currency)
Bedford	GB	(city)
Bedfordshire	GB	(county)
Beds.	GB	(county)

Be'eravon Moug'bal	IL	(company)	Bp.	HU	(city)
BEF	BE	(currency)	Bpk.	ZA	(company)
Bei	CN	north	B-r.	RU	(street)
Beijing	CN	(city)	B.R.A.	ID	(names)
Beit	IL	(offices)	Brasília	BR	(city)
BEL	BE	(currency)	BRC	BR	(currency)
Belfast	GB	(city)	BRD	DE	Germany
België	BE	Belgium	Bremen	DE	(city)
Belgique	BE	Belgium	brief	du,ge	letter
Belo Horizonte	BR	(city)	Brighton	GB	(city)
Benin City	NG	(city)	brinken	SE	(street)
Benue	NG	(state)	Bristol	GB	(city)
Bergen	NO	(city)	Britain	GB	(country)
Berks.	GB	(county)	British Colum-bia	CA	(province)
Berkshire	GB	(county)	British Isles	GB	(country)
Berlin	DE	(city)	Brm.	DE	(city)
Bern	CH	(city)	Brno	CS	(city)
Besöksadresse	SE	delivery address	Bromley	GB	(city)
			Bruges	BE	Brugge
Besøksadresse	NO	delivery address	Brugge	BE	(city)
			Brussel	BE	(city)
Betrieb	ge	factory	Brussels	BE	Bruxelles
Bey	TR	(names)	Bruxelles	BE	(city)
BFR	BE	(currency)	Bs.	VE	(currency)
Bharat	IN	India	Bs.As.	AR	Buenos Aires
Bilbao	ES	(city)	bt.	MY	(names)
bin	SA,MY	(names)	BTW	BE,NL	sales tax
bint	SA	(names)	Budapest	HU	(city)
binti	MY	(names)	bucho	JP	(title)
Birmingham	GB	(city)	Buckingham-shire	GB	(county)
biru	JP	Building			
bis	FR	(offices)	Bucks.	GB	(county)
Bl.	BR	(locality)	Buenos Aires	AR	(city)
Blk.	SG	(offices)	Bulacan	PH	(province)
Bln.	DE	(city)	Bulvar	RU	(street)
Bloemfontein	ZA	(city)	Bulvarı	TR	(street)
Blok	ID	(offices)	Bundesrepublik	DE	(country)
B.M.	IL	(company)	Bur.	CA	(offices)
Bogor	ID	(city)	Bureau	CA	(offices)
boîte	fr	box	bureaux	fr	offices
Boîte Postale	BE,FR	P.O.Box	Burgos	ES	(city)
Bolívar	VE	(state)	Büro	ge	office
bolívar	VE	(currency)	BV	BE,NL	(company)
Bologna	IT	(city)	BVBA	BE	(company)
Bolshoy	RU	large	by	GB	[city]
Bombay	IN	(city)	Bydgoszcz	PL	(city)
Bordeaux	FR	(city)	C	DK	center
Borisat Jamkad	TH	(company)	c.	SI	(street)
Borno	NG	(state)	C/	sp	Street
Boston	US	(city)	C/-	NZ	c/o
Bournemouth	GB	(city)	č.	CS	(offices)
B.P.	BE,FR	P.O.Box	CA	US	(state)

Cab.	FR	(company)
CAD	CA	(currency)
Cad.	TR	(street)
Cais	BR	(locality)
Calabar	NG	(city)
Calçada	PT	(street)
Calcutta	IN	(city)
Calgary	CA	(city)
California	US	(state)
Calle	sp	Street
Callejón	ES	(street)
Calz.	ES	(street)
Calzada	ES	(street)
Cambridge	GB	(city)
Cambridgeshire	GB	(county)
Cambs.	GB	(county)
Camp.	MX	(state)
Campeche	MX	(state)
Cand.	DK	(degree)
Cantab.	GB	(degree)
Cantabria	ES	(province)
Canton	CN	Guangzhou
CAP	IT	Postcode
Cape Town	ZA	(city)
Capital Federal	AR	Federal Capital
Capital Social	ES	(letterhead)
Capodistria	SI	(city)
Carabobo	VE	(state)
Caracas	VE	(city)
Cardiff	GB	(city)
Carolina,N.,S.	US	(state)
Carrer	ES	(street)
Carretera	sp	highway
Cartagena	ES	(city)
Casa	VE	(offices)
Casella Postale	it	P.O.Box
Case Postale	CA,CH	P.O.Box
Casilla de Correos	AR	P.O.Box
Casilla (Postal)	CL	P.O.Box
Catamarca	AR	(province)
Causeway Bay	HK	(locality)
Cav.	IT	(title)
Cavite	PH	(province)
CC	ZA	(company)
Cd.	sp	City
CE	BR	(state)
Ceará	BR	(state)
Cebu	PH	(province)
Cebu City	PH	(city)
CEDEX	FR	(postcodes)
cen.	ES	(offices)

centavos	Lat. Amer.	cents
centimes	fr	cents
centimos	VE	cents
Central	HK	(locality)
Centro	MX	(locality)
Centro	sp,it	(offices)
Česká Republika	CS	(country)
České Budějovice	CS	(city)
cesta	SI	(street)
CF	AR	Federal Capital
CH–	CH	(country)
Chaco	AR	(province)
Cha Jang	KR	(title)
Chambers	GB	(offices)
Changzhang	CN	(title)
Chantaburi	TH	(city)
Charleroi	BE	(city)
Chaussée	BE	highway
chaussée	FR,CH	(street)
Cheju	KR	(prefecture)
Chelmsford	GB	(city)
chemin	fr	(street)
Chengdu	CN	(city)
Cheshire	GB	(county)
Chester	GB	(city)
CHF	CH	(currency)
Chiang Mai	TH	(city)
Chiapas	MX	(state)
Chiba	JP	(prefecture)
Chih.	MX	(state)
Chihuahua	MX	(city)
Chihuahua	MX	(state)
Chis.	MX	(state)
cho	JP	[street]
Chollabuk	KR	(prefecture)
Chollanam	KR	(prefecture)
chome	JP	[offices]
Chon Buri	TH	(city)
Christchurch	NZ	(city)
Chubut	AR	(province)
Chun	TW	village
Chungchongbuk	KR	(prefecture)
Chungchongnam	KR	(prefecture)
chuo	JP	central
Cía.	sp	Company
Cie.	fr	(company)
CIF	ES	Co. Registration (names)
Cik	MY	(names)
Cinc.	US	(city)
Cincinnati	US	(city)

Desp.	MX	Suite
Despacho	MX	Suite
Detroit	US	(city)
Deutschland	DE	Germany
Devon	GB	(county)
DF	BR,MX, VE	[state]
Dgo.	MX	(state)
Dhahran	SA	(city)
di	it	of,from
DI	FI	(degree)
dijk	NL	(street)
Dijon	FR	(city)
Dipl.	ge	(degree)
Dirección	sp	address
District of Columbia	US	[state]
Distrito Federal	BR,MX, VE	[state]
Ditta	IT	(honorific)
Djurs	DK	(province)
Djursland	DK	(province)
DK–	DK	(country)
DKK	DK	(currency)
DKR	DK	(currency)
DM	DE	(currency)
DN	IL	(street)
do	KR	(prefecture)
do	pt	of,from
Do'ar Na	IL	(street)
Don	ES	(title)
Dong	CN	east
dong	KR	[street]
dono	JP	(title)
d.o.o.	SI	(company)
dori	JP	(street)
Dorset	GB	(county)
Dortmund	DE	(city)
Dott.	it	Doctor
Dott.ssa	it	Doctor (female)
Dpl.	ID	(names)
DR	NL	(province)
Dr.	many	Doctor
Dra.	sp,pt	Doctor (female)
drachma	GR	(currency)
Drammen	NO	(city)
dreef	BE	(street)
Dresden	DE	(city)
drève	BE	(street)
Drs.	GR	(currency)
Dsdn.	DE	(city)
D.ssa	it	Doctor (female)
Dssd.	DE	(city)
Dtmd.	DE	(city)
dto.	pt	(offices)
Duan	CN	(street)
Dublin	IE	(city)
Duesseldorf	DE	Düsseldorf
Dundee	GB	(city)
Dunedin	NZ	(city)
Durango	MX	(state)
Durban	ZA	(city)
Durchwahl	ge	direct dial
Düsseldorf	DE	(city)
E–	ES	(country)
Eastern Cape	ZA	(province)
East Sussex	GB	(county)
Edificio	it,pt,sp	Building
Edinburgh	GB	(city)
Edmonton	CA	(city)
Edms.	ZA	(company)
Edo	NG	(state)
Edo.	MX,VE	State
Edo. de México	MX	(state)
EDSA	PH	(street)
Egr.	IT	(honorific)
Egregio	IT	(honorific)
Ehime	JP	(prefecture)
Eindhoven	NL	(city)
Éire	IE	Ireland
Eixo	BR	(street)
Eje	MX	(street)
Ekon	FI	(degree)
Ellas	GR	Greece
Elsene	BE	(city)
En.	MY	(names)
Encik	MY	(names)
Eng.	pt	(degree)
England	GB	(country)
entlo.	ES	(offices)
Entre Ríos	AR	(province)
entresuelo	ES	(offices)
Enugo	NG	(city)
Enugu	NG	(state)
EO	GR	(street)
Er	SE	your
Ermita	PH	(locality)
ES	BR	(state)
ESB	ES	(currency)
ESC	PT	(currency)
escalier	fr	staircase
Escritórios	PT	Postal address

gässlein	CH	(street)		GRA	NG	(locality)
gata	NO	Street		graben	CH	(street)
gatan	SE	Street		gracht	NL	(street)
gate(n)	NO	Street		Granada	ES	(city)
Gauteng	ZA	(province)		gränden	SE	(street)
GBP	GB	(currency)		Graz	AT	(city)
Gdańsk	PL	(city)		GRD	GR	(currency)
gdč	SI	(names)		Great Britain	GB	(country)
Gdynia	PL	(city)		Greenland	DK	(country)
Gebietsbüro	ge	branch		Grenoble	FR	(city)
Gebou	ZA	Building		Gro.	MX	(state)
Gebouw	du	Building		groene	NL	(phones)
Geneva	CH	Genève		Groningen	NL	(city)
Genève	CH	(city)		Groschen	AT	cents
Genoa	IT	Genova		Groß-	ge	Greater
Genova	IT	(city)		groszy	PL	(currency)
Gent	BE	(city)		Gto.	MX	(state)
Gent.	IT	(honorific)		Gua Jang	KR	(title)
Gentile	IT	(honorific)		Guanajuato	MX	(state)
Gentilissima	IT	(honorific)		Guangdong	CN	(province)
Gent.ma	IT	(honorific)		Guangxi Zhuangzu	CN	(province)
Georgia	US	(state)		Guangzhou	CN	(city)
Germiston	ZA	(city)		Guernsey	GB	(country)
Geschäftsführer	DE	(title)		Guerrero	MX	(state)
Ges.m.b.H.	AT	(company)		guilder	NL	(currency)
G/Flr	PH	(offices)		Guipúzcoa	ES	(province)
Ghent	BE	Gent		Guizhou	CN	(province)
Gifu	JP	(prefecture)		gulden	NL	(currency)
giro	many	Postal bank a/c		gun	JP,KR	[city]
				Gunma	JP	(prefecture)
Gl.	DK	old		Győr	HU	(city)
Glasgow	GB	(city)		H	HU	(country)
GLD	NL	(province)		Haad Yai	TH	(city)
Glos.	GB	(county)		Haarlem	NL	(city)
Gloucester	GB	(city)		Hague, The	NL	Den Haag
Gloucestershire	GB	(county)		Haifa	IL	(city)
GmbH	DE	(company)		Hainan	CN	(province)
GmbH & Co KG	AT,DE	(company)		Hajah	ID	(names)
GN	NL	(province)		Haji	ID, MY	(names)
go	KR	[locality]		Hajjah	MY	(names)
GO	BR	(state)		hala	CS	(offices)
Goiás	BR	(state)		Halifax	CA	(city)
Gongyuan	CN	Park		hallalah	SA	(currency)
Gospa	SI	(names)		Hälsingborg	SE	(city)
Gospod	SI	(names)		Hamburg	DE	(city)
Gospodična	SI	(names)		Hamilton	NZ	(city)
Gospodin	RU	(names)		Hampshire	GB	(county)
Gospozha	RU	(names)		Han	TR	(offices)
Göteborg	SE	(city)		Han.	DE	(city)
Gothenburg	SE	Göteborg		Handelsregister	BE	Co. Regis-tration
GPO	AU,HK, IN	(boxes)		Hanım	TR	(names)
GR–	GR	(country)		Hannover	DE	(city)

Hanover	DE	Hannover		Ibadan	NG	(city)
Hants.	GB	(county)		Ibaraki	JP	(prefecture)
Happy Valley	HK	(locality)		Ibu	ID	(names)
Hauptverwaltung	ge	head office		ID	US	(state)
haven	NL	(street)		Idaho	US	(state)
Hawaii	US	(state)		IDR	ID	(currency)
HC	US	(street)		IEP	IE	(currency)
Hebei	CN	(province)		Ifj.	HU	(names)
Heilongjiang	CN	(province)		IH	US	(street)
Hellas	GR	Greece		Ikeja	NG	(locality)
Helsingfors	FI	(city)		IL	US	(state)
Helsinki	FI	(city)		Illinois	US	(state)
Helvetia	CH	Switzerland		Ill.mo	IT	(honorific)
Henan	CN	(province)		Illustrissimo	IT	(honorific)
Herefordshire	GB	(county)		Ilma.	BR	(honorific)
Herr	ge	Mr.		Ilmo.	BR	(honorific)
Herren	ge	(names)		Ilorin	NG	(city)
Herrn	ge	to Mr.		ILS	IL	(currency)
Hertford	GB	(city)		Immeuble	fr	Building
Hertfordshire	GB	(county)		Imo	NG	(state)
Herts.	GB	(county)		impasse	FR	(street)
het	NL	(names)		IN	US	(state)
Hgo.	MX	(state)		Indiana	US	(state)
HI	US	(state)		Industriegebiet	DE	(offices)
Hidalgo	MX	(state)		Industrieområdet	SE	(offices)
Higashi	JP	east		Ing.	many	graduate
Hiroshima	JP	(city)		ingresso	IT	entrance
Hiroshima	JP	(prefecture)		Innsbruck	AT	(city)
HKD	HK	(currency)		Insp.	ge	(degree)
Hmb.	DE	(city)		interno	IT	Suite
Hokkaido	JP	(prefecture)		Intramuros	PH	(locality)
Ho Man Tin	HK	(locality)		Invercargill	NZ	(city)
Hong Kong	HK	(city)		Inż	PL	(degree)
Island				Iowa	US	(state)
Hounslow	GB	(city)		Ipoh	MY	(city)
Houston	US	(city)		Ipswich	GB	(city)
HR	BE	Co. Regis-		Ir.	NL	(title)
		tration		Ireland,	GB	(country)
Hradec Králove	CS	(city)		N(orthern)		
Hsiang	TW	City		Ishikawa	JP	(prefecture)
Hsien	TW	(county)		Isle of Man	GB	(country)
HT	fr	excl. tax		İstanbul	TR	(city)
Hubei	CN	(province)		itä	FI	east
HUF	HU	(currency)		Italia	IT	Italy
Huis	ZA	(offices)		ITL	IT	(currency)
Huizu	CN	(province)		iur.	ge	(degree)
Hunan	CN	(province)		IVA	ES,IT,	sales tax
Hung Hom	HK	(locality)			PT	
Hutong	CN	(street)		Iwate	JP	(prefecture)
Hyderabad	IN	(city)		Ixelles	BE	(city)
Hyogo	JP	(prefecture)		İzmir	TR	(city)
I–	IT	(country)		izq(da).	ES	(offices)
IA	US	(state)		izquierda	ES	(offices)

J	DK	(province)
Jabotabek	ID	(city)
Jaffa	IL	(city)
Jaipur	IN	(city)
Jakarta	ID	(city)
Jal.	MX	(state)
Jalan	SG, ID, MY	(street)
Jalisco	MX	(state)
Jang	KR	(title)
Jardim	BR	(locality)
JD	US	(names)
Jeddah	SA	(city)
Jersey	GB	(country)
Jerusalem	IL	(city)
JFK	US	(street)
JH	KR	(company)
Jiangsu	CN	(province)
Jiangxi	CN	(province)
jiao	CN	Suburb
Jieu	CN	(street)
Jigawa	NG	(state)
Jihlava	CS	(city)
Jilin	CN	(province)
Jl.	ID	(street)
jo	JP	[street]
Jogjakarta	ID	(city)
Johannesburg	ZA	(city)
Johor Darul Takzim	MY	(province)
johtaja	FI	director
jomu	JP	(title)
JPY	JP	(currency)
Jr.	US	(names)
Juárez	MX	(city)
Juárez	MX	(locality)
Jubail	SA	(city)
Jujuy	AR	(province)
Jur.	DK	(degree)
Jusik Haesa	KR	(company)
Jyll	DK	(province)
Jylland	DK	(province)
K	DK	(city)
K	CS	near
K.	GR	Mr.
k.	RU	(offices)
K:	TR	(offices)
ka	KR	[street]
Ka.	GR	Ms.
Kaapprovinsie	ZA	(province)
Kaapstad	ZA	(city)
Kabupaten	ID	(locality)
Kabushiki Kaisha	JP	(company)

kacho	JP	(title)
kade	NL	(street)
Kaduna	NG	(city)
Kaduna	NG	(state)
Kagawa	JP	(prefecture)
Kagoshima	JP	(prefecture)
Kai	ge	(street)
kaicho	JP	(title)
kaisha	JP	(company)
kakricho	JP	(title)
Kalimantan	ID	(province)
kampung	MY	(locality)
Kanagawa	JP	(prefecture)
kančelar	CS	(offices)
Kangwon	KR	(prefecture)
Kano	NG	(state)
Kano	NG	(city)
Kanpur	IN	(city)
Kansas	US	(state)
Kansas City	US	(city)
Kaohsiung	TW	(city)
Karlovy Vary	CS	(city)
Katowice	PL	(city)
Katsina	NG	(state)
katu	FI	Street
Kaur	IN	(names)
Kav., Kavling	ID	(offices)
Kawasan Perindustrian	MY	(offices)
Kawasaki	JP	(city)
Kb	ID	(offices)
Kbh.	DK	(city)
Kblz.	DE	(city)
Kč	CS	(currency)
Kebbi	NG	(state)
Kecamatan	ID	(locality)
Kedah Darul Aman	MY	(province)
Keelung	TW	(city)
Kelang	MY	(city)
Kelurahan	ID	(locality)
ken	JP	(prefecture)
Kent	GB	(county)
Kentucky	US	(state)
Kfm.	ge	(degree)
Kft	HU	(company)
KG	ge	(company)
Kheifa	IL	(city)
Khobar	SA	(city)
Khon Kean	TH	(city)
Ki'kar	IL	square
Kita	JP	north
Kitakyushu	JP	(city)
KK	JP	(company)

kl.	PL	(offices)	KY	US	(state)
Klagenfurt	AT	(city)	Kyonggi	KR	(prefecture)
Klein-	ge	Lesser	Kyongsangbuk	KR	(prefecture)
Kln.	DE	(city)	Kyongsangnam	KR	(prefecture)
Km.	many	kilometer	Kyoto	JP	(city)
		(post)	Kyoto	JP	(prefecture)
Kni'ssa	IL	(offices)	L	DK	(province)
Ko.	GR	Mr.	L	DK,SE	small
Kobe	JP	(city)	L.	IT	(currency)
København	DK	(city)	L–	LU	(country)
Koblenz	DE	(city)	LA	US	(state)
Kochi	JP	(prefecture)	L.A.	US	(city)
Kogi	NG	(state)	laan	BE,NL,	(street)
Köln	DE	(city)		ZA	
Kompleks	MY	(offices)	La Coruña	ES	(city)
Koper	SI	(city)	Lagos	NG	(city)
Koruna	CS	(currency)	Lagos	NG	(state)
Körút	HU	(street)	Laguna	PH	(province)
Kota	ID	(locality)	lakh	IN	(currency)
Kota Baharu	MY	(city)	Lakó Telep	HU	(offices)
Kotak Pos	ID	(boxes)	Lampang	TH	(city)
Kowloon	HK	[city]	Lam Plai Mat	TH	(city)
KPO	KR	(boxes)	Lancashire	GB	(county)
Kr	DK,NO,	(currency)	Lancs.	GB	(county)
	SE		länsi	FI	west
Kr	ID	(offices)	Lantai	ID	(offices)
Kraków	PL	(city)	La Pampa	AR	(province)
Kranj	SI	(city)	La Plata	AR	(city)
Kristiansand	NO	(city)	Lara	VE	(state)
krone	DK,NO	(currency)	Largo	PT	(street)
kronor	SE	(currency)	La Rioja	AR	(province)
Krung Thep	TH	(city)	Larisa	GR	(city)
KRW	KR	(currency)	Lausanne	CH	(city)
KS	US	(state)	LB	CA	(province)
K/S	DK,NO	(company)	LB	NL	(province)
Ks	ID	(offices)	Leeds	GB	(city)
k.s.	CS	(company)	lei	BE	(street)
Kt	ID	(offices)	Leicester	GB	(city)
ku	JP,KR	(locality)	Leicestershire	GB	(county)
Kuala Lumpur	MY	(city)	Leics.	GB	(county)
Kuala Terengganu	MY	(city)	Leipzig	DE	(city)
Kuantan	MY	(city)	Leiter	DE	(title)
Kumamoto	JP	(prefecture)	Le Mans	FR	(city)
kun	KR	[city]	Leof.	GR	Ave.
Kúria	GR	Ms.	Leuven	BE	(city)
Kúrio	GR	Mr.	Level	AU,NZ	floor
Kv	HU	(company)	LGA	NG	(locality)
Kv.	RU	(offices)	Liaoning	CN	(province)
KvK	NL	Co. Regis-	Liberec	CS	(city)
		tration	Lic.	many	graduate
Kwangju	KR	(city)	Liechtenstein	CH	(country)
Kwara	NG	(state)	Liège	BE	(city)
KwaZulu-Natal	ZA	(province)	Likh'vod	IL	To:

nostro	it	our
Nottingham	GB	(city)
Nottinghamshire	GB	(county)
Notts.	GB	(county)
Nouveau Bruns-wick, le	CA	(province)
Nouvelle Écosse, la	CA	(province)
Nova Scotia	CA	(province)
Novy	RU	(city)
NP	MX	(currency)
N/ref	sp	our ref.
NS	CA	(province)
NS	IL	(currency)
Ns/Rif.	it	our ref.
NT	CA	(province)
NT$	TW	(currency)
NTD	TW	(currency)
Nua	TH	north
nuestra	sp	our
Nueva Esparta	VE	(state)
Nuevo Laredo	MX	(city)
Nuevo León	MX	(state)
Núm(ero)	sp	number
Numero	it	number
Nuremberg	DE	Nürnberg
Nürnberg	DE	(city)
NV	BE,NL	(company)
NV	US	(state)
Nwanyi	NG	(names)
Nwoko	NG	(names)
N.W.T.	CA	(province)
NY	US	(state)
Ny	DK	new
NY, NYC	US	(city)
Nyonya	ID	(names)
N. Yorks.	GB	(county)
NYSE	US	(company)
NZD	NZ	(currency)
NZE	NG	(names)
Ö	SE	east
Ø	DK	east
O.	CA	west
Oax.	MX	(state)
Oaxaca	MX	(state)
ob	SI	on
Oba	NG	(names)
OBE	GB	(title)
Ober-	ge	upper
Obi	NG	(names)
objet	fr	subject
Odense	DK	(city)
Odos	GR	Street
oec.	ge	(degree)
Oeste	sp	west
Of.	sp	Suite
Oficina	sp	Suite
OFS	ZA	(province)
Oga	NG	(names)
Ogbomosho	NG	(city)
oggetto	it	subject
Ogun	NG	(state)
OH	US	(state)
Ohio	US	(state)
Ohita	JP	(prefecture)
Ojota	NG	(locality)
OK	US	(state)
Øk	NO	(degree)
Okayama	JP	(prefecture)
Okinawa	JP	(prefecture)
Oklahoma	US	(state)
Oklahoma City	US	(city)
Oldham	GB	(city)
Olomouc	CS	(city)
ON	CA	(province)
Onchon	KR	(city)
onderwerp	du	subject
Ondo	NG	(state)
Ons	du	our
Ont.	CA	(province)
Ontario	CA	(province)
oos	ZA	east
Oostende	BE	(city)
oost(zijde)	du	east
op	NL	(names)
OR	US	(state)
Orange Free State	ZA	(province)
Oranje-vrystaat	ZA	(province)
öre	SE	(currency)
øre	DK,NO	cents
Örebro	SE	(city)
Oregon	US	(state)
Oriente	sp	east
Orléans	FR	(city)
öS	AT	(currency)
Osaka	JP	(city)
Osaka	JP	(prefecture)
Oshogbo	NG	(city)
Oslo	NO	(city)
Øst	DK	east
Ost-	ge	east
Ostend	BE	Oostende
Österreich	AT	Austria
Östra	SE	east
Ostrava	CS	(city)

østre	NO	east
Osun	NG	(state)
otdel	RU	(company)
otdeleniye	RU	(company)
Ottawa	CA	(city)
Oud	du	old
Oudergem	BE	(city)
ouest	fr	west
OV	NL	(province)
øvre	NO	upper
OVS	ZA	(province)
Oxford	GB	(city)
Oxfordshire	GB	(county)
Oxon.	GB	(county)
Oxon.	GB	(degree)
OY	FI	(company)
Oyo	NG	(state)
p,P	sp	floor
P	PL	(boxes)
P	PH	(currency)
p.	CS	(honorific)
p.	PL	floor
P–	PT	(country)
PA	BR	(state)
PA	US	(state)
päällikkö	FI	manager
Pahang Darul Makmur	MY	(province)
paise	IN	(currency)
Pak Chong	TH	(city)
Palazzo	IT	(offices)
Pampanga	PH	(province)
Pan	CS, PL	(honorific)
Pani	PL	(honorific)
Paní	CS	(honorific)
Pará	BR	(state)
Paraíba	BR	(state)
Paraná	AR	(city)
Paraná	BR	(state)
Parcela	ES	(offices)
Pardubice	CS	(city)
Paris	FR	(city)
Parque	BR	(locality)
parter	PL	(offices)
Paseo	sp	(street)
passage	FR	(street)
Passeig	ES	(street)
Path	IN	(street)
Patra	GR	(city)
paw.	PH	(offices)
PB	BR	(state)
PB	IN	P.O.Box
PB	sp	street level

PC	FR	(offices)
Pç	pt	square
P.C.	US	(company)
Pcia	AR	Province
PDG	FR	(title)
PE	BR	(state)
PE	CA	(province)
p.e.	SI	(company)
P.E.	US	(names)
Pécs	HU	(city)
P.E.I.	CA	(province)
Peiraias	GR	(city)
Peking	CN	Beijing
pence	GB,IE	cents
penni	FI	(currency)
Pennsylvania	US	(state)
Perak Darul Ridzuan	MY	(province)
Pereulok	RU	(street)
Perlis Indra Kayangan	MY	(province)
Pernambuco	BR	(state)
Perpignan	FR	(city)
Persiaran	MY	(offices)
peseta	ES	(currency)
peso	Lat. Amer.	(currency)
Peterborough	GB	(city)
Peti Surat	MY	(boxes)
Pf.	HU	(boxes)
pfennig	DE	cents
PH	sp	penthouse
Philadelphia	US	(city)
Phils.	PH	(country)
Phoenix	US	(city)
PHP	PH	(currency)
Phra-In Racha	TH	(city)
Phuket	TH	(city)
pí	CS	(honorific)
PI	BR	(state)
piano	IT	floor
Piauí	BR	(state)
Piazza	it	square
Piraeus	GR	(city)
piso	PH	(currency)
piso	sp	floor
Pittsburgh	US	(city)
P.K.	TR	(boxes)
Pl.	FI	P.O.Box
Pl.	many	square
Pl.	RU	(street)
Plaça	ES	square
place	fr	square

pladsen	DK	square		PR	BR	(state)
planen	SE	square		PR	US	[state]
planta	sp	floor		Pr.	RU	(street)
planta baja	sp	street level		Praça	pt	square
plass	NO	square		Praceta	PT	(street)
Plateau	NG	(state)		Praha	CS	(city)
Plateia	GR	square		Prathet Thai	TH	(country)
platz	ge	square		PRC	CN	(country)
Plaza	sp	square		Pref.	JP	(prefecture)
PLC,plc	GB,IE,	(company)		Pregiatissimo	IT	(honorific)
	NG			Preg.mo	IT	(honorific)
plein	du	square		prehod	SI	(street)
Ploshchad	RU	(street)		Pretoria	ZA	(city)
Plymouth	GB	(city)		pri	SI	beside
PLZ	ge	Postcode		Prince Edward	CA	(province)
PLZ	Pl	(currency)		Island		
Plzeň	CS	(city)		Privaatbus	ZA	P.O.Box
PMA	ID	(company)		Privaatsak	ZA	P.O.Box
P.M.B.	NG	(boxes)		Private Bag	many	P.O.Box
Po.	ES	(street)		Private Box	many	P.O.Box
POB.	many	P.O.Box		Prof.	GR	Prophet
Pod	CS	below		promenaden	SE	(street)
P.O. Drawer	US	P.O.Box		Prospekt	RU	(street)
pohjois	FI	north		Provincia	AR	(province)
pok.	PL	(offices)		Proyezd	RU	(street)
Polig.	ES	(offices)		Pt.,Pts.	ES	(currency)
Polígono	ES	(offices)		PT	ID	(company)
Polska	PL	(country)		pta.	ES	(offices)
Rzeczpospolita				ptas.	ES	(currency)
Poniente	sp	west		PTE	PT	(currency)
Porlamar	VE	(city)		Pte.	SG	(company)
Port Dickson	MY	(city)		Pty.	AU,ZA	(company)
Port Elizabeth	ZA	(city)		Puan	MY	(names)
Port Harcourt	NG	(city)		Pue.	MX	(state)
Porto	PT	(city)		Puebla	MX	(city)
Portsmouth	GB	(city)		Puebla	MX	(state)
portti	FI	(street)		puerta	ES	(offices)
Posbus	ZA	P.O.Box		Puerto Ordaz	VE	(city)
pošta	CS	(city)		Puerto Rico	US	[state]
Postafiók	HU	(boxes)		Pulau Pinang	MY	(city)
Postboks	DK,NO	P.O.Box		Pulau Pinang	MY	(province)
Postbus	du	P.O.Box		Pune	IN	(city)
Postfach	ge	P.O.Box		punt	IE	(currency)
Postilokero	FI	P.O.Box		Pusan	KR	(city)
Postleitzahl	ge	Postcode		Pusat	ID	central
pound	GB	(currency)		Pvt.	IN	(company)
Poznań	PL	(city)		P/YA	RU	(boxes)
PP	CS	(boxes)		Q	BR	(locality)
p.p.	SI	(boxes)		QC	CA	(province)
PPA	FI	(boxes)		Qiao	CN	Bridge
PQ	CA	(province)		Qinghai	CN	(province)
PqI	pt	Industrial		Q.R.	MX	(state)
		Park		Qro.	MX	(state)

qu	CN	district
quai	FR	(street)
Québec	CA	(province)
Querétaro	MX	(state)
Quezon City	PH	(city)
Quiapo	PH	(locality)
Quinta	VE	(offices)
Quintana Roo	MX	(state)
R	ZA	(currency)
R.A.	ID	(names)
rand	ZA	(currency)
ranta	FI	(street)
Ra'tsif	IL	(street)
RC	fr	street level
RC,RCS	fr	Co. Registration
r/c	pt	street level
RD	NZ	(street)
Reading	GB	(city)
Recife	BR	(city)
Redhill	GB	(city)
referanse	NO	reference
referencia	sp	reference
Regensburg	DE	(city)
Regina	CA	(city)
Registre de Commerce	fr	Co. Registration
Re'khov	IL	Street
renminbi	CN	(currency)
Rennes	FR	(city)
Repubblica	IT	Republic
República	sp	Republic
Republik	ge	Republic
Republika ng Pilipinas	PH	(country)
République	fr	Republic
rer.	ge	(degree)
Res.	US	(phones)
Résidence	fr	Building
Rev.	DK	Accountant
Revisor	DK	Accountant
Reynosa	MX	(city)
RF	FR	France
Rgsb.	DE	(city)
Rhode Island	US	(state)
ri	KR	[street]
RI	US	(state)
riferimento	it	reference
ring	ge	Loop
ringgit	MY	(currency)
Rio de Janeiro	BR	(city)
Rio de Janeiro	BR	(state)
Rio Grande do Norte	BR	(state)
Rio Grande do Sul	BR	(state)
Río Negro	AR	(province)
Riva	it	(street)
Rivers	NG	(state)
Riyadh	SA	(city)
riyal	SA	(currency)
Rizal	PH	(province)
RJ	BR	(state)
RM	MY	(currency)
R.M.	ID	(names)
RN	BR	(state)
RN	FR	(street)
ro	KR	[street]
RO	BR	(state)
R.O.C.	TW	Taiwan
Rodeløkka	NO	(boxes)
rodovia	pt	highway
Roi Et	TH	(city)
Roma	IT	(city)
Roma	MX	(locality)
Rome	IT	Roma
Romford	GB	(city)
Rondônia	BR	(state)
Roraima	BR	(state)
Rosario	AR	(city)
Rossiya	RU	(country)
Rotterdam	NL	(city)
rouble	RU	(currency)
Rouen	FR	(city)
route	fr	highway
Rp	ID	(currency)
RR	BR	(state)
R.R.	US	(street)
RS	BR	(state)
R.S.A.	ZA	South Africa
R.T.	ID	(names)
Rt.	HU	(company)
rua	pt	Street
rub.	RU	(currency)
rue	fr	Street
Ruko	ID	(offices)
rupee	IN	(currency)
rupiah	ID	(currency)
RUR	RU	(currency)
Ruta	sp	highway
S	AT	(currency)
S.	many	south
S–	SE	(country)
S.A.	many	Inc.
Saarbrücken	DE	(city)

shekel	IL	(currency)	Skt.	DK	Saint
Shenyang	CN	(city)	SL	ES	(company)
shi	JP	(locality),	slečna	CS	(honorific)
		(city)	Slough	GB	(city)
shi	KR	(city)	Slovenija	SI	(country)
Shiga	JP	(prefecture)	S.L.P.	MX	(state)
Shimane	JP	(prefecture)	Sn.	TR	(names)
Shizuoka	JP	(prefecture)	s/n	sp	unnumbered
SHN,SHS	BR	(locality)	sobre ático	ES	(offices)
Shosse	RU	(street)	soc.	ge	(degree)
Shri	IN	(title)	Soc.	fr	Co.
Shrimati	IN	(title)	Sociedad	sp	Company
Shropshire	GB	(county)	Sociedade	pt	Company
Shuji	CN	(title)	Società	it	Company
S. Humberside	GB	(county)	Société	fr	Company
shunin	JP	(title)	Södra	SE	south
Sichuan	CN	(province)	SOFN,SOFS	BR	(locality)
siège	fr	head office	Soi	TH	(street)
siège social	fr	registered	Sok.	TR	(street)
		office	Sokoto	NG	(state)
Sig.	it	Mr.	Somerset	GB	(county)
Sig.a	it	Ms.	Son.	MX	(state)
Sig.na	it	Miss	sønder	DK	southern
Signora	it	Mrs.	Songkhla	TR	(city)
Signore	it	Mr.	Sonora	MX	(state)
Signorina	it	Miss	søre	NO	south
Sig.ra	it	Mrs.	Southampton	GB	(city)
Simtat	IL	(street)	South Carolina	US	(state)
Sin.	MX	(state)	South Dakota	US	(state)
Sinaloa	MX	(state)	South Humberside	GB	(county)
singel	NL	(street)	South Yorkshire	GB	(county)
Singh	IN	(names)	SP	BR	(state)
Sint-Gillis	BE	(city)	s.p.	CS	(company)
Sint-Jans-	BE	(city)	SpA	IT	(company)
Molenbeek			Spettabile	IT	(honorific)
Sint-Lambrechts-	BE	(city)	Spett.le	IT	(honorific)
Woluwe			spol. s r.o.	CS	(company)
Sint-Pieters-	BE	(city)	Springs	ZA	(city)
Woluwe			SPRL	BE	(company)
Sint-Stevens-	BE	(city)	Sp. z o.o.	PL	(company)
Woluwe			Sr.	pt,sp	Mr.
Sir	GB	(title)	Sr.	US	(names)
Şirket	TR	(company)	Sra.	pt,sp	Mrs.
Şirketi	TR	(company)	Sráid	IE	Street
Si Sa Ket	TH	(city)	Sredny	RU	middle
SIT	SI	(currency)	S/ref	sp	your ref.
Siv. Ing.	NO	(degree)	Srl	IT	(company)
Sj	DK	(province)	SRL	ES	(company)
Sjælland	DK	(province)	s.r.o.	CS	(company)
SK	CA	(province)	Srta.	pt,sp	Miss
SKR	SE	(currency)	SS	IT	(street)
skr. poczt.	PL	(boxes)	ST	SE	big
skrytka pocztowa	PL	(boxes)	S:T	SE	Saint